Interpretive Approaches to Global Climate Governance

Global climate change is perceived to be one of the biggest challenges for international politics in the 21st century. This work seeks to fuse a global governance perspective together with different interpretive approaches, offering a novel way of looking at international climate politics. Equipped with a common interpretive tool-kit, the authors examine different issue-areas and excavate the contours of an overall pattern – the depoliticisation of climate governance. It is this concept which represents the overarching theme connecting the different contributions, addressing issues such as how the securitization of climate change conceals its socio-economic roots; how highly political decisions and value-judgements are couched in the terms of science; how the reframing of climate change as a matter of economic calculation and investment narrows the scope of political action; and how the prevailing concentration on technological solutions to climate change turns it into a mere administrative issue to be tackled by experts. Highlighting the depoliticisation of highly political issues provides a means to bring the political back into one of the most important issue areas of 21st century world politics.

The editors have assembled a series of 14 interpretive inquiries into discourses of global climate governance which aim to flesh out an interpretive methodology, demonstrating the value it offers to those seeking to achieve a better understanding of global climate governance.

This work will be of great interest to students and scholars of environmental politics, political theory and climate change.

Chris Methmann, Delf Rothe and **Benjamin Stephan** are all at the University of Hamburg, Germany.

Interventions
Edited by:
Jenny Edkins, Aberystwyth University and
Nick Vaughan-Williams, University of Warwick

As Michel Foucault has famously stated, 'knowledge is not made for understanding; it is made for cutting.' In this spirit the Edkins–Vaughan-Williams Interventions series solicits cutting edge, critical works that challenge mainstream understandings in international relations. It is the best place to contribute post disciplinary works that think rather than merely recognize and affirm the world recycled in IR's traditional geopolitical imaginary.

Michael J. Shapiro, University of Hawai'i at Mānoa, USA

The series aims to advance understanding of the key areas in which scholars working within broad critical post-structural and post-colonial traditions have chosen to make their interventions, and to present innovative analyses of important topics.

Titles in the series engage with critical thinkers in philosophy, sociology, politics and other disciplines and provide situated historical, empirical and textual studies in international politics.

Critical Theorists and International Relations
Edited by Jenny Edkins and Nick Vaughan-Williams

Ethics as Foreign Policy
Britain, the EU and the other
Dan Bulley

Universality, Ethics and International Relations
A grammatical reading
Véronique Pin-Fat

The Time of the City
Politics, philosophy, and genre
Michael J. Shapiro

Governing Sustainable Development
Partnership, protest and power at the world summit
Carl Death

Insuring Security
Biopolitics, security and risk
Luis Lobo-Guerrero

Foucault and International Relations
New critical engagements
Edited by Nicholas J. Kiersey and Doug Stokes

International Relations and Non-Western Thought
Imperialism, colonialism and investigations of global modernity
Edited by Robbie Shilliam

Autobiographical International Relations
I, IR
Edited by Naeem Inayatullah

War and Rape
Law, memory and justice
Nicola Henry

Madness in International Relations
Psychology, security and the global governance of mental health
Alison Howell

Spatiality, Sovereignty and Carl Schmitt
Geographies of the nomos
Edited by Stephen Legg

Politics of Urbanism
Seeing like a city
Warren Magnusson

Beyond Biopolitics
Theory, violence and horror in world politics
François Debrix and Alexander D. Barder

The Politics of Speed
Capitalism, the state and war in an accelerating world
Simon Glezos

Politics and the Art of Commemoration
Memorials to struggle in Latin America and Spain
Katherine Hite

Indian Foreign Policy
The politics of postcolonial identity
Priya Chacko

Politics of the Event
Time, movement, becoming
Tom Lundborg

Theorising Post-Conflict Reconciliation
Agonism, restitution and repair
Edited by Alexander Keller Hirsch

Europe's Encounter with Islam
The secular and the postsecular
Luca Mavelli

Re-Thinking International Relations Theory via Deconstruction
Badredine Arfi

The New Violent Cartography
Geo-analysis after the aesthetic turn
Edited by Sam Okoth Opondo and Michael J. Shapiro

Insuring War
Sovereignty, security and risk
Luis Lobo-Guerrero

International Relations, Meaning and Mimesis
Necati Polat

The Postcolonial Subject
Claiming politics/governing others in late modernity
Vivienne Jabri

Foucault and the Politics of Hearing
Lauri Siisiäinen

Volunteer Tourism in the Global South
Giving back in neoliberal times
Wanda Vrasti

Cosmopolitan Government in Europe
Citizens and entrepreneurs in postnational politics
Owen Parker

Studies in the Trans-Disciplinary Method
After the aesthetic turn
Michael J. Shapiro

Alternative Accountabilities in Global Politics
The scars of violence
Brent J. Steele

Celebrity Humanitarianism
The ideology of global charity
Ilan Kapoor

Deconstructing International Politics
Michael Dillon

The Politics of Exile
Elizabeth Dauphinee

Democratic Futures
Revisioning democracy promotion
Milja Kurki

Postcolonial Theory
A critical introduction
Edited by Sanjay Seth

More than Just War
Narratives of the just war and military life
Charles A. Jones

Deleuze & Fascism
Security: war: aesthetics
Edited by Brad Evans and Julian Reid

Feminist International Relations
'Exquisite Corpse'
Marysia Zalewski

The Persistence of Nationalism
From imagined communities to urban encounters
Angharad Closs Stephens

Interpretive Approaches to Global Climate Governance
(De)constructing the greenhouse
Edited by Chris Methmann, Delf Rothe and Benjamin Stephan

Interpretive Approaches to Global Climate Governance

(De)constructing the greenhouse

**Edited by
Chris Methmann, Delf Rothe
and Benjamin Stephan**

LONDON AND NEW YORK

First published 2013
by Routledge
2 Park Square, Milton Park, Abingdon, Oxfordshire OX14 4RN

Simultaneously published in the USA and Canada
by Routledge
711 Third Avenue, New York, NY 10017

First issued in paperback 2014

Routledge is an imprint of the Taylor and Francis Group, an informa business

© 2013 selection and editorial matter, Chris Methmann,
Delf Rothe and Benjamin Stephan; contributors, their contributions.

The right of Chris Methmann, Delf Rothe & Benjamin Stephan to be
identified as editors of this work has been asserted by them
in accordance with the Copyright, Designs and Patent Act 1988.

All rights reserved. No part of this book may be reprinted or reproduced
or utilised in any form or by any electronic, mechanical, or other means,
now known or hereafter invented, including photocopying and recording,
or in any information storage or retrieval system, without permission in
writing from the publishers.

Trademark notice: Product or corporate names may be trademarks or
registered trademarks, and are used only for identification and
explanation without intent to infringe.

British Library Cataloguing in Publication Data
A catalogue record for this book is available from the British Library

Library of Congress Cataloging in Publication Data
A catalog record for this book has been requested

ISBN 978-0-415-52188-8 (hbk)
ISBN 978-1-138-90930-4 (pbk)
ISBN 978-0-203-38557-9 (ebk)

Typeset in Times New Roman
by Swales & Willis Ltd, Exeter, Devon

Contents

Notes on contributors vii
Acknowledgements x

1 Introduction: how and why to deconstruct the greenhouse 1
CHRIS METHMANN, DELF ROTHE AND BENJAMIN STEPHAN

2 Discursive interplay and co-constitution: carbonification of environmental discourses 23
AYŞEM MERT

PART I
The economization of climate change

3 Climate politics as investment: understanding discourse through governmental practice 43
SIMON WOLF

4 How to trade 'not cutting down trees': a governmentality perspective on the commodification of avoided deforestation 57
BENJAMIN STEPHAN

5 Interpretive openness and climate action in an age of market environmentalism 72
LARRY LOHMANN

PART II
The securitization of climate change

6 Climate chains: neo-Malthusianism, militarism and migration 91
BETSY HARTMANN

7 Apocalypse now! From exceptional rhetoric to risk
management in global climate politics 105
CHRIS METHMANN AND DELF ROTHE

8 (In)convenient convergences: 'climate refugees', apocalyptic
discourses and the depoliticization of climate-induced migration 122
GIOVANNI BETTINI

PART III
The technocratization of climate change

9 My space: governing individuals' carbon emissions 139
MATTHEW PATERSON AND JOHANNES STRIPPLE

10 Governing knowledge through START and the expansion
of global environmental change research 152
OLA UHRQVIST

11 Climate engineering: spectacle, tragedy or solution?
A content analysis of news media framing 166
HOLLY JEAN BUCK

PART IV
Between de- and re-politicization

12 White ponchos dripping away? Glacier narratives in
Bolivian climate change discourse 183
ANNA KAIJSER

13 'Climate justice', 'green economy' or 'a one planet lifestyle':
hegemonic narratives in transnational NGOs and social
movements 198
PHILIP T. BEDALL

14 Building legitimacy: consensus and conflict over
historic responsibility for climate change 217
MATHIAS FRIMAN

15 Democratizing the global climate regime 232
JOHN S. DRYZEK AND HAYLEY STEVENSON

16 Reflections 248
CHRIS METHMANN, DELF ROTHE AND BENJAMIN STEPHAN

Index 257

Contributors

Philip T. Bedall is an Environmental Scientist (Diplom) pursuing a PhD in Political Science at Kassel University in Germany. His research interests revolve around climate politics – with a particular emphasis on NGOs and social movements – and post-structuralist discourse theory. In addition to his academic work he is involved in transnational social movements for global justice.

Giovanni Bettini is currently completing his PhD on environmental and climate migration at Lund University in Sweden. His research is concerned with the (re)production of environmental discourses at the intersection of research, policy and politics, with a focus on security, climate justice and post-foundational conceptualizations of the environment.

Holly Jean Buck studies the geopolitics of climate engineering, place-based geospatial technologies and environmentally induced migration. She earned her MSc in Human Ecology from Lund University in Sweden. She has worked as a geospatial humanitarian analyst, a mapping technician, a sustainability blogger and a writing teacher.

John S. Dryzek is Australian Research Council Federation Fellow and Professor in the School of Politics and International Relations at Australian National University. Recent books include *Foundations and Frontiers of Deliberative Governance* (Oxford University Press, 2010) and *The Oxford Handbook of Climate Change and Society* (co-edited with Richard Norgaard and David Schlosberg, 2011).

Mathias Friman is educated in environmental history and human ecology. A PhD student, he has focused on discursive mechanisms to deal with conflict in international negotiations; how constructions of history govern the present; and how modelling historic contributions to climate change contains assumptions about historical responsibilities for climate change.

Betsy Hartmann is the Director of the Population and Development Program and Professor of Development Studies at Hampshire College in Amherst, Massachusetts, USA. Her recent research focuses on the intersections between population, environment, climate change and security. Among her books are

Reproductive Rights and Wrongs: The Global Politics of Population Control and the co-edited anthology *Making Threats: Biofears and Environmental Anxieties*.

Anna Kaijser is a PhD candidate in Sustainability Science at Lund University, Sweden. In her research, she addresses the complex interactions and entanglements of environmental discourses, power, identity and social structures. These are explored through the case of ongoing debates around climate change policy and large-scale infrastructure projects in Bolivia.

Larry Lohmann works with The Corner House, a research and advocacy organization based in Dorset, UK. He has contributed to scholarly journals in sociology, politics, development, science studies, law, social policy, environment, accounting and Southeast Asian studies. His latest book is *Mercados de Carbono: La Neoliberalizacion del Clima* (Quito, 2012).

Ayşem Mert is a post-doctoral researcher at the Amsterdam Global Change Institute. She worked on a discourse theoretical study of sustainability partnerships for her PhD at the Institute for Environmental Studies, Vrije Universiteit Amsterdam. She is currently conducting research on democratization of transnational and/or hybrid governance mechanisms.

Chris Methmann is a fellow in International Relations at the University of Hamburg. In his PhD, he studied hegemony, governmentality and fantasy in global discourses of climate change. Other research interests include the political economy of environmental change, the role of civil society as well as the politics of climate refugees and climate conflicts.

Matthew Paterson is Professor of Political Science at the University of Ottawa. His main research interest is in the political economy of climate change. His most recent book is (with Peter Newell) *Climate Capitalism: Global Warming and the Transformation of the Global Economy* (Cambridge, 2010).

Delf Rothe has just finished his PhD project about the securitization of international climate politics at the department of International Relations, University of Hamburg with a scholarship from the Heinrich-Böll-Foundation. He is currently working as a research assistant to Prof. Annette Jünemann at the Helmut Schmidt University Hamburg. His main research interests are critical security studies, International Relations theory, post-structuralist and critical theory and international climate politics.

Benjamin Stephan is a research fellow at the Centre for Globalisation and Governance, part of the KlimaCampus at the University of Hamburg. He is currently working on his PhD in political science. His PhD project is concerned with the role of avoiding deforestation in the context of global climate governance.

Hayley Stevenson is a Lecturer in International Relations at the University of Sheffield, UK. Her book, *Institutionalizing Unsustainability: The Paradox of Global Climate Governance*, will be published in 2012 (University of

California Press). She has also published articles in the *Review of International Studies*, *Ecological Economics*, *Environmental Politics* and the *Australian Journal of International Affairs*.

Johannes Stripple is Associate Professor at the Department of Political Science, Lund University, Sweden. His research interests lie at the intersection of international relations theory and global environmental politics. His recent research has covered European and international climate policy, carbon markets, renewable energy, sinks, scenarios and governmentalities around climate change, carbon and the Earth System.

Ola Uhrqvist is a PhD student within the Earth System Governmentality project at the Centre for Climate Science and Policy Research (CSPR) and Department of Water and Environmental Studies at Linköping University. He studies how international research programmes rendered the Earth System and the Anthropocene thinkable, knowable and governable.

Simon Wolf holds a Diploma in Political Science from Free University Berlin and recently finished his dissertation on economic discourses in climate change governance. In recent years, he also worked as a writer and editor for the Earth Negotiations Bulletin at the International Institute for Sustainable Development (IISD).

Acknowledgements

This book would have not been possible without the support and encouragement of a number of people. We would like to thank the European Consortium for Political Research's Standing Group on International Relations to provide us with the funds to organize a Young Researcher's Workshop on Interpretative Approaches on Global Climate Governance at their 2010 meeting in Stockholm, Sweden. Particular credit goes to Stefano Guzzini, who, when listening to a few presentations at the workshop, encouraged us to turn it into a book project.

Furthermore we would like to thank the Cluster of Excellence 'Climate System Analysis and Prediction' (CliSAP) (EXC177), at the University of Hamburg, funded through the German Science Foundation (DFG), for providing financial support to put the proposal for this volume together.

Special thanks go to Jenny Edkins, Nick Vaughan-Williams, the editors of the Interventions book series and to Routledge for trusting three young researchers at the beginning of their academic careers with such a project, and providing the opportunity to publish this edited volume.

This book would not have been possible without the dedicated contributors providing these interesting chapters and of course the group of anonymous reviewers that ensured their scientific quality. Working with them turned putting this edited volume together into a delightful project.

Finally we would like to express our gratitude to Angela Oels, Cord Jakobeit and Anita Engels, who have supported our academic work over the past years and without whom we would have not been in the position to pursue such a project in the first place.

1 Introduction
How and why to deconstruct the greenhouse

Chris Methmann, Delf Rothe and Benjamin Stephan

> Just as the human transformation of the world's physical climate is now inescapable, so is personal engagement with the idea of climate change now unavoidable. It is an idea circulating anxiously in the fields of domestic politics and international diplomacy. It is an idea circulating with mobilising force in the fields of business, of law and of international trade. It is an idea circulating with potency in the fields of knowledge and invention, of development and welfare, of religion and ethics, and of public celebrity. And it is an idea circulating creatively in the fields of art, of cinema, of literature, of music and of sport.
>
> (Hulme 2010: 171)

In the 1980s, global warming started out as a problem concerning environmentalists and scientists. Today, it has reached the core of social life in societies around the globe. It constantly ranks among the most pressing issues of our times in the eyes of the public (Nielsen 2011). In the 1990s, international climate politics started out as a hopeful journey animated by the spirit of the Rio Earth Summit in 1992 and guided by the positive example of the Montreal Protocol's ban on ozone-depleting substances successfully negotiated in the 1980s. Today, however, international climate politics appears to be in a disastrous state. The failure of the Copenhagen summit and the several unsuccessful attempts to reboot negotiations since then represent a case in point. Ingolfur Blühdorn has called this 'curious simultaneity of an unprecedented recognition of the urgency of radical ecological policy change, on one hand, and an equally unprecedented unwillingness and inability to perform such change, on the other' an 'ecological paradox' (Blühdorn 2011: 36). This book has grown out of the contention that the two sides of this paradox create an urgent necessity to rethink the way we approach climate change in International Relations.

Climate change and International Relations: the story so far

It is especially the first side of the paradox – the proliferation of climate change discourses – which challenges the established theories of International Relations. The scholarly concern with the politics of global warming is as old as these politics themselves. During the 1980s, climate change increasingly became a concern of international negotiations. This decade also gave birth to the regime literature in International Relations, which was also triggered by the growing significance of international environmental agreements (Young 1989, 1994). Emerging right from the heart of the debate between neorealists and neoliberals this literature sought to show that international regimes – understood as 'implicit or explicit principles, norms, rules and decision-making procedures around which actors' expectations converge' (Krasner 1983: 2) – can indeed foster cooperation under the conditions of international anarchy.

This so-called 'neo-neo-synthesis' (Waever 1996) subsequently became the dominant approach for dealing with global climate politics (for an overview of the regime literature see Hasenclever et al. 1997; Vormedal 2010: 2–4). In this perspective, the emergence of international climate politics is a function of nation state's preferences. However, states are supposed to be trapped in the 'tragedy of the commons' (Hardin 1968) which keeps them from achieving a joint administration of the climate as a global public good (Victor 2001). The regime literature basically sketches two ways out of this cooperation dilemma. According to the neorealist theory of hegemonic stability (Webb and Krasner 1989), regimes have to be animated by a hegemon, the United States (recently Roberts 2011). Neo-liberal institutionalists, by contrast, focus on institutional design and seek to reveal the optimal conditions for the formation of an effective climate regime (Young 1989). Recent contributions, for example, discuss whether democracies are more cooperative in international climate negotiations (Bättig and Bernauer 2009).

The proliferation of climate change discourses described in the epigraph of this introduction consists of two dimensions, each of which meets with an important strand of criticism of the regime approach. On the one hand, climate change has turned from an issue to be dealt with by scientists and politicians to a concern that permeates all sectors of society. Climate change has become 'mainstream' (Methmann 2010). This development corresponds to the literature on global governance that highlights 'governance without governments' (Rosenau 1992) and criticizes regime theory for its state-centrism (Biermann 2010; Bulkeley and Newell 2010). The governance perspective highlights the fragmented character of climate politics (Zelli 2011) – including a broad variety of actors and taking place across different levels from the international to the local. Scholars have assessed the character and role of transnational networks (Bäckstrand 2008; Pattberg and Stripple 2008); activities of local or regional governments (Betsill and Bulkeley 2004); or the emergence of the carbon market as a novel policy tool (Voß 2007). As the global governance approach enables a much broader perspective on international climate politics, it represents a first step to approach the subject of this book.

Yet, the penetration of all parts of society with the issue of global warming does not only spawn a variety of new actors and spaces of climate governance, but also results in a proliferation of different meanings or perceptions of climate change. The geographer Mike Hulme, in his highly influential book *Why We Disagree about Climate Change*, highlights four such different discourses of climate change (Hulme 2009): climate change as a matter of science, as a matter of economics, as a matter of security, and as an inspiration for global networks of social movements to campaign for radical social and ecological change. They all problematize climate change in a different way and emphasize different options for action:

> Our discordant conversations about climate change reveal at a deeper level all that makes for diversity, creativity and conflict within the human story – our different attitudes to risk, technology and well-being; our different ethical, ideological and political beliefs; our different interpretations of the past and our competing visions of the future. If we are to understand climate change and if we are to use climate change constructively in politics, we must first hear and understand these discordant voices, these multifarious human beliefs, values, attitudes, aspirations and behaviours.
>
> (Hulme 2010: 172)

And these are not just different ideas, but they have material consequences – so that '[t]hey each invoke different "climate change", that are neither completely separate with no overlap, nor simply different representations of the same object. These invocations are enacted, they are practiced in ways that characterize the goods to be achieved and the bads to be avoided in different ways' (Randalls 2013). Climate change is far removed from being a single 'problem', to which we can simply apply political solutions. Instead, the social significance of climate change is constantly negotiated, but also constitutive of the practices of climate governance itself. And in our view, this insight is largely absent from the IR take on the politics of global warming.[1]

Parallel, but unrelated to the formation of international climate regime, constructivist scholarship emerged in the field of International Relations (Onuf 1989). A social-constructivist approach, which goes beyond the idea that cooperation is determined by countries' (fixed) interests, brings in socially constituted meaning as a relevant factor and argues that regimes provide the forum for policy learning and norm diffusion. With regard to the international climate regime the diffusion of emissions trading is a frequently cited example (Christiansen and Wettestad 2003; Damro and Mendez 2003) as well as the influence of 'epistemic communities' (Gough and Shackley 2001). However, instead of resulting in a broader inquiry into the formation of meaning, indeed, social constructivist interventions in IR successively turned into 'rearranging the deckchairs on the epistemological *Titanic*' (Jackson 2010, citing Smith 1994). And this applies especially to the study of climate politics. Norms and ideas turned into just another variable to explain the climate regime (e.g. Dimitrov 2003). In this sense, constructivist research hardly pays attention to the fact that the idea of 'climate change' has multiple identities and is far from producing stable and easy-to-transfer norms for appropriate behaviour. Social constructivism, thus, cannot account for the proliferation of different discourses on global warming.

A third strand criticizing the regime approach is rooted in the field of International Political Economy (IPE). In a sense, this literature is aware of the two tendencies – climate mainstreaming and 'climate change multiple' (Randalls 2013) – but only to a certain and limited extent. Critical IPE approaches grew out of the discontent with the separation between politics and the economy in most regime approaches (Paterson 1996). This critique involved highlighting the power of different non-state actors such as business lobbies (Newell and Paterson 1998; Levy and Newell 2002). Drawing on the Gramscian notion of hegemony, it also takes account of the discourses that influence how climate changed is governed internationally (Levy and Egan 2003; Stephan 2011) or considers the role of culture (Paterson 2000). It is, however, limited in the sense that these discourses often appear as economically determined, so that it in effect narrows these discourses down to 'neoliberalism' (Brunnengräber et al. 2008; Bailey 2007). To be precise: we agree that climate change is often depicted as an economic problem, resulting in a neoliberal stance on climate policy. In fact, this book itself presents evidence for such a claim (e.g. see the Chapters 5 or 13). However, there is much more to the proliferation of climate change discourses than just an economic explanation.

This book does not entirely depart from the existing literature on the global politics of climate change. First and foremost, it acknowledges the fact that climate change is governed by a multiplicity of agents and in a broad variety of spaces as discussed in the governance literature. However, this book seeks to infuse literature on global climate governance with a decidedly interpretive perspective. In doing so the volume links and contributes to the rich interpretive and discourse analytical literature on environmental issues in other disciplines and fields. Geographers as well as science and technology scholars have analysed the production of knowledge in climate science (Jasanoff 2001; Boykoff et al. 2010). Sociologists have inquired into political, science and media discourses of global warming (Weingart et al. 2000). Political scientists have put forth an interpretive perspective on environmental policies (Fischer and Hajer 1999; Dryzek 2005). In the discipline of International Relations, however, interpretive perspectives on climate change are mostly absent (for the few exceptions see Litfin 1994; Oels 2005; Bäckstrand and Lövbrand 2006; Pettenger 2007; Death 2010).

Interpretive theory

What connects this emerging literature in theoretical terms? What exactly do we mean with 'interpretive'? In very general terms, what sets apart interpretive analyses from a more traditional perspective on climate change can be boiled down to one formula: the latter takes global warming as a simply existing thing-in-the-world, and analyses how actors (at all different social and political levels) respond to this phenomenon. An interpretive perspective, by contrast, investigates the 'problematization' (Foucault 1994) of climate change: how global warming is rendered as an object and problem to be acted upon, how different meanings of climate change (e.g. as a global environmental threat, as an economic problem or as a security risk) emerge and become dominant, how the different meanings affect the toolkit of feasible political solutions, and what the effects of such practices are.

Since the end of the 1980s one can observe a so-called 'interpretive turn' in the discipline of International Relations (see e.g. Neufeld 1993) – as well as in other parts of the social sciences (Rabinow 1987). As Price (1994: 202) puts it, 'the chief concern for these scholars is not so much with providing a causal explanation for an outcome or event as with understanding the meaning of social practices and institutions'. However, what exactly this turn entails and where to draw its boundaries is a matter of fierce debate, the frontline of which can be demarcated somewhere around the terms 'realism' vs. 'reflectivism' (Keohane 1988), and 'moderate' vs. 'radical constructivism' (Wendt 1999: 11). Post-modernism and post-structuralism are terms that are often used to denote the 'extreme positions' (Campbell 1993) in this debate. Some observers have noted that the meta-theoretical foundations upon which these distinctions rest are not quite clear (Wight 2002). Moreover, others have demonstrated how categorizations like these often serve to demarcate a space of legitimate positions within the discipline, aiming to exclude and marginalize the 'extreme' positions (Hynek and Teti 2010).

We seek to evade stumbling into these deeply ingrained – and in our view, not very productive – trenches by adopting the term 'interpretive'. Whereas it is more explicitly used in the study of, for example, public policy (Yanow and Schwartz-Shea 2006), it is not commonly used in IR for demarcating different camps. Being interpretive is not only a matter of method (although it clearly excludes certain techniques of knowledge production), but entails a particular worldview in terms of ontology and epistemology (Jackson 2010: 36). With this definition, we take sides with Moore and Farrands who – in a slightly different context – invoke 'interpretive' as a means to 'open the doors of IR to [a] broader agenda of debate, not to reject something' (Moore and Farrands 2010: 4).

Therefore, we deliberately avoid a clear-cut definition of what it means to be interpretive, as this would reproduce the categorization trap. Instead of drawing boundaries, we would like to highlight some of the 'family resemblances' of an interpretive perspective (Tully 2002: 553). In this sense, the following paragraphs highlight various similarities of what we see as the family of interpretive perspectives on climate change.

The contributions assembled in this volume, *first*, share a commitment to a 'postfoundationalist' ontology and epistemology (Marchart 2005). To be precise, this does not, as often insinuated, involve the claim that reality would not exist or matter for interpretive approaches. Instead, it is based on the assumption that 'the very possibility of perception, thought and action depends on the structuration of a certain meaningful field which pre-exists any factual immediacy' (Laclau 1993: 431). Although, for example, a glacier is, in physical terms, a mass of ice with certain properties, it depends on its discursive representation whether it counts as an object of scientific inquiry, an emblem of pure nature or the witness of a dangerous global warming (see Chapter 12 in this volume). While some interpretive approaches define these perceptions in a hermeneutic sense as subjective perceptions, this book is based on a discursive understanding. 'Discourse', in John Dryzek's words, can be defined as 'a shared way of apprehending the world', which 'enables those who subscribe to it to interpret bits of information and put them together into coherent stories or accounts' (Dryzek 2005: 8). Meaning, hence, is a feature of supra-individual and rather unconscious webs of signification. Following Foucault, such a perspective is interested in the 'rules of formation', which make individual perceptions and statements possible in the first place (Foucault 1972). The aim of analysis is thus to reveal the infrastructure of a discourse, which generates the meaning of social and natural phenomena. Ayşem Mert (Chapter 2 in this volume), for instance, maps a range of different discursive arenas – environmental, economic and security discourses – which all depict climate change in a varying but coherent way. And she maps the processes of discursive translation between them through the concept of carbonification, which links the understandings of climate change between these arenas.

Second, the interpretive perspective employed in this book emphasizes the relationship between discursive and non-discursive practices. In our view, it is a common misunderstanding that interpretive works would only be interested in the linguistic (although broadly understood) practices of producing meaning. Yet discursive and non-discursive practices can hardly be separated, as every practice is also signifying to a certain extent. Simon Wolf (Chapter 3 in this volume) illustrates this perfectly in his analysis of economic discourses of climate change: he demonstrates that the emerging framing of climate change in finance terms is not something tied to the world of speech, but first and foremost roots in changing investment practices, that precede the emergence of a coherent governmental rationality. Thus, whereas some highlight the differences regarding the distinction between discursive and non-discursive practices in various interpretive approaches (Howarth 2000), we think that this is mostly a problem of terminology. In this sense, interpretive perspectives often hardly distinguish between material/ideational or discursive/non-discursive worlds.

A *third* proposition that guides an interpretive inquiry is that discourses are historically contingent. Contingency, first, means that discursive representations of any issue can vary over time. There is no inherently necessary way of depicting a certain phenomenon like climate change. Benjamin Stephan (Chapter 4 in this volume), for example, shows how within the last 15 years, deforestation has turned from a problem that is difficult to tackle into an object of government (REDD+), laden with optimism throughout the whole international climate negotiations. Paraphrasing Foucault, one can further distinguish between an archeological-synchronic (Chapter 7 in this volume) and a genealogical-diachronic (Chapter 10 in this volume) interpretive perspective. The former analyses a discourse at a particular point in time, interested in making the discursive rules of formation visible, while the latter traces the historical development of a discourse highlighting its shifts, break and changes. Combined, they make up what the later Foucault has called the study of 'problematizations' (Foucault 1994): the way we come to perceive a particular problem as problem. Contingency, second, refers to the fact that no discursive representation is necessarily determined by 'real' material forces (although it might be influenced by them to a certain degree). This rules out the possibility of understanding discourse as ideology, at least in the traditional Marxist conception of false consciousness. Obviously, from an interpretive perspective it is difficult to distinguish between true and false, if the yardstick of such judgments is dependent on the respective discursive context. In this sense, discourses are autonomous and cannot be subjugated under concepts such as 'bounded rationality' (regime theory) or 'base and superstructure' (IPE). Therefore, finally, the term contingency also refers to the fact that discourses are radically unstable. In this sense, the interpretive interest in contingency brings about an explicit interest in change, transformation and variety in the meaning of climate change. This change might take place rather incremental, often even unnoticed: because there is no natural or fixed relation between the term climate change and the 'physical thing out there'; and because the terms' meaning is continuously 'negotiated' through practices of reiteration and citation; a concept like that of climate change over time slightly alters its meaning (see Butler 1993). At the same time, there is also always the possibility for greater transformations. Although certain meanings and representations might have become hegemonic and thus 'sedimented' (Laclau 1990), 'dislocative moments', such as the recent global economic crisis, can subvert the established discursive order and trigger discursive change.

Fourth, interpretive approaches are often characterized by a particular perspective on agency and the subject. Other than most traditional approaches, which are based on some version of methodological individualism (such as regime theory or global governance, to name but two), most interpretive approaches assume that subjects are conditioned by discursive structures. Discourses create particular subject positions that create expectations about appropriate behaviour in the face of global warming. Paterson and Stripple (Chapter 9 in this volume) demonstrate how practices of individual carbon accounting create a particular way of acting on climate change – namely to count and take care of your personal carbon emissions. Here, the individual consumer becomes the main proponent in the fight against global warming. However, stating that discourses shape subjects is not to say that their behaviour would be determined. Maarten Haajer's influential work on 'discourse coalitions' has inspired a lot of work on collective attempts to transform structures of meaning and make particular framings of the world hegemonic (Hajer 1995). Philip Bedall (Chapter 13 in this volume), for example, is interested in how social movements constitute themselves in opposition or affirmation of a hegemonic order. The insight that agency is partly shaped by discursive structures, however, teaches that such attempts to shape these very structures are most likely to be successful in times of discursive dislocation.

Finally, *fifth*, interpretive approaches see discourses as laden with relations of power. On the one hand, this means that discourses are the outcome of discursive (power) struggles. Neatly tied into the question of agency and change, every part of a discourse, as deeply as it may be ingrained in our social lives, is the outcome of a discursive struggle and hence represents a relation of power. In this perspective, thus, power is a regular feature of society, and must not only be thought of in terms of domination. Yet, instead of being simply repressive, this form of discursive power has to be understood of making society possible in the first place. Ola Uhrqvist (Chapter 10 in this volume), for example, demonstrates how the creation of a global scientific authority on environmental change (the START programme), went hand in hand with the exclusion of certain scientific points of view within the community and the establishment of a dominant approach to 'measuring' environmental change. Although this has to be understood as a relation of power, it was constitutive for our knowledge about the biosphere – and hence productive. Discourse, however, is not only based on power, it also has power effects. Most of the contributions in this volume, in one form or the other, assess the power effects of discourse which amount, in our view, to a depoliticization in global climate governance. We will elaborate on this point below.

Interpretive methodology

Interpretive approaches to global climate governance are not only bound together by shared ontological assumptions about the role of knowledge and language in politics. In addition, interpretive accounts also share a common distrust of the neopositivist mainstream of International Relations and Social Sciences in general. Since the linguist turn 20 years ago, a multiplicity of different approaches that followed a post-positivist understanding of research evolved in IR. Their common ground is the rejection of an epistemic realism (Campbell 1993) or a causal-laws approach that aims at explaining and predicting social phenomena along the lines of the natural sciences. In this sense, interpretive approaches depart from the division between mind and world and adopt a 'mind-world-monist' perspective (Jackson 2010: 35). This philosophy-of-science trademark of interpretive approaches opposes the 'mind-world-dualist' position of neopositivism (and also critical realism), which

> maintains a separation between researcher and world such that research has to be directed toward properly crossing that gap, and valid knowledge must in the end be related to some part of accurate correspondence between empirical and theoretical propositions . . . [Mind-world monism], on the other hand, maintains that the researcher is a part of the world in such a way that speaking of 'the world' as divorced from the activities of making sense of the world is literally nonsensical: 'world' is endogenous to social practices of knowledge production, including (but not limited to) scholarly practices, and hence scholarly knowledge-production is in no sense a simple description or recording of already-existing stable worldly objects.
>
> (Jackson 2010: 35–36)

In other words, every inquiry into 'the world' is a historically contingent articulation. In effect, this relaxes the neopositivist obsession with proper methodology, and advocates a plurality of different styles of inquiry. Providing examples for this plurality is also the aim of this volume. The contributions represent a variety of different strategies of inquiry: discourse analysis (Chapters 2, 6 and 8); hegemony theory (Chapters 13 and 14); narrative analysis (Chapters 7, 12 and 13); actor-network-theory (Chapter 5); deliberative democracy (Chapters 14 and 15); governmentality studies (Chapters 2 and 9); Foucauldian archeology and genealogy (Chapters 3, 7 and 10) or content analysis (Chapter 11).

For many scholars adopting interpretive perspectives highlighting the contingent character of scientific knowledge, however, also means to refuse to deal with questions of methodology at all. Understood as an unchanging, quasi-universal set of rules of procedure for social scientific research, methodology clearly belongs into the realm of the positivist mainstream (Milliken 1999: 226). The dark side of this is twofold. On the one hand, implicitness prevents interpretive approaches from developing a proper methodological toolkit or entering into debates about strategies of empirical inquiry. As an upshot, many scholars often find it difficult to adopt a proper interpretive perspective without falling back onto neopositivist or critical realist conceptions of methodology. Therefore, contributors to this volume make their methodological strategy explicit and hence provide examples for different strategies of inquiry. In this sense, this book can also read as an exercise in 'practised methodology'. On the other hand, interpretivism is often used as a catch-all term for a whole variety of different and partially competing methods of textual analysis, whose methodological similarities and contradictions are seldom discussed. Mainstream scholars, then, criticize these approaches for their 'anything goes' relativism or even for not being scientific at all (Walt 1991: 195). But also post-positivist scholars themselves begin to show dissatisfaction with the aversion against any form of methodological consideration (see e.g. Milliken 1999; Glynos and Howarth 2007). In a sense, interpretive approaches are trapped in the 'post-positivist paradox' (Wullweber 2010: 49): whereas post-positivism as a methodological position champions a plurality of research styles and strategies of inquiry, any post-positivist explanation acquires its plausibility only against the backdrop of a positivist regime of truth. In this sense, engaging with methodological concerns also increases the plausibility of knowledge generated through interpretive inquiry. Discussing the implications of this claim could fill whole books – and indeed it has done so already (see for example Glynos and Howarth 2007; Jackson 2010). In the remainder of this section, we would like to revisit some of these implications in detail in order to lay the groundwork to the following contributions.

Understanding versus explaining

In the discipline of IR the distinction between positivism and post-positivism is often made on the ground of a binary differentiation between efforts to explain social phenomena on the one hand and attempts to understand them on the other (Hollis and Smith 1990). Thus, an ideal type of science derived from the natural sciences, seeking answers for why-questions, is contrasted with a reflectivist counterpart in the tradition of hermeneutics, which is interested in how-questions. While the former seeks to formulate robust and generalizable causal laws, the latter restricts itself to the study of subjective self-interpretations, not able to being generalized beyond a given context (Glynos and Howarth 2007: 51). It is important to note that this perspective was widely shared within the field of interpretive approaches, which tended to neglect the possibility to explain social phenomena in general (Dean 1999: 23; Wight 2002: 36).

This is clearly mirrored in recent interpretive approaches to study international climate governance. These, often influenced by the discourse analytical concepts of Michel Foucault, mainly revolved around the question of how climate change is discursively constructed or how it is governed (see e.g. Oels 2005; Bäckstrand and Lövbrand 2006). Studies asked for the discourses, i.e. rationalities and practices, for the identities and imaginaries that have played a role in governing climate change at different times. The causes for the evolution of these discourses – the driving factors of discursive change, however, have seldom been addressed from an interpretive perspective.

Different scholars from the philosophy of science have questioned the dichotomous of a explaining/understanding divide (see e.g. Wight 2002: 36ff.). According to them it is neither possible to explain social phenomena without asking how-questions, that is to understand the mechanisms, reasons, processes that stand behind correlations, nor is it desirable for interpretive approaches to restrict themselves to asking how-questions. In fact, the distinction is based on the – not very convincing – idea that there would be a proper 'scientific' approach to international relations (Jackson 2010: chapter 1). As Milja Kurki has argued:

> we can, in fact, think of causation as a 'common-sensical' intuitive notion with a multiplicity of different meanings, none of which entail laws or determinism. We can also understand social scientific causal analysis as epistemically reflective, methodologically pluralist and complexity-sensitive.
>
> (Kurki 2006: 190)

We agree. The present volume contributes to this growing debate in two different ways: first of all it shows that the best way to *explain* the outlined ecological paradox is to *understand* the different dimensions of this complex phenomenon. First, many contributions seek to *understand* recent discursive shifts (like a securitization, financialization, technocratization) or phenomena that have previously not been considered in international climate governance. They ask for example how existing hegemonic structures are being reproduced and challenged by discourses within social movements (see Chapter 13), how geoengineering is being framed in the news media and how this effects the modes of climate governance (see Chapter 11); or how climate change is governed at a distance through a variety of technologies of self-government (see Chapter 9). By bringing together and comparing their findings, we are able to identify a broader de-politicization trend in global climate governance, which can *explain* the ecological paradox. In this sense the book follows Max Weber's assumption that one cannot explain social behaviour without understanding it (Weber 1984: 28ff.).

Second, different contributions in this volume explicitly set out to bring forward or develop post-positivist methodological approaches that allow explaining trends and developments in global climate governance. In doing so they follow recent approaches by different scholars in IR and political science in general such as David Howarth and Jason Glynos (Glynos and Howarth 2007) with their 'logics of critical explanation' approach, Mitchell Dean's 'analytics of government' (Dean 1999) or the 'interpretative analytics' by Rainer Diaz-Bone (2006, 2007). In sum these authors stress that post-positivism is just not to be confused with anti-positivism – so there can be explanations for social phenomena, which certainly aren't objectively truer than others but still can be more plausible.

In line with this argument many of our contributors seek to explain recent changes in international climate governance like the growing importance of rationalities of finance in climate politics (see Chapter 3) and the increasing popularity of forest protection mechanisms in the international climate regime (see Chapter 4), or explore the question, why neo-Malthusian narratives have become so dominant in discourses on climate change, security and migration (see Chapter 6).

Finally, some contributions in this volume go even beyond the understanding/explanation dichotomy and show that interpretive approaches can even build the basis for normative judgments and suggestions for improving international climate governance. Dryzek and Stevenson (Chapter 15), for example, use a discourse analytical approach to identify a democratic deficit of climate governance in terms of deliberative possibilities. Friman (Chapter 14), on the other hand, calls for the possibility of using conflict within the UNFCCC negotiations for building legitimacy of international climate governance.

Plausibility as the methodological yardstick of interpretive approaches

Explanation, as understood in this volume, is getting possible if we give up the concept of a strict mechanistic causality (a causes b, if the conditions c–f are fulfilled). An explanation does not rely upon the identification of the sufficient conditions, or independent variables, that cause a certain phenomenon. This is not lastly due to the fact that any clear-cut distinction between an explanandum and an explanans is in fact impossible: discursive articulations on the one hand and their political effects on the other cannot be separated into two distinct spheres, as they are part of the same dispositif or discourse (see Wullweber 2010). Such an account relates to a more constitutive understanding of causation, in the sense that certain phenomena (ideas, knowledge, practices, etc.) can cause others by rendering them possible in the first place. The rejection of any mechanistic notion of causality, yet, also implies that the neopositivist yardsticks for explanation, i.e. the criteria of validity, reliability or objectivity, are inappropriate for our purpose.

The core quality criterion that guides explanatory approaches in this volume is the plausibility of an explanation (Flyvbjerg 2001: 137). A good explanation, then, is one that is plausible against the background of a specific regime of truth or a certain theoretical background, which is deliberately chosen by the contributors (see Laclau 1996). Explanation, thus, becomes a much more comprehensive and holistic endeavour than it is in a positivist research design. It involves the endeavour to understand phenomena in the first place, reveal their context conditions, formulate hypotheses or assumptions that could plausibly explain it, as well as the process to test these assumptions through discussions in different expert fora (Glynos and Howarth 2007: 38–40). This means that you – as the critical reader – become part of the explanatory process as well, as you reflect the hypotheses that our authors formulate, judge them against plausibility and possibly – if you disagree – even intervene into the research process by emailing us, contacting us at the next international conference or by writing a discussion piece.

Methodological holism

Methodology, as understood in this volume, thus, is not the result of a reflection on different means and procedures of research – it is the process of reflection itself. It acts as an intermediating instance, which helps translating theoretical assumptions into concrete methods and controls the fit or compatibility of these two levels. Diaz-Bone (2006) describes this function with the term methodological holism. Qualitative interviews, for example, by origin do not fit within a post-structuralist theoretical framework as method and theory here are characterized by different meta-theoretical assumptions. While the former tries to capture the individualistic self-interpretations of subjects under investigation post-structuralism denies the existence of any fully constituted subjectivity. However, methodology also means to produce a fit: by reflecting and unfolding the meta-theoretical behind certain methods one can find ways to modify or advancing them in order to fit into the research design.

Several contributions in this volume are providing examples of how this could be done. In his contribution on the role of social movements Bedall (Chapter 13), for example, draws on qualitative interviews and discusses the possibility to include this method into a post-structuralist hegemony-theoretical framework. Bettini (Chapter 8) uses narrative analysis as a possibility to translate post-structuralist discourse theory into a method of interpretive analysis. Buck (Chapter 11) presents frame-analysis as a possibility to grasp mass-media representations of geoengineering and combines it with Maarten Hajer's work on performance and authoritative governance to discuss the governance implications of these frames. Rothe and Methmann (Chapter 7), finally, present a possibility to include metaphor analysis into a post-structuralist framework to study securitization processes.

Just as there cannot be one universal methodology from a post-positivist perspective there is no single way of finding or fitting methods that are coherent with a theoretical framework. Rather than presenting the royal road to a discourse analytical methodology, thus, this volume provides a whole series of different examples and ways to work with interpretive methods. This means concretely that all contributions include a reflection of their methodological approach, together representing the whole variety of different interpretive methods available.

The red thread: the depoliticization of global warming

Returning to our initial observation, we have so far been concerned with how an interpretive perspective can shed light on the first side of the ecological paradox: the proliferation of climate change discourses in different political, economic and social fields. However, the contributions assembled in this volume also speak to the second side of the paradox: the simultaneous stalemate in global climate politics. As a common thread they diagnose the *depoliticization* of global climate governance as one of the root causes of its persistent failure to trigger sufficient social change. What do we mean with this term?

For the regular observer of global climate politics it might seem strange to diagnose a depoliticization trend. Very obviously, one could say, climate change is too politicized. The probably most-often discussed explanation for the stalemate in global climate politics is the conflict among nations – for example between China, the EU and the United States as well as the developing countries – that blocks the necessary consensus at international conferences. Copenhagen, for example, has been termed as the 'victory of climate realism' (Brunnengräber 2009). In this sense, climate change has become too politicized, indeed. However, from the theoretical point of view adopted in this volume, this interpretation sticks to a rather narrow conception of the political.

The chapters in this volume more or less explicitly put forth a much more encompassing understanding of the political. The political, as opposed to politics, 'has to do with the establishment of that very social order which sets out a particular, historically specific account of what counts as politics and defines other areas of social life as not politics' (Edkins 1999: 2). In this sense, the *political* of global climate governance defines the matter and limits of what climate politics is supposed to do.

Such an understanding of the political emerges from a branch of political theory that highlights 'the political dimension of the social' in general (Marchart 2005: 16). Laclau, for example, assumes a 'primacy of the political' in that he claims that all social relations have been instituted by a political act and could hence be repoliticized, at least in principle (Laclau 1990: 31–36). In a similar vein, Foucault notes that 'nothing is political, everything could be politicised, everything may become political' (quoted in Sennelart 2007: 390). In this understanding, the political is a latent feature in all areas of social life, which comes to the fore when their implicit foundations are challenged, when the taken-for-granted becomes questioned and 'the consensual' becomes contested. A politicizing treatment of a particular problem, in this sense, is one that brings the underlying antagonisms to the fore, opens up discursive contestation and aims for the transformation of sedimented social structures. Depoliticization, by contrast, involves all counter-strategies, which seek to conceal the contingency of social reality, disclose discursive struggle by silencing alternative views or channel dislocations in a way that fundamental social structures remain untouched.

In the light of this argument we can say that since the 1960s the growing perception of an environmental crisis has become a major discursive dislocation of Western societies (Stavrakakis 2000). The environmental crisis undermined the modern narrative of infinite progress and growth. Decline and scarcity, which for a long time defined the lives and fates of European societies but had been excluded from the discourses of advanced capitalist societies, returned in the figures of pollution, resource depletion and ecological catastrophe and put issues like limits to growth and renouncement of consumption on the political agenda. This dislocation, carried into public discourse through the efforts of scientists, environmental movements and green parties, clearly represents a politicization of

14 C. Methmann et al.

established social structures such as dependence on fossil fuels, industrial agriculture, consumer culture, growth orientation and the like. In short, then, a politicizing take would seek to save the climate by transforming these fundamental causes of climate change. A depoliticizing movement, by contrast, would save these very structures from climate protection; excluding them from political consideration and public debate (Swyngedouw 2010; Blühdorn and Welsh 2007).

It is this latter tendency – depoliticization – which runs as a common thread through the contributions assembled in this volume. The first three parts collect evidence of the depoliticization trend in climate governance in various forms from the field of economics, science and security – the first three of Hulme's (2009) interpretations of climate change. The final part turns to the dynamics of (re-)politicization and thereby also touches upon Hulme's fourth discourse – that of social movements.

In Chapter 2 *Ayşem Mert* provides a general and comprehensive analysis of recent discursive shifts in climate governance that sets up a frame for the following parts of the book. She uses a discourse analytical approach drawing on both Foucault's as well as Laclau and Mouffe's discourse theory to study how the issue of climate change could spread into the discourses on security, privatization and the financial crisis. In doing so, Mert is able to illuminate the central discursive dynamic behind this proliferation of climate discourses: carbonification. Carbonification refers to discursive strategies that reframe other environmental issues by relating them to climate change and promote tons of carbon dioxide equivalents as commodity and unit of measurement against which technologies and individual actions are evaluated. Mert shows that carbonification depoliticizes other issue areas by obscuring tensions and conflicts that exist in these fields.

Economization

The following part of this book comprises three contributions that take a closer look at the economization of global climate governance. In the first of these contributions *Simon Wolf* (Chapter 3) analyses recent political transformations that he describes as a 'financialization' of climate politics. Starting point of Wolf's detailed empirical analysis are novel governmental practices that aim at enabling or enhancing investment into means of climate protection and the transformation to low-carbon economies. The contribution builds on the work of Mitchell Dean (Dean 1999) to formulate a research strategy that focuses on the emergence and significance of governmental practices. The chapter argues that the turn to investment is embedded within a new kind of problematization that highlights the economic risk and opportunities related to climate change and asks for new strategies to align climate protection with economic objectives. Following such a discursive problematization the climate investment challenge emerged through the practices of a variety of actors in quite different contexts (private investment, public finance mechanisms, carbon offsetting), but increasingly coheres around common understandings of these actors.

Benjamin Stephan's contribution (Chapter 4) detects another example of the economization trend: He demonstrates how deforestation and degradation of the world's forest is currently being made governable through the adoption of market mechanisms. This development can be seen as the establishment of an advanced liberal governmentality in the forest sector. However, while such a governmentality is often detected in the field of environmental politics, the existing literature takes market mechanisms, which are central to it, for granted. Methodologically fusing Dean's analytics of government with the sociology of markets, Stephan examines how such an abstract thing as 'not cutting down trees' is turned into a tradable entity. Moreover, the governmentality perspective allows him to carve out how this process both detaches deforestation from its socio-economic causes and reduces forests to simple carbon storages. The integration of avoided deforestation into climate governance through technologies of advanced liberal governance hence represents a clear depoliticization trend.

Larry Lohmann (Chapter 5) contextualizes the economization of climate governance by, for example, comparing emissions trading and carbon offsetting to governmental technologies deployed in other areas of environmental policy making – such as fisheries or wetland preservation. He draws on Actor-Network-Theory (ANT) and Marxist IPE literature to understand how market environmentalist policies have become the dominant response to climate change. Lohmann's chapter is slightly different from the rest of the contributions to this volume, as he explores the possibilities to use interpretative approaches for activist purposes, with an eye to criticizing and challenging carbon markets. The contribution is an impressive and unique example of how to use interpretive approaches in a more political way.

Securitization

The second part of the book goes deeper into a securitization of climate change politics that could be observed over the last couple of years. *Betsy Hartmann* (Chapter 6) draws on Foucault's methods of archeology and genealogy to critically examine neo-Malthusian discourses about the risks of climate change-induced conflict and migration and their strategic uses by political and military interests. She offers a historical comparison between models of environmental security popular in the 1990s and their current transposition into related climate and security narratives. Thereby she is able to highlight the continuity of underlying assumptions about population, poverty, migration and resource scarcity. Hartman argues that the portrayal of climate change as a security threat could further militarize the provision of humanitarian and development aid.

Chris Methmann and *Delf Rothe* (Chapter 7) also discuss the military implications of climate change when scrutinizing what they call the security paradox in global climate governance. Even though climate change is increasingly rendered as a security threat, exceptional measures to handle this problem are missing. They deploy a metaphor and narrative analysis to reveal the discursive deep structures of the security discourse on climate change. Their results show that the different narratives in the discourse are bound together by an apocalyptic meta-narrative, which lays ground for a precautionary risk management logic. This precautionary logic draws on piecemeal and technocratic technologies of risk-management such as the flexible mechanisms of the Kyoto Protocol, rather than on exceptional political measures. Thereby security discourses rather reinforce a depoliticization trend in global climate governance than promoting discussion and increasing the publicity of the issue.

Giovanni Bettini's chapter (Chapter 8), at the end of this section, focuses on a central issue in current climate change and security discourses: the 'climate refugee'. Climate-induced migration is often used to give the impacts of global warming a human face. However, Bettini's discourse analysis of a wide range of publications from different types of actors within global climate governance reveals that all of them converge into several core assumptions, which paint an apocalyptic picture. His close investigation of central texts of the climate refugee discourse highlights that climate refugees are pictured as an anonymous mass of people, knocking on the doors of the Western world; a threat, deprived of their own agency.

Technocratization

The third part of the book sheds light on the growing role of expert knowledge and technocratic practices in global climate governance. The chapter by *Matthew Paterson* and *Johannes Stripple* (Chapter 9), for example, detects a recent growth in governmental technologies that seek enabling individuals to 'do their bit' in the struggle to limit climate change. Drawing on a governmentality perspective Paterson and Stripple examine five specific self-government technologies in climate governance: carbon footprinting; carbon offsetting; carbon dieting; carbon reduction action groups; and personal carbon allowances. Asking for the reasons for their recent proliferation as well as their function in broader schemes of global carbon governance the chapter argues that these technologies constitute a new form of carbon governmenality. Paterson and Stripple convincingly show how forms of carbon government work through calculative practices and technologies that simultaneously totalize (aggregating social practices, overall greenhouse gas emissions) and individualize (producing reflexive subjects actively managing their greenhouse gas practices). Their chapter moreover is a perfect example for how ethical questions, such as individual contributions to climate change, are transformed into a set of technical rules and procedures.

Ola Uhrquist (Chapter 10) combines Foucault's genealogy and governmentality approaches with science and technology studies to analyse the SysTem for Analysis, Research, and Training (START) project, a global expansion of research programmes in 'earth sciences' that took place since 1992. He examines the scientific rationalities and practices as they became visible when START emerged and expanded into new areas. Uhrquist's chapter demonstrates how the expansion of the Global Environmental Change research network was organized around a set of changing rationalities mixing policy impacts, infrastructure and scientific needs. Through scrutinizing central newsletters and reports Uhrquist shows how the present knowledge infrastructure developed and how the idea of the Earth

Introduction 17

system as an object of government emerged, associated with a certain rationality and technology.

Holly Buck's (Chapter 11) analysis of geoengineering in the print media and the blogosphere is an example of how the framing of particular issues in discourse influences how we act on them. Deploying Silverstone's mediapolis concept and combining it with Habermas', Fairclough's and Hajer's work, she develops an innovative approach to content analysis. Her empirical results show that the discourse on geoengineering is dominated by a catastrophic-managerial frame, implying that there is no alternative to geoengineering. This limits the possibilities to consider potential impacts of geoengineering or to take into account alternative approaches and hence results in a further depoliticization of climate governance.

Between re- and depoliticization

The last part of the volume turns to new fields of discursive struggle and contestation between re- and depoliticization. Lastly, it also asks for possibilities to actively reform and thereby (re-)politicize the current international climate regime. *Anna Kaijser*'s contribution (Chapter 12) on glacier narratives in Bolivian climate change discourses illustrates the dynamics between politicization and repoliticization in global climate governance. Drawing on a combination of discourse analysis, ethnography and interviews, she shows how Bolivian authorities, politicians and social movements succeeded in a redefinition of the glacier retreat as an emblematic image of global warming. Whereas global glacier discourses – centring on glaciers as an 'endangered species' – picture climate change as a global and environmental problem, Bolivian discourses of climate change have turned them into a symbol for the local impacts of climate change, which mostly affect the poor. Glacier retreat, moreover, is portrayed as a symptom for the exploitation of nature through capitalism. Her analysis provides an interesting example for how narratives can turn emblems of hegemonic depoliticizing discourses into a vehicle for re-politicization.

Philip Bedall (Chapter 13) provides another example of the heterogeneity of discourses and the possibilities for re-politicization. He examines the civil society discourses on global climate governance in the context of the fifteenth Conference of Parties (COP) in Copenhagen. Departing from the common assumption that grassroots movements are more critical of official climate politics, whereas institutionalized NGOs are more affirmative of the negotiations, the chapters paints a much more complex picture. Drawing on the theory of hegemony by Laclau and Mouffe, Bedall dissects the interviews he conducted with civil society representatives into individual demands. His combination of interview research and discourse analysis yields a fascinating picture of the contradictions within actors' discourses and thereby highlights the potential for counter-hegemonic projects as well as the power of consensus through civil society.

Mathias Friman (Chapter 14) takes up this lead and fathoms the potential of democratizing and hence re-politicizing global climate governance. Drawing on both Habermas and Laclau and Mouffe, he develops two ideal types of democracy:

a deliberative and an antagonistic one. His empirical applications demonstrate that the negotiations on historic responsibility within the UNFCCC have mostly followed a deliberative logic, which, however, has failed to create sufficient legitimacy. Instead, it has turned historic responsibility into a highly technical issue, evacuating it from moral and socio-political considerations. This narrowing resulted in a depoliticization of the issue. As a solution, Friman develops and promotes the idea of a subsidiary body to the UNFCCC, which would follow the second ideal type derived from Laclau and Mouffe's antagonistic understanding of democracy.

Finally, *Hayley Stevenson* and *John Dryzek* (Chapter 15) present us a promising possibility for how to (re-)politicize the international climate regime through the idea of a 'deliberative system'. Discourses, understood as shared sets of concepts, categories and ideas that provide their proponents with a framework for making sense of situations, constitute a central feature of such a deliberative system. In their chapter the authors develop a discourse analytic approach that is appropriate to the task of mapping the deliberative system for climate governance and evaluating its performance. This is illustrated in a case study of the United Nations Framework Convention on Climate Change, the main multilateral institution for debating international action on climate change. Their analysis reveals that a rudimentary deliberative system already exists in the arena of international climate politics but that its shortcomings are significant. The challenge for democracy and ecologically effective climate governance, they argue, is to find ways to overcome these shortcomings.

Apart from providing a host of insights into the present state of global climate governance, the contributions to this volume demonstrate one particular value of interpretive perspectives that sets them apart from conventional approaches: interpretive approaches enable us to dig deeper into the foundations of climate change policies, tracing the hidden origins of dominant understandings of global warming, revealing the discursive struggles that lead to their creation, and finally delineating the political consequences of these foundations. Highlighting the contingency of seemingly given and fixed framings, we think, is the competitive advantage of an interpretive perspective. This, most importantly, opens the possibility for new perspectives on the issue, which might help solving the climate crisis.

Note

1 This is not to say that ideas would not matter in the scholarship on the climate regime or climate governance in general.

References

Bäckstrand, K. (2008) 'Accountability of networked climate governance: the rise of transnational climate partnerships', *Global Environmental Politics* 8(3): 74–102.

Bäckstrand, K. and Lövbrand, E. (2006) 'Planting trees to mitigate climate change: contested discourses of ecological modernization, green governmentality and civic environmentalism', *Global Environmental Politics* 6(1): 50–75.

Bailey, I. (2007) 'Neoliberalism, climate governance and the scalar politics of EU emissions trading', *Area* 39(4): 431–442.
Bättig, M.B. and Bernauer, T. (2009) 'National institutions and global public goods: are democracies more cooperative in climate change policy', *International Organization* 63(2): 281–308.
Betsill, M. and Bulkeley, H. (2004) 'Transnational networks and global environmental governance: the cities for climate protection', *International Studies Quarterly* 38(2): 471–493.
Biermann, F. (2010) 'Beyond the intergovernmental regime: recent trends in global carbon governance', *Current Opinion in Environmental Sustainability* 2(4): 284–288.
Blühdorn, I. (2011) 'The politics of unsustainability: COP15, post-ecologism, and the ecological paradox', *Organization & Environment* 24(1): 34–53.
Blühdorn, I. and Welsh, I. (2007) 'Eco-politics beyond the paradigm of sustainability: a conceptual framework and research agenda', *Environmental Politics* 16(2): 185–205.
Boykoff, M.T., Frame, D. and Randalls, S. (2010) 'Discursive stability meets climate instability: a critical exploration of the concept of "climate stabilization" in contemporary climate policy', *Global Environmental Change* 20(1): 53–64.
Brunnengräber, A. (2009) 'Der Sieg des Klimarealismus vor Kopenhagen', *Informationsbrief Weltwirtschaft & Entwicklung* 2009(11): 2–4.
Brunnengräber, A., Dietz, K., Hirschl, B., Walk, H. and Weber, M. (2008) *Das Klima neu Denken: Eine sozial-ökologische Perspektive auf die lokale, nationale und internationale Klimapolitik*, Münster: Westfälisches Dampfboot.
Bulkeley, H. and Newell, P. (2010) *Governing Climate Change*, London: Routledge.
Butler, J. (1993) *Bodies that Matter: On the Discursive Limits of 'Sex'*, New York: Routledge.
Campbell, D. (1993) *Politics Without Principle: Sovereignty, Ethics, and the Narratives of the Gulf War*, Boulder: Lynne Rienner Publishers.
Christiansen, A.C. and Wettestad, J. (2003) 'The EU as a frontrunner on greenhouse gas emissions trading: how did it happen and will the EU succeed?', *Climate Policy* 3(1): 3–18.
Damro, C. and Mendez, P.L. (2003) 'Emissions trading at Kyoto: from EU resistance to union innovation', *Environmental Politics* 12(2): 71–94.
Dean, M. (1999) *Governmentality*, London: Sage Publications.
Death, C. (2010) *Governing Sustainable Development: Partnerships, Protests and Power at the World Summit*, London and New York: Routledge.
Diaz-Bone, R. (2006) 'Zur Methodologisierung der Foucaultschen Diskursanalyse', *Forum Qualitative Sozialforschung/Forum: Qualitative Social Research* 7(1): Art. 6.
Diaz-Bone, R. (2007) 'Die französische epistemologie und ihre revisionen. Zur rekonstruktion des methodologischen standortes der foucaultschen diskursanalyse', *Forum Qualitative Sozialforschung/Forum: Qualitative Social Research* 8(2).
Dimitrov, R.S. (2003) 'Knowledge, power, and interests in environmental regime formation', *International Studies Quarterly* 47(1): 123–150.
Dryzek, J.S. (2005) *The Politics of the Earth: Environmental Discourses*, 2nd edn, Oxford and New York: Oxford University Press.
Edkins, J. (1999) *Poststructuralism & International Relations: Bringing the Political Back in*, Boulder and London: Lynne Rienner.
Fischer, F. and Hajer, M.A. (1999) *Living with Nature: Environmental Politics as Cultural Discourse*, Oxford: Oxford University Press.
Flyvbjerg, B. (2001) *Making Social Science Matter: Why Social Inquiry Fails and How It Can Succeed Again*, Cambridge: Cambridge University Press.

Foucault, M. (1972) *The Archaeology of Knowledge*, New York: Pantheon Books.
Foucault, M. (1994) 'Polemics, power, and problematizations', in: Faubion, J.D. (ed.) *Ethics: Essential Works of Foucault 1954–1984*, London: Penguin, 112–119.
Glynos, J. and Howarth, D. (2007) *Logics of Critical Explanation in Social and Political Theory*, London and New York: Routledge.
Gough, C. and Shackley, S. (2001) 'The respectable politics of climate change: the epistemic communities and NGOs', *International Affairs* 77(2): 329–346.
Hajer, M.A. (1995) *The Politics of Environmental Discourse: Ecological Modernization and the Policy Process*, Oxford: Oxford University Press.
Hardin, G. (1968) 'The tragedy of the commons', *Science* 162(859): 1243–1248.
Hasenclever, A., Mayer, P. and Rittberger, V. (1997) *Theories of International Regimes*, Cambridge: Cambridge University Press.
Hollis, M. and Smith, S. (1990) *Explaining and Understanding International Relations*, Oxford: Oxford University Press.
Howarth, D. (2000) *Discourse*, Buckingham: Open University Press.
Hulme, M. (2009) *Why We Disagree About Climate Change: Understanding Controversy, Inaction and Opportunity*, Cambridge: Cambridge University Press.
Hulme, M. (2010) 'The idea of climate change: exploring complexity, plurality and opportunity', *GAIA - Ecological Perspectives for Science and Society* 19(3): 171–174.
Hynek, N. and Teti, A. (2010) 'Saving identity from postmodernism? The normalization of constructivism in international relations', *Contemporary Political Theory* 9(2): 171–199. Jackson, P.T. (2010) *The Conduct of Inquiry in International Relations: Philosophy of Science and Its Implications for the Study of World Politics*, London: Routledge.
Jasanoff, S. (2001) 'Image and imagination: the formation of global environmental consciousness', in: Edwards, P.N. and Miller, C.A. (eds) *Changing the Atmosphere: Expert Knowledge and Environmental Governance*, Cambridge, MA: MIT Press.
Keohane, R.O. (1988) 'International institutions: two approaches', *International Studies Quarterly* 32: 379–396.
Krasner, S.D. (1983) *International Regimes*, Ithaca: Cornell University Press.
Kurki, M. (2006) 'Causes of a divided discipline: rethinking the concept of cause in International Relations theory', *Review of International Studies* 32(2): 189–216.
Laclau, E. (1990) *New Reflections on the Revolution of Our Time*, London: Verso.
Laclau, E. (1993) 'Discourse', in: Goodin, R. and Pettit, P. (eds) *A Companion to Contemporary Political Philosophy*, Oxford: Blackwell.
Laclau, E. (1996) 'Subject of politics, politics of the subject', in: *Emancipation(s)*, London: Verso, 47–65.
Levy, D. and Egan, D. (2003) 'A neo-Gramscian approach to corporate political strategy: conflict and accommodation in the climate change negotiations', *Journal of Management Studies* 40(4): 803–829.
Levy, D. and Newell, P. (2002) 'Business strategy and international environmental governance: toward a neo-Gramscian synthesis', *Global Environmental Politics* 2(4): 84–101.
Litfin, K. (1994) *Ozone Discourses: Science and Politics in Global Environmental Cooperation*, New York: Columbia University Press.
Marchart, O. (2005) *Die Politische Differenz. Zum Denken des Politischen bei Nancy, Lefort, Badiou, Laclau und Agamben*, Frankfurt: Suhrkamp.
Methmann, C. (2010) '"Climate protection" as empty signifier: a discourse theoretical perspective on mainstreaming climate change in world politics', *Millennium: Journal of International Studies* 39(2): 345–372.

Milliken, J. (1999) 'The study of discourse in international relations', *European Journal of International Relations* 5(2): 225–254.

Moore, C. and Farrands, C. (2010) *International Relations Theory and Philosophy: Interpretive Dialogues*, London and New York: Routledge.

Neufeld, M. (1993) 'Interpretation and the "science" of international relations', *Review of International Studies* 19(1): 39–61.

Newell, P. and Paterson, M. (1998) 'A climate for business: global warming, the state, and capital', *Review of International Political Economy* 5: 679–703.

Nielsen (2011) *Sustainability Survey: Global Warming Cools Off as Top Concern*. Available at: www.nielsen.com/us/en/insights/press-room/2011/global-warming-cools-off-as-top-concern.html (retrieved: 29.3.2012).

Oels, A. (2005) 'Rendering climate change governable: from biopower to advanced liberal government', *Journal of Environmental Policy and Planning* 7(3): 185–207.

Onuf, N.G. (1989) *World of Our Making: Rules and Rule in Social Theory and International Relations*, Columbia: University of South Carolina Press.

Paterson, M. (1996) *Global Warming and Global Politics*, London and New York: Routledge.

Paterson, M. (2000) 'Car culture and global environmental politics', *Review of International Studies* 26: 253–270.

Pattberg, P. and Stripple, J. (2008) 'Beyond the public and private divide: remapping transnational climate governance in the 21st century', *International Environmental Agreements* 8(4): 367–388.

Pettenger, M.E. (2007) *The Social Construction of Climate Change: Power, Knowledge, Norms, Discourses*, Aldershot: Ashgate.

Price, R. (1994) 'Interpretation and disciplinary orthodoxy in international relations', *Review of International Studies* 20(2): 201–204.

Rabinow, P. (1987) *Interpretive Social Science: A Second Look*, Berkeley: University of California Press.

Randalls, S. (2013, forthcoming) 'Climate change multiple', in: Strippe, J. and Bulkeley, H. (eds) *Governing the Global Climate: Rationality, Practice and Power*, Cambridge: Cambridge University Press.Roberts, T.J. (2011) 'Multipolarity and the new world (dis)order: US hegemonic decline and the fragmentation of the global climate regime', *Global Environmental Change* 21(3): 776–784.

Rosenau, J.N. (1992) 'Governance, order, and change in world politics', in: Rosenau, J.N. and Czempiel, E.-O. (eds) *Governance Without Government: Order and Change in World Politics*, Cambridge: Cambridge University Press, 1–29.

Sennelart, M. (2007) 'Course context', in: Foucault, M. *Security, Territory, Population: Lectures at the Collège De France 1977–78*, New York: Picador, 369–401.

Smith, S. (1994) 'Rearranging the deckchairs on the ship called modernity: Rosenberg, epistemology and emancipation', *Millennium: Journal of International Studies* 23(2): 395–405.

Stavrakakis, Y. (2000) 'On the emergence of green ideology: the dislocation factor in green politics', in: Howarth, D., Stavrakakis, Y. and Norval, A. (eds) *Discourse Theory and Political Analysis: Identities, Hegemonies and Social Change*, Manchester: Manchester University Press, 100–118.

Stephan, B. (2011) 'The power in carbon: A neo-Gramscian explanation for the EU's changing stance on emissions trading', in: Engels, A. *Global Transformations Towards a Low Carbon Society (3)*, Hamburg: University of Hamburg (working paper series).

Swyngedouw, E. (2010) 'Apocalypse forever? Post-political populism and the spectre of climate change', *Theory, Culture & Society* 27(2–3): 213–232.

Tully, J. (2002) 'Political philosophy as a critical activity', *Political Theory* 30(4): 533–555.

Victor, D.G. (2001) *The Collapse of the Kyoto Protocol and the Struggle to Slow Global Warming*, Princeton: Princeton University Press.

Vormedal, I. (2010) 'States and markets in global environmental governance: on the role of tipping points in international regime formation', *European Journal of International Relations* (published online, 18 November).

Voß, J.P. (2007) 'Innovation processes in governance: the development of "emissions trading" as a new policy instrument', *Science and Public Policy* 34(5): 329–343.

Waever, O. (1996) 'The rise and fall of the inter-paradigm debate', in: *International Relations Theory: Positivism and Beyond*, Cambridge: Cambridge University Press, 149–187.

Walt, S.M. (1991) 'The renaissance of security studies', *International Studies Quarterly* 35(2): 211–239.

Webb, M.C. and Krasner, S.D. (1989) 'Hegemonic stability theory: an empirical assessment', *Review of International Studies* 15(2): 183–198.

Weber, M. (1984) *Soziologische Grundbegriffe, 6. Aufl*, Tübingen: Mohr.

Weingart, P., Engels, A. and Pansegrau, P. (2000) 'Risks of communication: discourses on climate change in science, politics, and the mass media', *Public Understanding of Science* 9(3): 261–283.

Wendt, A. (1999) *Social Theory of International Politics*, Cambridge: Cambridge University Press.

Wight, C. (2002) 'Philosophy of social science and international relations', in: Carlsnaes, W., Risse, T. and Simmons, B.A. (eds) *Philosophy of Social Science and International Relations*, London and New York: SAGE, 23–51.

Wullweber, J. (2010) *Hegemonie, Diskurs Und Politische Ökonomie: Das Nanotechnologie-Projekt*, Baden-Baden: Nomos.

Yanow, D. and Schwartz-Shea, P. (2006) *Interpretation and Method: Empirical Research Methods and the Interpretive Turn*, New York: ME Sharpe.

Young, O.R. (1989) *International Cooperation: Building Regimes for Natural Resources and the Environment*, Ithaca: Cornell University Press.

Young, O.R. (1994) *International Governance: Protecting the Environment in a Stateless Society*, Ithaca: Cornell University Press.

Zelli, F. (2011) 'The fragmentation of the global climate governance architecture', *Wiley Interdisciplinary Reviews: Climate Change* 2(2): 255–270.

2 Discursive interplay and co-constitution

Carbonification of environmental discourses

Ayşem Mert

Introduction

It is impossible to discuss the environmental crisis today without referring to global climate change. Besides threatening the survival of species and planetary ecological cycles, climate change challenges the existing social and economic system at various levels: everyday habits of individuals are under scrutiny as household energy use, fossil fuel-dependent transport and meat consumption all exacerbate global warming. At another level, climate change challenges the existing social and economic system in its very foundations: not only consumerism but also the assumptions of linear economic growth, the necessity of industrialization for progress and the unquestionable desirability of development need all be framed and discussed anew if the climate crisis is to be resolved. It is for this reason (together with its unpredictable planet-wide effects) that climate change is a difficult political issue.

The extent to which climate change captures the social imaginary in modernized, industrialized societies is discernible in the number of movies, social campaigns and Internet blogs, controversies represented in them, as well as the new Corporate Social Responsibility (CSR) programmes that prioritize it over other issues (cf. Kellow 2007: 73). Conversely, it is manifest in the discourses of the climate sceptics, that regard climate activism as global-scale 'scaremongering' by 'eco-doomsayers' (Congressional Records of the USA 2006: 326). It is this power climate change seems to exert on the social imaginary that concerns this chapter.

More specifically, this power causes a number of transformations at the eco-political realm. An increasing number of NGOs try to link their various causes and projects to climate change to secure funding.[1] Critical ecological issues, such as desertification, forests and biodiversity (Crist 2007; Wapner 2011: 140; Chapter 4, this volume), as well as sectors such as agriculture and fisheries are being either redefined in relation to climate change and carbon emissions, or otherwise risk being ignored (Jinnah 2011; Wapner 2011). Ultimately, the proposals to solve the climate crisis are increasingly expansive: with the Intergovernmental Panel on Climate Change (IPCC) one of the biggest scientific networks has been formed; the funding climate change is attracting and the scope of geo-engineering projects increasingly proposed as solutions are both gigantic. When taken together, these examples point towards a paradigmatic change in the political and scientific approaches to environmental issues. Climate change is increasingly formative over other discourses, taking over 'as the dominate narrative of environmental movements [and] the leading driver of the new development agenda' (Goodman and Boyd 2010: 7). Yet, as carbon gets commodified and marketized, it acquires a 'social life' (Appadurai 1986) beyond its material essence as the building block of all life (Roston 2008). This paradigmatic change can be called *carbonification*, as carbon emissions become an ambivalent measure for environmental problems, solutions and their governance (Mert 2009; Goodman and Boyd 2010).

It is to be expected that issues that make up the microcosm of environmental governance influence one another, as they are all related to ecosystems connected in complex ways. Discourses of biodiversity, agriculture, energy production, toxic pollution and so forth co-construct one another. Rationales, techniques and terms are continuously transferred from one discourse to the other. In what follows, I argue that the way climate change structures the eco-political realm is puzzling and problematic. Thus, this chapter aims to highlight this paradigmatic change in environmental governance, and the challenges it brings to the policy process.

Second, it aims to scrutinize how carbonification relates to other meta-narratives of global governance. To do this, I focus on the interplay of several discourses that influence global environmental governance today: security, privatization and the financial crisis. The last decade has seen the (non-linear and indirect) influence of these discourses on all political issues, including environmental discourses: voluntary and market-based mechanisms that parallel the neoliberal globalization trends became fashionable – a process called 'privatization of governance', 'private governance' (Hall and Biersteker 2002), or even 'governance without government' (Rosenau and Czempiel 1992). Environmental discourses have also been reflecting concerns over security in the post-9/11 era, and over economic stability after the 2007 financial crisis. To demonstrate: the first proposal for the organization of an international Rio+20 Summit asked for a human and environmental security focus (see below). After the financial crises, however, the foci of the conference were agreed to be green economy and the institutional framework for sustainable development (UN 2012).

Finally, this chapter aims to establish discursive interplay and discursive co-constitution as concepts and tools for interpretive policy research: while discourses affect each other in various ways, some description and categorization of these influences can clarify and enrich the analyses of dominant discourses. Discursive interplay and co-constitution are most evidently manifest in symbolic political events, where seemingly unrelated narrative lines cross each other's way for the first time (or at a critical point) on the public domain: new texts and reports are produced by political actors with the aim of shaping politics; unexpected alliances are formed around policy-makers; new actors, concepts or frames of reference are introduced to various institutional platforms. Such symbolic events gave the climate discourse a new twist, framing, or a new representation. Simultaneously, they show how carbonification took place, providing a background for the analyses in the other chapters of this volume, such as securitization, technocratization and economization of climate change. Thus, some critical events are presented as brief examples of interplay between carbonification and other trends. In order for these examples to reach their aim, the next section defines interplay and co-constitution. The following section describes the four dominant trends and their impact on environmental discourses. Some examples of interplay are then elaborated to demonstrate the concepts, followed by the conclusions.

Discursive interplay and discursive co-constitution

The theoretical concepts employed in this chapter can be defined as follows: *discursive interplay* refers to situations when the contents, practices or frames of reference that belong to a discourse are significantly affected by another discourse. Like the use of the term in regime theory suggests (cf. Stokke 2001), interplay includes the uncalculated, unplanned and unintended consequences and side effects of one discourse over others. Even though some regime theory scholars proposed that interplay is 'manageable' (Oberthür and Stokke 2011), this is not the case with discursive interplay: discourses are embedded in language, rationales and practices, which makes such planning a matter of politics and power rather than management. While some of the influences on a discourse can be planned and intended, agents would not be able to control the results of their efforts.[2] This takes place in the midst of various political forces with diverse aims and actions with as many unintended consequences as consciously planned ones.

Discursive co-constitution refers to the circular and continuous formational influence of a discourse over others, while simultaneously being formed by them. In this process, discourses receive semiotic, symbolic or rhetorical elements from one another and are transformed. Co-constitution results in paradigmatic harmony, wherein common elements emerge in various discourses. For instance, discourses on sustainable energy production, recycling and waste reduction have common elements such as aiming to achieve clean production and sustainable growth without the necessity of having to change lifestyles – only production and disposal patterns. This environmentalist/modernist paradigm is distinguishable from other eco-political discourses. It is different from the green/autonomous paradigm (e.g. green politics and humanist eco-Marxism), which has a sceptical attitude towards techno-science and an anti-industrial stance. It is also different from the industrialist/modernist paradigm (e.g. conservationism and eco-socialism), which has an instrumentalist attitude towards nature (cf. Eckersley 1996).

Co-constitution is at times difficult to distinguish from the *logic of difference*: in Ernesto Laclau's (2005) terminology, logic of difference describes a situation where the hegemonic system intentionally aims to pacify or domesticate emerging challenges by suggesting a harmonious solution to the problem at hand, within the existing system. As a result, the political movement demanding the change finds itself either mainstreamed or marginalized. In this process, the hegemonic discourse is often co-constituted as well (if not, the interplay between the hegemonic discourse and the popular demand is one-dimensional). In sum, the logic of difference is one of the political dynamics that bring about discursive interplay or discursive co-constitution: both the hegemonic and the popular discourses are influenced and transformed by each other through a political process.

In other words, the causality or direction of influences across and among discourses is ambivalent, although the process is co-constitutive. While discursive interplay describes the asymmetrical influence of one discourse over others, discursive co-constitution is the de facto situation in politics: any successful discourse affects and is affected by others, which is made visible through politics, wherein politics is understood in Gramscian terms as a *war of position* (Laclau 2005: 89; Glynos and Howarth 2007). According to this view, change takes place slowly and incrementally, and yet it is constant. The society is always open to new articulations of identity, to new democratic demands, in short to constant political change. The implication of this ontological position for this study is that the examples focus on interplay, while co-constitution remains the background.

To clarify: Foucauldian discourse analysis examines how meaning is governed by specific rules, such that it often demonstrates how seemingly opposing articulations are in fact governed by a system that defines what can be meaningfully said. To illustrate: in the contestation regarding the efficacy of carbon markets as a governance mechanism to mitigate climate change, all parties would agree that climate change does happen, that it can indeed be mitigated, that it can be mitigated through the reduction of greenhouse gases and that carbon dioxide is the most important greenhouse gas. They would also agree that these negotiations should be held at an international platform (e.g. the UNFCCC). Therefore, while at the level of manifest politics there are different, opposing articulations, agents in fact share a common code through which they relate to each other; they struggle, but they struggle over the same issues, and opponents try to establish their hegemony, again, over the meaning of the same points (Laclau and Mouffe 1985).

Accordingly, politics is a constant tug-of-war between demands to change or maintain the existing system; yet, these demands constitute a continuum, being incrementally rather than fundamentally different from one another. Politics takes place in the dynamic sphere of continuity and change: Overbeek and Apeldoorn (2012: 1–22) aptly call this process 'the life course of hegemonic projects', wherein a (hegemonic) discourse first emerges and deconstructs the existing power relations, then, normalizes its values, consolidates into institutions, matures (wherein its contradictions are revealed), and enters a full-scale crisis. In a similar fashion, Ole Wæver conceives international relations as composed of layered structures of successive depth-levels. His metaphor of placing Foucauldian boxes in each other ideates a dynamic analysis that can specify 'change within continuity':

> Change is not an either–or question, because we are not operating at one level only. The concept of a 'dominant' discourse becomes relative, too. That something is in 'opposition' or even 'marginalised' means only that it is 'outside' and 'different' at the level of manifest politics, while it probably shares codes at the next (deeper) level of abstraction . . . The depth-levels [refer] to degrees of sedimentation: the deeper structures are more solidly sedimented and more difficult to politicise and change, partly because they are more abstract and

thereby logically implied across a wide spectrum. But, principally, change is always possible since all these structures are socially constituted. [When a dominant discourse cannot] handle a problem anymore ('dislocation'), it is possible first to make 'surface changes' which keep all the deeper levels intact. This can become increasingly uncomfortable and unstable, however, and at some point a deeper change might happen.

(Wæver 2005: 36–38)

Even if dominant discourses are embedded within societal power structures, resistance emerges at several points, and challenges the status quo. Sometimes these challenges can be domesticated and handled by making 'surface changes' in the institutions of the existing power structure. When this is not possible, paradigmatic changes might take place, affecting the deeper layers. Therefore, society is never a fully fixed entity; it is always contingent. The extent to which each discourse is transformed is undecided, which reveals the contingent nature of politics. Therefore, the results of interplay among particular discourses require a careful and detailed historical and political study. Studies of this kind are available regarding the various discourses of environment, development and democracy (e.g. Sachs 1992; Rist 1997). As this chapter has the more specific aim of studying the interplay between carbonification and other dominant discourses in global politics, the next section attends to these influences on environmental governance.

Global influences on environmental discourses

The security turn

The relationship between environment and security has been discussed by international relations (IR) scholars since the early 1990s: on the one hand it is argued that linking the 'soft politics' of environment with the 'high politics' of security might give environmental problems a sense of urgency and political importance. This potential advantage is counterpoised by the argument that such an affiliation would result in the 'securitization' of the environment in the sense that it would limit 'the range of means available for resolving environmental problems' (Graeger 1996).

Securitization refers to the transformation of an issue into a matter of security, or 'politics of existential threat' (Buzan et al. 1998: 25). After 9/11 security concerns overwhelmed the global agenda in general, and 'environmental security' became a catchphrase in governance. The first development summit after 9/11, the 2002 UN Conference on Financing for Development, produced the Monterrey Consensus – a milestone in the securitization of sustainable development. It emphasized that 'fighting poverty must be the main goal of an effective security policy' (Hofmann and Drescher 2002). George W. Bush (2002) aligned the two concepts in his plenary speech: 'poverty and hopelessness [allow for] conditions that terrorists can seize'. Yet, proposals for a global council on sustainable development and security, such as the Zedillo Report and Jacques Chirac's call, did not materialize (Hofmann and Drescher 2002).

After the Monterrey Conference, other elements of the sustainable development discourse have also been equated to security, with a reference to the Brundtland Report (WCED 1987). One of the earliest analyses of this shift (Khagram et al. 2003: 290) argued that 'human security highlights the social dimension of sustainable development's three pillars'. Already in 2002, the authors submitted the study to the UN Commission on Human Security, for discussion at the World Summit on Sustainable Development (WSSD). In 2005, *Human and Environmental Security: An Agenda for Change* was published, highlighting the importance of the security–environment interplay (Dodds and Pippard 2005). The editor of this volume, Felix Dodds, subsequently argued for a 2012 Earth Summit on human and environmental security, a title that has been officially proposed albeit turned down (Dodds and Sherman 2007).

The security–environment nexus remains on the academic agenda: in the context of global warming, climatic disasters threaten both human safety (Biermann and Boas 2010) and economic security (Bouwer 2011). Climate change is a national security issue for a few states (e.g. small island states) and may undermine the capacity of many other states to provide for their citizens, possibly resulting in violent conflict (Barnett and Adger 2007). A 2011 *Nature* article argued that social stability strongly relates to global warming, and predicted increased civil conflict in the tropics due to climatic changes (Hsiang et al. 2011).

This redefinition of human security to include environmental challenges is often not related to the immediate security threats climate change poses. Securitization had a stronger influence on the climate change discourse, vis-à-vis other environmental issues, because of climate change's low-probability/high-impact consequences (Barnett 2001: 4). This element pertaining to climate change is often depicted in popular culture, such as the movie *The Day After Tomorrow*, wherein globally catastrophic effects of climatic change irreversibly undermine human civilization in a matter of days (see Chapters 7 and 8 in this volume). It is a powerful imaginary that reveals how deeply the concept of security is embedded in modern environmental consciousness. In fact, the birth of modern environmentalism was marked by low-probability/high-impact risks of nuclear warfare and other industrial disasters with greater and better documented ecological impacts (e.g. the toxic dumping in Love Canal, the meltdown in Three Mile Island nuclear plant, the industrial disaster resulting from the operations of Dow Chemicals in Bhopal, the Chernobyl explosion and the Exxon-Valdez oil spill) (Sachs 1992).

I return to the securitization/carbonification interplay with examples, after describing other recent discursive shifts.

Privatization of environmental governance

Rosenau and Czempiel's (1992) famous term 'governance without government' highlights the recent intensification of non-state actor involvement in politics. Some scholars attribute this change to the end of ideological clash (Keck and Sikkink 1998), others to democratization (Glasbergen 2002), or to the increasingly complex character of governance issues (Biermann and Dingwerth 2004).

Another vein of IR scholars labels it as 'privatization of governance', by focusing on the neoliberal economic connotations of this transformation (Sassen 1996; Cutler et al. 1999; Hall and Biersteker 2002). The main features of this process are deregulation (or selective regulation), with an emphasis on voluntary schemes of non-/self-regulation, deployment of market-based approaches, network type organizational models, and more non-state actor involvement in decision-making. On the basis of this list, privatization of governance can be defined as the process through which non-state actors are increasingly included in the political decision-making – either by state actors willingly relinquishing some of their functions, or by unwillingly responding to the emerging authority of non-state actors – and in which regulatory approaches based on state coercion are replaced by market-based and voluntary mechanisms.

Privatization of environmental governance can be juxtaposed to the context of globalization and liberalization, too. Debates around the participation of corporate actors in global governance parallel the contestations of the 1960s about their role in modern societies (Mert 2012). These contestations resulted in a general consensus on the so-called stakeholder view of the corporation, which emphasized the responsibility of firms towards employees, customers and the larger community, as opposed to profit-maximization. As this view gained acceptance CSR programmes, developmental and environmental projects, and partnerships with local and national governments settled into the agendas and operations of corporations.

The New Right ideology of the 1980s promoted the ideas of New Public Management, based on the assumptions that the private sector provides a more efficient mechanism in producing public goods and services, and in order to reduce the size of the government, the public sector should retreat from these areas. These ideas took the shape of new governance institutions, such as public–private partnerships, corporate reporting schemes, standard-setting and labelling practices.

Simultaneously, at the international level, corporations became increasingly visible economic agents, because of the foreign direct investment they brought into economies and due to the social, economic and environmental effects of their operations. This was a time when globalization became the prevailing background for developmental and environmental policies; embedding these issues in liberal markets dovetailed the neoliberal shifts in the international economy. The demands to moderate the impacts of financial globalization and to place liberalism in a broader set of values (such as environmental concerns, human rights, labour rights, etc.) resulted in the 'compromise of liberal environmentalism' (Bernstein 2001).

In the beginning of this process, 'sustainable development' was conceptualized, seemingly reconciling economic growth and environmental protection, and has become the dominant perspective of the UN system. It was subsequently institutionalized into treaties during the UN Conference on Environment and Development, wherein an open international economic system was regarded as a precondition for 'economic growth and sustainable development in all countries' (UN 1992). The assumption that free trade, economic growth and environmental protection are compatible was reinforced in the WSSD in 2002: the Johannesburg Declaration performed a 'legitimating function for major trade agreements, including the WTO' (Bernstein 2005: 159), and new private governance mechanisms (sustainability partnerships) were endorsed as the Type-II outcomes of the Summit, to provide more efficiently what governments failed to provide. The Global Compact and the partnerships registered with the UN Commission on Sustainable Development (UNCSD) were the most visible indicators of a change in UN–business relations. By promising improvements in their operations, corporations would receive UN endorsement and in return initiate projects and contribute to the UN funds. Other private governance mechanisms were also increasingly popular, as the UN's endorsement of the World Commission on Dams and the Forest and Marine Stewardship Councils demonstrates.

The financial crisis and 'win-win' narratives

The most recent, albeit significant, influence on the global environmental discourses presented here is that of the 2006–7 subprime mortgage crisis, and the following global recession. Although environmental issues have been framed in economic and financial terms earlier (see Chapters 3 and 4 in this volume), starting in the mid-2000s, this tendency intensified and a new approach has emerged, which I call 'the win-win narrative'. The win-win narrative implies the double solution to financial/economic and environmental/social problems through increased investment in environmentally friendly sectors, and the promotion of so-called sustainable industries for economic growth and jobs. This model is different from traditional green economics of Leopold Kohr and E.F. Schumacher, which emphasize autonomy, local initiatives and human-scale economies. The win-win narrative on the contrary highlights the economic value of natural 'capital' and ecological 'services', and suggests a double-solution to the ecological and economic crises, as represented in UNEP's Green Economy Initiative. One of the earliest prominent expressions of this narrative was the 2006 Stern Review, which framed climate change as a primarily economic peril (Stern 2007). Shortly afterwards, the term 'green new deal' was coined (see below), and it was decided that the 2012 Rio+20 Conference would focus on green economy.

What is novel in this interplay is that it transforms the classical economic conception of environmental problems as externalities, and their solutions as problematic under liberal capitalism. On the contrary, the 'green economic revival' paradigm suggests that solutions to the financial and ecological crises are the same. However, the win-win narrative does not suggest a fundamental change in the organization of economies. It is rather a manifestation of how financial and economic terminology and framing extends to environmental discourses. This strategy is also employed by Secretary-General Ban Ki-Moon as he stresses the importance of role of comparative advantages in creating effective governance solutions: 'Addressing global challenges requires a collective and concerted effort, involving all actors. Through partnerships and alliances, and by pooling comparative advantages, we increase our chances of success' (UN 2010).

The win-win narrative is afflicted by the superimposition of the economic rationale, wherein the competitive concept of 'winning' becomes the organizing principle of environmental governance. Not only does it equate the reduction of transaction costs with effectiveness, but it also uses this economic definition of effectiveness to legitimize certain governance models. In sum, it conceals the conflicts between economic growth and ecological conservation. This win-win strategy aligning environmental and economic interest is manifest for instance in the global food crises, which has almost exclusively been discussed in financial terms: the problem was defined as the increase in the prices of staple foods, and discussed solutions were solely framed in terms of global trade and 'food security' (von Braun 2007: 10; Collier 2008). This was significantly different from the global North versus global South framing, attached to food crises in the 1980s (Berry 1984; Friedmann 1993).

Carbonification of environmental discourses

As introduced at the beginning of this chapter, carbonification refers to the process through which other environmental issues are understood in terms of their relation to and interplay with climate change, while every solution to climate change is reduced to and evaluated in terms of carbon emissions. In the last decade, environmental issues as important as biodiversity, desertification and deforestation (see Chapter 4, this volume) have been redefined through their relationship with climate change. If the resolution of an environmental problem contradicts the proposed solutions for climate change, it is highly likely that its solution is postponed if not altogether excluded. Hence, every campaign finds ways of allying their themes and goals with those of climate change. However, 'that climate change and the carbon economy has successfully "hijacked" just about every other environmental cause or concern might certainly be justified but there is still the question about how "right" or "good" this is and of the geographical differentiations or similarities to this "rightness" or "goodness" across spaces, places and scales' (Goodman and Boyd 2010: 7).

Eileen Crist (2007: 33) points to the dangers of representing climate change as the most urgent problem humanity faces: not only does this kind of framing restrict solutions to technofixes 'by powerfully insinuating that the needed approaches are those that directly address the problem [but also] it detracts attention from the planet's ecological predicament as a whole, by virtue of claiming the limelight for the one issue that trumps all others'. While I agree with her position, I would like to add to these arguments.

Crist mainly disagrees with climate change taking the centre stage because other environmental issues and the combined planetary ecological crisis are downplayed. Her study of biodiversity/climate interplay reveals a marginalization of biodiversity and a misleading focus on the consequences of global warming for biodiversity (as bio-depletion predates climate change and cannot be solved by its technological resolution). Second, as climate change becomes 'The Problem', proposed solutions (e.g. nuclear power, renewable energy, carbon-sequestration, placing deflection mirrors in space) view it as a technological issue. Technological solutions to phase out, supersede, capture or mitigate the effects of greenhouse gasses also put them into the limelight as opposed to more structural reasons of climate change, such as industrial production and consumption patterns. These potential solutions frame climate change as a problem of greenhouse gas emissions, particularly carbon emissions. The effectiveness and necessity of every proposed solution is calculated in terms of the amount of carbon emissions it reduces.

Some results of carbonification are alarming: international climate negotiations almost exclusively focus on the reduction of carbon emissions, a goal that sets aside the common cause of many other problems, simply put, unsustainable lifestyles (O'Hara 2007). Environmental friendliness of new (and old) technologies is evaluated on the basis of how much carbon they emit. This is not only the case with environmental but also with financial, military, agricultural technologies, and causes contestations: the contestations on the legitimacy of framing biofuels as clean fuels and their interplay with agriculture and security is one example (Runge and Senauer 2007). Simultaneously, nuclear power is promoted as a sustainable energy source and biofuelled fighter jets are promoted as green technology as they decrease the amount of carbon that 'would have been produced' (GE 2011; NPR 2011). The next section demonstrates some of these aspects through examples of interplay among discourses.

Interplay and co-constitution: examples

Securitization and carbonification: the IPCC and Al Gore receive the Nobel Peace Prize

The Nobel Peace Prize is granted every year to 'the person who [has] done the most or the best work for fraternity between the nations, for the abolition or reduction of standing armies and for the holding and promotion of peace congresses' (Noble Foundation 2007a). While their work is difficult to categorize under these criteria, the 2007 Nobel Peace Prize was awarded to Al Gore and the IPCC, 'for their efforts to build up and disseminate greater knowledge about man-made climate change, and to lay the foundations for the measures that are needed to counteract [it]' (Noble Foundation 2007b). The symbolic value of the prize derives precisely from the fact that the accumulation and dissemination of knowledge on climate change have nothing to do with peace-building. By awarding IPCC and Al Gore, the Nobel Committee has frustrated the climate sceptics, and endorsed the security–climate link at the highest level.

In their Nobel lectures after receiving the prize, Al Gore and the IPCC chairman Rajendra Pachauri diverged in the ways they made use of this gap in the mission statement of the Prize Committee and their work: while Al Gore emphasized the requirement of 'making peace with the planet' (Noble Foundation 2007c), Pachauri remarked more that IPCC 'provided scientific assessment of what could be a basis for future conflict' (Noble Foundation 2007d).

Securitization and carbonification: climate change was the first environmental issue discussed at the UN Security Council

In April 2007, UK Foreign Secretary Margaret Beckett (2007) suggested that the UN Security Council should take a central role in responding to climate change, and the UK government brought the issue to the council despite opposition from the United States, Russia and China. Within the United States, the most interesting party to support this move was the Centre for Naval Analyses, which published a report on the security challenges posed by climate change and the necessity of governmental action. The authors were 11 retired US Army generals, who regarded climate change as a 'threat multiplier' which could further destabilize volatile countries, or intensify scarcity-related conflicts (*Guardian* 2007; CNA 2007). The meeting was a failure due to lack of participants. Moreover, developing countries[3] as well as NGOs, such as the Worldwatch Institute (Renner 2007), showed discomfort over the choice of platform.

Dodds and Sherman argued against the initiative on the basis that it was wrong to exclude over 180 countries that were not represented in the Security Council:

> The question is not whether climate change is a threat to international peace and security, but more about how and where the world should have a discussion on addressing these issues creatively ... By 2012, 20 years from Rio, we need another Earth Summit this time on human and environmental security. If we don't, then the agenda of sustainable development will be dictated by the security concerns bringing major impacts on our lives and our democracies.
> (Dodds and Sherman 2007)

Despite their disagreement on the appropriate platform, Dodds and Sherman seem to agree with Margaret Beckett that environmental issues (in the form of climate change) and security are related issue areas that should be tackled together. Moreover, the suggestion for a human and environmental security summit points to the security/climate interplay that was dominant between 2001 and 2007.

Privatization and carbonification: nuclear energy partnerships registered with the UNCSD

Carbonification has influenced all environmental discourses but particularly energy policies. First, the conception of clean/sustainable energy has been tied to carbon emissions rather than the complete production process, which in the past included criteria on renewability, durability, quality, social effects, health risks and waste issues, and habitat effects. This change has presented an invaluable opportunity for both renewable energy producers to receive subsidies, and for the nuclear industry that was almost out of business due to high construction costs, high risks and unresolved waste problems.

The 'sustainability' partnerships registered with the CSD immediately before the 15th meeting of the commission (CSD-15), namely The Generation IV International Forum (GIF) and World Nuclear University (WNU), demonstrate how sustainable development was subjugated to climate change and reduced to carbon emissions. Until 2007, the CSD had no nuclear partnerships on its portfolio. These partnerships had their stands at the Partnerships Fair that ran parallel to CSD-15, and the WNU organized a high profile side-event, titled *The Contribution of Nuclear Energy to Sustainable Development*, with presentations on the benefits of nuclear energy for sustainable development and the necessity to influence public opinion for this cause. One speaker noted that the public ('naturally') lacked the knowledge to understand the importance of nuclear energy for climate change, and demanded social campaigns to win women and the youth over. Another speaker introduced the idea of 'nuclear renaissance', and its indispensability:

> Nuclear energy is under review again [in the context of climate change] and for good reason. It has been and will continue to be the largest source of emission-free energy . . . Nuclear plants are responsible for half of the total voluntary [emission] reductions reported by US companies in 2001 . . . Nuclear energy is the only source of energy that can provide consistent and substantial levels of energy while reducing . . . [correction:] while producing emission-free.[4]

Leaving aside the controversies around nuclear energy production, it is important to note how the discourse around clean energy production is increasingly being subdued to concerns over carbon emissions. Both of these partnerships claim climate change and sustainable energy production as their primary goals (WNU's specific goal is to increase the 'use of nuclear power as the one proven technology able to produce clean energy on a global scale') (UNCSD 2007). Their contribution to UN sustainability policies are stated as protection of the atmosphere and freshwater resources, transfer of environmentally-sound technology, and contribution to sustainability science. In sum carbonification introduced a controversial technology to the UN platforms, subjugating other issues on the CSD agenda to technofixes to remedy climate change.

The financial crisis and carbonification: the Green New Deal

The term 'Green New Deal' echoes Franklin Roosevelt's economic package in the wake of the Great Depression, and was coined in 2008, in the report 'A Green New Deal: Joined-up Policies to Solve the Triple Crunch of the Credit Crisis, Climate Change and High Oil Prices' (NEF 2009). The main suggestions of the report were new regulations on financial sectors, increased taxation of carbon-emitting industries, and public investments to replace fossil-fuel dependency with renewable energy production. The idea has gained popularity especially after the Obama Administration has (at least rhetorically) endorsed it in November 2008 (Daley 2008). It has been officially adopted by the UNEP (2009) as the 'Global Green New Deal' in April 2009. In this process the emphases on regulation and taxation were replaced by emphases on subsidies and green jobs.

There were other, similar initiatives from different sectors: among NGOs, Greenpeace (2008a) started its Green Finance Initiative with the aim of 'realign[ing] global financial investment with Greenpeace's definition of sustainability [and] and promote a responsible corporate governance framework that addresses global warming'. They further questioned government support for 'unsustainable industries', largely defined by the kind of energy consumed. Shortly afterwards, Greenpeace (2008b) published 'The Corporate Governance Framework for Climate Change', which was a call for corporate action towards mitigating the effect of business on climate change, accountability to make absolute carbon reductions and disclose the level of emissions in products, and capacity building to increase energy efficiency.

Among businesses, the emphasis was on the profitability of sustainable industries, inadvertently limiting sustainability to renewable energy production. For instance, in a joint report of the UN and the New Economics Foundation, it is celebrated that 'total global investment in clean-energy technologies jumped 60% in 2007' while only 7 per cent was divided among low-carbon technologies and energy efficiency (Rombel 2008). The Green New Deal and the reports, policy recommendations and business strategies around it has been a demonstration of both the win-win strategy between the particular environmental and economic interests, and the interplay between carbonification and the financial crisis.

Conclusions

Some issues generate so much public attention or become so prolific that they re-structure environmental governance practices, institutions and discourses. This chapter looked into the interplay among such discourses, namely, security, financial crisis, privatization and carbonification. First, carbonification was defined on two premises: the reframing of environmental issues through their relation to climate change, and commodification of carbon as a unit of measurement for environmental friendliness of technologies, policies and actions.

Second, I highlighted the alarming influences of carbonification: international negotiations focus primarily on the reduction of carbon emissions, and the proposed solutions measure all greenhouse gases in carbon units. Environmental friendliness of new technologies is assessed (often solely) on the basis of how much carbon they emit. At times, this type of evaluation produces debates like those on biofuels, where the agricultural production of crops for climate-friendly energy might result in food scarcity and/or deforestation. Other times, nuclear energy or fighter jets running on biofuels are promoted as environmentally friendly technologies. In short, carbonification alters perceptions and evaluations of what is good for the environment, often generating a race to the bottom, as these calculations are mostly based on carbon that would have been emitted.

Another implication of carbonification is that several political demands are aligned with climate change, intentionally (as in the case of climate bandwagoning) or unintentionally (as the structures, rationales and techniques dictate). As a result, climate change starts to signify several other environmental demands, it becomes a 'colossal' problem, and an apocalyptic view settles in. This view encourages direct and one-off solutions and limits the scope of 'legitimate and worthwhile solutions to climate change' to technofixes despite their potential risks.

I also argued that carbonification undermines other environmental issues on the political agenda and diverts attention from more fundamental causes of ecological degradation. As various discursive elements co-constitute climate discourses, it becomes increasingly intricate to negotiate international agreements and to generate legally coherent environmental governance. Effective climate governance requires 'everyone in the room'; but when the number of involved actors and aligned issues increase, less can be achieved (Wapner 2011).

How the competing discourses will sediment into new or existing institutions of global environmental governance remains to be seen. Yet, it seems reasonable to argue that a competition will take place between the existing hegemonic discourse of sustainable development and the newly emerging trends of carbonification, environmental security, private environmental governance and the win-win trend of the Green New Deal.

Notes

1 Interview with NGO representative to the UN Commission on Sustainable Development (UNCSD), New York, May 2008.
2 This aspect also differentiates the concept of discursive interplay from 'bandwagoning'. Recently, the term climate bandwagoning has been used to describe the conscious efforts of interested parties to link other issues with climate change in order to increase the amount of attention and/or funding these issues receive (cf. Jinnah 2011; McDermott *et al.* 2011; Conliffe 2011). Stakeholders 'jump on the climate bandwagon partly because they think they know both how to steer the cart and the direction it should go' although often this is not the case (Wapner 2011: 139). Similarly, actors might assume that they have control over discursive interplay, but the term incorporates the unintended dimension of discursive influences, as well.
3 On the surrounding UN debates see the UN media releases on the issue (UN 2011).
4 Transcribed from the presentations held in the Side Event to the CSD-15, 1/5/2007.

References

Appadurai, A. (1986) *The Social Life of Things*, Cambridge, Cambridge University Press.
Barnett, J. (2001) 'Security and Climate Change', *Tyndall Centre Working Paper* 7, October 2001.
Barnett, J. and Adger, N. (2007) 'Climate Change, Human Security and Violent Conflict', *Political Geography* 26: 639–655.
Beckett, M. (2007) 'The Case for Climate Security'. Online. Available at: www.rusi.org/events/past/ref:E464343E93D15A/info:public/infoID:E4643430E3E85A (retrieved: 16.11.2011).
Bernstein, S. (2001) *The Compromise of Liberal Environmentalism*, New York: Columbia University Press.
Bernstein, S. (2005) 'Legitimacy in Global Environmental Governance', *Journal of International Law and International Relations* 1(1–2): 139–166.
Berry, S. (1984) 'The Food Crisis and Agrarian Change in Africa', *African Studies Review* 27(2): 59–112.
Biermann, F. and Boas, I. (2010) 'Preparing for a Warmer World: Towards a Global Governance System to Protect Climate Refugees', *Global Environmental Politics* 10(1): 60–88.

Biermann, F. and Dingwerth, K. (2004) 'Global Environmental Change and the Nation State', *Global Environmental Politics* 4(1): 1–22.
Bouwer, L. (2011) 'Have Disaster Losses Increased Due to Anthropogenic Climate Change?', *Bulletin of the American Meteorological Society* 92(1): 39–46.
Bush, G.W. (2002) 'Remarks by Mr. George W. Bush (President of the United States of America) at the International Conference on Financing for Development, Monterrey, Mexico'. Online. Available at: www.un.org/ffd/statements/usaE.htm (retrieved: 10.8.2007).
Buzan, B., Wæver, O. and de Wilde, J. (1998) *Security: A New Framework for Analysis*, Boulder: Lynne Rienner Publishers.
CNA (2007) 'National Security and the Threat of Climate Change'. Online. Available at: www.cna.org/reports/climate (retrieved: 2.5.2011).
Collier, P. (2008) 'The Politics of Hunger: How Illusion and Greed Fan the Food Crisis', *Foreign Affairs* 87(6): 67–79.
Congressional Record of the United States of America (2006), No. 19598, 152(14): 326.
Conliffe, A. (2011) 'Combating Ineffectiveness: Climate Change Bandwagoning and the UN Convention to Combat Desertification', *Global Environmental Politics* 11(3): 44–63.
Crist, E. (2007) 'Beyond the Climate Crisis: A Critique of Climate Change Discourse', *Telos* 4: 29–55.
Cutler, C., Haufler, V. and Porter, T. (1999) *Private Authority and International Affairs*, New York: State University of New York Press.
Daley, B. (2008) 'Obama Urged to Create "Green New Deal"'. Online. Available at: www.boston.com/news/science/articles/2008/11/24/obama_urged_to_create_green_new_deal (retrieved: 16.11.2011).
Dodds, F. and Pippard, T. (2005) *Human and Environmental Security: An Agenda for Change*, London: Earthscan.
Dodds, F. and Sherman, R. (2007) 'Climate and the UN: A New Bid for Control?'. Online. Available at: news.bbc.co.uk/2/hi/science/nature/6665205.stm (retrieved: 16.11.2011).
Eckersley, R. (1996) 'Socialism and Ecocentrism: Toward a New Synthesis', in Benton, T. (ed.) *The Greening of Marxism*, New York: The Guilford Press, 272–297.
Friedmann, H. (1993) 'The Political Economy of Food: A Global Crisis', *New Left Review* 1(197): 29–57.
GE, General Electric (2011) 'GE Powers "Green Hornet" Fighter in Biofuel Flight'. Online. Available at: www.gereports.com/ge-powers-green-hornet-fighter-in-biofuel-flight/ (retrieved: 26.9.2011).
Glasbergen, P. (2002) 'The Green Polder Model: Institutionalizing Multi-Stakeholder Processes in Strategic Environmental Decision-Making', *European Environment* 12(6): 303–315.
Glynos, J. and Howarth, D. (2007) *Logics of Critical Explanation in Social and Political Theory*, Abingdon: Routledge.
Goodman, M. and Boyd, E. (2010) 'A Social Life for Carbon? Commodification, Markets and Care', Environment, Politics and Development Working Papers 36. Online. Available at: www.kcl.ac.uk/schools/sspp/geography/research/epd/working.html (retrieved: 11.2.2012).
Græger, N. (1996) 'Environmental Security?', *Journal of Peace Research* 33(1): 109–116.
Greenpeace (2008a) 'Green Finance Initiative'. Online. Available at: www.greenpeace.org/usa/campaigns/global-warming-and-energy/green-solutions/green-finance-initiative/ (retrieved: 17.10.2011).

Greenpeace (2008b) 'A Corporate Governance Framework for Climate Change'. Online. Available at: www.greenpeace.org/usa/Global/usa/binaries/2008/9/corporate-governance-for-clima.pdf (retrieved: 17.10.2011).

Guardian (2007) 'UK to Raise Climate Talks as Security Council Issue'. Online. Available at: www.guardian.co.uk/world/2007/apr/16/greenpolitics.climatechange (retrieved: 27.1.2012).

Hall, R. and Biersteker, T. (2002) *The Emergence of Private Authority in Global Governance*, Cambridge: Cambridge University Press.

Hofmann, M. and Drescher, R. (2002) 'The Monterey Consensus: A New Development Partnership', *D+C Development and Cooperation* 4(4–5): 26.

Hsiang, S., Meng, K. and Cane, M. (2011) 'Civil Conflicts are Associated with the Global Climate', *Nature* 476(25): 438–441.

Jinnah, S. (2011) 'Climate Change Bandwagoning: The Impacts of Strategic Linkages on Regime Design, Maintenance, and Death', *Global Environmental Politics* 11(3): 1–9.

Keck, M.E. and Sikkink, K. (1998) *Activists Beyond Borders: Advocacy Networks in International Politics*, Cambridge: Cambridge University Press.

Kellow, A. (2007) *Science and Public Policy: The Virtuous Corruption of Virtual Environmental Science*, Cheltenham: Edward Elgar.

Khagram, S., Clark, W.C. and Raad, D.F. (2003) 'From the Environment and Human Security to Sustainable Security and Development', *Journal of Human Development* 4(2): 289–313.

Laclau, E. (2005) *On Populist Reason*, London: Verso.

Laclau, E. and Mouffe, C. (1985) *Hegemony and Socialist Strategy: Towards a Radical Democratic Politics*, London: Verso.

McDermott, C., Levin, K. and Cashore, B. (2011) 'Building the Forest-Climate Bandwagon: REDD+ and the Logic of Problem Amelioration', *Global Environmental Politics* 11(3): 85–103.

Mert, A. (2009) 'Partnerships for Sustainable Development as Discursive Practice: Shifts in Discourses of Environment and Democracy', *Forest Policy and Economics* 11(5–6): 326–339.

Mert, A. (2012) 'The Privatisation of Environmental Governance: On Myths, Forces of Nature and other Inevitabilities', *Environmental Values* 21(4): 475–498.

NEF (2009) 'The Green New Deal'. Online. Available at: www.neweconomics.org/projects/green-new-deal (retrieved: 11.2.2011).

Nobel Foundation (2007a) 'Alfred Nobel's Will'. Online. Available at: nobelpeaceprize.org/eng_com_will2.html (retrieved: 22.9.2007).

Nobel Foundation (2007b) 'The Nobel Peace Prize 2007'. Online. Available at: nobelpeaceprize.org/ (retrieved: 22.9.2007).

Nobel Foundation (2007c) 'Al Gore's Noble Lecture'. Online. Available at: <nobelprize.org/nobel_prizes/peace/laureates/2007/gore-lecture_en.html> (retrieved: 10.12.2007).

Nobel Foundation (2007d) 'R.K. Pachauri's Noble Lecture'. Online. Available at: nobelprize.org/nobel_prizes/peace/laureates/2007/ipcc-lecture.html (retrieved: 10.12.2007).

NPR (2011) 'Air Force And Navy Turn To Biofuels'. Online. Available at: http://www.npr.org/2011/09/26/140702387/air-force-and-navy-turn-to-bio-fuels (retrieved: 12.3.2012).

Oberthür, S. and Stokke, O. (2011) *Managing Institutional Complexity: Regime Interplay and Global Environmental Change*, Cambridge: MIT Press.

O'Hara, E. (2007) 'Focus on Carbon "Missing the Point"'. Online. Available at: news.bbc.co.uk/2/hi/science/nature/6922065.stm (retrieved: 13.9.2007).

Overbeek, H. and van Apeldoorn, B. (2012) 'Introduction: The Life Course of the Neoliberal Project and the Global Crisis', in Overbeek, H. and van Apeldoorn, B. (eds) *Neoliberalism in Crisis*, London: Palgrave Macmillan, pp. 1–20.

Renner, M. (2007) 'Security Council Discussion of Climate Change Raises Concerns About "Securitisation" of Environment'. Online. Available at: www.worldwatch.org/node/5049 (retrieved: 16.11.2011).

Rist, G. (1997) *The History of Development: From Western Origins to Global Faith*, London: Zed Books.

Rombel, A. (2008) 'Cover Story: Green Finance'. Online. Available at: www.gfmag.com/archives/29-sept2008/86-green-finance.html#axzz0wRz3H4HP (retrieved: 16.11.2011).

Rosenau, J. and Czempiel, O. (1992) *Governance without Government: Order and Change in World Politics*, Cambridge: Cambridge University Press.

Roston, E. (2008) *The Carbon Age: How Life's Core Element Has Become Civilization's Greatest Threat*, New York: Walker and Company.

Runge, F. and Senauer, B. (2007) 'How Biofuels Could Starve the Poor', *Foreign Affairs* 86(3): 41–54.

Sachs, W. (1992) 'Environment', in Sachs, W. (ed.) *The Development Dictionary: A Guide to Knowledge as Power*, London: Zed Books, 1–5.

Sassen, S. (1996) *Losing Control? Sovereignty in an Age of Globalization*, New York: Columbia University Press.

Stern, N. (2007) *Stern Review: The Economics of Climate Change*, London: HM Treasury.

Stokke, O. (2001) 'The Interplay of International Regimes: Putting Effectiveness Theory to Work', *FNI Report* 14/2001.

UN (1992) 'Rio Declaration on Environment and Development', UN Doc. A/CONF.151/26, Vol. 1, Annex 1.

UN (2010) 'United Nations Office for Partnerships'. Online. Available at: www.un.org/partnerships (retrieved: 1.11.2010).

UN (2011) 'Security Council Holds First-Ever Debate on Impact of Climate Change on Peace, Security. Hearing over 50 Speakers'. Online. Available at: www.un.org/News/Press/docs/2007/sc9000.doc.htm (retrieved: 4.5.2011).

UN (2012) 'Rio+20 United Nations Conference on Sustainable Development – Objective and Themes'. Online. Available at: www.uncsd2012.org/rio20/objectiveandthemes.html (retrieved: 2.2.2012).

UNCSD (2007) 'World Nuclear University'. Online. Available at: webapps01.un.org/dsd/partnerships/public/partnerships/1859.html (retrieved: 01.8.2007).

UNEP (2009) 'The UNEP Report on Green Economy, 2009'. UNEP Website. Online. Available at: www.unep.org/greeneconomy/GlobalGreenNewDeal/tabid/1371/Default.aspx (retrieved: 6.11.2011).

von Braun, J. (2007) *The World Food Situation: New Driving Forces and Required Actions*, Washington, DC: IFRPI.

Wæver, O. (2005) 'European Integration and Security: Analysing French and German Discourses on State, Nation and Europe', in Howarth D. and Torfing J. (eds) *Discourse Theory in European Politics: Identity, Policy, Governance*, Basingstoke: Palgrave, 33–67.

Wapner, P. (2011) 'The Challenges of Planetary Bandwagoning', *Global Environmental Politics* 11(3): 137–144.

WCED (1987) *Our Common Future: Report of the World Commission on Environment and Development*, Oxford: Oxford University Press.

Part I
The economization of climate change

3 Climate politics as investment

Understanding discourse through governmental practice

Simon Wolf

Introduction

Investment talk has loomed large in climate politics in recent years: governments consider ways to engage the private sector for financing climate protection activities, the UN Secretary General has invited banks to join his High Level Advisory Group on Climate Finance, and investor organizations urge governments to agree on an ambitious climate deal. The message from these and similar processes is usually the same: the amount of investment needed for climate protection is enormous, but can be achieved when private investors are engaged. A great number of new instruments and policies seek to stimulate low-carbon investment, accordingly. The World Bank and national governments have created climate investment funds; low-carbon strategies aim at enhancing investment to low-carbon economies; and the objective to enhance clean investment also plays a role in the governance of carbon market instruments like the Clean Development Mechanism (CDM).

This chapter seeks to explain the new emphasis on investment, and to reflect its significance within the greater picture of climate change governance. In doing so, it closes a gap in the social science literature on finance and investment in climate politics that has largely focused on carbon markets thus far, but missed to create a broader perspective on financing climate protection that has emerged in recent years and has also changed the role of carbon markets. The chapter argues that the turn to investment is embedded in a changing understanding of the climate challenge that can be described as financialization: starting from the increasing awareness of the economic risks and opportunities related to climate change, governmental strategies seek to align economic and climate protection objectives by raising finance for climate related activities; enhancing the contribution of private investors can be considered as a crucial part of these strategies.

This analysis applies a governmentality approach (Foucault 2007), in order to study how this financialization changes existing attempts to govern climate change. A governmentality perspective highlights the mutual constitution of governmental rationalities and practices, and shows how governmental activities constitute the objects they address. Methodologically, the chapter largely follows the heuristic that Dean (2010) develops for his analysis of *regimes of practices*, and combines it with insights from the Foucault's *dispositif* concept. The objective is to develop a methodology that does not start from the diagnosis of a particular governmentality, but focuses on the emergence and significance of governmental practices.

After outlining this particular research perspective in the following section, the chapter proceeds by describing the discourses that problematize a lack of private investment for climate protection and the low-carbon transformation. This section moreover provides a terminology and rationality for addressing this lack. It then discusses Public Finance Mechanisms and proposals for reforming the Clean Development Mechanism as governmental practices that aim at enabling low-carbon investment, and contribute to the emergence of a climate investment dispositif. The empirical analysis forms the basis for reflecting the significance of the investment turn within the greater context of climate change governance: The government of investment can be understood as a part of the *return of the state* in global climate governance, which aims at making markets work for climate protection; it is important therefore to have a closer look at what is made visible and invisible in the strategies that target investment for climate protection. The last section concludes and reflects difficulties encountered with the research perspective applied in this chapter.

Theory and methodology

Foucault did not develop a methodology for the analysis of governmentalities, and the governmentality literature offers different, but sometimes also problematic, approaches: these do not always distinguish accurately between governmentality as an analytical perspective and the diagnosis of specific governmentalities, and have a tendency to overemphasize the rationalities compared to the practices of government (Rose *et al.* 2006). This section, thus, starts by reflecting how Foucault addresses the power/knowledge nexus, in particular the role of practices in the formation of rationalities.

Foucault and the power–knowledge nexus

In one of the interviews in which Foucault reflects on his work, he suggests that the main objective of his empirical studies was to identify problematizations as the ensemble of discursive and non-discursive practices that constitute something as an object of thought (Foucault 1985). Through the notion of problematization, Foucault emphasizes both thinking as a driver of historical change, and the structural conditions that enable and constrain these processes of thought. Problematizations, in that sense, 'define the conditions in which human beings "problematize" what they are, what they do, and the world in which they live' (Foucault 1986: 10).

From a methodological point of view, the concept links and reorganizes Foucault's two central research methods, *archaeology* and *genealogy* (Lemke 1997). Archaeology aims 'to examine the forms of problematization themselves' (Foucault 1986: 11–12), and genealogy scrutinizes the formation of problematizations or rationalities 'out of the practices and their modifications' (Foucault 1986: 11–12). In another interview, Foucault explains the emphasis on the practices of government present in the genealogical style of analysis that is central to his later work. Genealogy accounts for moments of discontinuity or change by rediscovering the elements and practices 'which at a given moment establish what subsequently counts as being self-evident, universal and necessary' (Foucault 1991: 76). It thus replaces strong causal explanation with a pluralization of causes.

The other important point that Foucault makes here is that the link between rationalities and practices of government is not a one-way relationship. Governmental practices are informed by rationalities or governmental programmes on different levels, but are not determined by these; rather, they 'possess up to a certain point their own specific regularities, logic, strategy, self-evidence and "reason"' (Foucault 1991: 75). The objective is thus to analyse how practices – as always meaningful – contribute to the formation of knowledge and rationalities.

Foucault has constantly pointed out this co-constitution of forms of power and historical knowledge in his empirical studies and through concepts like disciplines and biopower. Against this background, the governmentality notion serves, on the one hand, as an analytical perspective that highlights the relation of strategies, programmes and technologies of government (Rose *et al.* 2006). On the other hand, the governmentality concept also describes a specific power-knowledge formation. Introducing the concept in his 1978 lectures, Foucault focused on governmentality as the specific Western form of (state) power that 'has as its target population, as its principal form of knowledge political economy, and as its essential technical means apparatuses of security' (Foucault 1998: 108). In this context he described government as specific form of power that works through shaping the field of possible actions for others (Foucault 2007).

Combining regimes of practice with a dispositif perspective

Dean (2010) has developed a methodology for studying governmentality in form of an *analytics of regimes of practice*. It highlights the 'complex and variable relations' (Dean 2010: 27) between governmental practices and (historical forms of) truth. Dean's framework focuses on practices of government, understood as 'any more or less calculated and rational activity, undertaken by a multiplicity of authorities and agencies, employing a variety of techniques and forms of knowledge, that seeks to shape conduct by working through the desire, aspirations, interests and beliefs of various actors' (Dean 2010: 18).

Dean's heuristic for the analysis of regimes of practice builds on the insight that governmental practices do not merely address an object of government but constitute it in its concrete form, and it makes use of how Deleuze (1992) systemizes the dispositif concept in this respect. Practices, or regimes of practices, first, produce a *field of visibility*, including maps, charts and other media, that make the object of government visible and understandable, and indicate what problems are to be solved; second, they deploy a certain *technical dimension* of government in form of tactics, techniques or procedures; third, regimes of practices are informed by the *episteme of government*, that is, the forms of knowledge and rationality that arise from and inform the practices of governing; fourth, they produce certain forms of *identities* through which government operates, on both the side of the governing (experts, politicians, etc.) and the governed (workers, consumers, etc.).

This research strategy can be further defined by building on the dispositif concept and its application in recent studies. Dispositifs are power-knowledge formations that relate discursive orders to forms of power and practices. Foucault describes the dispositif as a *thoroughly heterogeneous ensemble* that contains discourses, institutions and practices; it is also the web that links these elements and directs them towards a strategic objective (Foucault 1980).

A change in the environment of governmental practices, rather than the interests or intentions of a certain actor, is the starting point for the emergence or evolution of a dispositif. The dispositif is a

> formation which has as its major function at a given historical moment that of responding to an *urgent need*. The apparatus thus has a dominant strategic function. This may have been, for example, the assimilation of a floating population found to be burdensome for an essentially mercantilist economy.
> (Foucault 1980: 195)

This strategy links the elements of the dispositif and emerges from their interplay at the same time.

As analytical tool or *grid of interpretation*, the dispositif helps to account for the emergence of practices and institutions within a certain rationality or discursive constellation (Howarth 2000). The dispositif perspective defines the object of analysis as practices that cohere around a similar objective, and asks how their emergence is related to changes of governmental rationality. Such an understanding of the dispositif also helps to address another important issue in the analysis of governmentality – the question of agency and, related to this, change. Governmentality studies are sometimes accused of focusing on the systematic nature and internal coherence of discursive or governmental constellations, but they do not account for their emergence and change. In that sense, they seem to have a structural bias and lack an agency perspective.

Such critique, however, 'ignore[s] governmentality's genealogical foundations and thus its emphasis on the contingent and invented (and thus always mutable) nature of governmental thought and technique' (Rose *et al.* 2006: 99). We have seen that Foucault highlights – through the notion of problematization – both thinking as a driver of historical change and the (structural) conditions for governmental thought and practice. Governmental practice takes place within these conditions but is not their necessary consequence; rather, it is an attempt by governmental agencies to make sense of and cope with certain social conditions.

The dispositif concept is well suited to capture this interplay of structural conditions and agency: it highlights how the strategies of different actors cohere around a common strategic objective, without the need for a hegemonic force or a congruence of interests between all actors. Rather than to ask, who pushed through her interests, dispositif analysis examines the contexts and practices that contribute to the emergence of a problematization, and how it is accessible for a variety of strategies and interests.

Heuristically, it makes sense therefore to distinguish an archaeological from a genealogical dimension in the dispositif analysis: archaeology focuses on the coherence of governmental formations, it seeks to identify the common ground in the strategies or practices of different actors. Genealogy, on the contrary, takes up a much wider perspective, to capture the many elements that contribute to the formation of a problematization. In this sense then for Foucault, a genealogical style of explanation replaces strong causality with a pluralization of causes, and leads to an 'increasing polymorphism' of elements and the relations between them (Foucault 1991: 77). Dean (2010: 39) suggests that analysing governmental practice means to 'examine all that which is necessary to a particular regime of practices of government, the conditions of government in the broadest sense of that word. In principle, this includes an unlimited and heterogeneous range of things'. Clearly, as Dean also highlights, genealogical analysis does not simply list these things, but reflects how they are rationalized in governmental thought and practice.

The climate investment dispositif

The first step of empirical analysis shows how the discourses in two particular contexts – Public Finance Mechanisms and proposals for reforming the Clean Development Mechanism – construct and make visible a lack of private investment for climate protection and the low-carbon transformation. While these discourses overlap in many ways, scrutinizing them separately highlights their particular contributions to the emergence and framing of the investment challenge.

Climate finance: from compensation to investment

The provision of climate finance from developed to developing countries has been an issue in the UNFCCC negotiations almost from the beginning. Initially, the primary objective was to support adaptation in those (developing) countries that are most vulnerable to climate change through several climate funds created at COP 7 in Marrakesh in 2001. Subsequently, however, the climate finance debate widened its scope and changed its character after COP 13 in Bali in 2007. Since then, climate finance increasingly targets mitigation in the Global South as well.

Two main arguments can be found in the literature that account for the increasing role of mitigation in the Global South. These are a growing awareness of the magnitude of the climate challenge and the increasing contribution of developing countries to global emission levels on the one hand and new calculations that highlight the availability of comparably cheap abatement opportunities in developing countries on the other.

Following the perception that existing climate finance funds offer much less than what is needed for emission reductions in developing countries, the climate finance debate in recent years turned towards the private sector. Studies, including reports from the UNFCCC and the UN Secretary General's High Level Group on Climate Finance, started to consider potential contributions from private sources.

Many developing countries, however, refuse to accept private money as counting towards the obligations of developed countries.

Climate funds remain an important issue in the international climate regime; increasingly, however, governments and international organizations also consider strategies beyond the UNFCCC context to encourage climate related investment to developing countries. The creation of the World Bank Climate Investment Funds (CIFs) that aim at joint investments with the private sector played a crucial role here (see below).

The new interest in private sector contributions also brought new actors to the climate finance debate. One example is a cooperation between McKinsey, members of the British government and the finance industry organized by Nicholas Stern in the run-up to COP 15 in Copenhagen in 2009. Actors in this initiative quickly agreed that private investment will play a crucial role for achieving the necessary levels of climate finance, but also that little is known about how to encourage investment to climate related activities. Their publication, accordingly, focuses on constraints to low-carbon investment and ways to overcome them, and is an important part of formation of *knowledge* on the government of investment (Romani 2009).

Another influential tool in the climate finance and investment debate is the McKinsey's Global Greenhouse Gas Abatement Cost Curve: the initial version displayed the cost-effectiveness of mitigation opportunities on a global scale, and helped to make the argument for cost-effectiveness in developing country mitigation (McKinsey 2009). Increasingly, it is applied to national contexts as well, in particular in developing countries: it makes investment opportunities related to climate change visible and in this way allows framing climate protection strategies around the investment needs and opportunities in different sectors.

Going low-carbon: from threat to opportunity in climate protection

Enabling clean investment also plays an important role in the strategies governments formulate to put economies on a low-carbon growth track – hence, to align climate protection with economic objectives. The low-carbon economy narrative gained track through proposals for a Green New Deal (GND) after the global financial crisis of 2007. But whereas GND proposals largely focus on greening financial stimulus packages, low-carbon strategies aim at a more fundamental economic transformation (European Commission 2011).

In the form of low-carbon development strategies, the focus of climate policy shifts from international negotiations to domestic activities. One crucial task for states in orchestrating the low-carbon transformation is to address the obstacles that prevent higher levels of low-carbon investment (UNDESA 2011). This new emphasis on raising finance and investment for climate protection is met by the increasing interest of investors in financing climate related activities. During the climate negotiations in Copenhagen in 2009, investor networks from Europe and the United States launched the *Investor Statement on the Urgent Need for a Global Agreement on Climate Change*, highlighting that investors are concerned with climate impacts and interested in the opportunities created by its regulation: 'It is therefore critical that heads of state and policymakers understand how climate change related public policy will influence investment decisions' (IIGCC *et al.* 2009: 1). One year later, the same investor groups highlighted that private finance is crucial to close the 'climate investment gap' (IIGCC *et al.* 2010: 1).

Renewable energies: understanding investment behaviour

Since the early 1990s, organizations like Greenpeace and the UNEP Finance Initiative (FI) have sought to raise the awareness of the finance industry for the risks and opportunities of climate related investment. More recently, the UNEP FI also tried to articulate and communicate a finance sector perspective on the role of climate regulation for clean investment to the climate policy arena.

Investors as new actors in climate politics are accompanied by all kinds of financial experts that analyse the climate challenge from an investment perspective. According to them, it is most important to address the risks and uncertainties related to low-carbon investment. The risk terminology translates the obstacles to climate protection or the low-carbon transformation into specific investment risks that can be addressed by technical interventions. The challenge is not, as Hamilton (2009: 2) emphasizes, to find 'a large pot of money quickly', but to create conducive and reliable investment frameworks.

Governing investment for climate protection

This section analyses governmental activitities that address investment for climate protection from different directions: Public Finance Mechanisms seek to lower the risks related to low-carbon investment, and proposals for reforming the Clean Development Mechanism aim to enhance the environmental performance of carbon finance.

Public Finance Mechanisms

Public Finance Mechanisms (PFMs) most explicitly take up the objective to enable low-carbon investment, through public–private investment schemes or risk-sharing products. The British government created a Green Investment Bank (GIB), to address the barriers to low-carbon investment in the UK. The GIB is meant to support, not replace, private investment: 'Wherever private sector activity is viable, the private sector, banks and investors should lead and execute deals. The GIB would act as an enabler for the private sector [and] commit the minimum resources required to support these functions' (GIB 2010: 14).

Whereas one part of the GIB, the UK Fund for Green Growth, can support low-carbon innovation and new clean tech enterprises through grants, subsidies and low-interest loans, the majority of GIB activities should be self-funding and aim for commercial rates of return, raising money from capital markets. 'This would allow the UK to . . . open up high growth opportunities to business without significantly increasing the public sector commitment' (GIB 2010: 26). To that end, the

Banking Division of the GIB deploys various finance products that address investor concerns: public equity co-investment in low-carbon projects in the development phase is intended to lower the concerns of private investors; investing specific types of debt like mezzanine debt, the GIB would receive lower returns than other investors and thus raise the returns of the latter; and a variety of insurance products address specific investment risks. In developing countries different types of PFMs play an increasingly important role in financing mitigation and enabling low-carbon investment activities, as well. As in the case of the GIB, their task is not to duplicate private sector activities, but to 'perform roles that the private sector cannot or will not play' (Ward et al. 2009: 15).

The World Bank Climate Investment Funds are thus far the largest PFMs that target clean investment to developing countries. The World Bank began to expand its climate funding activities based on a mandate given at the G8 meeting in Gleneagles in 2005. In 2008, the Board of Executive Directors formally approved the creation of the Clean Technology Fund (CTF) and the Strategic Climate Fund (SCF), which have similar funding principles and ways of engaging the private sector. In the following, the focus is on the Clean Technology Fund (CTF).

The provision of finance or guarantees to private companies takes place within a country investment plan in which governments, together with the private sector and other stakeholder groups, define how CTF finance can help to scale-up low-carbon activities. Both public and private sector activities with CTF support are assessed according to their potential for cost-effective emissions savings, and how they address barriers to further low-carbon investment.

The objective, thus, is to reduce risks or costs that prevent companies from investing or entering a new market, as early movers usually face higher risks and costs than the later entrants to a market. Buying down these costs or mitigating these risks would thus not only enable initial market activities, but demonstrate the viability of a certain technology or industry and thus allow for replication without – or at least with lower – subsidies.

To this end, the CTF offers financing and risk management tools, all of which include a grant element to lower the additional costs of investment or the risks that lenders and investors are not willing to accept. The objective is, however, to intervene into markets or investment decisions only to the degree that is necessary to avoid distortions and crowd-in the maximum possible level of investment. The CTF does not support projects that are expected to produce losses, but only projects where 'the real market risks are lower than the market perceives them to be' (World Bank 2010: 3).

Making carbon markets work for clean investment: the reform of the CDM

In recent years carbon markets have become the centrepiece of global climate regulation. They have been fundamental in bringing about an understanding of the investment opportunities related to climate protection and have thus 'mobilized the world of private capital to work in favour of protecting the environment'

(World Bank 2008a: 22). Today, a great variety of companies – including investment banks, carbon finance start-ups, law firms, auditors and consultancies – seek return from low-carbon investment.

The focus in this case is on how the climate investment discourse influenced recent proposals to reform carbon market governance and improve the contribution of carbon market finance to climate protection objectives. This is particularly obvious in proposals for reform of the CDM. The CDM as an offset mechanism was created with two objectives: to enhance sustainable investment in developing countries, and to lower the costs of emissions reductions for industrialized countries. But whereas it helped lowering the compliance costs for the latter, it was less successful in financing sustainable development (Sutter and Parreño 2007).

Many assessments identify a systematic problem and a trade-off between the two CDM objectives: the focus on cost-effectiveness in reducing emissions sets a barrier to financing projects that provide wider social and environmental benefits, as these goals are not monetized and play a limited role in investment decisions (Holm Olsen 2007). Thus, what has been regarded as one of the primary strengths of market mechanism turns out to be the central problem: the high diversity of project types within the CDM and carbon markets in general offers profitable investment opportunities, but limits the influence of governments in directing resources to the right places and projects (Wara 2007).

Increasing emphasis is therefore given to reforms that would make the CDM work for sustainable investment. This is strengthened by the investment turn in climate governance, as carbon markets are generally seen to have great potential as a tool for raising climate finance and leveraging low-carbon investment to developing countries (Clifton 2009). However, fundamental reform are deemed necessary both to scale-up carbon finance and to improve its contribution to sustainable and low-carbon development, in particular with respect to energy and infrastructure development (World Bank 2008b). A great number of proposals seek to improve the geographical equity of the CDM and enhance the market value of projects with greater social and environmental benefits, through the discrimination of CDM project types and certificates, the transformation of the CDM into a sector crediting mechanism, or intermediary carbon banks. These proposals have in common that they replace carbon market flexibility with a greater number of specific criteria. They reflect the understanding 'that left to itself, the market will not finance high quality projects' (Pearson 2007: 251). While the creation of carbon markets was embedded in an efficiency narrative that posits the superiority of markets in identifying cost-effective mitigation projects, the need for state intervention has been increasingly emphasized to make carbon markets work as a tool for financing climate protection and the low-carbon transformation. A reformed CDM, then, would replace a bottom-up approach with more top-down regulation (Stripple 2010).

A new problematization of climate change

The investment dispositif is part of a changing problematization of the climate challenge in recent years, as it is acknowledged that enhanced state intervention is required to align climate protection and economic objectives. A critical perspective on these processes must highlight what is made visible and invisible in this problematization.

The return of the state in climate governance

The growing awareness for the economic risks and opportunities related to climate change, together with the limited success of mitigation strategies in recent years, contribute to a changing understanding of the role of states and markets in aligning climate protection with economic growth. The transformation to low-carbon economies requires, according to Giddens (2009: 8), a 'return of planning' and 'active state intervention'; Nicholas Stern calls for a new industrial revolution led by policy (Gordon 2011), and Newell and Patterson (2010: 161ff.) highlight the crucial role of governments in making carbon markets work for climate protection.

The return of the state, however, is not to be confused with a return to top-down government; rather, the *ensuring state* should act as a facilitator or enabler for private activities, and 'allow market forces to become centred upon promoting environmental benefits' (Giddens 2009: 92). What is needed is 'a framework for the entrepreneurship and discovery across the whole of business and society, which can show us how to achieve a cleaner, safer, more sustainable pattern of growth and development' (Stern 2009: 7).

The analysis of the investment dispositif allows to take a closer look at the new role that is ascribed to the state. Both Public Finance Mechanisms and the reform of the CDM are state interventions that aim at enabling and stimulating low-carbon investment and, ultimately, at contributing to the creation of markets. The climate investment discourse, apparently, formulates a strategy for aligning climate regulation with commercial activities by addressing obstacles for climate related investment activities. Public Finance Mechanisms show that mitigation activities must be viable in financial market terms: it is the risk–return expectations of large investors that decide whether certain projects are realized, and governments have to organize climate protection around these expectations. Likewise, the CDM reform proposals highlight the need for technical interventions that enhance its contribution to sustainability while maintaining the attractiveness for investors.

Visibilities and invisibilities

Creating markets for climate protection, however, starts long before the first money flows or the first contracts for public–private cooperations are signed; the more fundamental contribution of the climate investment discourse is framing climate protection as commercial activities. 'In speculative enterprises', Tsing (2004: 84) writes, 'profit must be imagined before it can be extracted'. The climate investment discourse is such a form of imagination, as it allows for solving the climate challenge through finance and investment.

This *performativity* of the investment discourse is best visible in how forest protection is described from an investment perspective: the Informal Working Group on Interim Financing for REDD+ suggests that deforestation is a market failure that can be corrected by providing the appropriate level of finance (see Chapter 4 in this volume). Furthermore, the publications by Nicholas Stern and McKinsey, together with representatives from the finance industry and the British government, describe the root causes of deforestation as 'economic in nature, stemming from under-investment in the sustainable production of land-based commodities' (Romani 2009: 17).

It is obvious that these are contingent framings of the challenge to reduce emissions from forests, as the root causes of deforestation – through a different lens – could be described as overexploitation of forest resources at the community level or the consequence of global demand for forest products; these framings would enable and require different solutions. Framing climate protection or low-carbon activities in terms of investment risks and opportunities helps to imagine and create space for commercial activities. The need for national governments to ensure a 'viable deal flow' (Romani 2009: Summary, 11) or 'a pipeline of investment-ready projects' (Maclean *et al.* 2008: 6) points to the current non-existence of markets for profitable low-carbon investment in some countries or sectors; state intervention is meant to enable low-carbon economic activities therefore. However, the (discursive) processes that make an object or particular characteristics of it visible, render others *in*visible at the same time. The following paragraphs highlight two ways in which the climate investment discourse insulates issues from the discussion.

On the one hand, the climate investment discourse is largely embedded within a positive narrative that highlights the economic opportunities from climate protection and the low-carbon transformation. Investors, as the potential winners of this transformation, are seen as a powerful ally in establishing the frameworks for a decarbonization of economies (Newell and Patterson 2010). While this is understood as a more realistic approach to climate protection, it obscures all those economic activities that contribute to the climate crisis, and instead seeks to replace them by building low-carbon alternatives quickly. On the other hand, the climate investment discourse points to the links between the low-carbon transformation and financial market organization. But it is widely silent on the necessary changes to the financial system. Exceptions can be found, for instance, in the Green New Deal debate. The Green New Deal Group claims that reducing the structural power of capital markets is a precondition for regulation that directs investment towards climate protection (Green New Deal Group 2008: 23).

Usually, however, the climate investment discourse helps to maintain rather than question the picture of a bounded and thus powerful financial system. Strategies for the low-carbon transformation thus build on the fundament of global financial markets and they have to cope with the constraints they impose on organizing transformational change. In general, the climate investment discourse suggests a technical approach to governing investment for climate protection, and thus helps to maintain finance as one of 'modern society's most depoliticized areas of activity' (de Goede 2005: 2).

Conclusion

This chapter analysed recent changes in climate change discourse, focusing on new governmental practices that aim at investment for climate protection. Though they address the investment challenge from different angles, it was argued that they are part of and contribute to the emergence of an investment dispositif in climate governance.

Dean's heuristic for the analysis of regimes of practices helped to identify important processes in the formation of investment for climate protection as an object of government: the *visibility* of the investment challenge is related to the discourses and developments in three overlapping contexts; the *knowledge* on the investment challenge and the *rationality* for addressing it is strongly influenced by the increasing activities of investors in climate politics. Seeing climate protection from an investment perspective allows for *technical interventions* that enable low-carbon investment while making more fundamental changes unnecessary.

The dispositif perspective helped to understand the emergence of the investment challenge in climate politics not as the expression of the interests of a hegemonic force, but rather as a loose coupling of strategies around increasingly common understandings and interests: addressing climate change from an investment perspective is attractive for state actors and various businesses alike, even though they follow different objectives.

Combining the regimes of practices approach with the dispositif perspective thus allowed for an innovative perspective on current climate governance. Nevertheless, a number of open questions remain for an approach that aims at analysing discourse through practices. One issue that deserves particular attention is the formation and transformation of identities. Whereas Dean suggests that these processes play a role on both the side of the governing and the governed, the question that arises is if and how this perspective can be fruitfully applied to the practices of professionals that address the behaviour of other professionals. In the case of investment for climate protection, one would have to ask who is governing whom, as both governments and investors shape the field of possible actions of the other side.

With respect to the future of climate governance, the chapter showed that the climate investment discourse is only evolving, and that its future direction is thus still wide open. Nevertheless, in the context of the increasing attention for the economic opportunities of low-carbon growth and development (with or without climate change regulation) on the one hand, and the highly insecure prospects for meaningful international agreement on climate change on the other, it is highly probable that domestic climate protection strategies framed around economic and investment opportunities will play a more important role in the future.

In that sense, the climate investment discourse offered a number of important insights for further analyses and considerations. First of all, the investment perspective on climate change does not point to a lack of financial capital for climate protection and the low-carbon transformation; the question is, instead, how existing financial sources should be used on challenges like the transformation of energy systems, and whether broader societal interests will be represented in the enabling frameworks and regulation.

The climate investment discourse also brings to mind the degree to which financial markets and investment activities depend on state intervention and regulation; this could be a starting point for a broader discussion of state influence in setting the frameworks for future economic development. To be clear: it is certainly a task too big for low-carbon strategies alone to turn financial markets into a servant of the real economy again (or even for the interests of societies); nevertheless, the discussions and activities to realize the low-carbon transformation will either contribute to highlighting the need for steps in that direction, or to strengthening the image of financial markets as powerful entities beyond the control of societies.

References

Clifton, S.-J. (2009) 'A dangerous obsession: the evidence against carbon trading and for real solutions to avoid a climate crunch', London: Friends of the Earth. Online. Available at: foe.co.uk/resource/reports/dangerous-obsession.pdf (accessed 26 March 2012).

De Goede, M. (2005) *Virtue, fortune and faith: a genealogy of finance*, Minneapolis: University of Minnesota Press.

Dean, Mitchell (2010) *Governmentality: power and rule in modern society*, London: Sage.

Deleuze, G. (1992) 'What is a dispositif', in T. Armstrong (ed.) *Michel Foucault: philosopher*, Hemel Hempstead: Harvester Wheatsheaf, 159–168.

European Commission (2011) *A roadmap for moving to a competitive low carbon economy in 2050*, Communication from the Commission to the European Parliament, the Council, the European Economic and Social Committee and the Committe of the Regions, COM (2011) 112 final, Brussels.

Foucault, M. (1980) 'The confession of the flesh', interview in C. Gordon (ed.) *Power/knowledge: selected interviews and other writings*, New York: Harvester Wheatsheaf, 194–228.

Foucault, M. (1985) 'Geschichte der Sexualität', *Ästhetik und Kommunikation*, 57/58: 157–164.

Foucault, M. (1986) *The use of pleasure: the history of sexuality: volume Two*, New York: Vintage.

Foucault, M. (1991) 'Questions of method', in G. Burchell, C. Gordon and P. Miller (eds) *The Foucault effect: studies in governmentality*, Chicago: The University of Chicago Press, 73–86.

Foucault, M. (1998) *The history of sexuality vol. 1: the will to knowledge*, London: Penguin.

Foucault, M. (2007) *Security, territory, population: lectures at the College de France*, Basingstoke: Palgrave Macmillan.

GIB (2010) *Unlocking investment to deliver Britain's low carbon future*, London: Green Investment Bank Commission.

Giddens, A. (2009) *The politics of climate change*, Cambridge: Polity Press.

Gordon, L. (ed.) (2011) *World future energy summit bulletin: a summary report of the World Future Energy Summit (WFES) 2011*, Winnipeg: International Institute for Sustainable Development.

Green New Deal Group (2008) *A green new deal: joined-up policies to solve the triple crunch of the credit crisis, climate change and high oil prices*, London: New Economics Foundation.

Hamilton, K. (2009) *Unlocking finance for clean energy: the need for 'investment grade' policy*, London: Chatham House.

Holm Olsen, K. (2007) 'The clean development mechanism's contribution to sustainable development: a review of the literature', *Climatic Change* 87: 59–73.

Howarth, D. (2000) *Discourse*, Buckingham: Open University Press.

IIGCC, INCR, IGCC and UNEP FI (2009) *2009 investor statement on the urgent need for a global agreement on climate change*, Geneva: UNEP Finance Initiative.

IIGCC, INCR, IGCC and UNEP FI (2010) *Global investor statement on climate change: reducing risks, seizing opportunities & closing the climate investment gap*, Geneva: UNEP Finance Initiative.

Lemke, T. (1997) *Eine Kritik der politischen Vernunft. Foucaults Analyse der modernen Gouvernmentalität*, Argument: Hamburg.

McKinsey (2009) *Pathways to a low carbon economy*, Executive Summary, London.

Maclean, J., J. Tan, D. Tirpak, V. Sonntag-O'Brien and E. Usher (2008) *Public finance mechanisms to mobilise investment in climate change mitigation*, Paris: UNEP Sustainable Energy Finance Initiative.

Newell, P. and M. Patterson (2010) *Climate capitalism*, Cambridge: Cambridge University Press.

Pearson, B. (2007) 'Market failure: why the clean development mechanism won't promote clean development', *Journal of Cleaner Production* 15: 247–252.

Romani, M. (2009) *Meeting the climate challenge: using public funds to leverage private investment in developing countries*. Summary for policy makers, London: London School of Economics.

Rose, N., P. O'Malley *et al.* (2006) 'Governmentality', *Annual Review of Law and Society* 2: 83–104.

Stern, N. (2009) *A blueprint for a safer planet*, New York: Random House.

Stripple, J. (2010) 'Weberian climate policy: administrative rationality organized as a market', in K. Bäckstrand, J. Khan, A. Kronsell and E. Lövbrand (eds) *Environmental politics and deliberative democracy*, Cheltenham: Edward Elgar Publishing, 67–84.

Sutter, C. and J.C. Parreño (2007) 'Does the current clean development mechanism (CDM) deliver its sustainable development claim? An analysis of officially registered CDM projects', *Climatic Change* 84: 75–90.

Tsing, A. (2004) 'Inside the economy of appearances', in A. Amin and N. Thrift (eds) *The Blackwell cultural economy reader*, Oxford: Blackwell, 83–100.

UNDESA (2011) *World economic and social survey 2011: the great green technological transformation*. Overview, New York: United Nations Department of Economic and Social Affairs.

Wara, M. (2007) 'Is the global carbon market working?', *Nature* 445(8): 595–596.

Ward, J., S. Fankhauser, C. Hepburn, H. Jackson and R. Rajan (2009) *Catalysing low-carbon growth in developing economies: public finance mechanisms to scale up private sector investment in climate solutions*, Geneva: UNEP and Partners.

World Bank (2008a) *State and trend of the carbon market 2008*, Washington, DC: World Bank.

World Bank (2008b) *Carbon finance for sustainable development*, Washington, DC: World Bank.

World Bank (2010) *CTF financing products, terms and review procedures for private sector operations*, Washington, DC: World Bank.

4 How to trade 'not cutting down trees'

A governmentality perspective on the commodification of avoided deforestation[1]

Benjamin Stephan

Introduction

Protecting tropical rainforests – and thereby Reducing Emissions from Deforestation and Degradation (REDD+) in developing countries – has become one of the 'hot topics' within global climate governance. A REDD+ mechanism was first proposed in a 2005 submission to the UNFCCC by the Coalition for Rainforest Nations. Today, the topic receives broad support from most UNFCCC parties, and from a wide variety of non-state actors. Even with broad agreement that REDD+ should consist of performance-based payments that compensate for the opportunity costs of avoided deforestation, the exact details of the mechanism have yet to be finalized within the UNFCCC. Such payments could be realized through a fund, or through the integration of REDD+ into the carbon market. In the latter case, REDD+ credits could be used by industrialized countries, and companies, to fulfil their respective international and domestic emissions reduction requirements. While a final agreement within the UNFCCC is still missing, institutions like the World Bank's Forest Carbon Partnership Facility and UN-REDD are conducting pilot and capacity building projects. And the first voluntary carbon market REDD+ projects have started to issue credits (Volcovici 2011). This chapter focuses on the integration of REDD+ into the carbon market, as a trading mechanism will very likely form at least part of the final REDD+ mechanism.

During the past 15 years, creating markets has become a widespread, broadly accepted approach in global climate governance. As the example of the CDM shows, these markets are expected to reward project developers for implementing technologies that reduce greenhouse gas emissions. The case of REDD+ strikes the casual observer as particularly odd: in this context, doing nothing – 'not cutting down trees' – is turned into a commodity. This chapter investigates this peculiarity, and tries to solve the following research questions: how is avoided deforestation being made tradable? What steps are being taken to make not-cutting-down-trees a commodity that can be sold to a fund, or traded on the carbon market?

Governmentality scholars have described the increased use of market tools in the climate policy realm as a shift from biopolitics to advanced liberal government (Oels 2005). Such tools have been acknowledged as central elements of a 'global carbon governmentality', where they function as 'technologies of agency and performance' (Methmann 2011: 12). Despite a rich governmentality literature on global climate governance in general,[2] and on carbon markets in particular (Bäckstrand and Lövbrand 2006; Lovell and Liverman 2010; Paterson and Stripple 2010; Methmann 2011; Paterson and Stripple 2012), there is a lack of literature analysing the *process* of commodification and market creation from a governmentality angle.[3] This chapter tries to close this gap by developing a governmentality perspective on commodification itself, drawing on insights from the sociology of markets (Fligstein and Dauter 2007; Engels 2009) and the commodification of nature literature (Prudham 2009). Furthermore, I identify a number of advantages to using a governmentality approach to scrutinize the commodification process.

With regard to methodology, my research has followed a retroductive approach (Glynos and Howarth 2007). Beginning with an active problematization (*What must be done in order for avoided deforestation to be successfully commodified?*), I iterated between the empirical material and the development of an analytical approach, drawing on Mitchel Dean's (2003) analytics of government, a heuristic based on Foucault's governmentality lectures. In addition to using primary sources (IPCC reports, UNFCCC negotiation texts and submissions, voluntary market documentation and manuals) and secondary literature, interviews with stakeholders in the forest carbon market (consultants, verifiers, forest specialists from voluntary standard organizations and developers) provided important background information for developing the theoretical perspective.

The chapter proceeds as follows: first, a governmentality perspective on commodification is developed. Second, this perspective is applied to the case of REDD+. By outlining how the rationale for the commodification of REDD+ emerged, I discuss how measurement and accounting practices create a particular field of visibility – allowing for the commensuration of avoided deforestation. I continue by highlighting how many of these practices depended on the appearance of a new type of subjectivity: the carbon forester. The chapter closes by discussing the degree by which avoided deforestation currently presents a disentangled commodity.

Making governmentality studies fruitful for the analysis of commodification and market creation processes

Foucault developed his governmentality concept in a series of lectures (Foucault 2007, 2008), in an attempt to understand the character and genesis of modern forms of rule. He suggested that modern forms of rule no longer relied primarily on sovereign power – repressive, and tied to the sovereign centre. Instead, Foucault focused on the indirect and the productive aspects of power – which he called government. Foucault's understanding of government can best be described by the expression 'conduct of conduct' (Gordon 1991: 2). This definition includes both the self-conduct of individuals, as well as the conducting others (Foucault 1982: 789–790).[4]

Foucault neither developed a full-fledged theory of governmentality, nor did he provide a manual on how to apply his concept methodologically. Despite this, governmentality has seen wide reception within social sciences. For the purpose of this chapter, I will draw on Dean's (2003) analytics of government. It is a practical heuristic, developed by Dean using Foucault's lectures, for analysing different regimes of practices (e.g. the way we try to govern and regulate deforestation). Dean's approach has been applied within a number of governmentality studies – including the field of climate governance (Oels 2005; Paterson and Stripple 2010). In his analytics of government, Dean outlines four dimensions for determining how a particular phenomenon is governed, and for determining the effects a given mode of governing entails. These dimensions are: (1) rationalities and forms of knowledge, (2) technologies of government, (3) fields of visibility and (4) identities (Dean 2003: 30–33). Every regime of practice is based on particular rationalities and forms of knowledge. These underwrite concrete governmental technologies, deployed to reach specific goals – or policy tools, as the mainstream literature calls them. Creating markets – such as emissions trading schemes – to regulate particular behaviour is a widely adopted strategy in advanced liberal government settings. Dean's third dimension refers to the fact that, depending on how an issue is made governable, certain aspects of the issue move to the centre of attention, while other aspects are ignored and become invisible. Hence, every form of governmentality generates its particular field of visibility. With the fourth dimension, Dean's heuristic points us to the nexus of structure and subject: every regime of practice generates particular forms of subjects (e.g. the 'entrepreneur of himself' (Foucault 2008: 226) in advanced liberal government), but also depends on specific roles to be filled, in order for the regime to function.

As mentioned before, the governmentality concept has inspired assessments in a wide variety of policy fields. Based on Foucault's lecture series, many of these studies identified forms of advanced liberal government, and highlighted the importance of creating markets as governmental technologies. This focus has resulted in the criticism that governmentality studies have become analytically depleted (Keller 2010: 44–48); like a self-fulfilling prophecy, say the critics, governmentality studies only find forms of advanced liberal government in ever more deeply social contexts (Rothe 2011: 2). I do not fully share this critique. However, it is interesting to note that despite this emphasis on advanced liberal government, governmentality studies have yet to develop an understanding of what occurs when new markets are being created and previously uncommodified goods are being commodified.

This chapter will take the first steps to develop a governmentality perspective on the creation of markets. The aim is to understand how the implementation of this technology of government works, and how commodification takes place. I will disassemble Dean's heuristic, and use the rationality, field of visibility and subjectivity dimensions to understand how the market – the technology dimension, of this regime of practice – is being constituted.

To think about commodification from a governmentality perspective, one needs not start from scratch. The sociology of markets (Fligstein and Dauter 2007; Engels 2009), and the literature on the commodification of nature (Prudham 2009), have generated interesting insights, which I draw upon in order to develop a governmentality perspective.

Following the literature on the sociology of markets, the following tasks must be performed successfully in order to turn an ordinary object into a commodity: qualification, legitimization, commensuration and disentanglement. An object has to be qualified, meaning knowledge of its attributes and characteristics must be socially established and shared through processes of qualification (Carruthers and Stinchcombe 1999: 357; Engels 2009: 72). Furthermore, individuals must perceive it to be legitimate to trade a particular object (for example, see: Zelizer 1983). As the third section of this chapter will show, scrutinizing the rationale underpinning a regime of practice in which markets are being deployed provides us with the necessary information on how an object is being constructed – or qualified – and how trading it is rendered a legitimate and rational thing to do.

Commensuration has been identified as another important step in the literature, defined as: 'the expression or measurements of characteristics normally represented by different units according to a common metric' (Espeland and Stevens 1998: 315). The qualitative characteristics of an object, established through the process of qualification, have to be turned into a quantitative measure, comparable ranking, ratio or price. Information regarding some qualities of an object is discarded, while information regarding other qualities is organized into new forms. The result of this process, the obfuscation of the multiplicity of meanings of an object, constitutes part of what Marxist scholars call the commodity fetish (Kosoy and Corbera 2010). A governmentality perspective highlights how measurement and accounting practices create a field of visibility that enables successful commensuration.

Taking into account the subject dimension, a governmentality perspective can identify various forms of identities that emerge in the context of the commodification processes, and that are necessary for the processes' success. As I will show later in the chapter, the successful commodification of avoided deforestation is dependent on the emergence of a new type of subject – the carbon forester.

To have a good that is not just exchanged between two persons, but actually traded on an ongoing basis among a large group, there must be consensus on the underlying rationale, and the accounting and measurement practices that construct the commodity. Only if a certain degree of discursive closure is achieved can an object be traded among many people. One could speak of a 'discursive disentanglement'. Coined by Callon (1998: 19), the term refers to the disentangling of an object from its immediate context. The object must become something delimitable – an object of its own, no longer requiring the continued existence of its creator (Engels 2009: 71–72). Marxist authors call this the abstraction and individuation of an object (Castree 2003: 279–280).

As the subsequent analysis will underline, the added value of a governmentality perspective on commodification is twofold. On one hand, it provides a critical approach, problematizing commodification and market creation on a micro level – fleshing out important details often overlooked from other theoretical angles (e.g. the interplay between scientific practices and the functioning of a market). On the other hand, the governmentality approach allows a holistic view on commodification, including highly diverse elements (rationalities, technical practices and subjectivities) – and accounting for both the prerequisites and consequences of commodification.

Why to trade not cutting down trees: the rationale for commodifying avoided deforestation

The idea that avoiding deforestation is something that could, and should, be made tradable on the carbon market emerged from an understanding that deforestation is a key driver of anthropogenic climate change – and by framing deforestation as an opportunity cost problem. The following section details when these perceptions appeared, how the rationale to address deforestation through the carbon market developed and how people started to perceive avoided deforestation as a legitimate way to deal with the problem.

The discursive links made between forests and the climate system date back to the origins of the scientific debate on climate change (Arrhenius 1907: 51–52). Within the scientific discourse, forests have been articulated both as carbon sinks, and in the sense of deforestation as an important source of anthropogenic greenhouse gas emissions. This dual construction, including an emphasis on the role of tropical forests, plays prominently in the IPCC's first assessment report (e.g. IPCC 1990a: xxxii; IPCC 1990b: xiii).[5]

During the late 1980s and early 1990s, deforestation was increasingly framed in economic terms, and constructed as an opportunity cost problem. As the IPCC notes:

> The forest crisis is rooted in the agricultural sector and in people's needs for employment and income. Deforestation will be stopped only when the natural forest is economically more valuable for the people who live in and around the forests than alternative uses for the same land.
>
> (IPCC 1990b: xlii)

In line with this problem construction, the rationale to address deforestation through the creation of environmental markets emerged. In the international context, the Environmental Defense Fund was the first to publish a proposal on *Preserving Brazil's Tropical Forests through Emissions Trading* (Dudek and LeBlanc 1991), advocating both the creation of an international emissions trading system and the commodification of avoided deforestation.

Though the rationale underpinning the commodification of avoided deforestation, and rendering such commodification a reasonable thing to do, had already been developed in the early 1990s, commodification did not initially prevail in the international climate policy discourse. Tropical deforestation was a marginal issue in the early life of the UNFCCC, as the world's focus was on industrial countries' emissions. Avoided deforestation only achieved importance between COP 3, in 1997, and COP 9, in 2003, during the course of a heated debate on the question of whether afforestation, reforestation and avoided deforestation projects should become eligible project categories under the CDM. Ultimately, avoiding deforestation was excluded (UNFCCC 2001: 60); scepticism of the feasibility of accurate, reliable accounting and monitoring of forest carbon, and major objections to the legitimacy of such projects, led many actors – mainly the EU, a large number of developing countries and most major, international, environmental NGOs (excluding US-based conservation organizations) – to oppose its inclusion (Lövbrand 2009: 409; Schlamadinger *et al.* 2007: 278).

The push to commodify avoided deforestation was reintroduced to international climate negotiations via a submission by Costa Rica and Papua New Guinea on behalf of the Coalition for Rainforest Nations in 2005. In the submission, deforestation was framed as one of the most pressing issues in the quest to tackle global warming. Deforestation was articulated as 'the single largest source category of emissions in the developing world' (Papua New Guinea and Costa Rica 2005: 3–4). The submission further argued that 'Without a more complete market valuation standing forests cannot overcome the economic opportunity costs associated with their conservation' (Papua New Guinea and Costa Rica 2005: 7).

Backed by calculations in the *Stern Review,* which articulated avoiding deforestation as a 'highly cost-effective way of reducing greenhouse gas emissions' (Stern 2006: xxv), the submission on avoided deforestation sparked a major discussion. Initially pushed by an actor coalition consisting only of tropical developing countries, a number of North American conservation NGOs (e.g. Conservation International, The Nature Conservancy, The Rainforest Alliance) and various carbon market consultancies, the issue was soon picked up by a broad array of state and non-state actors. A number of discursive shifts have occurred since avoided deforestation was excluded from the CDM, and many of the issues that had been contentious earlier are no longer perceived to be overly problematic (for a detailed discussion, see Stephan 2012a). For example, even though the legitimacy of offset projects – and therefore, avoided deforestation projects – in the Global South used to be heavily contested during the earlier CDM debate, the expectation of large quantities of REDD+ credits isn't a problem for most contemporary actors. Actually, it's the opposite: the fact that REDD+ has the potential to generate reduction credits on a large scale is presented as an advantage – allowing industrialized countries to take on higher reduction commitments (see for example Eliasch 2008: xii).[6]

Within two years, REDD+ had become a key element of international climate policy making. In 2007, it was included in the Bali Action Plan, becoming a central element of a post-Kyoto agreement. Today, actors like the World Bank – with its Forest Carbon Partnership Facility – and Norway – which has provided several billion Euros to get REDD+ off the ground, funding initiatives like UN-REDD (a corporation between various UN agencies working on avoided deforestation) – have become the leading players on REDD+.

Making forest carbon (visible)

In addition to an underlying logic that renders trading avoided deforestation a rational thing to do, legitimizes this trade and constructs the qualities of the commodity – avoided deforestation must be commensurable. As avoided deforestation is being integrated into an existing market, a common metric – the ton of carbon dioxide equivalents, or tCO_2e (for a detailed discussion see Paterson and Stripple 2012) – already exists. Through the process of commensuration, a particular field of visibility is created that is necessary for the successful commodification of avoided deforestation: the non-carbon characteristics of a forest are being obscured, and the meaning of a forest is being reduced to that of a carbon stock. This section outlines how commensuration is achieved in the case of avoided deforestation, and what consequences such commensuration entails.

Commensurating avoided deforestation, and converting avoided deforestation into tCO_2e, depends on the potential to measure a forest's carbon stock, and the ability to convincingly construct a baseline – a counterfactual story on what would have happened without REDD+ measures.

Thus far, there are no technical devices for direct measurement of forest carbon. Instead, carbon content is estimated based on a forest's biomass. Forest inventories, biome averages and remote sensing are three approaches currently being used (often in combination) to determine a forest's biomass. These approaches require greatly varying efforts in order to obtain results – and are inconsistent in the quality of their respective measurement results (for example, see Köhl et al. 2011). To date, biome average data sets have been the main approach for determining tropical forest carbon stocks (Westholm et al. 2009: 29). Gibbs et al. (2007) have compared different data sets to compute the carbon stock in tropical developing countries. The results are inconsistent: depending on the chosen data set, the highest and lowest estimates differ by 51 per cent in the case of Brazil, 79 per cent in case of the Congo and 149 per cent in the case of Indonesia.

The difference between claiming 50, 100 or 150 tCO_2e for a hectare of avoided deforestation is significant, and such variance poses a serious challenge for the commodification of avoided deforestation. In his work on wetland banking, Robertson (2006) showed that unsettled scientific debates, and other forms of uncertainty, must be 'silenced' for commodification to take place. With its good practice guidance (Penman et al. 2003; Aalde et al. 2006) on measuring and monitoring forest carbon, the IPCC has silenced some of this scientific debate within the climate policy and carbon market domains. However, even the emissions factors the IPCC provides include a large range – and a significant amount of uncertainty (Penman et al. 2003: Table 3A.1.2). To deal with this, the 'principle of conservativeness'[7] has evolved within the discourse: project developers and national governments are supposed to use the most conservative estimate when calculating a forest's carbon stock and potential emissions reductions through REDD+ activities (see also Grassi et al. 2008).

The measurement results are combined with the baseline – also called the 'business as usual scenario' – to determine the number of reduction credits generated through REDD+ activities. A baseline consists of counterfactual arguments and hypothetical assumptions about the likely outcome of a forest without any REDD+ measures. This is figured using the extrapolation of historical deforestation rates, and predictions for the future development path of a forest region, including estimates about population, economic development or infrastructure changes.

Many issues regarding REDD+ baselines are similar to those in the CDM (see Lohmann 2005). However, REDD+ baselines depend on hypothetical assumptions, and counterfactual arguments, to a much larger extent than CDM baselines. While one can count planted trees in afforestation and reforestation projects, and monitor the progress of tree growth, there is no way to determine the exact number of trees that would have been cut down if a REDD+ measure had not taken place. This drawback of counterfactual reasoning has already been discussed in the CDM context (Methmann 2011: 14–15): due to methodological design, counterfactual arguments cannot deviate far from the status quo. And the possibility for drastic changes cannot be accounted for using counterfactual calculations. Instead, present trends are extrapolated into the future. By doing so, critics argue that the CDM perpetuates the status quo – and acts as an obstacle to substantial change. Following Bigo (2007), Methmann refers to this as 'governing the future perfect', and argues that the 'CDM simply administers a present which has always-already become our future' (Methmann 2011: 15).

Through measurement and baseline modelling practices, forests are being articulated solely as carbon stocks – and all their other meanings are being obscured. The field of visibility being created is limited to a forest's carbon qualities. Hence, we can talk about the *carbonification*[8] *of forests*. This is similar to what Marxist scholars describe as the fetishizing effect of a REDD+ mechanism (Kosoy and Corbera 2010: 1230). Avoided deforestation becomes commensurable on the carbon market as a result of carbonification. For instance, avoided deforestation in the Congo Basin can be directly compared and related to a coal-fired power plant in Poland, a wind farm in India or a refrigerator plant in China.[9]

While the carbonification of forests enables the commensuration of avoided deforestation, it also results in effects that run counter to the claims of REDD+ proponents. Most of these proponents take every chance to highlight that REDD+ will provide multiple benefits beyond mere emissions reductions. For instance, the protection of biodiversity and indigenous peoples' livelihoods are two commonly mentioned examples (Stephan 2012a). From a carbon market perspective – where the carbon characteristics of a forest are all that is visible – cutting down an area of high-biodiversity tropical forest poses no problem as long as the felling of trees is compensated by the construction of wind turbines or the retirement of a coal-fired power plant. From a biodiversity perspective, however, such action represents a massive problem. Even if REDD+ was not linked to the carbon market, carbonification presents problems. As the degree of biodiversity doesn't necessarily correlate with the amount of carbon stored in a forest, concerns have been raised that a REDD+ mechanism would shift deforestation from high-carbon, low-biodiversity forests to low-carbon, high-biodiversity forests. To address this problem, in an attempt to minimize perverse incentives, a significant amount of effort is being spent to develop the idea of 'safeguards'. More recent proposals have called for additional commodification of other ecosystem services provided by forests. According to this logic, the 'stacking' of payments for different services should generate broader revenue streams and prevent any distorting effects. It remains to be seen how well these measures will work. It is unlikely that such disruptions can be eliminated entirely, even if the worst can be prevented. Accounting for the complete value of forests is too complex, and would entail a reversal of carbonification – which in turn would challenge the commensurability of avoided deforestation.

The emergence of the carbon forester

The chapter now turns to the subject, or identity dimension, of Dean's heuristic. This dimension further adds to our understanding of how the initial controversy on the commodification of avoided deforestation is resolved.

A number of scholars (see for example Boyd 2010) and many of the non-forester REDD+ experts that I interviewed have argued that the commodification of avoided deforestation is perceived to be feasible today – as opposed to the CDM debate ten to 15 years ago – because of technological advancements which have improved our ability to measure forest carbon. Not all the foresters I interviewed agreed; one said that while there have been incremental improvements in remote sensing, the basics of measuring forest biomass through forest inventories have not changed much in the past 200 years (interview with a forest carbon expert, from a carbon market verifier, June 2011).[10] Instead, what had been missing was 'how you model hypothetical baselines, how you deal with leakage and temporality' (interview with a forest carbon expert from a consultancy, June 2011). Avoided deforestation baselines consist of a higher number of counterfactual assumptions, which makes them more complex than baselines from industrial sector CDM projects. Initially, this made such baselines more controversial than they are now, and resulted in their exclusion from the CDM. Today, however, counterfactual baselines, and other accounting practices, are no longer controversial.

On a macro level, one can conclude that this normalization is a result of the increased use of market tools in global climate governance – hence the consequence of a marketization of global climate governance. A closer look at the micro level helps us understand how this normalization took place. The introduction of the first emissions trading schemes and offset mechanisms has given rise to the carbon market industry. Simultaneously, a new type of subject – the carbon market professional (Voß 2007: 340; Methmann 2011: 16–17) – emerged. Through their daily routines and practices these professionals routinized previously controversial aspects, like counterfactual baselines, and normalized them. But the normalizing effect goes far beyond the community of carbon market professionals. Today, policy-makers and other individuals take the CDM's routines and methodologies for granted. Furthermore, carbon market professionals themselves are actively looking for new contexts to deploy the routines and logics they developed.

The emergence of the carbon industry also brought together previously divergent areas of scientific knowledge. Foresters, biochemists and remote sensing specialists started to combine their respective expertise. In doing so, they tried to find common ground with the demands of project developers, and developed the skill set necessary for the commodification of avoided deforestation (interview with the forest carbon expert at a consultancy, June 2011; interview with the methodology expert at a project developer, June 2011). The 'carbon forester', a new type of expert, emerged. Only in rare cases do single individuals possess a combination of all the necessary skills for modelling, measuring and monitoring. But in order to do their work, organizations that want to run REDD+ projects, or are asked to audit such projects, require interdisciplinary teams that possess these skills. In this light, it is not surprising that Wildlifeworks, the company running the first voluntary market project to issue REDD+ credits, is based in San Francisco. The proximity to big research centres, like the University of California, Berkeley, made it relatively easy for Wildlifeworks to gain access to people with the right skills.[11]

Avoided deforestation: fully disentangled?

The previous sections have shown how a rationale for REDD+ has developed, and how initial concerns about legitimacy have disappeared. Furthermore, we have seen how the emergence of the carbon industry has resulted in the normalization of various carbon accounting practices, and how the appearance of the carbon forester has provided the necessary skill set to develop and run REDD+ projects. It is yet to be seen whether this is enough to fully disentangle avoided deforestation as a tradable commodity on the carbon market. Thus far, REDD+ projects are not accepted in any compliance market.[12] And in the case of voluntary market REDD+ projects, we cannot speak of full disentanglement. Credits from these projects – as from voluntary forest carbon projects in general – tend to be bought by companies for marketing and CSR purposes, because they are 'easier to communicate than other types of offsets, as well as visually compelling through images of forested ecosystems, thereby potentially yielding brand-enhancement benefits' (Waage and Hamilton 2011: 6).

> Forestry is a very attractive emission reduction investment for many [investors], because it has so many Corporate Social Responsibility benefits. To be able to say that you are getting emissions reductions and you are also protecting elephants or tigers, and to say that you are also providing an income to communities that are desperate and schools and this and that. It is very attractive.
> (Interview with a project developer, running voluntary market REDD+ projects, June 2011)

Voluntary forestry credits are sold directly by the project developer to a company that then exploits the investment for CSR or marketing reasons. Generally, these credits are not resold on the secondary market – as their value draws on a direct connection to the project they originated from.

In this context, a forest is not fully carbonified; its biodiversity and livelihood-meaning play an important role in the value of the credits. As opposed to a forest's carbon stock function, these aspects can be documented easily, and visualized in colourful videos and photos. As a consequence, full commensurability is not achieved. In this case, we cannot speak of full disentanglement of avoided deforestation.

Conclusion

This chapter has developed a governmentality perspective on commodification, and applied this perspective in order to understand the current attempts to make avoiding deforestation tradable. Even though governmentality studies are often concerned with markets as technologies of government, the commodification and market creation process itself has yet to be discussed from this perspective. Besides closing a gap within the governmentality literature, a governmentality perspective on commodification adds value beyond existing approaches – particularly with regard to its micro-level problematizations, and its holistic take on a wide array of facets of the commodification process.

Looking at REDD+, this chapter has reconstructed how a rationale for commodification emerged, and how – to use the sociology of markets terminology – avoided deforestation has been qualified and legitimized as a tradable object. Furthermore, this chapter has shown how a particular field of visibility has been created through the use of measuring and accounting practices: forests are being carbonified, and all their non-carbon characteristics are being obscured. This carbonification is necessary for avoided deforestation to become commensurable on the carbon market.

This chapter has also shown that the full commodification of avoided deforestation within a compliance market, which was ruled out during the CDM negotiations, is becoming increasingly likely – in part, because new types of subjects, such as carbon professionals, have normalized initially contested accounting and modelling practices. In this context, this chapter highlights the emergence of the carbon forester – a role able to connect previously divergent scientific fields, and providing the skill set necessary for REDD+ projects. As long as REDD+ is not part of a compliance market, however, full disentanglement of avoided deforestation cannot be achieved. Voluntary market REDD+ credits rely on a direct connection to their respective projects in order to realize their value.

As this chapter could only devote limited space to development of a governmentality perspective on the commodification of avoided deforestation, not every aspect has been considered. A governmentality approach also offers interesting insights on the consequences of commodification. In the case of REDD+, for instance, it is crucial to understand how the commodification process plays out on the ground. Further research is necessary in order to gain a full understanding on how REDD+ impacts local communities and other actors.

Notes

1 The research for this chapter was supported through the Cluster of Excellence 'Climate System Analysis and Prediction' (CliSAP) (EXC177), University of Hamburg, funded by the German Science Foundation (DFG). I had the chance to write it, while I was a visiting scholar at Lund University, Sweden, funded through its strategic research area 'Biodiversity and Ecosystem Services in a Changing Climate' (BECC). I would like to thank Lund University's Environmental Politics Research Group – in particular Johannes Stripple and Karin Bäckstrand – as well as Chris Methman, Delf Rothe and two anonymous reviewers for helpful comments on earlier versions of this chapter.

2 For an excellent overview of the climate governmentality literature see Rothe (2011).
3 In an earlier article on the commodification of avoided deforestation (Stephan 2012b) I developed a discourse theoretical perspective on commodification drawing on Laclau and Mouffe's (2001) hegemony and discourse theory. This chapter builds on some of the same empirical material.
4 For a more detailed introduction see Chapter 3 by Simon Wolf.
5 For a more detailed analysis on how deforestation was articulated as a climate change issue see Boyd (2010).
6 Low costs for offset certificates lead to low overall abatement costs for industrialized countries, which subsequently might be more likely to agree to higher reduction commitments. As offset certificates are a zero-sum game at best (every reduced ton is offset by prolonging emissions in industrialized countries), this line of reasoning is being criticized.
7 This has come up in several interviews, and has been part of a REDD+ expert meeting I have observed.
8 I borrow this term from Mert (2009) who has used carbonification to describe the re-articulation of environmental discourses according to a climate change logic (see also Mert's contribution to this volume in Chapter 2).
9 This is based on the assumption that the different emission trading systems and offset mechanisms are fully interconnected, which is currently not the case (e.g. while the EU ETS is linked to the CDM, credits from some particular CDM project types are not being accepted).
10 Field inventories, conducted with the help of a tape measure to determine a tree's breast height diameter and an inclinometer to determine its height, were the 'key elements of a new "scientific forestry"' (Boyd 2010: 859) developed by German foresters in the late eighteenth and early nineteenth centuries and have not changed much since. Furthermore, even though there is a lot of effort in installing and developing new remote sensing techniques (e.g. radar or laser sensors) (Boyd 2010: 885–892) most of the analysis currently deployed in REDD+ contexts is based on satellite imagery that was already available at the end of the 1990s (Westholm *et al.* 2009).
11 Wildlifeworks' Vice President, responsible for Carbon Development, used to work for Berkeley's Geospatial Innovation Facility. Ecopartners, the consultancy they hired to develop the methodology for their first project, consists of PhD students from UC Berkeley working on 'Biometrics and Remote Sensing', 'Climate Science and Monitoring' as well as 'Forest Ecology' (Ecopartners 2011).
12 A UNFCCC mechanism where this might be an option is still under negotiation. Furthermore there are discussions to include REDD+ type offsets from Acre, Brazil, and Chiapas, Mexico, into the California ETS.

References

Aalde, H., Gonzalez, P., Gytarsky, M., Krug, T., Kurz, W.A., Ogle, S., Raison, J., Schoene, D., Ravindrath, N.H., Elhassan, N.G., Heath, L.S., Higuchi, N., Kainja, S., Matsumoto, M., Sánchez, M.J.S. and Somogyi, Z. (2006) 'Forest Land', in S. Eggleston, L. Buendia, K. Miwa, T. Ngara and K. Tanabe (eds) *IPCC Guidelines for National Greenhouse Gas Inventories – Volume IV: Agriculture, Forestry and Other Land Use*, Geneva: IPCC.

Arrhenius, S. (1907) *Das Werden der Welten*, Leipzig: Akademische Verlags-Gesellschaft.

Bäckstrand, K. and Lövbrand, E. (2006) 'Planting Trees to Mitigate Climate Change: Contested Discourses of Ecological Modernization, Green Governmentality and Civic Environmentalism', *Global Environmental Politics* 6(1): 50–75.

Bigo, D. (2007) 'Detention of Foreigners, States of Exception, and the Social Practices of Control of the Panopticon', in P.K. Rajaram and C. Grudy-Warr (eds) *Borderscapes:*

Hidden Geographies and Politics at Territory's Edge, Minneapolis: University of Minnesota Press, 3–34.

Boyd, W. (2010) 'Ways of Seeing in Environmental Law: How Deforestation Became an Object of Climate Governance', *Environmental Law Quaterly* 37(3): 843–916.

Callon, M. (1998) *The Laws of the Markets*, Oxford: Blackwell Publishers.

Carruthers, B.G. and Stinchcombe, A.L. (1999) 'The Social Structure of Liquidity: Flexibility, Markets, and States', *Theory and Society* 28(3): 353–382.

Castree, N. (2003) 'Commodifying what Nature?', *Progress in Human Geography* 27(3): 273–297.

Dean, M. (2003) *Governmentality: Power and Rule in Modern Society*, London: Sage Publications.

Dudek, D.J. and LeBlanc, A. (1991) *Preserving Brazil's Tropical Forests through Emissions Trading*, New York: Environmental Defense Fund.

Ecopartners (2011) *Ecopartners: People*. Online. Available at: www.ecopartnersllc.com/people.aspx (retrieved: 8 September 2011).

Eliasch, J. (2008) *Climate Change: Financing Global Forests – The Eliasch Review*, London: Earthscan.

Engels, A. (2009) 'Die Soziale Konstitution von Märkten', in J. Beckert and C. Deutschmann (eds) *Wirtschaftssoziologie. Sonderheft 49 der Kölner Zeitschrift für Soziologie und Sozialpsychologie*, Wiesbaden: Springer VS, 67–86.

Espeland, W.N. and Stevens, M.L. (1998) 'Commensuration as a Social Process', *Annual Review of Sociology* 24(1): 313–343.

Fligstein, N. and Dauter, L. (2007) 'The Sociology of Markets', *Annual Review of Sociology* 33: 105–128.

Foucault, M. (1982) 'The Subject and Power', *Critical Inquiry* 8(4): 777–795.

Foucault, M. (2007) *Security, Territory, Population: Lectures at the Collège de France, 1977–1978*, New York: Palgrave Macmillan.

Foucault, M. (2008) *The Birth of Biopolitics: Lectures at the Collège de France, 1978–79*, New York: Palgrave Macmillan.

Gibbs, H.K., Brown, S., Niles, J.O. and Foley, J.A. (2007) 'Monitoring and Estimating Tropical Forest Carbon Stocks: Making REDD a Reality', *Environmental Research Letters* 2(4): 1–13.

Glynos, J. and Howarth, D.R. (2007) *Logics of Critical Explanation in Social and Political Theory*, London: Routledge.

Gordon, C. (1991) 'Governmental Rationality: An Introduction', in G. Burchell, C. Gordon and P. Miller (eds) *The Foucault Effect: Studies in Governmentality*, London: Harvester Wheatsheaf, 119–150.

Grassi, G., Monni, S., Federici, S., Achard, F. and Mollicone, D. (2008) 'Applying the Conservativeness Principle to REDD to Deal with the Uncertainties of the Estimates', *Environmental Research Letters* 3(3): 1–12.

IPCC (1990a) *First Assessment Report – Working Group One 'Scientific Assessment of Climate Change'*, Geneva: IPCC.

IPCC (1990b) *First Assessment Report – Working Group Three 'The IPCC's Response Strategies'*, Geneva: IPCC.

Keller, R. (2010) 'Nach der Gouvernementalitätsforschung und jenseits des Poststrukstrukturalismus? Anmerkungen aus Sicht der Wissenssoziologischen Diskursanalyse', in J. Angermüller and S.V. Dyk (eds) *Diskursanalyse meets Gouvernementalitätsforschung*, Frankfurt: Campus Verlag, 43–70.

Köhl, M., Lister, A., Scott, C.T., Baldauf, T. and Plugge, D. (2011) 'Implications of

Sampling Design and Sample Size for National Carbon Accounting Systems', *Carbon Balance and Management* 6(1): 1–20.

Kosoy, N. and Corbera, E. (2010) 'Payments for Ecosystem Services as Commodity Fetishism', *Ecological Economics* 69(6): 1228–1236.

Laclau, E. and Mouffe, C. (2001) *Hegemony and Socialist Strategy: Towards a Radical Democratic Politics*, London: Verso.

Lohmann, L. (2005) 'Marketing and Making Carbon Dumps: Commodification, Calculation and Counterfactuals in Climate Change Mitigation', *Science as Culture* 14(3): 203–235.

Lövbrand, E. (2009) 'Revisiting the Politics of Expertise in Light of the Kyoto Negotiations on Land Use Change and Forestry', *Forest Policy and Economics* 11(5–6): 404–412.

Lovell, H. and Liverman, D. (2010) 'Understanding Carbon Offset Technologies', *New Political Economy* 15(2): 255–273.

Mert, A. (2009) 'Partnerships for Sustainable Development as Discursive Practice: Shifts in Discourses of Environment and Democracy', *Forest Policy and Economics* 11(5–6): 326–339.

Methmann, C.P. (2011) 'The Sky is the Limit: Global Warming as Global Governmentality', *European Journal of International Relations*.

Oels, A. (2005) 'Rendering Climate Change Governable: From Biopower to Advanced Liberal Government?', *Journal of Environmental Policy & Planning* 7(3): 185–207.

Papua New Guinea and Costa Rica (2005) *Submission to COP 11, Agenda Item 6: 'Reducing Emissions from Deforestation in Developing Countries: Approaches to Stimulate Action'*, Bonn: UNFCCC.

Paterson, M. and Stripple, J. (2010) 'My Space: Governing Individuals' Carbon Emissions', *Environment and Planning D: Society and Space* 28: 341–362.

Paterson, M. and Stripple, J. (2012) 'Virtuous Carbon', *Environmental Politics* 21(4): 563–582.

Penman, J., Gytarsky, M., Hiraishi, T., Krug, T., Kruger, D., Pipatti, R., Buendia, L., Miwa, K., Ngara, T., Tanabe, K. and Wagner, F. (eds) (2003) *Good Practice Guidance for Land Use, Land-Use Change and Forestry*, Geneva: Intergovernmental Panel on Climate Change.

Prudham, S. (2009) 'Commodification', in N. Castree, D. Demeritt and D. Liverman (eds) *A Companion to Environmental Geography*, Malden: Wiley-Blackwell, 123–142.

Robertson, M.M. (2006) 'The Nature that Capital Can See: Science, State, and Market in the Commodification of Ecosystem Services', *Environment and Planning D: Society and Space* 24(3): 367–387.

Rothe, D. (2011) 'Cleaning Foucault's Glasses: Problems and Blind-Spots of a Governmentality Approach to Global Climate Governance', paper presented on 20 June 2011 at *Governing the Global Climate Polity: Rationality, Practice and Power*, Lund, Sweden.

Schlamadinger, B., Bird, N., Johns, T., Brown, S., Canadell, J., Ciccarese, L., Dutschke, M., Fiedler, J., Fischlin, A. and Fearnside, P. (2007) 'A Synopsis of Land Use, Land-Use Change and Forestry (LULUCF) under the Kyoto Protocol and Marrakech Accords', *Environmental Science & Policy* 10(4): 271–282.

Stephan, B. (2012a) 'From Pariah to Messiah: Avoided Deforestation in Global Climate Governance', paper presented on 4 April 2012 at the *International Studies Association's Annual Convention*, San Diego, USA.

Stephan, B. (2012b) 'Bringing Discourse to the Market: The Commodification of Avoided Deforestation', *Environmental Politics* 21(4): 621–639.

Stern, N. (2006) *The Economics of Climate Change: The Stern Review*, Cambridge: Cambridge University Press.

UNFCCC (2001) *FCCC/CP/2001/13/Add.1.* Bonn: COP 7.
Volcovici, V. (2011) *Kenyan Project Issues First REDD Carbon Credits*, Oslo, Point Carbon. Online. Available at: www.pointcarbon.com/1.1504259 (retrieved: 30 July 2011).
Voß, J.-P. (2007) 'Innovation Processes in Governance: The Development of Emissions Trading as a New Policy Instrument', *Science and Public Policy* 34(5): 329–343.
Waage, S. and Hamilton, K. (2011) *Investing in Forest Carbon: Lessons from the First 20 Years*, Washington, DC: Ecosystem Marketplace.
Westholm, L., Henders, S., Ostwald, M. and Mattsson, E. (2009) 'Assessment of Existing Global Financial Initiatives and Monitoring Aspects of Carbon Sinks in Forest Ecosystems: The Issue of REDD', *Focali Report* 2009(1).
Zelizer, V.A. (1983) *Morals and Markets*, New Brunswick: Transaction Books.

5 Interpretive openness and climate action in an age of market environmentalism

Larry Lohmann

Introduction

Action on climate change, like any other kind of politics, consists largely of a process of continuous interpretation and reinterpretation. How to understand the climate crisis? How to understand the market environmentalist policies that have become the dominant official response to it? How to understand groups and networks with which one wants to build alliances? Such questions demand openness to whatever languages, cultures, disciplines and tools can help make sense of the current impasse and open up ways out of it. This chapter draws on three interpretive approaches from the academic world that all have contributions to make.

One resource consists of the studies critical geographers and sociologists have made of a range of contemporary ecosystem service markets and other manifestations of 'market environmentalism' that do not directly relate to climate change. Such studies offer a comparative perspective on carbon markets that helps in grasping their evolution, nature and limitations. A second resource is science and technology studies and the social study of finance, particularly actor-network theory, which provide tools for understanding the ascent to prominence of such markets and for engaging with the particular forms of expert power they embody and the objects they create. A third resource is the body of broadly Marxist literature that tries to comprehend the conditions that make it possible for one global regime or cycle of accumulation to succeed another. This tradition of thought can help evaluate the claims of the new 'green capitalism' to be capable of overcoming – or providing a transitory 'fix' for – the trend towards catastrophic climate change.

This chapter will begin by sketching some of the immediate historical background that has contributed to the 'economization' of the climate crisis, drawing in an abstract way on actor-network theory. It will then try to enrich this account by folding into it some comparative case-study material from the critical geography (and actor-network theory) literature. Finally, it will suggest ways in which the study of the history of accumulation regimes might help address challenges in the global warming debate. A brief conclusion will then attempt to draw the threads together.

Creating commodification-ready environmental objects

In the 1970s, global warming barely registered on the political radar. Nevertheless, the decade saw two developments that powerfully shaped subsequent official responses to the climate crisis. One was the proliferation of new environmental regulation in countries such as the United States. The other was the beginnings of a growing profitability crisis that ushered in the current period of financialization and neoliberalization (Peck 2010; Mirowski and Plehwe 2010).

These contrasting developments combined to produce a novel vector. On the one hand, it could no longer be questioned that land, water, forests and air required protection on a national, even international, scale. On the other, pressures grew to roll back the 'costly' legislation of the 1970s while rolling out new regulation that could help redistribute more wealth upwards to profit-challenged private corporations (Peck and Tickell 2002). An increasingly institutionalized neoliberal consensus made it necessary to ask how much societal and environmental protection was really necessary, and for what purposes. Could protection be calibrated more precisely to business needs for the sake of greater 'balance'? Could business perhaps even produce its own conditions of production as an outright commodity, thus maximizing efficiency and launching a lucrative new economic sector into the bargain? It began to seem both necessary and possible to bring the provision of the environmental conditions for survival and production into closer alignment with what the late Giovanni Arrighi (1994) called the 'economizing logic of capitalist enterprise'.

In ways that have been illuminated by actor-network theorists such as Michel Callon and Timothy Mitchell, institutions began to be organized in ways that devised a progressively more abstract and calculable 'environment' (Callon 1998; Holm 2001, 2002; MacKenzie 2009) and integrated it with the similarly abstract, calculable 'economy' whose construction had begun in the early postcolonial era between the 1930s and the 1950s (Mitchell 2002). Through process of 'framing' or 'disentanglement' (Thomas 1991), 'the environment' and 'the economy' were not only described, defined and measured, but also constituted, nurtured, 'performed' and transformed by a multitude of practices of calculation originating in academia, government bureaucracies and other institutional settings, as well as 'in the wild' among economic agents at large (Callon 2005).[1] Thus by 1972, the Club of Rome, alarmed by the long-term implications of resource depletion across the board, called for management of global environmental systems as a way of keeping 'the economy' going – a message that influenced the first UN conference on the environment. Environment ministries were subsequently set up in many countries and environment departments at international financial institutions. Economists and systems analysts drew diagrams with boxes or circles labelled 'the environment', often containing, contained by, situated alongside or intersecting boxes or circles representing 'the economy', while debates pitting fans of a 'steady-state economy' against advocates of 'green growth' reflected the emerging consensus that that 'environment' and 'economy' could be isolated, then commensurated with each other in a way that would allow either one to condition the other.

The ecological modernization theorists of the 1980s and 1990s spoke of the simultaneous 'ecologization of economy' and 'economization of ecology' (Mol 1995): as an unprecedented number of scientists and other experts found themselves working on market quantification, an equally unprecedented number of neoclassical economists, property lawyers and enforcement agencies found themselves toiling away on environmental projects. Not only did the new environmental professionals go to work calculating the value of an abstract, external nature to production and the value of production to nature, while simultaneously expanding cost–benefit analysis in an attempt to refine earlier rough-and-ready efforts to safeguard the background conditions for societal well-being and successful business enterprise. They also joined policymakers, environmental organizations, economists, derivatives traders and green entrepreneurs in building an infrastructure to seize and trade those conditions for profit, creating new areas for economic activity in which the financial sector played a central part. Production itself was expanded to create new values, including new natures. If nature could be fully commodified and properly priced, it was argued, capitalism could be made ecologically benign.[2]

One result was that new institutions began to produce vast numbers of what actor-network theorists, keen to emphasize what they see as mixed social-natural-technical nature of agency, call 'hybrids' or 'monsters' (Law 1991). Examples of such odd creatures included 'statistical persons', non-human collections of risks embodying the work of economists, lawyers, physical objects, bureaucrats and others interested in helping to specify monetary equivalents for the lives of individuals (Heinzerling 2000); 'contingent valuation subjects' (Lohmann 2009), semi-human agents schooled in assigning a cash value to unmarketed items like clean air; and 'biodiversity credits', abstract, mobile tokens of ecosystem value created through interactions among economists, plants, animals, bankers and scientists. As such entities multiplied, the English language and thinking in English themselves changed.[3] 'Environmental degradation' and 'environmental harm', as well as 'environmental cost' and 'environmental benefit,' started to come into widespread use about 1965, becoming rapidly more popular from about 1980. The term 'environmental risk', which started its career before 1970, built steadily to a peak around 2000. 'Market failure' – a phrase implying confidence that environmental externalities could be internalized, bringing about 'market success' – began its rise about 1970, peaking in the 1990s. Mentions of the environmental 'Kuznets curve' – according to which continued development of 'the market' leads to a decline in environmental impact – took off in the late 1970s. 'Environmental economics' began its career around 1970, 'ecological economics' a bit before 1990. 'Natural capital' began to go into linguistic circulation around 1985. During the first George Bush regime in the United States, the phrase 'no net loss' reflected the growth of a set of institutions devoted to equating biota in different locations with each other as a prelude to trading (Robertson 2000). 'Ecosystem services', a phrase that implies commensurability between clean water or air and the outputs of fast-food restaurants or auto repair shops, made its first significant appearance just before 1980 and has risen in popularity ever since (Gómez-Baggethun et al. 2010); by 1997, it was possible for the environmental economist Robert Costanza to characterize the Earth itself as a 'very efficient, least-cost provider of human life-support services', with a value of between US$16–54 trillion. In 2006, 'carbon neutral' – a phrase connoting the presence of institutions for valuing and trading increments of climate benefit – became the *New Oxford American Dictionary*'s 'word of the year'.

Of course, like all radical innovations, such post-1970 environment-economy confections were made from ingredients assembled in earlier eras, some of which had been known under other names. The phrase 'natural resource management', for example, which made a slow start into common usage in English around 1965 prior to a very steep increase starting in the early 1980s, combined a particular nature/society divide that had been built up since at least the eighteenth century with the equally hoary notion that the resulting 'nature' could be construed as raw material and subjected to rational planning. Similarly, the idea that pollution could in theory be 'optimized' through market bargaining, which eventually developed into the carbon trading of the Kyoto Protocol and the EU Emissions Trading Scheme, originated in the late 1950s with the US economist Ronald Coase, who had been working with an idea of 'externalities' formalized by Arthur Pigou in the earlier twentieth century and invented by the philosopher Henry Sidgwick in the nineteenth century. The term 'ecosystem', similarly, had been invented in the 1930s (by Arthur Tansley) before being developed by Howard Odum in the 1950s through calculable models based on electrical circuits, which found an echo not only in the perspex pipes of A.W. Phillips's 1949 MONIAC hydraulic economics computer modelling a 'national economy' but also in the Global Circulation Models and other 'worlds within machines' that began to emerge in the late 1950s in climatology. None of this, however, should obscure the significance of the wave of environment-economic hybrids that began to populate the world after 1970.

To sum up, the need to contend simultaneously with imperatives to protect conditions of production and to cope with profitability crisis necessitated decades of hard, culture-changing work in thousands of offices, field sites, computers, labs, meeting rooms, classrooms, trading floors and airplanes. It was, in part, the resulting matrix of new, commodification-ready environmental objects that made it so easy for a relatively small group of actors to insert what might otherwise seem the far-fetched construct of carbon trading into global policy.

Parallel developments

By the late 1990s, a growing technocracy devoted specifically to carbon trading was busy creating yet further novel objects such as 'tons of CO_2 equivalents' (Bumpus 2011). Carbon trading's two components – emissions trading (cap and trade) and offset trading – have been analysed at length elsewhere (Gilbertson and Reyes 2009; Lohmann 2005, 2009, 2010b). However, they have seldom been compared in much detail with other, similar markets developed during the neoliberal era. Putting carbon trading in this wider context helps highlight some of its salient features while enabling fresh perspectives on the development of climate politics.

Cap and trade and fishery quotas

One fascinating parallel is with the markets in 'tradable quotas' (TQs) legislated into existence in several Atlantic and Pacific ocean fisheries during the 1990s. The TQ system is a sort of 'cap and trade for fish', and cap and trade a sort of TQ system for greenhouse gases. Both systems trade in 'rights to exploit' – whether fish stocks or the earth's carbon-cycling capacity. Both systems, too, use dispossession to prepare a regime in which 'efficiency' purportedly coincides with environmental protection. In Norway, fish previously 'regarded as a common heritage of the coastal people' are 'expropriated, without compensation, and given, free of charge, as private property to a small elite' (Holm 2002). In various US Pacific fisheries, rights to fish for halibut and sablefish are divided among individual fishers, and rights to Alaska pollock among processors and fishing cooperatives. Under the Kyoto Protocol and EU ETS, meanwhile, the earth's carbon-cycling capacity is distributed, again usually free of charge, to Northern industrialized nation-states, according to the principle (known as 'grandfathering') that the most pollution rights should be awarded to those who have polluted most in the past.

In the carbon case, of course, the rights issued to Northern industry are not exclusionary (nor are they permanent, since the number of rights given out can be reduced over time). Nations and industries in the global South are allowed to continue using global carbon sinks without restriction. Nonetheless, the creation of tradable emissions rights is a form of privatization channelling disproportionate benefits to Northern industry and finance. For one thing, the rights granted to richer countries under Kyoto and the EU ETS come in the form of commodities, unlike the permissions allowed to the global South. These commodities have proved lucrative to many fractions of capital: electricity generators, steel firms, speculators and many others.[4] In addition, the rights that European and some other industrialized country governments distribute to their major polluting industries – again for the most part free of charge – can be conceptualized in part as legal and economic guarantees protecting Northern industries' power to harm others through their overuse of global carbon-cycling capacity.[5] In this respect, carbon trading bears a resemblance to the characteristic trade treaties of the neoliberal era, such as the North American Free Trade Agreement and Host Government Agreements, which enhance profits by effectively granting corporations' immunity from local environmental laws (McCarthy 2007).

Tradable quota regimes in fisheries are supposed to encourage the exit of 'inefficient' fishers from an overcapitalized industry (Mansfield 2007), leaving a 'new class' of fish-owners who are 'intensely preoccupied with the health of the resource, since the return on their investments depends on it' (Holm 2002). So, too, carbon cap and trade regimes are intended to recruit the private sector to environmentalism via imposed restrictions on emissions and a mounting 'carbon price' incorporated into business decision-making. Both regimes, in addition, devolve private property rights to corporations, groups or individuals through an enormous prior expansion of state control. As Becky Mansfield emphasizes in her work on 'neoliberalism in the oceans', TQ systems became possible only after seacoast states had enclosed 30 per cent of the oceans and 95 per cent of the world's fisheries through the establishment of 200-mile zones ultimately enshrined in the Law of the Sea (Mansfield 2007: 65). Under the EU ETS, similarly, European states had to entitle themselves to global carbon sinks before calculating and 'producing' commodified rights for donation to high-emitting corporate sectors – although in this case the objective from the outset was much more clearly to set up a trading system.[6]

In transforming environmental challenges (overfishing, global warming) into questions of capital management, TQs and cap and trade also both put distinctive, and similar, structural stresses on the scientific framework that is supposed to ensure their effectiveness. TQ systems require fishery science to come up with some approximation to 'sustainable limits' to fish catches and to subscribe to a belief in 'equilibrium' – requirements that are at odds with both vernacular and chaos theory-influenced conceptions of the marine environment (Smith 1990).[7] Similarly, cap and trade's reduction of the challenge of climate prescription to the simplified measure of setting probabilistic 'safe' limits to flows of greenhouse gas molecules abstracts from uncertainty, indeterminacy and the complex question of how to build a politics capable of ensuring that most remaining fossil fuels stay in the ground. Cap-setting in climate markets, however, appears to be more frankly determined by rent-seeking and international political horse-trading than is quota-setting in fishery TQ systems (Liverman 2009).

A final parallel is the tendency of both TQ and cap and trade systems to institute or exacerbate owner–worker divides of a kind familiar from histories of industrial capitalism. In Norway, fisher organizations 'are split right down the middle, with the fish-owners joining ranks on the one hand, sharply divided from the newly-formed class of fishermen-workers on the other' (Holm 2002: 18; see also Pálsson 1998). In cap and trade systems, a division between haves and have-nots was built in from the beginning. Under the Kyoto Protocol, Northern states are granted rights to global carbon-cycling capacity; the South is not. Under the EU ETS, similarly, it is the heaviest polluters of the private sector who are granted the largest chunk of rights and have reaped the most financial rewards, including 'carbon fat cats' such as Arcelor Mittal, Lafarge, Thyssen Krupp and Holcim Cement (Sandbag 2011b). Lower-emitting or 'greener' businesses get fewer rights, while individuals, communities and environmental organizations are left out entirely. In the global South, meanwhile, it is large and often heavily polluting industries that dominate production of cheap supplementary pollution rights (offsets) for sale to the industrial North (UN Risoe Centre 2012). Communities that have always acted in ways that maintain the earth's carbon-cycling capacity, such as small peasant farmers and many indigenous groups, are usually excluded from the market – although many would resist, or are resisting, attempts to integrate them into it – as are movements battling extractive industries or developing new low-carbon ways of life.

Environmentally, the record of TQs is mixed, reflecting, among other things, the fact that the biological management regime associated with TQs does not allow fish to be a 'complex, fragmented and unstable entity' (Holm 1999: 10; see also Bavington 2010). Even more embarrassing, however, is the record of the world's leading cap and trade programme, the EU Emissions Trading Scheme, which has ended up subsidizing carbon-profligate practices, coal-fired electricity generation in particular (Reyes 2011; Pahle et al. 2011; Sandbag 2010), and remains in perpetual tension with efforts to promote renewable energy and other reforms aimed at 'carbon efficiency' (Reuters 2011). For most European countries, not even the modest government-mandated targets that underpin the scheme can be met without importing extra pollution rights from abroad, and have been rendered meaningless even in their own terms by Europe's continued outsourcing of emissions to Asia and the rest of the world (Peters et al. 2011). Carbon prices, which have no prospect of attaining levels that would incentivize structural change, are uncertain and declining (Point Carbon 2012a, 2012b, 2012c).[8]

Carbon offsets and wetlands banking

The second component of carbon trading – carbon offsets – also finds instructive parallels among other ecosystem markets that have sprung up in recent decades. One example is wetlands banking – a scheme developed in the United States during the 1980s and 1990s as a way of making it easier for builders to comply with restrictions on dredging or dumping in swampy areas (Robertson 2004). Under wetlands banking, developers, instead of having to suspend operations, move to another site, or fashion 'compensatory wetlands' on the same parcel of land they are building on, can buy pre-packaged 'wetlands credits' from other locations to cover the damage they do. Just as carbon offsets produced through the Kyoto Protocol's Clean Development Mechanism (CDM) allow their ultimate buyers (mainly in Europe) to go on burning fossil fuels at the same rate at a time of incipient emissions caps, wetlands credits confer on builders the right (which regulation would otherwise curtail) to bulldoze unique sites. In addition to loosening regulatory constraints on business, carbon offset trading offers lucrative speculative opportunities, and not surprisingly is today dominated by the City of London and Wall Street (UNDP 2011).[9]

Unlike carbon offset trading, wetlands trading was not legislated into existence by national states and international treaties. Rather, as Morgan M. Robertson recounts in a series of brilliant papers, it was the brainstorm of state and federal highway agencies and Illinois private building contractors looking for innovative ways of complying with 1970s US federal clean water legislation (Robertson 2007: 115–116). Yet carbon credits and wetland credits are similar in that they are both created through techniques that reduce qualitative ecological/social processes to a simplified, standardized set of quantifiable 'ecosystem services', thus redefining nature as a 'stable external presence'. 'Wetland loss at the site of impact must be rendered commensurable with wetland gain at the site of banking in a regular and reliable way' (Roberston 2007: 118).

The consequence is what Robertson calls an 'inconcludable dynamic of contradictory, and perhaps cyclic impulses' (Robertson 2007: 122). On the one hand, scientists working for wetland banks use algorithms and professional judgment to assign numerical scores to the various 'functional benefits' of banking sites (habitat provision, plant diversity, peak flow attenuation, floodwater storage and so forth). On the other hand, the US Army Corps of Engineers, tasked with quantifying the impacts of construction, has little choice, due to lack of time and expertise, but to measure damage in acres. Bankers, suspicious that the mismatch is costing them profits, have proposed multiplying the number of commodities on offer, so that a builder who has reduced 'hydrologic function' at a certain site by three units and 'duck habitat' by four units can purchase separate credits, perhaps even at different banks, in mitigation. But the more ecological sensitivity is incorporated into the commodity, the less trade and liquidity is possible. It would be impossible, for instance, to create the ecosystem function 'floodwater storage for the Kishwaukee River basin' outside the Kishwaukee River basin. Ecosystem science eventually comes up hard against the 'generalizing abstractions that characterize the internal logic of capital', setting off conflicts among bankers, regulators and scientists alike. The institutions of wetlands banking, Robertson concludes, 'have not even agreed upon what the commodity *is* that they wish to measure' – in contrast with the institutions structuring markets in, say, wheat or microchips.

The parallels with carbon offset markets are unmistakable. Here, too, commodity construction requires heroic abstractions and (as also with TQ fishery systems) institutions that attempt to restructure nature as a stabilizable external entity. In order to be made quantifiable, divisible, standardizable and tradable, climate benefit and climate harm are conceptualized, in linear fashion, in terms of the flow of CO_2 molecules:

a better climate = reductions in CO_2 emissions

thus obscuring both uncertainty and the geo-ecological roots of the climate crisis in the unsustainable transfer of fossil carbon into an above-ground system comprising atmosphere, oceans, vegetation, soils and so forth. Supplementary acts of commensuration quickly follow:

CO_2 reduction in place A = CO_2 reduction in place B

CO_2 reduction through technology A = CO_2 reduction through technology B

CO_2 reduction through conservation of biota = CO_2 reduction through keeping fossil fuels in the ground[10]

A new construction, 'carbon dioxide equivalent', or CO_2e, is derived from further gross oversimplifications:

CH_4 = 21 X CO_2

N_2O = 310 X CO_2

HFC-23 = 11,700 X CO_2[11]

Carbon dioxide reductions mandated by cap and trade schemes are then made equivalent to offsetting activities outside the jurisdiction of the scheme:

CO_2e reduction under a cap = 'avoided' CO_2e outside the cap

Activities at a wide variety of 'mitigation sites' can accordingly be used to generate credits enabling the continued use of fossil fuels at 'impact sites' such as power stations and iron and steel factories. For example, two dozen giant hog farms operated by Granjas Carroll de Mexico, a subsidiary of the US-based Smithfield Farms, today capture and burn the methane given off by the huge volumes of pig excrement they produce (hence 'avoiding' biotic CH_4 emissions by replacing them with CO_2 emissions, thus reducing CO_2e and quantifiably 'benefiting' the climate), then sell the resulting carbon credits to Cargill International and EcoSecurities (UN Risoe Centre 2012).

Ultimately, as in wetlands trading, attempts to 'push ecological knowledge towards spawning further rounds of accumulation' via construction of such shaky equations 'may disrupt the very mechanics of accumulation' (Robertson 2007: 123).[12] In carbon trading, the equivalence 'CO_2e reduction under a cap = "avoided" CO_2e outside the cap', which underpins all offset commodities, generates particular mayhem. For example, the EU, noting that refrigerant gas producers have upped their production of HFC-23 merely to be able to sell carbon credits for 'avoiding' it later, recently decided to ban such credits from the EU ETS as of 2013, citing their 'total lack of environmental integrity' (Connie Hedegaard quoted in Reyes 2011). But the contradictions generated by attempts to apply the equation are far more general. To manufacture offsets by counting 'avoided CO_2 emissions', a baseline must first be established with which to compare current molecular activity. The baseline must be unique, since exchange requires a single value. Hence the calculation of 'avoided emissions' not only demands the sort of knowledge human beings have never before attained, attempted or believed possible. (Which of all the scenarios that counterfactual historians and novelists have imagined might have followed a Nazi invasion of Britain is the 'true' one?) It also demands, impossibly, that this knowledge come in the form of an extremely precise quantification of the associated molecular movements and that this quantification be open to a process of checking and verification that in fact will never become available to anyone.[13] Corporations are able to print climate money without much fear of sanction, since no stable distinction between counterfeit and legitimate currency can be maintained (The Munden Group 2011: 17). Already, different methodologies for singling out a baseline have resulted in calculations of forest carbon credits that range over two orders of magnitude (Griscom *et al.* 2009). Ultimately, this may be a step too far even for a financial system accustomed to lax reserve capital controls and complex financial derivatives such as credit default swaps (The Munden Group 2011).[14] As Robertson puts it, if some ecological knowledges 'work' for capital, others do not.

A longer-term historical logic

A final social-science tool can help place carbon trading in an even broader context, that of historical cycles of accumulation, by drawing on the work of historians, sociologists and geographers such as Giovanni Arrighi (1994, 2007), David Harvey (1982, 2003) and Jason W. Moore (2011a, 2011b). Such theorists take a long view, arguing that profit crises, financialization and attempts to 'internalize' threats to business expansion created by previous expansions have unfolded time and again over many centuries in varied ways.

Arrighi, for example, posits a succession of global 'systemic cycles of accumulation', each with a different geographical centre and each characterized by a different attempt to bring certain (emergent or long-standing) 'costs' within the 'economizing logic of capitalist enterprise'. In one such cycle centred on the Netherlands during the seventeenth and eighteenth centuries, Arrighi argues, a Dutch business class organized in the state found it to its advantage to internalize increasingly expensive 'protection costs' – costs of exercising force and making war – that an earlier, Genoese cycle between about 1450 and 1625 had found easier to 'externalize' to the Iberian imperial-territorial states. By 'economizing' on brutality and making it pay to a greater extent than other, more territory-obsessed powers could, Dutch chartered companies were able to become 'self-sufficient and competitive in the use and control of violence' in the East Indies (Arrighi 1994), 'producing' their own protection at costs that were lower and more predictable than the tribute or extortions extracted from caravans and ships by local powers (Steensgard 1981). Similar innovations allowed the Dutch to squeeze out Spanish influence in the Baltic and gain power over the Atlantic slave trade (Arrighi 1994: 155).

The British-centred cycle that followed from about 1775 to 1925, while continuing to internalize protection costs (ensuring agro-industrial imports), superseded the increasingly crisis-ridden Dutch cycle partly by bringing production, especially industrial production, 'within the *organizational* domain of capitalist enterprises', subjecting them to the investment planning and 'economizing tendencies typical of those enterprises' (Arrighi 1994: 177). This cycle – to whose productivity and flexibility coal, railroads and an increasingly commercialized agriculture were crucial – in turn succumbed to a US-dominated cycle in which oil-based processes of suburbanization, globalization and Green Revolution agriculture became essential. This cycle internalized not only protection and production costs, but also transaction costs, vertically integrating business organizations within a single organizational domain in a way that made the costs associated with the transfer of intermediate inputs through the long chain between production and consumption more predictable and calculable (Arrighi 1994: 218, 240, 241, 287). Railways, marketing, mail order, mass retail, computers all helped structure a high volume of market transactions within single enterprises. Capital sunk in specialized machinery mandated corporate control over prices and thus suspension or supersession of ordinary market mechanisms (Galbraith 1967). Post-1980 developments such as just-in-time production and containerized shipping further rationalized the process (Mirowski 2011; Levinson 2008). Eventually, however, as in previous cycles, a profitability crisis followed by a bout of speculative excess and financialization began to generate 'the chaotic ferment' (to use the words of another theorist of long capitalist cycles, David Harvey) out of which yet another mode of organization, with its own physical infrastructure, is now growing

(Arrighi 2007: 223). Arrighi thus anticipates the rise, in the twenty-first century, of a new, China-centred cycle.

An interpretive framework that emphasizes the importance of accumulation cycles explains a great deal about carbon markets that baffles and frustrates their mainstream proponents. According to mainstream accounts, for example, carbon trading will work if states follow the findings of scientific bodies in setting and enforcing stringent, progressive emissions caps (Sandbag 2011a; California Environmental Protection Agency 2011). Trading in emissions and offsets will then ensure that this scientifically 'correct' outcome is achieved at the lowest cost. Presupposing the existence of a technocratically rational, strong state independent of business, and conceiving of markets primarily as 'efficiency machines', this account tends to downplay the role of profits, productivity, accumulation crisis, commodification and regulatory capture in market construction and market performance. Phenomena such as the inability of states to set strict emissions caps, identify the commodity being traded or control carbon scams appear as irksome pathologies or side issues. When such phenomena persist despite their supposed 'abnormality', well-intentioned mainstream observers find themselves at sea, impotent to suggest any solutions other than more 'political will' or better technique.

Theories of accumulation cycles provide useful interpretive tools for avoiding this quagmire. Instead of treating the environmental ineffectiveness of carbon markets as a worrying but temporary anomaly, the theory treats it as a predictable – and partly successful – response to the stresses on capital building up at the tail end of a fossil-fuelled US-centred accumulation cycle. Such theories, grasping the enduring importance of state action in safeguarding conditions for accumulation, as well as the key role that fossil fuels continue to play in labour productivity throughout industrialized societies, find the unambitious emissions targets and production of implausible emissions-cut 'substitutes' that have characterized carbon markets entirely unsurprising. Well aware of the nature of the 'turn to finance' that typically occurs at the close of accumulation cycles, such theories also make explicable why carbon trading – along with other 'green capitalist' initiatives – originated partly from, and continues to be dominated by, a financial sector whose bias is towards creating novel sources of profit rather than halting the flow of fossil fuels out of the ground.[15] From this perspective, it is only to be expected that emissions caps will be set, at best, just strictly enough to create scarcity for a new market, but not strictly enough to threaten the role of coal and oil in capital accumulation, and that further plans to financialize forests and land as carbon sinks will proceed apace under the supportive eyes of many on Wall Street (Carbon Trade Watch 2010). The theory of accumulation cycles thus usefully redirects the attention of strategy-minded activists to the underlying drivers of global warming while explaining why carbon trading, and the 'market environmentalist' ideology that supports it, will remain less than credible responses to climate crisis. By linking false climate solutions to other manifestations of the neoliberal response to profit crisis, it also suggests the importance of alliance-building between carbon market critics and wider social movements countering privatization, appropriation and commodification.

Conclusion

In 2010, data from BP has shown, CO_2 emissions from burning fossil fuels rose at their fastest rate in four decades. So devastating are the implications of this trend that many Northern debates about how to reverse it seem to have little time to pause to consider lessons from history and sociology. This chapter has tried to suggest the strategic hazards of this short-sightedness, as well as the advantages of openness to more varied interpretive approaches to climate change politics.

Building more effective climate movements is largely a matter of interpretation and reinterpretation, which are in turn a matter of contextualization and re-contextualization. Climate activists can benefit from 'going wide' into the study of market environmentalisms that have evolved together with carbon trading; from 'going deep' into the insights of actor-network theory about the genesis and limitations of commodity-ready environmental objects; and from 'going long' into the historical investigation of accumulation cycles. Rather than being forced to beat their heads against the wall erected by the economistic premise that, given enough time and tweaks, carbon trading 'must' someday be made to work, climate activists can thereby gain a more detailed, nuanced and encouraging picture of the field of possible action on climate change.

Notes

1 'Expert knowledge', in the words of Mitchell, 'works to format social relations, never simply to report or picture them' (Mitchell 2002: 118). For example, double-entry bookkeeping 'was devised to account for business transactions, but once established, it altered these transactions by changing the way businessmen interpreted and understood them' (Carruthers and Espeland 1991; see also MacKenzie 2009). For an application to carbon markets specifically, see, for example, Lohmann (2005).
2 Al Gore, for example, has attributed environmental crisis mainly to the incorrect 'calculations by which our economy is governed' (Independent, 7 July 2007).
3 Google's Ngram Viewer is a useful way of tracking word usage over the centuries.
4 Offsets, while not distributed free, also allow for enhanced profits under regulatory regimes that would otherwise require emissions reductions at source. Diana Liverman gives one reason: 'the rationalities are of financial markets – the carbon credits (Certified Emission Reductions or CERS) are cheaper because investments in the developing world are considered riskier' (Liverman 2009).
5 Liverman (2009) glosses this 'grandfathering' regime as follows: 'Because the baseline for the reductions was based on emissions in 1990 the atmosphere was effectively "enclosed" according to pollution levels in 1990. The larger environmental narrative here is that of "prior appropriation" whereby those who first polluted the atmosphere then acquire a right to pollute under international law.'
6 The subsequent legal wrangles also appear to be harder to sort out than in the case of fisheries. All of the following questions, for example, have been the subject of extended dispute in the arenas of law and diplomacy: Who owns the rights to the carbon in New Zealand forests (Lohmann 2006: 127)? Who owns the millions of tonnes of stolen EU pollution rights that went into widespread circulation in early 2011 before anyone had rumbled the computer hackers that had lifted them (Lohmann 2010a: 117–120; Carbon Finance Online 2012)? Whose legal responsibility are the carbon dioxide molecules coming out of smokestacks in Shenzen if they are being emitted in the course of producing consumer goods for the United States or Europe (Peters *et al.* 2011)?

Is the EU exceeding its legal authority by bringing aviation under the EU ETS and thus regulating molecules emanating from machines that are used to start jet engines in Los Angeles or Beijing (Clark 2011)?

7. As Holm (2001) notes dryly, sociologists of fisheries tend to have better biological theories of fish than do the fish biologists who are constrained to work across disciplinary boundaries with the economist-managers of TQ systems. The latter are in turn better at sociology than the card-carrying academic fishery sociologists who are skeptical of TQs, as shown by the superior social and political influence they have been able to exert in entrenching the social-technical infrastructure required for TQs.

8. On the inability of price generally to achieve structural change, see, for example, Buck (2007).

9. The financial sector, however, is growing increasingly sceptical of the carbon market, with many banks and funds closing carbon trading desks, withdrawing from exchanges, divesting themselves of carbon businesses and shedding staff.

10. In current CDM forestry offsets, temporary CERs (or tCERs) must in the end be replaced with energy-based offsets. However, this does not eliminate dependence on this equation. The hundreds of millions of tons of offsets that would be produced by offsets under proposals for Reducing Emissions from Deforestation and Forest Degradation (REDD) also rely utterly on this equation.

11. All these equations oversimplify in the sense that each gas behaves qualitatively differently in the atmosphere and over different time spans, and the control of each has a different effect on fossil fuel use. Even the IPCC finds itself revising its calculations of the CO_2-calibrated 'Global Warming Potential' (GWP) of various gases every few years, and insists on giving gases different GWPs over 20-year, 100-year and 500-year time horizons. But even such token caveats cannot be accommodated by a market that requires a single, stable number in order to make exchange possible. The UN carbon market, for example, disregards its own IPCC's recent revisions in GWP figures, discards 20-year and 500-year figures, and ignores the (misnamed) 'error bands' specified by the IPCC (in the case of HFC-23, plus or minus 5,000 CO_2-equivalents). For further discussion, see, for example, MacKenzie (2009). In one example of the fragility of such equations, in 2007 the 'global warming potential' or GWP of HFC-23 was revised upwards from 11,700 to 14,800 by the Intergovernmental Panel on Climate Change – although the UN carbon market continues to use the earlier equation.

12. For a more gingerly treatment of some of these issues as they relate to carbon, see Bumpus (2011).

13. Technocratic institutions that reflect on this problem tend in the end to throw up their hands and bequeath the whole question to what they hope will be the greater 'technical' expertise of posterity. See, for example, United Nations Development Programme (2012). As Michael Gillenwater (2012) of the Greenhouse Gas Management Institute confesses, 'we don't appear to have a handle on a concept we have championed as integral to the policies we have created'.

14. As The Munden Project (2011) notes, the difficulty of verifying commodity quality eclipses those experienced even in financial derivatives markets. Oil futures markets, for instance, work with an underlying asset that, although infinitely variable, can be located, divided up, and its quality verified at any point along the user chain according to workable, standard criteria. The carbon offset commodity cannot be specified in the same way.

15. For example, members of the International Emissions Trading Association promote, in addition to increased use of the emissions 'equivalences' outlined above, sweeping standardization of climate commodities, rubber-stamp regulation, banking and borrowing of carbon pollution credits across compliance periods, increased participation of financial intermediaries, no buyer liability for fake products and an unregulated over-the-counter market that would encourage speculation. Some also make money by inducing carbon price volatility (Lohmann 2011).

References

Arrighi, G. (1994) *The Long Twentieth Century: Money, Power and the Origins of our Time*, London: Verso.
Arrighi, G. (2007) *Adam Smith in Beijing: Lineages of the 21st Century*, London: Verso.
Bavington, D. (2010) 'From Hunting Fish to Managing Populations: Fisheries Science and the Destruction of Newfoundland Cod Fisheries', *Science as Culture* 19(4): 509–528.
Buck, D. (2007) 'The Ecological Question: Can Capitalism Prevail?', *Socialist Register* 2007: 60–71.
Bumpus, A.G. (2011) 'The Matter of Carbon: Understanding the Materiality of tCO_2e in Carbon Offsets', *Antipode* 43(3): 612–638.
California Environmental Protection Agency, Air Resources Board (2011) *Supplement to the AB 32 Scoping Plan Functional Equivalent Document*, Sacramento: California Environmental Protection Agency.
Callon, M. (ed.) (1998) *The Laws of the Markets*, Oxford: Blackwell.
Callon, M. (2005) 'Why Virtualism Paves the Way to Political Impotence: Callon Replies to Miller', *Economic Sociology European Electronic Newsletter*, 6, 2, 3–20: 9.
Carbon Finance Online (2012) 'Court Rules EUA "Phishing" Victim Entitled to Compensation', *Carbon Finance Online*, 18 January.
Carbon Trade Watch (2010) *No REDD: A Reader*, Barcelona: Carbon Trade Watch.
Carruthers, B.G. and Espeland, W. (1991) 'Accounting for Rationality: Double-Entry Bookkeeping and Emergence of Economic Rationality', *American Journal of Sociology* 97: 36.
Clark, P. (2011) 'United Warns EU on Emissions Scheme', *Financial Times*, 3 April.
Galbraith, J.K. (1967) *The New Industrial State*, London: Penguin.
Gilbertson, T. and Reyes, O. (2009) *Carbon Trading: How it Works and Why it Fails*, Uppsala: Dag Hammarskjold Foundation.
Gillenwater, M. (2012) 'How Do You Explain Additionality?'. Online. Available at: ghginstitute.org/2012/01/25/how-do-you-explain-additionality (retrieved 1.2.2012).
Gómez-Baggethun, E.R., de Groot, P.L. and Lomas, C.M. (2010) 'The History of Ecosystem Services in Economic Theory and Practice: From Early Notions to Markets and Payment Schemes', *Ecological Economics* 69: 1209–1218.
Griscom, B., Shoch, D., Stanley, B., Cortez, R. and Virgilio, N. (2009) 'Sensitivity of Amount and Distribution of Tropical Forest Carbon Credits Depending on Baseline Rules', *Environmental Science and Policy* 12: 897–911.
Harvey, D. (1982) *The Limits to Capital*, London: Verso.
Harvey, D. (2003) *The New Imperialism*, Oxford: Oxford University Press.
Heinzerling, L. (2000) 'The Rights of Statistical People', *Harvard Environmental Law Review* 24: 189–207.
Holm, P. (1999) 'Fisheries Resource Management as a Heterogeneous Network', paper presented at the Eco-Knowledge Working Seminar, Nova Scotia, May.
Holm, P. (2001) *The Invisible Revolution: The Construction of Institutional Change in the Fisheries*, unpublished PhD thesis, Tromso: Norwegian College of Fishery.
Holm, P. (2002) 'Which Way is up on Callon? A Review of a Review: Daniel Miller's "Turning Callon the Right Way Up." On Michel Callon: The Laws of the Markets'. Online. Available at: www0.nfh.uit.no/dok/which_way_is_up0.pdf (retrieved: 22.3.2012).
Law, J. (ed.) (1991) *A Sociology of Monsters: Essays on Power, Technology, and Domination*, New York: Routledge.

Levinson, M. (2008) *The Box: How the Shipping Container Made the World Smaller and the World Economy Bigger*, Princeton: Princeton University Press.

Liverman, D.M. (2009) 'Conventions of Climate Change: Constructions of Danger and the Dispossession of the Atmosphere', *Journal of Historical Geography* 35(2): 279–296.

Lohmann, L. (2005) 'Marketing and Making Carbon Dumps: Commodification, Calculation and Counterfactuals in Climate Change Mitigation', *Science as Culture* 14(3): 203–235.

Lohmann, L. (ed.) (2006) *Carbon Trading: A Critical Conversation on Climate Change, Privatization and Power*, Uppsala: Dag Hammarskjold Foundation.

Lohmann, L. (2009) 'Toward a Different Debate in Environmental Accounting: The Cases of Carbon and Cost-Benefit', *Accounting, Organisations and Society* 34(3–4): 499–534.

Lohmann, L. (2010a) 'Los "Mercados Extraños" y la crisis climática', in Bravo, E. (ed.) *Crisis financiera o crisis civilizatoria*, Quito: Manthra Editores, 98–122.

Lohmann, L. (2010b) 'Uncertainty Markets and Carbon Markets: Variations on Polanyian Themes', *New Political Economy* 15: 225–254.

Lohmann, L. (2011) 'Financialization, Commodification and Carbon: The Contradictions of Neoliberal Climate Policy', *Socialist Register 2012*, 85–107.

McCarthy, J. (2007) 'Privatizing Conditions of Production: Trade Agreements as Neoliberal Environmental Governance', in Heynen, N. *et al.* (eds) *Neoliberal Environments: False Promises and Unnatural Consequences*, London: Routledge.

MacKenzie, D. (2009) 'Making Things the Same: Gases, Emissions Rights and the Politics of Carbon Markets', *Accounting, Organizations and Society*, 34(3–4): 440–455.

Mansfield, B. (2007) 'Neoliberalism in the Oceans: "Rationalization", Property Rights, and the Commons Question', in Heynen, N., McCarthy, J., Prudham, S. and Robbins, P. *et al.* (eds) *Neoliberal Environments: False Promises and Unnatural Consequences*, London: Routledge, 38–50.

Mirowski, P. (2011) *Science-Mart: Privatizing American Science*, Cambridge, MA: Harvard University Press.

Mirowski, P. and Plehwe, D. (eds) (2010) *The Road from Mont Pelerin: The Making of the Neoliberal Thought Collective*, Cambridge, MA: Harvard University Press.

Mitchell, T. (2002) *Rule of Experts: Egypt, Technopolitics, Modernity*, Berkeley: University of California Press.

Mol, A.P.J. (1995) *The Refinement of Production*, Utrecht: International Books.

Moore, J.W. (2011a) 'Transcending the Metabolic Rift: A Theory of Crises in the Capitalist World-Ecology', *The Journal of Peasant Studies* 38(1): 1–46.

Moore, J.W. (2011b) 'Ecology, Capital and the Nature of our Times: Accumulation and Crisis in the Capitalist World-Ecology', *Journal of World-Systems Research* 17(1): 108–147.

The Munden Group (2011) *REDD and Forest Carbon: Market-Based Critique and Recommendations*, New York: The Munden Group.

Pahle, M., Fan, L. and Schill, W.-P. (2011) 'How Emission Certificate Allocations Distort Fossil Investments: The German Example', *Energy Policy* 39(4): 1975–1987.

Pálsson, G. (1998) 'The Virtual Aquarium: Commodity Fiction and Cod Fishing', *Ecological Economics* 24(2–3): 275–288.

Peck, J. (2010) *Constructions of Neoliberal Reason*, Oxford: Oxford University Press.

Peck, J. and Tickell, A. (2002) 'Neoliberalizing Space', *Antipode* 34(3): 380–404.

Peters, G.P., Minx, J.C., Weber, C.L. and Edenhofer, O. (2011) 'Growth in Emission Trans-

fers via International Trade from 1990 to 2008', *Proceedings of the National Academy of Sciences* 108(21): 8903–8908.
Point Carbon (2012a) 'Barclays Shutters U.S. Emissions Trading Desk', 19 January; 'Rock-Bottom AAU Prices Could Spur CER Sell-off: Sources', *Point Carbon*, 12 January.
Point Carbon (2012b) 'Carbon Stocks Suffer as Investors Quit the Market', *Point Carbon*, 16 January.
Point Carbon (2012c) 'CERs Fall 5 pct, Hit Record Low on Oversupply, Weak Demand', *Point Carbon*, 16 January.
Reuters (2011) 'Polluters Winners from Carbon Scheme', *Reuters*, 23 June.
Reyes, O. (2011) *The EU Emissions Trading System: Failing at the Third Attempt*, Barcelona: Corporate Europe Observatory and Carbon Trade Watch.
Robertson, M.M. (2000) 'No Net Loss: Wetland Restoration and the Incomplete Capitalization of Nature', *Antipode* 32(4): 463–493.
Robertson, M.M. (2004) 'The Neoliberalization of Ecosystem Services: Wetland Mitigation Banking and Problems in Environmental Governance', *Geoforum* 35(3): 361–373.
Robertson, M.M. (2007) 'The Neoliberalization of Ecosystem Services: Wetland Mitigation Banking and the Problem of Measurement', in Heynen, N., McCarthy, J., Prudham, S. and Robbins, P. (eds) *Neoliberal Environments: False Promises and Unnatural Consequences*, London: Routledge: 114–125.
Sandbag (2010) *The Carbon Rich List*, London: Sandbag.
Sandbag (2011a) *Buckle Up! Tighten the Cap and Avoid the Carbon Crash*, London: Sandbag.
Sandbag (2011b) *Carbon Fat Cats 2011*, London: Sandbag.
Smith, M.E. (1990) 'Chaos in Fisheries Management', *Maritime Anthropological Studies* 3(2): 1–13.
Steensgard, N. (1981) 'Violence and the Rise of Capitalism: Frederic C. Lane's Theory of Protection and Tribute', *Review* 5(2): 259–260.
Thomas, N. (1991) *Entangled Objects: Exchange, Material Culture, and Colonialism in the Pacific*, Cambridge, MA: Harvard University Press.
UNDP (2011) 'Forest Carbon Accounting: Overviews and Principles'. Online. Available at: www.undp.org/climatechange/carbon-finance/CDM/resources.shtml (retrieved: 15.3.2011).
UN Risoe Centre (2012) 'CDM Pipeline'. Online. Available at: cdmpipeline.org/cdm-projects-type.htm (retrieved: 1.2.2012).

Part II
The securitization of climate change

6 Climate chains
Neo-Malthusianism, militarism and migration

Betsy Hartmann

Introduction

The year 2007 witnessed growing concern about the threats posed by 'climate refugees' and 'climate conflict' to international security.[1] First the *Atlantic Monthly* (Faris 2007), then the UN Environment Programme (UNEP 2007), then even UN Secretary General Ban Ki-Moon (2007) attributed violence in Darfur to a combination of demographic pressures, resource scarcities and climate change. Along with the Darfur stories came other dire predictions about the threat of so-called 'climate refugees' spilling across the globe and wreaking havoc (Christian Aid 2007a, 2007b).

In April that year the British government brought the issue of climate change before the UN Security Council for the first time, citing the Darfur case (Harvey 2007). In the United States, the defence think tank, Center for Naval Analysis (CNA), produced a report, *National Security and the Threat of Climate Change*, which argued that global warming could help trigger widespread political instability in poor regions and large refugee movements to the United States and Europe (CNA 2007). Towards the end of the year, the Norwegian Nobel Committee (2007) warned that climate-induced migration and resource scarcity could cause violent conflict and war within and between states when it awarded the Nobel Peace Prize to Al Gore, Jr. and the Intergovernmental Panel on Climate Change (IPCC).

For me these alarmist narratives rang a familiar bell. In the late 1990s, I researched the evolution and impact of environmental conflict discourse, focusing on the work of Canadian political scientist Thomas Homer-Dixon. I was interested not only in critiquing the assumptions underlying his models, but exploring why they gained so much currency in US and international policy circles. I interviewed 70 people in government and multilateral agencies, research and policy institutes, foundations, universities and non-governmental organizations (NGOs) in the United States and Europe. While the story was complex, an overarching theme emerged: environmental conflict models enjoyed (undue) influence because of their *usefulness* to a variety of policy interests and their funding by private foundations. Their usefulness in turn depended on the widespread *acceptability* of neo-Malthusian crisis narratives about the links between population, migration, environmental degradation and conflict as well as popular but unsubstantiated claims about the threat of millions of environmental refugees (Hartmann 2003).

In this chapter I probe why a similar discourse about climate conflict and climate refugees is gaining traction. Critical development studies literature on crisis narratives, especially in regard to Africa, informs the investigation. In the mid-1990s Emery Roe coined the term 'crisis narrative' to describe the stereotypical 'overpopulation causes scarcity causes political unrest' storylines applied indiscriminately to different African countries and designed to justify the intervention of Western development agencies (Roe 1995). More recent case studies show how these narratives survive and thrive despite a significant body of serious field research that calls them into question (e.g. Milligan and Binns 2007; Verhoeven 2011). Understanding their endurance requires looking at the diversity of interests they serve, their institutional rootedness and reproduction, the deep well of colonial and neo-Malthusian stereotypes on which they draw, and the role of private and public funding streams in rewarding their purveyors.

Some of the insights I offer in this chapter are speculative since I have not had the opportunity, as I did in my previous work on environmental conflict, to conduct interviews in the policy arena or closely follow the funding trail, both important avenues for further research. But what I have uncovered so far is troubling. Crisis narratives around climate conflict and climate refugees are closely linked to current worst-case scenarios and counterinsurgency strategies of Western defence interests. This linkage helps weaken the already porous boundaries between environment, development and humanitarian agencies, on the one hand, and the military on the other.

The chapter is organized in four sections. The first and second sections look at the transition from environmental conflict to climate conflict, and environmental refugees to climate refugees respectively. The third section considers the strategic value of these climate and security narratives for US defence interests and their potential to further militarize humanitarian aid. The final section offers some thoughts about the reasons for their staying power.

From environmental conflict to climate conflict

For those familiar with the environmental security field, particularly neo-Malthusian models of environmental conflict developed in the 1980s and 1990s, climate conflict and refugee narratives seem very much like old wine in a new bottle. The vintage goes back even further, however, to a powerful policy narrative that I call the 'degradation narrative' (Hartmann 2003, 2006). Drawing on old colonial stereotypes of destructive Third World peasants and herders, degradation narratives go something like this: population-pressure induced poverty makes Third World peasants degrade their environments by over-farming or over-grazing marginal lands. The ensuing soil depletion and desertification then lead them to migrate elsewhere as 'environmental refugees', either to other ecologically vulnerable rural areas where the vicious cycle is once again set in motion or to cities where they strain scarce resources and become a primary source of political instability.

Despite salient critiques by international development scholars and practitioners,[2] the degradation narrative has proved particularly popular in Western policy circles because it kills a number of birds with one stone: it blames poverty on population pressure, and not, for example, on lack of land reform or off-farm employment opportunities; it blames peasants for land degradation, obscuring the role of commercial agriculture and extractive industries; and it targets migration both as an environmental and security threat.

In the 1990s Canadian political scientist Thomas Homer-Dixon propelled the degradation narrative and its negative depiction of migration into the 'high politics' of national security. Homer-Dixon's environmental conflict model maintains that scarcities of renewable resources such as cropland, fresh water and forests, induced in large part by population growth, contribute to migration and violent intrastate conflict in many parts of the developing world (Homer-Dixon 1999). This conflict, in turn, can potentially disrupt international security as states fragment or become more authoritarian.[3]

Homer-Dixon's work proved useful to a number of government institutions and initiatives during the Clinton administration. With the end of Cold War clientism, a series of 'state failures', notably in Somalia, posed new challenges to the US foreign policy establishment and led to a more anticipatory strategy of 'preventive defence'. Homer-Dixon's model of environmental conflict provided the kind of causal reasoning policymakers were looking for. By emphasizing the role of migration in fomenting conflict, the model also meshed well with growing anti-immigrant sentiment in Washington, DC. Environmental security in general became an 'engagement tool' for US defence and intelligence interests to build bridges with foreign military officials in strategic areas as well as to US-based NGOs and academics. Homer-Dixon's neo-Malthusian ideas struck a particularly sympathetic chord among funders targeting population growth, who had been eager to get the national security community on board for the 1994 UN population conference in Cairo. In fact, private population funding was instrumental in propelling Homer-Dixon into Washington policy circles (Hartmann 2003, 2006).

The legacy of environmental conflict models persists today in the climate change arena where degradation narratives again link environmental change to migration and violent conflict. A UN Environment Program (UNEP) report on Sudan, for example, draws on Homer-Dixon's model and related research to make claims that overpopulation of both people and livestock, coupled with environmental stresses such as water shortages related to climate change, are at the root of conflict in the region (UNEP 2007). This analysis all but ignores the predatory policies of the Sudanese state – in fact, it actively supports them. As Verhoeven notes, 'The regime loves the "climate" war rhetoric because it obscures its own role, and, above all, Sudan's fundamental problem since independence: Khartoum's logic of rule is inextricably linked to exclusion, patronage and violence' (Verhoeven 2011: 695).

Moreover, such threat scenarios ignore the way many poorly resourced communities manage their affairs without recourse to violence. Brown *et al.* (2007) cite the case of the semi-arid regions of Northern Nigeria where conflicts between pastoralists and agricultural communities occur over water and fodder, but seldom spread because of the existence of traditional conflict resolution institutions. They argue that helping these communities adapt to climate change should involve strengthening such institutions.

Research in the drylands of Marsabit District in Northern Kenya found that in times of drought and water scarcity there was actually less violence, not more. Poor herdsmen were not inclined to start fights during droughts, and despite poverty and population growth in the region, strong but flexible common property regimes governing water helped people adjust to its scarcity. 'If at any time a conflict over a scarce natural resource like water exists', the authors write, 'it can be a sign that local resource users themselves have been made powerless and that their negotiating system has been paralyzed, either by external agencies or local elites' (Witsenburg and Roba 2007: 235).

In fact, there is a rich body of empirical case studies of African agriculture, pastoralism and forestry that challenges conventional neo-Malthusian narratives about population, scarcity and conflict (e.g. Leach and Mearns 1996; Gausset *et al.* 2005; Derman *et al.* 2007). Yet it is hardly ever cited in the environmental or climate conflict literature. A certain exceptionalism is at work – while it is commonly assumed that scarcity can lead to institutional and technological innovation in the Global North, just the opposite is assumed for poor people in the Global South. Scarcity renders them as victims/villains, incapable of innovation or livelihood diversification and naturally prone to violence.

Today critiques of 'climate conflict' are emerging. For example, in a study commissioned by the World Bank on the implications of climate change for armed conflict, Buhaug *et al.* note the difficulty of coming up with any generalizable model since increased likelihood of organized violence 'depends crucially on country-specific and contextual factors' (Buhaug *et al.* 2008: 2). The report concludes that alarm about climate conflict is not based on substantive evidence. Despite the growing critical literature, the purported threat of climate conflict continues to circulate vigorously in both popular and policy circles (Dyer 2010). The same is true of climate refugees.

From environmental refugees to climate refugees

Along with environmental conflict, the notion of 'environmental refugees' took root in policy circles in the 1990s, based on similar neo-Malthusian reasoning (Saunders 2000). Norman Myers, one of the main architects of the term, in fact wrote that environmental refugees are actually 'population pressure' refugees (Myers 1995: 63). He made the statistical claim that there were at least 25 million environmental refugees in the world, compared with 22 million refugees of 'traditional kind' (Myers 1995: 1). Despite the fact that the 25 million figure was arrived at more by conjecture than scientific method,[4] it began to circulate widely in the international policy arena and became an accepted 'fact' (Saunders 2000; Nordas and Gleditsch 2007).

The environmental refugee concept naturalizes the economic and political causes of environmental degradation and masks the role of institutional responses to it. Rooted as it is in neo-Malthusian thinking, it overemphasizes the role of demographic pressures in migration. The causes of migration are extremely complex and context-specific, and moreover, there is little evidence to support the view that demographic pressure is at the root of many population movements (Suhrke 1997). In addition, negative neo-Malthusian narratives of migration obscure the positive roles migration can play in improving people's livelihoods and diminishing vulnerability to environmental change. Often migration from rural areas is not a linear phenomenon or a rejection of rural livelihoods, but instead a vital part of sustaining them (Black 1998).

Despite such shortcomings, the environmental refugee concept was deployed by a variety of political actors. Sustainable development advocates found it useful to focus policy attention on environmental degradation issues (Black 1998) and it also appealed to Western interests in favour of more rigid immigration controls, including limiting the grounds for political asylum (Kibreab 1997). As the concept gained favour, environmental refugees were increasingly portrayed as a security threat, even though there was little serious research to substantiate the claim (Black 1998).

In the population field an interesting synergy emerged between environmental conflict and environmental refugees. A report commissioned by the Pew Global Stewardship Initiative, the main funder of Homer-Dixon's work, argued that as part of a 'grand strategy' to increase international family planning assistance, Americans would have to be convinced that unchecked population growth and environmental degradation are the key national security threats of the twenty-first century. Stoking fears of migration was part of the strategy. 'Unfortunately', the authors note, 'the specter of "environmental refugees" driven by scarcity of resources and flooding American borders may be necessary to build the public support necessary for required increases in funding for population and sustainable development'. They recommended using visual tools, such as computerized mapping, which overlays information about 'population growth, resource depletion, overt conflict and refugee movements' (PGSI 1994: 13, 33).

Seamlessly, environmental refugees morphed into climate refugees, with Norman Myers again playing a key role in their enumeration. In 2005 Myers estimated there would be 50 million climate refugees by 2010, and he has also claimed that there will be 200 million by 2050. The 50 million figure, embraced by both UNEP and the UN University, speedily made its way into the media and policy documents, with a map showing where these refugees were likely to come from posted on the UNEP website (Bojanowski 2011; Pearce 2011). The 200 million figure also gained wide currency, even though Myers himself acknowledged that the estimate is based on 'heroic extrapolations' (Brown 2008: 8).

Like climate conflict, the term 'climate refugees' is coming under increased scrutiny on a number of grounds. First, while climate change is likely to cause displacement, the extent of that displacement will not only depend on how much the temperature rises and affects sea-levels, rainfall patterns and the severity of storms, but on the existence and effectiveness of adaptation measures that help individuals and communities cope with environmental stresses. Whether or not such measures are in place in turn depends on political economies at the local, regional, national and international levels that are often conveniently left out of the discussion of so-called 'climate refugees'. And as one report points out, larger climate-related humanitarian emergencies may be in places 'where people *cannot* afford to move, rather than the places to which they do move' (GECHS 2008: 24).

Second, as recent case studies reveal, migration is much too complex a process to label simply as environmental or climate-induced (Morrissey 2008: 28; Tacoli 2011). Moreover, much displacement due to climate-related factors is likely to be internal in nature, without the crossing of international borders (UNHCR 2008). A third area of concern is how the label 'climate refugee', like 'environmental refugee' before it, could further undermine the rights and protections of traditional refugees as defined by the 1951 UN Refugee Convention (UNHCR 2008; IOM 2009). Human rights law may be a more appropriate legal regime for climate-related migration (McAdam and Saul 2008).

In April 2011, embarrassed that the 50 million forecast didn't pan out, UNEP took down the map of climate migration from its website (Bojanowski 2011). Hopefully, the extreme hype about climate refugees is giving way to a more sober assessment of climate-related displacement (Commission on Climate Change and Development 2009; COIN 2010). Yet the basic assumptions underlying the notion of climate refugees and climate conflict as *threats* to security have not been adequately challenged. Like a rhizome, you can pull out one plant, but the roots continue to spread underground.

Part of the endurance of such ideas lies in the ways they draw on a reservoir of deep-seated fears and stereotypes of the dark-skinned, over-breeding, dangerous poor (Hartmann 2009). For example, a June 2009 ABC prime time television documentary on climate change, *Earth 2100*, scared the viewers with scenes of future apocalypse in which starving Africans take to arms against the West, desperate Mexicans storm the American border, and half the world population dies of a new plague so humans can get back into balance with nature again.

In policy circles, the persistence of these narratives is tied to their usefulness to a variety of interests, including the military. The next section looks at the US security establishment as a case study of how these narratives function to further militarize development and humanitarian assistance.

White knights and black swans: military intervention

In 2003 the Pentagon entered the climate and security fray by sponsoring a scenario of the impacts of abrupt climate change. Widely reported in the press, the scenario painted a familiar neo-Malthusian nightmare of poor, starving populations overshooting the reduced carrying capacity of their lands, engaging in violent conflict over scarce resources, and storming en masse towards US and European borders (Schwartz and Randall 2003). Similar apocalyptic scenarios were generated by influential security think tanks connected to the Democratic Party in the run-up to the 2008 presidential election (Campbell 2008).

Today, climate change has been officially endorsed as a potential national security threat, albeit in less apocalyptic terms. According to the Department of Defense (DoD) 2010 *Quadrennial Defense Review*:

Assessments conducted by the intelligence community indicate that climate change could have significant geopolitical impacts around the world, contributing to poverty, environmental degradation, and the further weakening of fragile governments. Climate change will contribute to food and water scarcity, will increase the spread of disease, and may spur or exacerbate mass migration. While climate change does not alone cause conflict, it may act as an accelerant of instability or conflict, placing a burden to respond on civilian institutions and militaries around the world. In addition, extreme weather events may lead to increased demands for defense support to civil authorities for humanitarian assistance or disaster response both within the United States and overseas. In some nations, the military is the only institution with the capacity to respond to large-scale disaster. Proactive engagement with these countries can help build their capability to respond to such events.

(DoD 2010: 85)

This embrace of climate change as a national security threat has to be viewed in the context of larger developments in US national security policy. While development assistance and humanitarian aid have long been strategically deployed as an element of defence policy, in recent years the military has encroached much further into civilian territory. Observers are beginning to speak of an 'aid-military complex' – in 2005 the share of official US development assistance dispersed by the Pentagon was 22 per cent, up from 6 per cent three years before (Easterly 2008). The State Department's role in both diplomacy and development has been severely weakened as a consequence, and disaster response is increasingly becoming the purview of the military (Berrigan 2008). This so-called 'whole-of-government' approach masks the tighter integration of the national security state.

It also reflects a strategic shift in defence thinking towards a focus on counterinsurgency and associated 'stability operations' (Bacevich 2010). In 2005 the DoD issued a directive stating that 'stability operations' such as providing security to the local populace, meeting humanitarian needs and developing a robust market economy and civil society shall be given equal priority to combat operations (DoD 2005: 2). To this end, the US military should mainly work through 'indigenous, foreign, or U.S. civilian officials' or 'military-civilian teams' which shall be open to representatives of international organizations, NGOs and the private sector (DoD 2005: 3). The Army's 2008 manual on stability operations cites climate change as a driver of conflict (Department of the Army 2008).

From 2007 on, Africa has been the primary focus of climate conflict discourse. Coincidence or not, this development has coincided with the establishment of the new US military command for Africa, AFRICOM. The reasons for the creation of AFRICOM are multi-faceted and include the protection of US access to African oil and other strategic resources, the War on Terror, and countering increasing Chinese influence in the continent (Volman 2008). By its very institutional structure, AFRICOM represents the blurring of military/civilian boundaries. Among its staff AFRICOM includes senior USAID officials to 'help us plan our own military tasks supportive of USAID efforts' (USAID 2009). In general, AFRI-COM seeks to integrate US military objectives more firmly with economic and political ones.

Constructing climate conflict as a particularly African security threat meshes well with these objectives. CNA's 2007 report on the threat of climate change specifically linked potential insecurity caused by climate change to the proposed mission of AFRICOM (CNA 2007). While it is highly unlikely that the United States would send in the troops or base strategic development assistance solely on a perceived risk of climate conflict, the promotion of that risk helps to make such interventions more palatable, especially in liberal foreign policy circles. Indeed, a report by the Center for American Progress, a think tank close to the Obama administration, calls for protecting the United States through 'sustainable security' (Brigety and Dewan 2009). It seeks to tie US development assistance to strategic defence and intelligence objectives. 'Climate-induced resource conflicts' are cited as a potential 'significant source of political instability and violence' (Brigety and Dewan 2009: 14).

But perhaps most important is the role of climate change in the increasing involvement of military forces in humanitarian assistance. Since the early 1990s, the humanitarian mission has become increasingly politicized and militarized. Especially in conflict situations, humanitarian aid agencies are deeply worried about the evolving doctrine of military-civilian operations promoted by the United States and NATO. Under this doctrine, military forces are seeking a larger and larger role in the delivery of aid, undermining the independence, neutrality and safety of humanitarian aid workers (Barry and Jefferys 2002). They are also pushing for more involvement in humanitarian assistance during natural disasters (Hofmann and Hudson 2009). Arguably, there are times when military assets such as transport vehicles may be required to respond to a humanitarian crisis, but that should be the exception, not the rule.

A 2010 report by the CNA think tank on *Climate Change: Potential Effects on Demands for U.S. Military Humanitarian Assistance and Disaster Response* (McGrady *et al.* 2010) provides an interesting window on current defence thinking. The report uses a conventional neo-Malthusian environment and security framework to argue that climate change stresses may tip 'marginally stable' countries into instability and violence. Along with extreme weather events, this could cause humanitarian and disaster response operations to occur in unstable environments, increasing 'the demand for US military forces to conduct security or stabilization missions' (McGrady *et al.* 2010: 3). Key vulnerable regions are Central and Eastern Africa, the Middle East, South Central Asia, parts of the Far East and Central America.

According to the report, the US military may even need to intervene to create the conditions under which countries can *adapt* to climate change:

> Large-scale events, such as hurricanes or typhoons, or poorly managed responses might tip a country where adaptation is ongoing into an unstable state where adaptation is less possible. The need to stabilize these countries,

and to decrease violence so that adaptation may proceed, may drive the U.S. military into simultaneous disaster relief and security missions.

(McGrady *et al.* 2010: 35)

The report also highlights the role of the military in the identification of and planning for 'potential futures' through scenario-building and gaming exercises (McGrady *et al.* 2010: 79). These include consideration of 'black swan' low-probability, high-impact events that would be the result of abrupt or catastrophic climate change.

It is worth asking whether we want the vision of the future to lie in the Pentagon's hands. One of the main battles today in the climate change arena is over who gets to predict the future and which assumptions frame the games and models employed. Security scenario-building is a deeply political exercise – it not only helps determine external defence policy, internal policing and the allocation of public resources, but impacts popular media and thus shapes public opinion (Price 2011). Drum up enough fear of black swans and people are more willing to bring in the white knights. Increasingly, military worst-case scenarios about climate change are being cited as undisputed evidence by non-military researchers. A January 2012 report by the Center for American Progress, for example, uncritically accepts recent intelligence reports and war games that drum up fears of climate conflict and migration (Werz and Conley 2012). The result is a vicious knowledge cycle: crisis narratives misinform military scenarios, and the scenarios are then used to legitimize the crisis narratives.

While many in the humanitarian aid community are worried about the growing encroachment of the military, there are troubling signs that the line is becoming further blurred. In June 2011, for example, CNA and Oxfam America produced a joint report on how climate change necessitates greater involvement of the US military in humanitarian and disaster response (CNA and Oxfam America 2011). The report uncritically repeats CNA's analysis of the impact of climate change on political instability and accepts the 200 million climate refugee figure proffered by Myers. Military security operations, it argues, may be necessary to support aid providers. It calls for joint planning exercises between civilian agencies and the military in preparation for black swan events. That a liberal NGO would go this far in cooperating with defence interests does not bode well for the future independence of the humanitarian aid community.

Staying power

Clearly, given the high policy stakes, there is an urgent need for more critical scholarship that challenges the prevailing orthodoxies around climate, population, migration and security. However, one must stay attuned to the possibility that while terms like climate refugees and climate conflict may be discredited and go out of fashion, the degradation narratives, and colonial and racial stereotypes at their root, will continue to wield undue influence as they assume new forms and new names.

As in the heyday of environmental security, one reason for their staying power is the entrenchment and generous funding of neo-Malthusian ideas, projects and policies. Today, in the United States, for example, influential members of the lobby targeting population growth are strategically deploying the idea that population growth is a major cause of climate change, environmental degradation, poverty and political instability in order to build support for an increase in international family planning assistance (Sasser 2011; Hartmann 2011). Funded by the United Nations Foundation, a recent report for the Council on Foreign Relations on *Family Planning and US Foreign Policy* espouses such views (Coleman and Lemmon 2011).

The Woodrow Wilson Center's Environmental Change and Security Program, which played a key role in the promotion of Homer-Dixon's views (Hartmann 2003), is again serving as a focal point for the coming together of neo-Malthusian academics and policymakers from the population, environment and defence communities with funding from USAID and UNEP, among others. 'We shatter the boundaries separating environment, population, and security, and reveal the links that connect our natural resources – air, water, land, forests – to conflict and cooperation', states its website (ECSP 2011). Those boundaries have long been shattered, however – at least since the 1960s when population control became a key component of US foreign policy and came to dominate American perceptions of the dynamics of poverty, insecurity and environmental degradation in the Global South. The remarkable endurance of neo-Malthusianism, even in an era of declining population growth rates and falling family size, is testament to how strong a hold it has over American liberal thought (Hartmann 2011).

Conclusion

In the end, it is necessary but not sufficient to critique these problematic climate chains. Ultimately, freeing climate policy from the shackles of neo-Malthusianism and militarism requires the political imagination to articulate a different and compelling set of potential futures in which an ethic of justice, equality and peace is at the centre. In that process progressive climate scholars need to practice some boundary crossing of their own, reaching beyond the confines of the academy and research institutes to engage in the messy politics of policy change, grassroots education and activism, and the shaping of public opinion. The stakes are too high to stay on the sidelines.

Notes

1 Portions of this chapter are drawn from my earlier article, 'Rethinking climate refugees and climate conflict: rhetoric, reality and the politics of policy discourse', *Journal of International Development* 22, 233–246 (2010).
2 For example, Boserup (1965), Blaikie and Brookfield (1987), Williams (1995), Thompson (2000), Leach and Mearns (1996).
3 For a critique of his model, see Hartmann (2001).
4 While doing PhD research on environment and security in 1997, I was told by someone who was present during the process that the figure was essentially conjured up by clustering groups of refugees and immigrants on the basis of already dubious statistics.

References

Bacevich, A.J. (2010) *Washington Rules: America's Path to Permanent War*, New York: Metropolitan Books.

Barry, J. and Jefferys, A. (2002) 'A bridge too far: aid agencies and the military in humanitarian response', *Humanitarian Practice Network, Paper 37*. London: Overseas Development Institute.

Berrigan, F. (2008) 'Entrenched, embedded and here to stay: the Pentagon's expansion will be Bush's lasting legacy'. Online. Available at: www.tomdispatch.com/post/174936 (retrieved: 27.9.2009).

Black, R. 1998. *Refugees, Environment and Development*, New York: Longman.

Blaikie, P. and Brookfield, H. (1987) *Land Degradation and Society*, London: Methuen Publishers.

Bojanowski, A. (2011) 'UN embarassed by forecast on climate refugees'. Online. Available at: www.spiegel.de/international/world/0,1518,757713,00.html (retrieved: 3.7.2011).

Boserup, E. (1965) *The Conditions of Agricultural Growth: The Economics of Agrarian Change Under Population Pressure*, Chicago: Aldine Publishers.

Brigety, E and Dewan, S. (2009) 'A national strategy for global development: protecting America and our world through sustainable security'. Online. Available at: www.americanprogress.org/issues/2009/05/pdf/brigety_dewan_security.pdf (retrieved 26.9.2009).

Brown, O. (2008) 'The numbers game', *Forced Migration Review* 31: 8–9.

Brown, O., Hammill, A. and McLeman, R. (2007) 'Climate change as the new security threat: implications for Africa', *International Affairs* 83(6): 1141–1154.

Buhaug, B., Gleditsch, N.P. and Theisen, O.M. (2008) 'Implications of climate change for armed conflict', paper presented at the World Bank Workshop on Social Dimensions of Climate Change in Washington, DC, 25 February 2008. Online. Available at: siteresources.worldbank.org/INTRANETSOCIALDEVELOPMENT/Resources/SDC-CWorkingPaper_Conflict.pdf (retrieved: 25.9.2009).

Campbell, K.M. (ed.) (2008) *Climatic Cataclysm: The Foreign Policy and National Security Implications of Climate Change*, Washington, DC: Brookings Institution Press.

Christian Aid (2007a) 'Human tide: the real migration crisis'. Online. Available at: www.christian-aid.org.uk (retrieved: 31.5.2007).

Christian Aid (2007b) 'World facing worst migration crisis'. Online. Available at: www.christian-aid.org.uk/news/media/pressrel/070514p.htm (retrieved: 31.5.2007).

CNA (2007) *National Security and the Threat of Climate Change*, Alexandria: CNA Corporation. Online. Available at: http://securityandclimate.cna.org/report (retrieved: 5.7.2007).

CNA and Oxfam America (2011) 'An ounce of prevention: preparing for the impact of a changing climate on US humanitarian and disaster response'. Online. Available at: www.cna.org/sites/default/files/news/2011/CNA%20Oxfam.pdf (retrieved: 7.7.2011).

COIN, Climate Outreach and Information Network (2010) *Forced Migration and Climate Change: The Challenge for Refugee and Environmental NGOs in the UK*, London: COIN.

Coleman, I. and Lemmon, G.T. (2011) 'Family planning and U.S. foreign policy'. Online. Available at: i.cfr.org/women/family-planning-us-foreign-policy/p24683 (retrieved: 7.7.2011).

Commission on Climate Change and Development (2009) 'Closing the gaps: disaster risk reduction and adaptation to climate change in developing countries', Stockholm, 1–107. Online. Available at: www.ccdcommission.org/Filer/report/CCD_REPORT.pdf (retrieved: 27.9.2009).

Department of the Army (2008) 'Stability operations. Field manual No. 3-07'. Online. Available at: www.fas.org/irp/doddir/army/fm3-07.pdf (retrieved: 25.9.2009).

Derman, B., Odgaard, R. and Sjaastad, E. (eds) (2007) *Conflicts over Land and Water in Africa*, Oxford: James Currey.

DoD, Department of Defense (2005) 'Military support for stability, security, transition and reconstruction. Directive 3000.05'. Online. Available at: www.dtic.mil/whs/directives/corres/pdf/300005p.pdf (retrieved: 6.10.2007).

DoD, Department of Defense (2010) *Quadrennial Defense Review Report*, Washington, DC: Department of Defense.

Dyer, G. (2010) *Climate Wars: The Fight for Survival as the World Overheats*, Oxford: Oneworld.

Easterly, W. (2008) 'Foreign aid goes military', *New York Review of Books* 55(19).

ECSP (2011) 'Environmental change and security program'. Online. Available at: www.wilsoncenter.org/index.cfm?topic_id=1413&fuseaction=topics.intro (retrieved: 7.7.2011).

Faris, S. (2007) 'The real roots of Darfur', *Atlantic Monthly*, April 2007. Online. Available at: www.theatlantic.com/doc/200704/darfur-climate (retrieved 27.9.2009).

Gausset, Q., Whyte, M. and Birch-Thomsen, T. (eds) (2005) *Beyond Territory and Scarcity: Exploring Conflicts over Natural Resource Management*, Stockholm: Nordiska Afrikainstitutet.

GECHS (2008) 'Disaster risk reduction, climate change adaptation and human security: a commissioned report for the Norwegian Ministry of Foreign Affairs'. Online. Available at: www.gechs.org/downloads/GECHS_Report_3-08.pdf (retrieved: 27.9.2009).

Hartmann, B. (2001) 'Will the circle be unbroken? A critique of the Project on Environment, Population and Security', in Peluso, N.L. and Watts, M. (eds) *Violent Environments*, Ithaca: Cornell University Press, 39–62.

Hartmann, B. (2003) *Strategic Scarcity: The Origins and Impact of Environmental Conflict Ideas*, PhD thesis. Development Studies Institute, London School of Economics and Political Science.

Hartmann, B. (2006) 'Liberal ends, illiberal means: national security, "environmental conflict" and the making of the Cairo consensus', *Indian Journal of Gender Studies* 13(2): 195–227.

Hartmann, B. (2009) 'From climate refugees to climate conflict: who is taking the heat for global warming?', in Salih, M. (ed.) *Climate Change and Sustainable Development: New Challenges for Poverty Reduction*, Cheltenham: Edward Elgar Publishers, 142–155.

Hartmann, B. (2011) 'Challenging the population/climate connection', in Sengupta, A. (ed.) *Global Health Watch 3*, London: Zed Books.

Harvey, F. (2007) 'UN climate panel detailed potential for global conflict', *Financial Times*, 13 October.

Hofmann, C. and Hudson, L. (2009) 'Military responses to natural disasters: last resort of inevitable trend?', *Humanitarian Exchange* 44: 29–31.

Homer-Dixon, T. (1999) *Environment, Scarcity and Violence*, Princeton: Princeton University Press.

IOM (2009) 'Migration, climate change and the environment', Policy Brief, May 2009, 1–8. Online. Available at: www.iom.int/jahia/webdav/shared/shared/mainsite/policy_and_research/policy_documents/policy_brief.pdf (retrieved: 3.6.2009).

Kibreab, G. (1997) 'Environmental causes and impact of refugee movements: a critique of the current debate', *Disasters* 21(1): 20–38.

Leach, M. and Mearns, R. (1996) *The Lie of the Land: Challenging Received Wisdom on the African Environment*, London: International African Institute.

McAdam, J. and Saul, B. (2008) 'An insecure climate for human security? Climate-induced displacement and international law', *Sydney Center for International Law Working Paper 4*. Online. Available at: www.law.usyd.edu.au/scil/pdf/SCIL%20WP%204%20Final.pdf (retrieved: 27.9.2009).

McGrady, E., Kingsley, M. and Stewart, J. (2010) 'Climate change: potential effects on demands for US military humanitarian assistance and disaster response'. Online. Available at: www.cna.org/research/2010/climate-change-potential-effects-demands-us (retrieved: 7.7.2011).

Milligan, S. and Binns, T. (2007) 'Crisis in policy, policy in crisis: understanding environmental discourse and resource-use conflict in northern Nigeria', *The Geographical Journal* 173(2): 143–156.

Moon, B.K. (2007) 'A climate culprit in Darfur', *Washington Post*, 16 June.

Morrissey, J. (2008) 'Rural-urban migration in Ethiopia', *Forced Migration Review* 31: 28–29.

Myers, N. (1995). *Environmental Exodus: An Emergent Crisis in the Global Arena*, Washington, DC: The Climate Institute.

Nordas, R. and Gleditsch, N.P. (2007) 'Climate change and conflict', *Political Geography* 26(6): 627–638.

Norwegian Nobel Committee. (2007) Press release. Online. Available at: nobelprize.org/nobel_prizes/peace/laureates/2007/press.html (retrieved: 27.9.2009).

Pearce, F. (2011) 'Searching for the climate refugees', *New Scientist*, 27 April. Online. Available at: www.newscientist.com/article/mg21028104.600-searching-for-the-climate-refugees.html (retrieved 7.7.2011).

PGSI, Pew Global Stewardship Initiative (1994) *Building a Coordinated Campaign on Population and Sustainable Development Policy*, Washington, DC: The Pew Charitable Trust.

Price, S. (2011) *Worst-Case Scenario: Governance, Mediation and the Security Regime*, London: Zed Books.

Roe, E.M. (1995) 'Except Africa: postscript to a special section on development narratives', *World Development* 23(6): 1065–1069.

Sasser, J. (2011) 'Une vision progressiste de la question démographique? La croissance démographique, le changement climatique et la nouvelle approche "gagnant-gagnant"', *Ecologie et Politique* 41: 73–84.

Saunders, P.L. (2000) 'Environmental refugees: the origins of a construct', in Stott, P. and Sullivan, S. (eds) *Political Ecology: Science, Myth and Power*, London: Arnold Publishers, 218–246.

Schwartz, P. and Randall, D. (2003) 'An abrupt climate change scenario and its implications for United States national security'. Online. Available at: www.gbn.com/articles/pdfs/Abrupt%20Climate%20Change%20February%202004.pdf (retrieved: 27.9.2009).

Suhrke, A. (1997) 'Environmental degradation, migration and the potential for conflict', in Gleditsch, N.P. (ed.) *Conflict and the Environment*, Dordrecht: Kluwer Academic Publishers, 255–272.

Tacoli, C. (2011) 'Not only climate change: mobility, vulnerability and socio-economic transformations in environmentally fragile areas of Bolivia, Senegal and Tanzania', *IIED Human Settlements Working Paper Series, Rural-Urban Interactions and Livelihood Stategies, 28*. Online. Available at: pubs.iied.org/10590IIED.html (retrieved: 7.7.2011).

Thompson, M. (2000) 'Not seeing the people for the population', in Lowi, M.R. and Shaw, B.R. (eds) *Environment and Security: Discourses and Practices*, London: Macmillan, 173–192.

UNEP (2007) 'Sudan Post-Conflict Environmental Assessment'. Online. Available at: www.unep.org/Sudan/ (retrieved: 7.7.2007).

UNHCR (2008) 'Climate change, natural disasters and human displacement: a UNHCR perspective'. Online. Available at: www.unhcr.org/refworld/pdfid/492bb6b92.pdf (retrieved: 6.3.2009).

USAID (2009) 'AFRICOM general hails USAID-military links', *Frontlines*, December 2008 – January 2009. Online. Available at: www.usaid.gov/press/frontlines/fl_decjan09.html (retrieved: 27.9.2009).

Verhoeven, H. (2011) 'Climate change, conflict and development in Sudan: global meo-Malthusian narratives and local power struggles', *Development and Change* 42(3): 679–707.

Volman, D. (2008) 'Why is the Pentagon marching into Africa?'. Online. Available at: concernedafricascholars.org/african-security-research-project/?p=11 (retrieved: 27.9.2009).

Werz, M. and Conley, L. (2012) *Climate Change, Migration and Conflict: Addressing Complex Crisis Scenarios in the 21st Century*, Washington, DC: Center for American Progress. Online. Available at: www.americanprogress.org/issues/2012/01/pdf/climate_migration.pdf (retrieved 20.1.2012).

Williams, G. (1995) 'Modernizing Malthus: the World Bank, population control and the African environment', in Crush, J. (ed.) *Power of Development*, London: Routledge, 158–175.

Witsenburg, K. and Roba, A.W. (2007) 'The use and management of water sources in Kenya's drylands: is there a link between scarcity and violent conflicts?', in Derman, B., Odgaard, R. and Sjaastad, E. (eds) *Conflicts over Land and Water in Africa*, Oxford: James Currey, 203–215.

7 Apocalypse now!
From exceptional rhetoric to risk management in global climate politics

Chris Methmann and Delf Rothe

Introduction

Climate change has turned from an environmental problem into a high politics issue.[1] Two debates in the UN Security Council in 2007 and 2011, supported by increased activities of governmental and non-governmental organizations, and surrounded by a growing public and academic awareness to 'climate wars' and 'climate refugees', indicate that global warming is more and more perceived as a matter of international peace and security.[2] The most prominent approach within critical security studies, the Copenhagen School, would expect that securitization in general results in the adoption of exceptional measures (Buzan *et al.* 1998).[3] However, the politics of global warming seems to be far removed from exceptionalism. The 2011 Security Council meeting on climate change serves as a case in point. It has been widely perceived as a failure, not being able to break with the usual routines of global climate politics. And exceptional measures such as, for example, Ban Ki-Moon's call for a 'green helmet' force under the auspices of the UN found no support from the council at all (Goldenberg 2011). Instead, the securitization of climate change seems to reinforce the mundane routine practices of risk management such as embodied by the Kyoto Protocol (Oels 2012).

A number of explanations have been provided for this conundrum. The Copenhagen School assumes that climate change has not been securitized enough: every 'securitizing move', in order to result in bold and exceptional political action, depends on the acceptance by an audience – and this public consent is still lacking (Buzan and Wæver 2009: 271–272). For others, the securitization of climate change is an undecided discursive struggle about different conceptions of security (Trombetta 2008; Brzoska 2009; Detraz and Betsill 2009). The aim of this chapter is to show that the securitization of climate change is neither incomplete nor a failure. Nor is it undecided and simply contingent on discursive struggles. We argue that, although there indeed is a discursive struggle, the storylines put forth by different discourse coalitions are all permeated by a common logic of apocalypse. And this logic makes the securitization of climate change result in the piecemeal and technocratic approach of Foucauldian 'risk management' (Aradau *et al.* 2008) instead of exceptional measures.[4]

It has to be emphasized, though, that our principal aim is not to prove the Copenhagen School wrong, nor do we want to champion a Foucauldian approach. Our research is not theory-, or method-, but problem-driven. Theories form a particular 'problematization' (Glynos and Howarth 2007: 167) that represents the starting point for a process through which we try to excavate a plausible explanation in a constant 'to-and-fro movement' between different theories and empirical material (Glynos and Howarth 2007: 34). Accordingly, this chapter is organized in four parts. The first section turns to the field of critical security studies and seeks to destabilize the established distinction between risk and security. In particular, we introduce the notions of catastrophe and apocalypse and show how they are connected to particular types of risk management. The second section discusses the methodological implications of our claim and proposes metaphors and narrative analysis as a tool for security analysis. These methods are then applied to the two debates in the Security Council on climate change (2007 and 2011) as well as the climate–security debate in the UN General Assembly in 2009, which can be seen as 'paradigmatic cases' (Flyvbjerg 2006) of the climate–security nexus due to the authority of the UN in both fields. The third section explores the metaphoric deep structure of these debates, while the fourth shows how an apocalyptic narrative draws on this structure in order to link various security narratives with risk management.

Theory: securitization, apocalypse, risk

The field of Critical Security Studies, which is helpful in elucidating the emergence of security issues broadly understood, is usually distinguished in two different approaches: those working on security and those working on risk (Aradau and van Munster 2011; Balzacq 2010).[5] Both depart from studying the supposedly objective nature of a threat (as realists do, see Walt 1991) and seek to understand their discursive emergence and perception. Despite this common interpretive framework, both schools focus on different *loci* for studying the emergence of such a construction. The Copenhagen School's theory of securitization concentrates on the speech acts of authoritative politicians that declare something an existential threat to a valued reference object (Buzan et al. 1998). This is supposed to remove this issue from the regular field of politics and legitimates the urgent adoption of exceptional measures. Those working in the tradition of Foucault and Bourdieu, by contrast, highlight the politics of security below the threshold of exceptionalism (Aradau et al. 2008). Drawing on the concept of 'risk' derived from Foucault's understanding of security (Rose 2001), they study the different rationalities and technologies for managing threats in the face of uncertainty, mostly employed by 'security professionals' (Bigo 2002).[6]

We doubt that the stark separation between the two lines of thought is justified. The work of Claudia Aradau and Rens van Munster (2011) is incisive in this regard. They argue that even the Cold War – the paradigmatic example for the Copenhagen School's 'macro-securitization' (Buzan and Wæver 2009) – was simultaneously made governable by a logic of risk (Aradau and van Munster 2011: 18). The dawning nuclear catastrophe essential for this securitization was not a clearly observable threat but an almost virtual entity (Derrida 1984). It thus became subject to technologies and practices of risk management in order to make it thinkable and actionable despite its absence. Aradau and van Munster's 'genealogy of the unknown' traces different rationalities and practices to think about the uncertain impacts of existential threats – among them 'crisis', 'disaster' and 'catastrophe' that subsequently built upon each other (Aradau and van Munster 2011: chapter 2). And as we will see below, the rationality of catastrophe resonates well with our own case of climate change politics. However, at this stage, the crucial point for our own argument is that an analysis of Cold War security politics demonstrates the close entanglement of risk and security: the virtuality of most macro-securitizations makes it necessary to enact practices of risk management in order to make the unknown future actionable.

Other studies make it possible to add more detail to this general insight. Drawing on the examples of terrorism and climate change, Marieke de Goede and Sam Randalls introduce the notion of 'apocalypse' as another way of articulating security.[7] They argue that both are usually perceived as 'total threats' (de Goede and Randalls 2009: 859), so that the danger of total annihilation paired with radical uncertainty about the exact timing and location of impacts gives rise to politics of 'precaution' (in the field of climate change) and 'preemption' (in the field of terrorism). Highlighting the joint genealogy of these two forms of managing risks, they reveal that even apocalyptic securitizations result in 'banal' political measures of 'institutional preparation and routinized imagination' (de Goede and Randalls 2009: 871). In a similar vein, Ben Anderson distinguishes between three types of risk management in the face of catastrophe: precaution, preparedness and preemption (Anderson 2010).[8] *Precaution* tries to keep a threatening development below a certain dangerous threshold beyond which catastrophe would become inevitable. *Preparedness*, by contrast, acknowledges the impossibility of entirely ruling out the occurrence of high impact/low probability events and thus invests in the resilience of subjects, infrastructures and governance mechanisms in general. *Preemption* differs from both in that it seeks to completely alter the course of action and generates an entirely new path for future development. Whereas precaution is conservative, preemption 'unashamedly makes and reshapes life' (Anderson 2010: 790). This most radical form of action, in our view, comes closest to the exceptional measures predicted by the Copenhagen School.[9] In climate politics, for example, precaution is embodied by mitigation policies such as carbon offsetting (Anderson 2010), whereas preparedness features more prominently in the field of adaptation (Oels 2012). Preemption, however, seems to be absent. It might be detected in plans for large-scale geo-engineering (Cooper 2006), or would correspond to the creation of an UN force of 'green helmets' (Goldenberg 2011).

These brief remarks show that a particular macro-securitization – such as climate change or terrorism – can be made thinkable in different forms (e.g. disaster, crisis, catastrophe, apocalypse) and that this may result in a variety of political practices (e.g. precaution, preemption, preparedness). Put simply: the political measures brought about by securitization depend on its actual discursive articulation. In the following, we attempt to show that climate change takes the form of a dawning apocalypse that results in the banal and mundane practices of precaution and preparedness – but leaves no space for preemptive action. Before we turn to this claim, though, we discuss how discursive articulations of security could be studied.

Methodology: digging deeper

The Copenhagen School locates securitization in individual speech acts of authoritative actors that declare something an existential threat for a certain reference object and so justify the adoption of exceptional measures. From a theoretical point of view, the problem with this approach is that security is understood as a predefined speech act and tied to a certain type of politics. This treats security as an a-historic and essential concept (Stritzel 2011) and downplays the role of its discursive (Stritzel 2007) and social context (Balzacq 2005). Neither security nor the politics associated with it are simply given, but are products of discourse. So if we contend that securitization can take multiple forms and can have various political consequences, this methodologically implies that we have to leave the superficial level of the simple speech act and dig deeper into the meaning of security and the implicated political consequences. In other words, one must not only analyse the speech acts themselves (*what* they say; what it declares a security issue), but the discursive context that enables these statements in the first place (*how* they are possible; how security is understood in this context, and how it affects politics).

In our view, a Foucauldian discourse analysis lends itself perfectly to this task. Foucault's method of archaeology treats discourses, first of all, as an ensemble of 'statements', and takes these statements as 'simple positivities' (Foucault 1972: 79). But instead of analysing them as such, an archaeological perspective seeks to infer from their 'regularities in dispersion' (Foucault 1972: 49) towards the 'rules of formation' (Foucault 1972: 32) that make these statements possible in the first place. This discursive 'deep structure' (Diaz-Bone 2007: 65), upon which speakers draw unconsciously in their statements, defines what can and cannot be said in certain discursive context. Although this structure may be incomplete, incoherent or even contested, it makes the discourse hang together and so provides a common point of reference for all actors.

In line with Hajer (2010), we claim that metaphors and narratives provide a helpful path to uncovering discursive deep structures. On the one hand, we focus on metaphors as analytic micro-units. Metaphors[10] provide an essential but unconscious device for human beings to make sense of the world (Lakoff and Johnson 1980). Translated from the individual level to that of social discourses, metaphors thus open a viable way for accessing a discursive deep structure (Milliken 1999: 235–236). This is all the more important as metaphors represent an important means of linking different discursive arenas by providing a conceptual vocabulary to render the themes of one discourse (e.g. climate change) intelligible in another discourse (e.g. security) (Link 2011). On the other hand, we employ the concept of narratives. Narrative discourse analysis assumes that all discourses are organized by virtue of narrative structures (Somers 1994). Moreover, narratives connect the discursive deep structure with the level of the actual statements (Viehöver 2011). They combine collective symbols into more overarching and comprehensive structures of meaning. Narratives, for instance, constitute causal relationships (Somers 1994) as well as responsibilities and recipes for action (Hajer 2010). We thus assume that analysing metaphors reveals the actual meaning and conception of security underpinning any act of securitization. A closer inspection of the narratives in which these are organized then indicates the associated political measures that flow from this very conception. Together, both highlight the structures of meaning that make certain speech acts of securitization possible in the first place and so connect a particular type of securitization with certain sets of governmental practices.

Based on these general methodological considerations, the following analysis was conducted in three steps. First, we have coded the Security Council debate for metaphors and collective symbols in general with the qualitative data analysis software MaxQDA. This coding was guided by several coding families such as metaphors and other collective symbols, like analogy and metonymy. Second, we tried to identify the core storylines, in which these metaphors were embedded through an interpretive discourse analysis. Finally, we distilled the common essence in these storylines, which is made up by a certain meta-narrative that we would call a logic of apocalypse.

The metaphorical structure of the Security Council debates

A metaphor analysis of the two Security Council and the UN General Assembly debates on climate change and security reveals the discursive deep structure of all arguments and speech acts in the debate.[11] This deep structure is similar across the three debates (see Table 7.1). This comes as no surprise as collective symbols are deeply ingrained discursive elements. In the case of the climate–security discourse the most prominent metaphorical concept is WAR and STRUGGLE. The mere existence of WAR metaphors alone does not yet imply a securitization of a particular discourse. Nevertheless, as we could see from the examples, war metaphors and collective symbols convey certain irreducible implications: they always articulate an antagonistic relation – between an enemy/threat and something threatened – and they produce a certain sense of urgency. The nature of the threat as well as the measures that are brought forward, yet, depend on the specific storylines and narratives in the discourse.

A trope closely related to the war metaphors in the discourse is the personification of climate change. Climate change appears as a clearly identifiable external entity with the possibility to act. This allows for predicating it with certain human attitudes such as being *unfair*, *cruel*, *grim*, *erratic* or *dangerous*. This already indicates one of the most prominent narrative scripts in the discourse, stating that 'nature rebels against humans' (Flores in Security Council 2011b: 12).

Further important nodal points in the discourse on climate change and security are different motional as well as topological metaphors. CLIMATE CHANGE IS A VEHICLE: 'Climate change . . . is accelerating in a dangerous manner . . .

we were on the cusp of a global climate disaster without an urgent and ambitious collective response' (Goddard in Security Council 2011b: 228). In a similar vein, climate politics is depicted as a JOURNEY or a RACE between humanity and climate change. Movement, however, also entails a vertical dimension: as a substance, which is rising. This concept draws on the metaphors of THE EARTH IS A CONTAINER (for states, people, nature, etc.) and ABOVE IS MORE/BELOW IS LESS. Other than the horizontal dimension, however, there is no critical threshold in this type of movement; it simply depicts a linear increase. The vertical axis is dealing with quantitative changes, while the horizontal dimension involves qualitative change. Together the two-dimensional movement creates a specific notion of urgency and provides the discursive background for a precautionary risk-management as outlined below.

Another important set of topological metaphors is related to the human body or organism: NATIONAL STATES ARE BODIES; THE EARTH IS A BODY and CLIMATE CHANGE IS A DISEASE. These metaphors treat collectives such as nation states as individuals and identify potential harms, pathogenic agents or vulnerable parts of the earth *organism*. Finally, different religious metaphors revolving around notions of apocalypse and damnation characterize the deep structure of the climate security discourse. These are used to demonstrate the unprecedented magnitude of the climate threat but also to argue for 'the historic and overriding need to take decisive action to assuage the scourge' (Rodríguez in Security Council 2011b: 23). Religious collective symbols link up with the motion metaphors described above, thereby constructing a coherent religious teleology of climate change.

These metaphors create a repertoire for argumentation at the level of discursive struggle. They are either filled up with content (e.g. by identifying heroes and anti-heroes, competitors, etc.) or combined to construct larger storylines or narratives. We identify three such storylines and demonstrate how a fourth permeates them – apocalypse – that implies risk management.

The evil deeds of a rebelling climate

The first storyline sets the general stage. It defines the problem at stake and negotiates causalities, actors, norms and values. A large part of the statements in the sample start with calling climate change 'one of the major challenges facing the international community' (see e.g. Morgan in Security Council 2011b: 9). This already points to the dominant actant-structure of the climate-security plot. Personification presents climate change as the anti-hero. This role is further specified through the negative attributes mentioned above and by providing examples for the evil deeds of climate change.[12] The victims, by contrast, are the vulnerable countries and communities; the small island states and other low lying developing states as well as the 'poorest of the poor' (UN Secretary General 2009: 11). Yet climate change also threatens the planet as a whole. Accordingly, although there is no present hero in the climate change discourse – there is only a potential one: humanity or the international community as a collective: 'this is a universal

Table 7.1 Narratives in the climate security discourse and examples from the empirical material (source: own depiction; italics highlight the metaphorical/crucial parts of articulations)

Narratives	Metaphors	Actants	Pairs of opposition
The evil deeds of a rebelling climate	War metaphors: 'We are confronted with a *chemical war of immense proportions*' (Weisleder in Security Council 2007b: 32); 'the *warming war*' (Pita in Security Council 2007b: 8) Personification: '*Climate change can further erode state capacity*' (Rice in Security Council 2011a: 7); 'I would like to underscore some of the *havoc that climate change has been wreaking in my country*' (Rodriguez in Security Council 2011b: 23) '*Climate change is not fair*' (Lucas in Security Council 2011b: 3) Anti-hero: dangerous climate change:	'Global warming in different parts of the world is already *compelling us to face* erratic climatic behaviour and witness increasing natural catastrophes' (Momen in Security Council 2011a: 25) Victims: communities; national states, international community: 'Climate change poses serious challenges to our planet' (Sammis in UN General Assembly 2009: 19); 'We will all suffer sooner or later. No country is immune to the impacts of climate change' (Moses in UN General Assembly 2009: 2) Potential hero: humanity, international community: 'This is a universal phenomenon that can be addressed only through joint coordination, solidarity and responsibility by all of us' (Laiglesia in Security Council 2011b: 40)	The social world versus the natural world: 'I think we can all agree that the threat of climate change to the livelihood, well-being and security of all our peoples and countries is real and upon us' (Elisaia in UN General Assembly 2009: 17) 'Because of climate change, our islands face dangerous and potentially catastrophic impacts that threaten to destabilize our societies and political institutions' (Stephen in Security Council 2011a: 22) Manageable versus uncontrollable climate change: 'we know from past experience that such challenges can be addressed before they reach crisis point' (Simpson in Security Council 2011b: 5)
Precautionary tales	Motional metaphors: '*Climate change … is accelerating in a dangerous manner … We were on*	The tragic hero: humans 'Let me now take the Council back in time and history. While the	Action (positive) versus inaction (negative): 'The price for inaction now will be immeasurably high in the future' (Daunivalu

Table 7.1 Continued

Narratives	Metaphors	Actants	Pairs of opposition
	the cusp of a global climate disaster without an urgent and ambitious collective response' (Goddard in Security Council 2011b: 228); 'The planet will not wait patiently' (Brockmann in UN General Assembly 2009: 3); 'if we do not bring climate change under control' (Sefue in Security Council 2011b: 38) 'Without an effective global agreement . . . on Climate Change, the human and economic costs of climate change and its impact on security will only grow and be perpetuated indefinitely' (Ragaglini in Security Council 2011b: 40); 'Time is not just moving ahead; time is running out' (Rice in Security Council 2011a: 6)	Mediterranean world was mired in the dark ages, in Mexico there existed a "one world", much like what we have at the United Nations today. They read the heavens, preceded Copernicus's heliocentric theory and devised a calendar accurate until 2012. Thousands of years ago, the Olmecas built the pyramid of Cholula, one-third larger than the great pyramids of Giza; the Mayas build their famous city of Uxmal; and the Toltecs, their fabled Tula. And then: destruction! They had problems frighteningly similar to our own' (Haroon in Security Council 2011b: 42)	in Security Council 2011b: 37 Predictable/calculable versus unpredictable/incalculable 'Before we reach the ultimate crisis level when nation States drown, all efforts to prevent this from happening through adaptation and mitigation must be exhausted' (Cabactulan in Security Council 2011b: 31); 'what emerged from that research is that, at a certain point of warming, an entire ecosystem ceases functioning in the way that is functions today' (Steiner in Security Council 2011a: 5)
Climate conflict or the vulnerable becoming dangerous	Health and disease: 'The spread of environmental migration' (Lambert in Security Council 2011b: 22); 'the Earth's life-support systems' (Steiner in Security Council, 2011a: 4); 'Scarcity breeds fear, which in turn fuels conflict' (Ogwu in Security Council 2011a: 10)	Episode 1: the poor as victims 'As many least developed countries are both highly exposed and highly vulnerable to climate change, and as the poor within countries are usually the most vulnerable, climate change is likely to exacerbate inequalities both between and within countries' (UN Secretary General 2009: 11)	North versus South; developed versus underdeveloped; active versus passive (subject versus object), resilient versus helpless 'Environmental factors that "push" people to migrate' (UN Secretary General 2009: 17); 'Small island States have become victims of a devastating phenomenon' (Vunibobo in UN General Assembly 2009: 15); 'more

Mechanical metaphors:

'in the case of countries characterized by fragile States and internal tensions, increased climate-induced environmental stress could overstretch existing coping strategies and, in combination with a number of political, economic, and societal factors, could result in: (a) growing tensions over increasingly scarce natural resources; (b) decreased State authority and increased risk of domestic strife; and (c) political instability and radicalization' (UN Secretary General 2009: 15)

Episode 2: the poor becoming dangerous 'The areas most affected will be those under strong demographic pressure and with a massive influx of environmental migrants. That will lead to political, religious and ethnic radicalization' (Aitimova in Security Council 2011b:21); 'These multiple disasters – shrinking farmlands, pandemic wildfires and food and water scarcity compounded by dwindling energy reserves, are destabilizing the world's most violently troubled nations. By destroying people's livelihoods, aggravating poverty and fuelling terrorism among the have-nots, can we even begin to fathom what we have wreaked?' (Haroon in Security Council 2011b: 42)

and more people become displaced' (Beck in UN General Assembly 2009: 13); 'triggering environmentally induced migration' (Vunibobo in UN General Assembly 2009: 15); 'developing countries – particularly the least developed countries ... are most harmed by the negative effects of climate change' (Alotaibi in Security Council 2011b: 20); 'Vulnerable societies ... could be overwhelmed by such events' (Kőrösi 2011b: 27); 'Populous and underdeveloped countries, particularly those that are geographically disadvantaged, will be the hardest hit' (Sorcar in Security Council 2007b: 9) phenomenon that can be addressed only through joint coordination, solidarity and responsibility by all of us' (Laiglesia in Security Council 2011b: 40).

The narrative is constructed upon several pairs of opposition, such as the strict division between the social and the natural worlds. This first binary stems mainly from the prominence of WAR and PERSONIFICATION metaphors in the discourse that construct climate change as an enemy or foe, external and independent from the social (human) referent objects it threatens (see also Swyngedouw 2010).

A second boundary is drawn between a 'normal' status of nature, i.e. the climate and related ecosystems in a stable equilibrium, and a 'dangerous' state of these systems. This is rooted in the general climate change discourse, which has declared the 2°C target a threshold between a manageable and an uncontrollable version of climate change, the latter involving large-scale discontinuities or irreversible extreme changes, such as a collapse of the Gulf Stream (Liverman 2009). These are represented by the metaphor of a 'tipping point' – the notion that an initially gradual development, when crossing a critical threshold, might become irreversible and uncontrollable. And in the climate security discourse this tipping point does not only refer to natural changes but links them with chaotic developments of social phenomena:

> Much of the concern for the security implications of climate change relates to the possible consequences of large-scale and/or rapid disruptions to economies, societies and ecosystems. In that event, adaptive capacities of individuals, communities and even nation States may be severely challenged if not overwhelmed. In that event, uncoordinated coping and survival strategies may come to prevail, including migration and competition for resources, possibly increasing the risks of conflict.
>
> (UN Secretary General 2009: 15)

Tales of precaution

A second set of storylines is closely related to the fear of a nature out of control and the tipping point metaphor. In short these precautionary tales – as we call them – all follow the same narrative script: the tragedy. First of all, there is a political subject – the tragic hero – confronted with a problem or an enemy, whose development or future actions are obscure. The hero deduces her predictions about the future development of this threat from her past experiences, thereby assuming a linear development. The threat, however, takes some unexpected turn and our tragic hero dies or at least suffers considerably.[13] In the climate change and security discourse this tragedy is commonly narrated along historical analogies to past civilizations or populations. Given their lack of experience with climatic changes for example the Maya or the Egyptian civilizations were overwhelmed by a sudden climatic shift. This led ultimately to their decline as civilizations (see e.g. Haroon in Security Council 2011b: 42). These precautionary tales are organized around the motional and biological collective symbols outlined above. And

Apocalypse now! 115

they construct certain oppositional values or binaries. This is first the opposition action/inaction, while action is the positive value and inaction – as reason for the tragedy – is negatively connoted. A further opposition differentiates between the old continuous world and the modern status of complexity and unpredictability. The moral of this story should have become clear: given the threat of climate change, the international community must act now – even in absence of any concrete knowledge. At the same time one must always be prepared for the very worst – or the unexpected (see UN Secretary General 2009: 28).

Climate conflict storylines

A last set of narratives revolves around climate change induced conflicts. It is structured in two, partly contradictory, episodes, the first expressing humanitarian concerns for the victims of climate change, and the second constructing failed states and other climate hot-spots itself as a source of danger and insecurity. In the studied material there is widespread consent that 'today, we generally regard climate change as a threat multiplier' (Štiglic in Security Council 2011b: 2). What is crucial about this metaphor is on the one hand its ambiguity and vagueness. It is ambiguous because to act as a multiplier could either mean to amplify single factors or to increase the total number of threats. And it is vague as it leaves completely open how this multiplication of threats actually happens.

The technical tone of the 'threat multiplier' concept is complemented by a normative tone, characterizing both Western humanitarian discourses and ethical discourse about responsibility brought forward by developing countries. It is seen as a moral obligation for the industrialized countries to assist the developing world to cope with dangerous climate changes (see e.g. Mohamad in Security Council 2007b: 12). The two framings – technical and normative – resonate quite well as they both draw on the same image of victims as objects. The victim is marked by its vulnerability against the climate change threat; it is depicted as passive and helpless. This first episode thus constructs a moral obligation for the West to help the passive victims in the Global South. Pairs of opposition and binaries are quite obvious in this narrative: first, there is a series of binaries dividing the world in two parts: North/South; developed/developing; rich/poor, etc.; second we can find binaries of normative values like responsible/irresponsible; caring/uncaring; passive/active, etc.

Yet, the second episode of climate conflict storylines turns the actant-structure of the humanitarian episode upside down. Here the vulnerable and poor become the source of danger (see Oels 2012) – either in the form of tragic heroes or anti-heroes. The most important tragic heroes in this episode are climate refugees, which are passive victims that unintentionally become a danger for the Western world by carrying diseases or further destabilizing target-countries (concerning the Malthusian background of this idea see Hartmann, Chapter 6 in this volume). The figure of the climate refugee is important in several ways. First of all, climate-induced migration is a central and major issue across the whole sample. Second, it is a cross-cutting issue as it concerns very different policy fields like security, environment, development policy as well as international law. It is also a consent-producing issue, as it produces resonances between climate conflict and humanitarian thinking. Besides becoming refugees, there is a range of mechanisms how the poor can become dangerous, referring to further figures in this episode of the climate conflict narrative. Already fragile states might be tipped into chaos by climate change. These failed states then become a source and breeding ground for a series of dangers like global pandemics, international terrorism or regional instability.

The logic of apocalypse: the war of all against nothing

'Climate change rebelling against humanity', 'Humanity as a tragic hero', 'The poor as vulnerable victims', 'The vulnerable becoming dangerous' – so far we have seen that the climate security discourse revolves around a number of different and partly contradictory storylines. Their common point of reference is a securitization of climate change. Nonetheless, exceptional measures are largely absent. And this is because all storylines are permeated by an apocalyptic meta-narrative. It takes up and exaggerates the notion of 'catastrophe' discussed above in a couple of points and results in banal practices of risk management.

First of all, apocalypse puts the whole of humanity at risk. Unlike other threats such as catastrophes, which affect a clearly delimited political community or region, climate change puts each and every one at risk: 'It is about our collective security in a fragile and increasingly interdependent world' (Becket in Security Council 2007b: 19). There are no sides in the battle against climate change. Instead, humanity is constituted as a homogeneous social space that can be governed according to a logic of risk – we will return to this below.

Second, the logic of apocalypse constructs a specific temporality. While catastrophe represents the interruption of a linear development by an unknowable event, the apocalypse represents the (sometimes even teleological) endpoint of an accelerating development. Hence, 'the way in which we deal with climate change today will have a direct impact on the development prospects of many countries and humankind's very survival' (Benítez Versón in Security Council 2011b: 11). Climate change is not only external to 'humanity' as a spatial category (each and every inhabitant of the planet), but also seems to constitute a temporal limit to society.

Third, apocalypse involves a different epistemology: 'In today's world, there are no longer solely concrete and easy to discern and understand threats, such as those stemming from an armed conflict or terrorist acts. Instead, we face amorphous, complex and multidimensional threats' (De Laiglesia in Security Council 2011b: 39). This complexity and the resulting contingency means that conventional security measures (as well as traditional risk-management based on calculation and probability) do not work in the case of climate change.

Fourth, the logic of apocalypse draws upon the common dichotomization between a tolerable and a dangerous climate change in terms of the 2°C limit (see e.g. Ban Ki-Moon in Security Council 2011a: 3). Beyond this limit, climate change

Apocalypse now! 117

is supposed to 'lead us into chaos, tension and potential conflict' (Steiner in Security Council 2011a: 6). Hence, as second order threats like uncontrollable migratory flows mainly evolve under dangerous climate change, mitigation becomes the best measure of conflict prevention. Despite the different narratives explained above, this storyline of apocalyptic climate change is largely shared throughout the entire discourse. It incorporates elements of previous episodes and condenses them into the image of climate change as an overwhelming, unpredictable collective enemy – supported by the religious metaphorical structure described above.

So, while the climate/humanity antagonism is still most dominantly couched in metaphors of war ('the two world wars', 'chemical war', 'warming war'), the unification of humanity implies that this particular war is fought against an entirely spectral enemy: 'this is not a struggle against anyone' (Weisleder in Security Council 2007b: 32). And this war of all against nothing is the crucial point for the logic of apocalypse that connects security and risk and thus excludes exceptional measures – because this particular war cannot be fought with the traditional toolkit of military security and preemptive measures: 'Our conflict is not being fought with guns and missiles but with weapons from everyday life – *chimney stacks and exhaust pipes*' (Pita in Security Council 2007b: 8, emphasis added).

Though there is a clear securitization of the vulnerable as it was shown in the previous section, this does not come along with calls for exceptional measures such as humanitarian interventions, geo-engineering, or calls to fence off against the rising 'tides' of environmental refugees. Instead, the solution to the danger of apocalypse lies in a common effort of the international community to implement risk management practices in both precautionary and preparatory manner: 'the responsibilities of Member States to avert the threat of climate change lie in making progress through mitigation and adaptation under the UNFCCC framework' (Sefue in Security Council 2011b: 39).

Mitigation, on the one hand, is informed by the rationality of precaution. It shall prevent future climate conflicts by keeping climate change below the dangerous threshold of 2°C. The emission of CO_2 above a critical threshold is no longer just an economic or environmental problem, but a security concern that is linked to migration, instability and even terrorism. The contribution of risk management, then, is to identify this particularly dangerous amount of CO_2 and prevent it from being released. This is the kernel of a 'carbon governmentality', which characterizes the current international climate regime UNFCCC and concentrates on carbon trading and carbon offsetting technologies (Methmann 2011; Chapter 9, this volume). As 'dangerous climate change' cannot be dealt with, it has to be prevented.

On the other hand, also adaptation, by increasing the preparedness of the vulnerable, becomes a form of conflict prevention: 'We are convinced that mitigation and adaptation are two sides of the same risk-management coin' (Webster in Security Council 2011b: 11). The logic behind this call is straightforward: if the vulnerable are better prepared to cope with climate change, they won't produce the different security threats that are articulated in the sample. Instead of preemptive fencing or military interventions, global climate governance should focus on reducing vulnerability, increasing resilience, empowering communities – the toolkit of preparedness.

It is hence 'required to move the international community from a culture of reaction to one of preparedness' (Stephen in Security Council 2011a: 23). The only way to deal with complex risks, due to their high degree of contingency and uncertainty, is thus to increase the resilience or preparedness of the communities at risk through information and empowerment. The severity of the threat, hence, paradoxically does not lead to a whole-of-government approach in the adaptation field but to rather piecemeal and indirect forms of risk-management at the individual level.

And the moral is . . .

The interpretive perspective on the climate–security discourse provides an alternative account for securitization paradox: just because it constructs climate change as a universal threat of apocalyptic dimensions, no preemptive or security measures are adopted. Rather, the international community further relies on precautionary mitigation and preparatory adaptation policies of the international climate regime UNFCCC. Together, they represented rather piecemeal and technocratic forms of governance than exceptional measures in the sense of the Copenhagen School of securitization. And the resulting 'carbon governmentality' strongly resembles the notion of depoliticization that runs through this book (Methmann 2011).

Yet, the most surprising fact is that all this happens in a highly politicized discursive arena. At the surface the Security Council debates appear as highly controversial. Industrialized states, the G77, small island developing states or the Group of Arab states advocated completely different arguments about the security implications of climate change. However, our analysis revealed that even those arguing that climate change did not represent a security issue at all, framed their articulations in line with the apocalyptic narratives and its discursive deep structure. Hence, we conclude: interpretive methods find the political where other approaches did not look for it. And, more importantly, they can diagnose its disappearance where other approaches would expect it the least.

Notes

1 We would like to thank Giovanni Bettini, Rita Floyd, Angela Oels and Benjamin Stephan for their helpful comments on earlier drafts of this chapter.
2 It has to be noted that although the securitization of climate change only recently received widespread attention, its roots can be traced back to a Pentagon Study in 2003 or even fears of a nuclear winter that emerged in the 1980s (de Goede and Randalls 2009).
3 Exceptional measures as defined in the Copenhagen School's approach of securitization refer to the breaking of accepted rules (Buzan et al. 1998: 24); here it could mean, e.g., limiting national sovereignty for the sake of climate protection, restricting individual liberties through rationing carbon emissions, or opposing existing ethical rules, e.g.

Apocalypse now! 119

by legitimizing geo-engineering. A more radical version of exceptionalism could put it under the responsibility of security professionals: arming for dealing with 'climate wars' or raising fences against 'climate refugees'. Although some instances of this do indeed exist – for example, fencing off the Indian border to keep Bangladeshi migrants out – it is fair to the say that such exceptionalism remains the exception in global climate governance.

4 Mind our wording here: the most obvious response from scholars working with the Copenhagen approach would hold that the securitization of climate change has not been successful so far – due to a lack of consensual acceptance by an audience. We counter this claim in two ways: by focusing on discourses, we dissolve the causal separation between speaker and audience. And we demonstrate that already the different 'securitizing moves' – regardless of their success in terms of securitization (see Buzan *et al.* 1998: 25) imply risk practices. We would like to thank Rita Floyd for raising this issue.

5 The space provided keeps us from discussing the field of security studies in detail. For a more elaborate version of our theoretical argument see Methmann and Rothe (2012). Especially those who doubt that the risk literature is part of security studies, see Aradau and van Munster (2011: 130, footnote 4).

6 A case in point would be the securitization of transnational terrorism in the aftermath of 9/11, which did not only result in military interventions but sought to control the risks inherent in Western populations through security technologies (Dillon 2007).

7 Unfortunately, they do not clearly distinguish between 'catastrophe' and 'apocalypse' and use both terms almost interchangeably – we will return to a clearer elaboration of the differences between the concepts below.

8 We are aware that the literature on rationalities of catastrophic risks is highly incoherent regarding its terminology. There are, for example, slight differences between the usage of precaution in Aradau and van Munster (2007) and de Goede and Randalls (2009). And while the latter stress the similarity between precaution and preemption, Anderson (2010) is it at pains to set the two apart. Others, by contrast, mix preemption, precaution and preparedness into a single 'paradigm of prudence' (Diprose *et al.* 2008), thereby neglecting the severe differences among them. Since these are mainly analytical distinctions which may overlap in reality, we stick to Anderson's terminology here for the sake of simplicity.

9 It is clear that exceptionalism includes much more than just preemption, for example, as deterrence or compellence. Nonetheless, the 'dangerous' part of climate change is yet to come, so every action to deal with its security implications is preemptive in nature. Moreover, other than deterrence and compellence, preemption allows for including non-militarist conceptions such as geo-engineering. Therefore, we narrow our analysis to preemption as an exceptional measure.

10 In line with Link (2011) we propose to broaden the notion of metaphors towards all 'collective symbols' – analogy, catachresis, metonymy, etc. – which render something intelligible in terms of something else. Focusing only on metaphors in the strict sense of the term would neglect important aspects through which discourses are organized. Nonetheless, we will stick to the term of metaphors for the sake of simplicity.

11 The following text just briefly summarizes our empirical results. For more empirical backing, refer to Table 7.1.

12 The Sudan conflict (see e.g. Osman in Security Council 2011a: 34) or the recent drought at the Horn of Africa (Kamau in Security Council 2011a: 32) are prominent examples in this sense. The discursive strategy behind this equals the rhetorical trope *pars pro toto* (a part represents the whole): a single conflict is presented as an expression of a broader phenomenon (climate change as a threat multiplier).

13 A similar type of tragedy is informing climate mitigation discourses in general, where human nature is believed to undermine the capacity to solve major problems that lie in the future (Methmann and Rothe 2012).

References

Anderson, B. (2010) 'Preemption, precaution, preparedness: anticipatory action and future geographies', *Progress in Human Geography* 34(6): 777–798.

Aradau, C. and van Munster, R. (2007) 'Governing terrorism through risk: taking precautions, (un)knowing the future', *European Journal of International Relations* 13(1): 89–115.

Aradau, C. and van Munster, R. (2011) *Politics of Catastrophe: Genealogies of the Unknown*, London and New York: Routledge.

Aradau, C., Lobo-Guerrero, L. and van Munster, R. (2008) 'Security, technologies of risk, and the political: guest editors' introduction', *Security Dialogue* 39(2–3): 147–154.

Balzacq, T. (2005) 'The three faces of securitization: political agency, audience and context', *European Journal of International Relations* 11(2): 171–201.

Balzacq, T. (2010) 'A theory of securitization: origins, core assumptions, and variants', in: Balzacq, T. (ed.) *Securitization Theory: How Security Problems Emerge and Dissolve*, London and New York: Routledge, pp. 1–30.

Bigo, D. (2002) 'Security and immigration: toward a critique of the governmentality of unease', *Alternatives: Global, Local, Political* 27: 63–92.

Brzoska, M. (2009) 'The securitization of climate change and the power of conceptions of security', *Security and Peace* 27(3): 137–145.

Buzan, B. and Wæver, O. (2009) 'Macrosecuritisation and security constellations: reconsidering scale in securitisation theory', *Review of International Studies* 35(2): 253–276.

Buzan, B., Wæver, O. and de Wilde, J. (1998) *Security: A New Framework for Analysis*, Boulder: Lynne Rienner Publishers.

Cooper, M. (2006) 'Pre-empting emergence', *Theory, Culture & Society* 23(4): 113–135.

de Goede, M. and Randalls, S. (2009) 'Precaution, preemption: arts and technologies of the actionable future', *Environment and Planning D: Society and Space* 27: 859–878.

Derrida, J. (1984) 'No apocalypse, not now (full speed ahead, seven missiles, seven missives)', *Diacritics* 14(2): 20–31.

Detraz, N. and Betsill, M. (2009) 'Climate change and environmental security: for whom the discourse shifts.', *International Studies Perspectives* 10(3): 303–320.

Diaz-Bone, R. (2007) 'Die französische Epistemologie und ihre Revisionen. Zur Rekonstruktion des methodologischen Standortes der Foucaultschen Diskursanalyse', *Forum Qualitative Sozialforschung/Forum: Qualitative Social Research* 8(2).

Dillon, M. (2007) 'Governing terror: the state of emergency of biopolitical emergence', *International Political Sociology* 1(1): 7–28.

Diprose, R., Stephenson, N., Mills, C., Race, K. and Hawkins, G. (2008) 'Governing the future: the paradigm of prudence in political technologies of risk management', *Security Dialogue* 39(2–3): 267–288.

Flyvbjerg, B. (2006) 'Five misunderstandings about case-study research', *Qualitative Inquiry* 12(2): 219–245.

Foucault, M. (1972) *The Archaeology of Knowledge*, New York: Pantheon Books.

Glynos, J. and Howarth, D. (2007) *Logics of Critical Explanation in Social and Political Theory*, London and New York: Routledge.

Goldenberg, S. (2011) 'UN security council to consider climate change peacekeeping', *Guardian*, 20 July.

Hajer, M. (2010) 'Argumentative Diskursanalyse – Auf der Suche nach Koalitionen, Praktiken und Bedeutung', in: Keller, R., Hirseland, A., Schneider, W. and Viehöver, W. (eds) *Handbuch sozialwissenschaftliche Diskursanalyse Bd. 2*, Wiesbaden: VS Verlag, pp. 271–298.

Lakoff, G. and Johnson, M. (1980) *Metaphors We Live By*, Chicago: University of Chicago Press.
Link, J. (2011) 'Diskursanalyse unter besonderer Berücksichtigung von Interdiskurs und Kollektivsymbolik', in: Keller R., Hirseland, A., Schneider, W. and Viehöver, W. (eds) *Handbuch sozialwissenschaftliche Diskursanalyse Bd. 1*, Wiesbaden: VS Verlag, pp. 433–458.
Liverman, D.M. (2009) 'Conventions of climate change: constructions of danger and the dispossession of the atmosphere', *Journal of Historical Geography* 35(2): 279–296.
Methmann, C. (2011) 'The sky is the limit: global warming as global governmentality', *European Journal of International Relations* (published online first, 27 October).
Methmann, C. and Rothe, D. (2012) 'Politics for the day after tomorrow: the logic of apocalypse in global climate governance', *Security Dialogue* 43(4): 323–344.
Milliken, J. (1999) 'The study of discourse in International Relations', *European Journal of International Relations* 5(2): 225–254.
Oels, A. (2012) 'Rendering climate change governable by risk: from probability to contingency', *Geoforum* (forthcoming).
Rose, N. (2001) 'The politics of life itself', *Theory, Culture & Society* 18(6): 1–30.
Security Council (2007a) *5663rd Meeting* (Part 1). S/PV.5663.
Security Council (2007b) *5663rd Meeting* (Part 2). S/PV.5663 (Resumption 1).
Security Council (2011a) *6587th meeting* (Part 1). S/PV.6587.
Security Council (2011b) *6587th meeting* (Part 2). S/PV.6587 (Resumption 1).
Somers, M. (1994) 'The narrative constitution of identity: a relational and network approach', *Theory and Society* 23(5): 605–649.
Stritzel, H. (2007) 'Towards a theory of securitization: Copenhagen and beyond', *European Journal of International Relations* 13(3): 357–383.
Stritzel, H. (2011) 'Security, the translation', *Security Dialogue* 42(4–5): 343–355.
Swyngedouw, E. (2010) 'Apocalypse forever? Post-political populism and the spectre of climate change', *Theory, Culture & Society* 27(2–3): 213–232.
Trombetta, M. (2008) 'Environmental security and climate change: analysing the discourse', *Cambridge Review of International Affairs* 21(4): 585–602.
UN General Assembly (2009) *85th Plenary Meeting*. A/63/PV.85.
UN Secretary General (2009) *Climate Change and its Possible Security Implications. Report of the Secretary-General*. A/64/350.
Viehöver, W. (2011) 'Diskurse als Narrationen', in: Keller, R., Hirseland, A., Schneider, W. and Viehöver, W. (eds) *Handbuch Sozialwissenschaftliche Diskursanalyse Bd. 1*, Wiesbaden: VS Verlag, pp. 177–206.
Walt, St. (1991) 'The renaissance of security studies', *International Studies Quarterly* 35(2): 211–239.

8 (In)convenient convergences
'Climate refugees', apocalyptic discourses and the depoliticization of climate-induced migration

Giovanni Bettini

Introduction

In 1992, the first report by the Intergovernmental Panel on Climate Change (IPCC) stated that '[t]he gravest effects of climate change may be those on human migration as millions are displaced by shoreline erosion, coastal flooding and severe drought' (IPCC 1992: 103). Since then, the connections between ecological conditions and migration[1] have attracted growing attention. The topic has reached the highest levels of (environmental) politics, to the point that the Cancun Adaptation Framework signed by the parties to the United Nations Framework Convention on Climate Change in December 2010 urges member countries to implement '[m]easures to enhance understanding, coordination and cooperation with regard to climate change induced displacement, migration and planned relocation' (UNFCCC 2010: 5).

Climate-induced migration (hereafter CM) is spoken of and represented in contrasting ways.[2] Some talk of CM as a security threat possibly igniting violent conflicts;[3] others, such as small island states, instead treat CM as a matter of national survival. Some fear the occurrence of a global humanitarian crisis,[4] while others cite CM as a case of climate (in)justice.[5]

Even though CM is represented in various ways and meanings, it seems consistently to lead the actors involved to express themselves in vigorous terms. Academic publications, policy briefs and NGO reports often convey images of inexorable floods of 'climate refugees' fleeing from the global South. Words like catastrophe, threat, frightening, urgency are widely used – with emblematic titles such as *Here Comes the Flood* (Bogardi and Warner 2009), *The Human Tide* (Christian Aid 2007) or *The Human Tsunami* (Knight 2009).

There are good reasons to employ strong language. Climate change threatens a large share of the world's population and scientists suggest that it may be even more severe than predicted by the IPCC (Schneider 2009; Parry *et al.* 2009). How would a 4°C-plus warming impact migration? The complexity of CM makes straightforward answers impossible (Gemenne 2011a), but changes of such magnitude set the stage for dark scenarios. For instance, what if climate change exacerbated the 'slumification' of human settlements already occurring in the global South (Davis 2006)? It would be irresponsible to evade, or seek to deny or obfuscate, these troubling questions.

(In)convenient convergences 123

Nevertheless, the purpose of this chapter is to offer a criticism of such narratives. It first develops an interpretive framework inspired by poststructuralist discourse theory, before conducting a narrative analysis of major policy documents on CM. This analysis highlights the apocalyptic character of the narratives centred on the floating signifier 'climate refugees'. The chapter argues that the convergence of conflicting discourses into an apocalyptic storyline paves the way for a depoliticization of CM and that it is therefore 'counterproductive' for those pursuing a radical political agenda on climate change.

Beyond words: a discursive reading

This analysis does not trivialize the impacts of climate change – whether on people trapped in places made inhospitable or on those displaced from them. In fact, this chapter is informed by a 'postfoundationalist' ontology (Marchart 2007; see also Chapter 1, this volume). In other words, it rests upon the belief that although climate change exists and has physical effects whether one thinks about it or not, it becomes an object of social meaning and practices only through human signification. Even 'climate science' does not handle or produce transparent images of biophysical phenomena. In this sense climate change and CM are to be regarded as constructs. A surplus of non-factual meaning is always added during the process of describing and developing intelligible narratives and this is not inherently a matter of rhetorical manipulation.[6]

This chapter's theoretical skeleton is drawn from Laclau's elaboration of discourse theory (Laclau 1996, 2005; Laclau and Mouffe 2001), complemented with elements of Hajer's (1995, 2006) Argumentative Discourse Analysis. Laclau's and Hajer's analytics are mobilized at different levels: the former is applied to the ontological and political dimensions of the convergence between different CM narratives, while the latter provides tools for the analysis of the 'micro-interactions' of the narratives and is thus limited to the argumentative dimension.

This chapter defines 'discourse' as practices constituting and determining social relations and objects; discourse is thus more than a cognitive or linguistic entity (Laclau and Mouffe 2001: 96; Laclau 2005; see also Chapter 1, this volume, as regards the relationship between discursive and non-discursive practices). Discourse goes beyond the linguistic or argumentative sphere[7] to which 'narratives' belong. A narrative is understood here as a generative 'sequence of events, experiences, or actions with a plot that ties together different parts into a meaningful whole' (Feldman *et al.* 2004: 148).

The concepts of 'climate refugees' or CM are read as a 'floating signifiers' (Laclau 2005) – signifiers whose meaning is not yet settled and fought over. These signifiers, which float between different meanings, are articulated differently by competing discourses which attempt to enforce a particular take on CM as the right one – by inscribing them into different chains of equivalence with other discursive elements (concerning the role of difference and equivalence in Laclau's concept of discourse see Chapter 13, this volume). In this light, the polarizations and ambiguities that surround the concept of climate refugees do not solely result from (mis)communication among different academic disciplines, disagreements over theoretical or empirical aspects, and strains in the interaction between policy and research.[8] On the one hand, the ambiguity of the term 'climate refugees' is a symptom of the problems and strains encountered by discourses that attempt drawing clearer frontiers in a discursive landscape still dislocated by CM. On the other hand, the very ambiguities make the convergence among discourses possible: the 'imprecision' and indeterminacy of the term 'climate refugees' permit that several conflicting discursive formations mobilize it (Laclau 1996: 36). Hajer (1995, 2006) provides further details on how different discourses converge into a certain narrative (a storyline in Hajer's terminology). A convergence ('a coalition' in Hajer's vocabulary) lives by 'discursive affinities' – that is, a certain narrative resonates with those discourses and 'sounds right'. The narrative makes sense of a phenomenon and is sufficiently compatible with the structure of the discourse.

Notably, objects and narratives assume divergent meanings in conflicting discourses (Laclau 2005; Laclau and Mouffe 2001; Stavrakakis 1997; Žižek 2008). Depending on the discourse in which it is inscribed rather than on some essential characteristics, the undocumented migrant (a good example of a floating signifier) can be a threat, a source of cheap labour, or the subject of an emancipatory struggle.

Therefore, discourses that converge into a narrative are not necessarily assimilable. That a 'capitalist' and a 'radical' discourse share a set of apocalyptic narratives does not imply that the two see and react to climate change in the same way, share common goals, or form a hegemonic coalition. Nonetheless, convergences structure a discursive landscape and influence how an issue may legitimately be handled.

In this chapter, the word *apocalyptic* denotes something qualitatively different from the distinction between alarmist and alarming – a distinction about whether a narrative or explanation is a *fair* representation of scientific knowledge or distorts it (see e.g. Risbey 2008). The point here is not whether a narrative exaggerates the seriousness of global warming and of CM, but *how* the (grave) matter is signified and incorporated into discourses (see also Chapter 7, this volume). An apocalyptic reading of CM conveys an image of an escalating event (such as the tsunami of climate refugees), producing a discrete rupture between the 'normal' present and the post-apocalyptic times. 'Apocalyptic' thus consists in raising a matter to a peculiar ontological novelty and degree of exceptionality. An apocalyptic narration envisions an ultimate threat, evoking the imperative 'If I don't do this . . . some unspeakably horrible X will take place' (Žižek 1991: 35), thereby mobilizing fear. The events leading to the rupture are isolated from 'ordinary' phenomena. Indeed, apocalyptic narratives favour the detachment of present and future CM from existing population movements and political dynamics, and exclude the possibility that the event(s) will be re-absorbed through a reproduction – or exacerbation – of existing patterns.

The discursive landscape

This section analyses the narratives about CM and climate refugees expressed in six publications chosen as 'paradigmatic cases' (Flyvbjerg 2001) of discourses on climate change. Four discourses are examined, which I name the scientific, the capitalist, the humanitarian and the radical discourse (see Table 8.1). The identification of these discourses draws upon previous studies on the discursive landscape of climate change (Adger *et al.* 2001; Clapp and Dauvergne 2005; Chapter 15, this volume). I would like to emphasize, however, that the distinction between the discourses serves only a heuristic function. It demonstrates that even though the discourses all display a different stance towards climate change, they converge on certain narratives – as I establish below.

The IPCC reports represent the scientific discourse on climate change. The IPCC is marked both by the ambition to represent a neutral compilation of best climate science and an indisputable politicization (evidenced by the fact that the reports are subject to negotiation by national governments), and are thus not free from friction and contention. These reports are extremely influential and have a performative impact on climate change discussions. Any topic included in the IPCC's account is automatically accorded much greater attention within the academy, the political arena, the media and public opinion.

The Stern Review (2007) represents a capitalist discourse on climate change. Commissioned by the UK government, it portrays climate change as an economic externality and market failure that threatens global politico-economic stability. By calculating the economic costs of the impacts of climate change, the review argues that to address climate change is beneficial even in strictly economic terms. In a nutshell, a discourse of this kind advocates market-based policies for curbing CO_2 emissions.

The reports by the Environmental Justice Foundation (EJF 2009) and Christian Aid (2007), two UK-based NGOs, represent a northern humanitarian discourse. Climate change is framed as a threat to human rights and as a hindrance to development. Ethical arguments have a prominent role in the narratives mobilized by this discourse.

The Agreement signed at the World People's Conference (WPC) on Climate Change and the Rights of Mother Earth held in Cochabamba, Bolivia, is chosen as emblem of a radical southern discourse. It sees global warming as a systemic failure, with a clear 'cause, which is the capitalist system' promoted by 'the corporations and governments of the so-called "developed" countries' (WPC 2010a). The discourse advocates an equity of substance among humans, and proposes systemic shifts.

Table 8.1 Mapping of discourses dealing with climate-induced migration within the discursive field of climate change

Discourse	Document(s)
Scientific	IPCC Assessment Reports 2001 and 2007
Capitalistic	Stern Review
Humanitarian	Christian Aid, *Human Tide: The Real Migration Crisis* (2007) Environmental Justice Foundation, *No Place Like Home – Where Next for Climate Refugees?* (2009)
Radical	Agreement at the People's Conference on Climate Change and the Rights of Mother Earth, Cochabamba (Bolivia)

(De)constructing the apocalypse

The narrative analysis in this chapter deconstructs the picture of CM in these five texts. The analysis reveals a contrast between the capitalist, the radical and the humanitarian discourses, which paint CM in apocalyptic colours and the IPCC's recent milder tones. To highlight this contrast, two ingredients of the apocalyptic narratives (the securitization of CM and numerical estimates) will be examined more closely, in order to identify the differing approaches employed by the IPCC and the other discourses and thereby to shed light on the convergence.

Apocalyptic tones in the humanitarian, capitalist and radical discourses

Several of the traits designated above as apocalyptic appear in the texts emanating from the EJF, WCD, Christian Aid and Stern. Words such as 'threat', 'fear' and 'danger' recur. While Stern argues that '[m]ajor areas of the world could be devastated by the social and economic consequences of very high temperatures' (Stern 2007: 173), according to the EJF, '[t]he overall impacts for the developing world are sobering: within this century, hundreds of millions of people are likely to be displaced' (2009: 6). Christian Aid warns that, as climate change adds to other drivers of displacement, we may see an emerging migration crisis that 'threatens to dwarf even that [crisis] faced by the war-ravaged world all those decades ago' (Christian Aid 2007: 1). The semantic of 'crisis' recurs extensively in all the documents. It expresses fear of an impending epochal, exceptional and unprecedented calamity and is carried to the point that, in the EJF's terms, '[t]he world has not previously faced a crisis on this scale' (2009: 6). The texts convey a sense of urgency: the 'time for action is now' (Christian Aid 2007: 1) and 'the severity of the situation demands urgent action' (Environmental Justice Foundation 2009: 7). Christian Aid is furthermore worried about the possibility that 'an emerging migration crisis will spiral out of control' (Christian Aid 2007: 1).

IPCC: from the exploratory approach of the 1990s to the cautious tone of 2007

Such tones contrast with the IPCC's narrative on CM, which has become milder over the years (Morrissey 2009; Tacoli 2009; Warner *et al.* 2009). The tone in the 1990 report is simultaneously grave and exploratory. Strong language appears when the IPCC hypothesizes that '[m]igration and resettlement may be the most threatening short-term effects of climate change on human settlements' (IPCC 1990: 5–10), or that '[t]he gravest effects of climate change may be those on human migration as millions are displaced by shoreline erosion, coastal flooding and severe drought' (IPCC 1992: 103). However, the report presents hypotheses rather than conclusions, uses the conditional 'may be', and utilizes only general terms such 'out-migration' or 'resettlement'.

The 2007 report dedicates two text boxes (IPCC 2007: 365, 736) to 'Environmental Migration'.[9] However, they are accompanied by a softening of tone. In

(In)convenient convergences 127

a nutshell, the IPCC's message is: 'caution'. Indeed environmental migration, climate refugees and related terms are discussed as contested and controversial concepts.

Several explanations for the shift are plausible. Some relate to the IPCC's growing orientation towards adaptive capacity (Tacoli 2009: 516). Others point to the profound polarization and politicization in the debate: Morrissey (2009: 13) claims that the IPCC distanced itself from the maximalist tradition,[10] while Sam Knight (2009) argues that the competing schools may have cancelled one another out.

These explanations should be read against the backdrop of the mainstreaming and politicization that climate change has undergone (Methmann 2010). If the politically loaded character of migration is added into the account (Black 2001; Castles 2010; Hartmann 2010), it seems understandable that the IPCC (subject to various processes of political scrutiny) did not compromise itself by a specific account of CM and climate refugees. This gives support to the reading of climate refugees as a floating signifier (rather than an empty signifier[11]), illustrating the mounting struggles on CM and the openness of the issue.[12] Hence, the softening of tone may also be attributed to the political implications that would arise from an IPCC endorsement of securitized and policy prescriptive concepts such as climate refugees.

A global security crisis: the migration–conflict nexus

A prominent (and contentious) ingredient of apocalyptic narratives is the hypothesis that CM will have destabilizing impacts well beyond the areas impacted by displacement. The texts acknowledge (e.g. EJF 2009: 4) that the direct influence of climate change will be mainly on local or intra-regional patterns of mobility, but they nonetheless excite fears of domino effects. The troubles in 'the developing world may have knock-on consequences for developed economies, through disruption to global trade and security . . . population movement and financial contagion' (Stern 2007: 173). Images of crisis and conflicts are just a few steps away. The idea that ecological stresses lead to conflicts is prominent both in the Stern Report (2007: vii–viii) and in Christian Aid's report. The logic may seem straightforward:

> [t]he danger is that this new forced migration will fuel existing conflicts and generate new ones in the areas of the world – the poorest – where resources are most scarce. Movement on this scale has the potential to de-stabilize whole regions where increasingly desperate populations compete for dwindling food and water.
>
> (Christian Aid 2007: 3)

Christian Aid thus accepts the (neo-)Malthusian rationale that links demographics, environmental degradation and violent conflicts (for critique, see Haas 2002; Hartmann 2010; White 2011). Put simply, ecological stresses and scarcity, by worsening the conditions of the poor, foment migration and conflicts – the two being mutually reinforcing processes that feed an uncontrollable spiral.

These matters are at the crux of the lively academic debate on 'environmental security' and on the hypothesis that environmental stresses cause violent conflicts (Homer-Dixon 1994; Burke *et al.* 2009; Zhang *et al.* 2007). Several documents explicitly discuss climate or ecological migration among the 'environmental' causes of violent conflicts (Myers 2005; Reuveny 2007). However, such views face strong critiques of their assumptions, methodologies, empirical consistency and implications (Baechler 1998; Barnett 2000; Dalby 2009; Detraz and Betsill 2009; O'Lear and Diehl 2007; Chapter 6, this volume). At minimum, one can say that there is no consensus on the validity of such hypotheses (Salehyan 2008).

The IPCC suggests caution about linking climate change, migration and conflict (e.g. 2007: 365). On the contrary, the innocence with which the other texts endorse the hypothesis confirms that it is 'becoming "conventional wisdom" in some policy and activist circles' (Salehyan 2008: 318). At all events, the reports promote a contested and normative rationale as a settled truth – *assuming* that the deterioration in the socio-ecological conditions of poor populations will generally lead to violent conflicts.

Heavy numbers with thin evidence

The huge figures foreseeing hundreds of millions of climate refugees are another necessary ingredient of the apocalyptic narratives. Without such numbers, the 'doom and gloom' idea would be unspectacular. Such figures are one of the debated aspects of CM and have received a huge volume of criticism over the years (Black *et al.* 2008; Kniveton 2008; Morrissey 2009; Piguet 2010; Gemenne 2011c; Jakobeit and Methmann 2012). As reconstructed by the *Foresight Report* (2011: 28), the majority of the estimates in circulation actually derive from Myers' controversial work (Kerr 2009; Myers 2005; Myers and Kent 1995).

The IPCC's 2007 report dismisses these figures, stating that '[e]stimates of the number of people who may become environmental migrants are, at best, guesswork' (IPCC 2007: 365). The story is again very different for the other texts. The EJF accepts the estimates and builds them into their scenarios without any deeper reflections on their robustness.[13] The other four have an ambiguous relation to the projections. They present a series of substantial points (echoing the academic debates) that seem to undermine the credibility of the estimates,[14] but they nevertheless use the 'old and widely disputed figures' (Christian Aid 2007: 2). While the IPCC adopts a cautious stance, the other texts unhesitatingly construct their narratives on contested scientific bases, which are anything but sober facts.

Cementing a coherent picture: complexity and uncertainty disappear

The comparison with the IPCC's caution highlights the contrast between the bold terms employed by Stern, WPC, Christian Aid and the EJF and their shaky grounds (as we saw in terms of numbers and of the security/conflict rationale). The complexities involved in CM are acknowledged by all the texts, yet they are radically downsized in the overall picture the texts paint. The case of the People's

Agreement is a clear example: the preparatory discussions[15] gave ample space to the complexities, which nonetheless disappear in the declaration.[16] The resulting picture displays clearer contours, and CM can be spoken of in a way that makes sense and appeals to other moments of the discourse (such as the need for urgent action).

The absence of complexity in the construction of a narrative is not (necessarily) a matter of inconsistency or a mystification. Some sort of 'black boxing' (Hajer 1995), i.e. recurring to some simplified image and story that cannot accommodate all the complexities and disorder of the real, is normal rather than pathological. What is interesting, from an interpretive perspective, are the ways in which black boxing takes place in the construction of intelligible narratives, and the meanings that come into play in such a process.

In our case, what is problematic is not the simplification per se, but the implicit claim that these narratives are grounded solely on 'facts'. A heading in the EJF's report is revealing: 'The numbers speak for themselves' (EJF 2009: 8). At a first glance, this seems an innocent statement: the evidence for global warming is so overwhelming that climate science in many ways seems to speak for itself. However, the question is more complicated: biophysical measures or projections do not provide any formula for how to connect ecological conditions with migration. Even less they do speak of 'climate refugees'. The numbers *do not* speak for themselves and neither relate to nor mandate the way in which populations will respond to ecological stresses.

This reveals a conflation of 'matters of concern' with 'matters of fact' (Latour 2004): the biophysical changes giving rise to the risks of mass displacements (the latter) determining the political questions about how to understand and act upon them (the former). This conflation paves the way for determinism, and certain narratives become an unavoidable 'datum of reality'. This has deep political implications: it short-circuits the discursive struggles and prompts a closure of the debate.

Apocalypse and its inconveniences

What are the implications of these narratives, and what does the convergence mean? First, apocalyptic narratives risk becoming a counterproductive strategy for communicating the urgency of climate change (Ereaut and Segnit 2006; Hulme 2007; O'Neill and Nicholson-Cole 2009). The fear they engender can also lead to 'denial, paralysis, apathy or even perverse reactive behaviour' (Hulme 2007: 818). It can undermine the credibility attached to an issue and give rise to scepticism ('can this really be true?'), as well as create emotional inflation (Ereaut and Segnit 2006; O'Neill and Nicholson-Cole 2009). Moreover, the fear and/or refusal of an emergent danger can prove volatile, creating an environment where the impossible becomes possible. Žižek (2010: 329–330) provides an example, namely the 're-normalization' of climate change: dismissed by large parts of the establishment as an ideologically charged and impossible apocalypse until a few years ago, it is increasingly treated as a business-as-usual part of the political and economic routine.

Second, by creating anxiety and a sense of an impending catastrophe, apocalyptic narratives reinforce the representation of migration as a threatening dysfunction. In the words of Stephen Castles:

> a dominant political discourse sees migration as a problem that needs to be 'fixed' by appropriate policies. The repressive variant is tight border control, the more liberal one is addressing the 'root causes' of migration especially poverty and violence in origin countries so that people do not have to migrate.
>
> (Castles 2010: 3)

Apocalyptic narratives that foresee hordes of climate refugees knocking on developed countries' doors might prove grist to the mill of both the liberal and the repressive variant – opening the way for more restrictive policies or even for a militarization of the issue (Chapter 6, this volume; Smith 2007).

Third, the disempowering construction of the affected (migrants or refugees) embedded in the apocalyptic narratives on climate refugees is problematic. As noted by Kate Manzo (2010: 99), 'at the epicentre' of narratives based on fear and apocalypse 'stands the figure of the vulnerable being'. Reinforcing postcolonial imaginaries (see e.g. Manzo 2010; Doulton and Brown 2009; O'Brien et al. 2007), climate refugees are constructed as voiceless victims – either to protect or to fear.

It is remarkable that the People's Agreement endorses such a construction. Climate refugees are indeed depicted as victims that developed countries should protect, by 'offering migrants a decent life [sic] with full human rights guarantees in their countries' (WPC 2010a). This is a far cry from the conflictual attitude and the claim for radical shifts, for 'real' changes and not simply rearrangements of the present situation that permeate the text. The revolutionary spark fades away. One no longer hears the voice of any struggling subject, but an appeal for pity for a third subject – a construction that (re)produces asymmetrical relations to destitute victims rather than to subjects whose struggle and interests one supports.

Fear of politics or politics of fear?

After this summary of the apocalyptic tones that permeate the texts, it may seem surprising that the policy approaches they suggest do not have the same 'exceptional' character of the catastrophe looming on the horizon. Indeed, the narratives on 'climate refugees' advocate legal instruments and related governance measures. The Stern Review suggests that 'the international community should support greater investment in managing and reducing the consequences of climate change ... including improving mechanisms for refugee resettlement' (Stern 2007: 566). Following a similar line, the EJF 'suggests a new category definition of refugee is needed to reflect this unprecedented upheaval facing millions of people across our planet' (EJF 2009: 7). According to this NGO, 'a new multi-lateral legal instrument – either a Protocol under the United Nations Framework Convention on

(In)convenient convergences 131

Climate Change, or a stand-alone Convention – is required to specifically address the needs of "climate refugees"' (EJF 2009: 25).

It is not immediately understandable why apocalyptic imaginaries should suggest governance solutions to CM – why one should deal with a looming catastrophe with the calm, moderate, incremental mechanisms of governance. This contrast between an exceptional threat and 'mild' governance responses is similar to the paradox highlighted by Swyngedouw (2010, 2011) in his discussion of the post-politicization of environmental matters, in which apocalyptic imaginaries play an important role. Indeed, with the negation of matters of concern and the related determinism, the apocalyptic narratives about CM become a datum of reality, and the 'phantom' of climate refugees takes centre stage. There will be massive displacements of people, as a result of ecological degradation, and the discursive structuration highlighted here leaves the implementation and improvement of governance and legal instruments as the only remaining way to deal with them (for a similar argument with regard to climate and security in general see Chapter 7, this volume).

This has a depoliticizing potential in various ways. The construct of climate refugees disempowers those concerned, who, treated as victims (see above), are excluded from the determination of the field(s) of the possible. Someone else is defining how to speak about their future.

Constructing the concerned as victims and dealing with them through improved governance does something more: it fills the gap between the unimaginable, unprecedented humanitarian catastrophe, and the acceptance of climate-induced 'resettlements' as part of business-as-usual. CM risks becoming *de facto* an unavoidable element of business-as-usual, to be governed (controlled and curbed) with the instruments and mechanisms of governance – governance that is essentially incapable of hosting struggles on goals and alternative futures. This dismisses the political; it inhibits the envisioning of radically alternative futures. The existing relations (and their discursive representation), those seen as the root of the problem by a radical discourse such as WPC's (2010b), those very factors putting the dwellings of huge numbers of people at risk, are left untouched.

An inconvenient convergence?

Summing up, the interpretive approach delineated here allowed us to see in a different light some aspects of the lively discursive field of CM. In exploring apocalyptic narratives on climate refugees, the chapter avoided the deadlock of the binary alarmist/alarming and discussed the imaginaries and political meanings mobilized around CM. Reading climate refugees as a floating signifier, the chapter argues that the convergence into apocalyptic narratives does not mean that the discursive field has undergone a closure: the contradictions among and within discourses manifest the still open character of the CM debate. Nevertheless, since floating signifiers are related to the establishment of chains of equivalence, and, as noted by Laclau, the distance between empty and floating signifiers 'is not that great' (Laclau 2005: 133), the convergence may facilitate the affirmation of 'climate refugees' as an empty signifier. Given the characteristics of these narratives (which conflate matters of concern and of fact, are deterministic, disempower the concerned and favour a depoliticization of CM), such an outcome would imply a structuration of the discursive field that leaves existing hegemonic relations substantially untouched.

The chapter thus articulates a qualified but firm critique of the deployment of the apocalyptic narratives on climate refugees. Qualified in the sense that it does not assimilate the goals of agents (discourses) that share narratives, nor blame them for hidden agendas or intentional manipulation. Firm, since the discursive structuration (re)produced by such narratives is shown to be counterproductive for radical agendas.

Notes

1 Several disciplines have explored the connections between ecological conditions and population movements, but the topic was brought to the fore in the early 1980s when influential reports by the UN Environmental Programme (El-Hinnawi 1985) and the Worldwatch Institute (Jacobsen 1988) launched the term 'environmental refugees'.
2 Representations are of course connected to definitions, on which there is a heated debate. On this, see Bates (2002), Brown (2008), Castles (2002), Foresight (2011), IPCC (2007), Kälin (2010) and Suhrke (1994).
3 See for instance Myers (2005), Stern (2007), Reuveny (2007), the European Commission (EU 2008) and German Advisory Council on Global Change (WBGU 2008).
4 E.g. Christian Aid (2007), Docherty and Giannini (2009) and Westra (2009).
5 E.g. the declaration at the World People's Conference on Climate Change (WPC 2010a) or Greenpeace's campaign Blue Alert.
6 See, for example, the work of Laclau on populism (2005).
7 Others restrict discourse to 'meaning' and words. For instance Hajer (1995: 60) describes discourse as 'ensemble of ideas, concepts, and categorizations that is produced, reproduced, and transformed in a particular set of practices and through which meaning is given to physical and social realities'.
8 On these aspects, see Bardsley and Hugo (2010), Barnett and Webber (2009), Bates (2002), Massey et al. (2010), Black et al. (2008), Castles (2002), Gemenne (2011b) and Kälin (2010).
9 Migration is discussed also elsewhere, such as in chapter 16 (IPCC 2007: 734–736), chapter 18 and chapter 10 (IPCC 2007: 488).
10 This term refers to Suhrke's (1994) classification of the debate on environmental migration into a maximalist and a minimalist tradition.
11 An empty signifier is an element that, voided of its specific meaning, supports a chain of equivalence between different discursive elements. The emergence of an empty signifier testifies the occurrence of a discursive closure, an (in)stable fixation of meaning in a discursive field (Laclau 1996, 2005).
12 The comments by an anonymous reviewer stimulated me to remark the contentious character of the concept of 'climate refugee' and to illustrate it by pointing to the difference between the 'empty' and 'floating' signifiers (on this, see Laclau 1996: 36ff.).
13 See EJF (2009: 14, footnote 8).
14 See for instance Stern (2007: 77, 112, 199) and Christian Aid (2007: 2, 22).
15 See the preparatory discussions (WPC 2010b).
16 The fact that projections 'suggest that between 200 million and 1 billion people will become displaced by situations resulting from climate change by the year 2050' dominates the narrative of the declaration.

References

Adger, W.N., Tor, A.B., Katrina, B. and Hanne, S. (2001) 'Advancing a political ecology of global environmental discourses', *Development and Change* 32: 681–715.

Baechler, G. (1998) 'Why environmental transformation causes violence: a synthesis', *Environmental Change and Security Project Report* 4: 24–44.

Bardsley, D.K. and Hugo, G.J. (2010) 'Migration and climate change: examining thresholds of change to guide effective adaptation decision-making', *Population and Environment* 32: 238–262.

Barnett, J. (2000) 'Destabilizing the environment-conflict thesis', *Review of International Studies* 26(2): 271–288.

Barnett, J. and Webber, M. (2009) *Accommodating Migration to Promote Adaptation to Climate Change*, Melbourne: Commission on Climate Change and Development, University of Melbourne.

Bates, D.C. (2002) 'Environmental refugees? Classifying human migrations caused by environmental change', *Population and Environment* 23: 465–477.

Black, R. (2001) 'Environmental refugees: myth or reality?', *New Issues in Refugee Research* – UNHCR working paper 70, Geneva: UNHCR.

Black, R., Kniveton, D., Skeldon, R., Coppard, D., Murata, A. and Schmidt-Verkerk, K. (2008) 'Demographics and Climate Change: Future Trends and their Policy Implications for Migration', *Working Paper 27*, Brighton: University of Sussex.

Bogardi, J. and Warner, K. (2009) 'Here comes the flood', *Nature Reports Climate Change*, 9–11.

Brown, O. (2008) 'Migration and climate change', *IOM Migration Research Series* 31, Geneva: International Organization for Migration.

Burke, M.B., Miguel, E., Satyanath, S., Dykema, J.A. and Lobell, D.B. (2009) 'Warming increases the risk of civil war in Africa', *Proceedings of the National Academy of Sciences* 106: 20670–20674.

Castles, S. (2002) 'Environmental change and forced migration: making sense of the debate', *New Issues in Refugee Research* – UNHCR working paper 70, Geneva: UNHCR.

Castles, S. (2010) 'Understanding global migration: a social transformation perspective', *Journal of Ethnic and Migration Studies* 36: 1565–1586.

Christian Aid (2007) *Human Tide: The Real Migration Crisis*, London: Christian Aid.

Clapp, J. and Dauvergne, P. (2005) *Paths to a Green World: The Political Economy of the Global Environment*, Cambridge, MA: MIT Press.

Dalby, S. (2009) *Security and Environmental Change*, Cambridge: Polity.

Davis, M. (2006) *Planet of Slums*, London: Verso.

Detraz, N. and Betsill, M.M. (2009) 'Climate change and environmental security: for whom the discourse shifts', *International Studies Perspectives* 10(3): 303–320.

Docherty, B. and Giannini, T. (2009) 'Confronting a rising tide: a proposal for a convention on climate change refugees', *Harvard Environmental Law Review* 33: 349–403.

Doulton, H. and Brown, K. (2009) 'Ten years to prevent catastrophe?', *Global Environmental Change* 19: 191–202.

El-Hinnawi, E. (1985) *Environmental Refugees*, Nairobi: UNEP.

Environmental Justice Foundation (2009) *No Place Like Home: Where Next for Climate Refugees?*, London: Environmental Justice Foundation.

Ereaut, G. and Segnit, N. (2006) *Warm Words: How Are We Telling the Climate Story and Can We Tell it Better?*, London: Institute for Public Policy Research.

EU (2008) *Climate Change and International Security*, paper from the High Representative and the European Commission to the European Council. Available at: www.consilium.europa.eu/ueDocs/cms_Data/docs/pressData/en/reports/99387.pdf [retrieved: 10.2.2012].

Feldman, M.S., Brown, R.N. and Horner, D. (2004) 'Making sense of stories: a rhetorical approach to narrative analysis', *Journal of Public Administration Research and Theory* 14: 147–170.

Flyvbjerg, B. (2001) *Making Social Science Matter: Why Social Inquiry Fails and How it Can Succeed Again*, Cambridge: Cambridge University Press.

Foresight (2011) *Final Project Report – Foresight: Migration and Global Environmental Change*, London: The Government Office for Science.

Gemenne, F. (2011a) 'Climate-induced population displacements in a 4°C+ world', *Philosophical Transactions of the Royal Society A* 369: 182–195.

Gemenne, F. (2011b) 'How they became the human face of climate change: research and policy interactions in the birth of the "environmental migration" concept', in: Piguet, E., Pécoud, A. and de Guchteneire, P. (eds) *Migration and Climate Change*, Cambridge: Cambridge University Press, 225–259.

Gemenne, F. (2011c) 'Why the numbers don't add up: a review of estimates and predictions of people displaced by environmental changes', *Global Environmental Change* 21: S41–S49.

Haas, P.M. (2002) 'Constructing environmental conflicts from resource scarcity', *Global Environmental Politics* 2: 1–11.

Hajer, M.A. (1995) *The Politics of Environmental Discourse: Ecological Modernization and the Policy Process*, Oxford: Clarendon Press.

Hajer, M.A. (2006) 'Doing discourse analysis: coalitions, practices, meaning', in: van den Brink, M. and Metze, T. (eds) *Words Matter in Policy and Planning: Discourse Theory and Method in the Social Sciences*, Utrecht: Netherlands Graduate School of Urban and Regional Research, 65–74.

Hartmann, B. (2010) 'Rethinking climate refugees and climate conflict: rhetoric, reality and the politics of policy discourse', *Journal of International Development* 22: 233–246.

Homer-Dixon, T.F. (1994) 'Environmental scarcities and violent conflict', *International Security* 19: 5–41.

Hulme, M. (2007) 'Newspaper scare headlines can be counter-productive', *Nature* 445: 818.

IPCC (1990) *First Assessment: Report Prepared for IPCC by Working Group II*, Geneva: WMO.

IPCC (1992) *IPCC First Assessment Report*, Geneva: WMO.

IPCC (2007) *Climate Change 2007: Impacts, Adaptation and Vulnerability. Contribution of Working Group II to the Fourth Assessment Report of the Intergovernmental Panel on Climate Change*, Cambridge and New York: Cambridge University Press.

Jacobsen, J.L. (1988) *Environmental Refugees: A Yardstick of Habitability*, Washington, DC: World Watch Institute.

Jakobeit, C. and Methmann, C. (2012) '"Climate Refugees" as Dawning Catastrophe? A Critique of the Dominant Quest for Numbers', in: Scheffran, J., Brzoska, M., Brauch, H.G., Link, P.M. and Schilling, J. (eds) *Climate Change, Human Security and Violent Conflict: Challenges for Societal Stability*, New York: Springer, 301–314.

Kälin, W. (2010) 'Conceptualising climate-induced displacement', in: McAdam, J. (ed.) *Climate Change and Displacement: Multidisciplinary Perspectives*, Oxford: Hart Publishing, 81–103.

Kerr, R.A. (2009) 'Amid worrisome signs of warming, "climate fatigue" sets in', *Science* 326: 926–928.
Knight, S. (2009) 'The human tsunami', *The Financial Times, 19 June*.
Kniveton, D.R. (2008) 'Climate change and migration: improving methodologies to estimate flows', *IOM Migration Research Series* 33, Geneva: International Organization For Migration.
Laclau, E. (1996) *Emancipation(s)*, London: Verso.
Laclau, E. (2005) *On Populist Reason*, London: Verso.
Laclau, E. and Mouffe, C. (2001) *Hegemony and Socialist Strategy: Towards a Radical Democratic Politics*, London: Verso.
Latour, B. (2004) *Politics of Nature: How to Bring the Sciences into Democracy*, Cambridge, MA: Harvard University Press.
Manzo, K. (2010) 'Imaging vulnerability: the iconography of climate change', *Area* 42: 96–107.
Marchart, O. (2007) *Post-Foundational Political Thought: Political Difference in Nancy, Lefort, Badiou and Laclau*, Edinburgh: Edinburgh University Press.
Massey, D.S., Axinn, W.G. and Ghimire, D.J. (2010) 'Environmental change and out-migration: evidence from Nepal', *Population and Environment* 32: 109–136.
Methmann, C. (2010) '"Climate protection" as empty signifier: a discourse theoretical perspective on climate mainstreaming in world politics', *Millennium* 39: 345–372.
Morrissey, J. (2009) *Environmental Change and Forced Migration: A State of the Art Review*, Oxford: Refugee Studies Centre.
Myers, N. (2005) 'Environmental refugees: an emergent security issue', paper presented at the *13th Economic Forum*, Prague, 23–27 May.
Myers, N. and Kent, J. (1995) *Environmental Exodus: An Emergent Crisis in the Global Arena*, Washington, DC: Climate Institute.
O'Brien, K., Eriksen, S., Nygard, L.P. and Schjolden, A. (2007) 'Why different interpretations of vulnerability matter in climate change discourses', *Climate Policy* 7: 73–88.
O'Lear, S. and Diehl, P.F. (2007) 'Not drawn to scale: research on resource and environmental conflict', *Geopolitics* 12(1): 166–183.
O'Neill, S. and Nicholson-Cole, S. (2009) '"Fear won't do it": promoting positive engagement with climate change through visual and iconic representations', *Science Communication* 30: 355–379.
Parry, M., Lowe, J. and Hanson, C. (2009) 'Overshoot, adapt and recover', *Nature* 458: 1102–1103.
Piguet, E. (2010) 'Linking climate change, environmental degradation, and migration: a methodological overview', *Wiley Interdisciplinary Reviews: Climate Change* 1: 517–524.
Reuveny, R. (2007) 'Climate change-induced migration and violent conflict', *Political Geography* 26: 656–673.
Risbey, J.S. (2008) 'The new climate discourse: alarmist or alarming?', *Global Environmental Change – Human and Policy Dimensions* 18: 26–37.
Salehyan, I. (2008) 'From climate change to conflict? No consensus yet', *Journal of Peace Research* 45: 315–327.
Schneider, S. (2009) 'The worst-case scenario', *Nature* 458: 1104–1105.
Smith, P.J. (2007) 'Climate change, mass migration and the military response', *Orbis* 51: 617–633.
Stavrakakis, Y. (1997) 'Green ideology: a discursive reading', *Journal of Political Ideologies* 2: 259–279.

Stern, N. (2007) *The Economics of Climate Change: The Stern Review*, Cambridge: Cambridge University Press.
Suhrke, A. (1994) 'Environmental degradation and population flows', *Journal of International Affairs* 47: 473–496.
Swyngedouw, E. (2010) 'Apocalypse forever? Post-political populism and the spectre of climate change', *Theory, Culture & Society* 27: 213–232.
Swyngedouw, E. (2011) 'Interrogating post-democratization: reclaiming egalitarian political spaces', *Political Geography* 30: 370–380.
Tacoli, C. (2009) 'Crisis or adaptation? Migration and climate change in a context of high mobility', *Environment and Urbanization* 21: 513–525.
UNFCCC (2010) The Cancun Agreements: Outcome of the Work of the Ad-Hoc Working Group on Long-term Cooperative Action under the Convention. Online. Available at: http://unfccc.int/resource/docs/2010/cop16/eng/07a01.pdf (retrieved: 15.7.2012).
Warner, K., Hamza, M., Oliver-Smith, A., Renaud, F. and Julca, A. (2009) 'Climate change, environmental degradation and migration', *Natural Hazards 55(3): 689–715*.
WBGU (2008) *Climate Change as a Security Risk*, London: Earthscan.
Westra, L. (2009) *Environmental Justice and the Rights of Ecological Refugees*, London: Earthscan.
White, G. (2011) *Climate Change and Migration: Security and Borders in a Warming World*, Oxford: Oxford University Press.
WPC (2010a) *People's Agreement. World People's Conference on Climate Change and the Rights of Mother Earth*. Online. Available at: http://pwccc.wordpress.com (retrieved: 20.6.2010).
WPC (2010b) *Working Group 6: Climate Change and Migrations. World People's Conference on Climate Change and the Rights of Mother Earth*. Online. Available at: http://pwccc.wordpress.com/category/working-groups/06-climate-migrants (retrieved: 10.12.2011).
Zhang, D.D., Brecke, P., Lee, H.F., He, Y.-Q. and Zhang, J. (2007) 'Global climate change, war, and population decline in recent human history', *Proceedings of the National Academy of Sciences* 104: 19214–19219.
Žižek, S. (1991) *Looking Awry: An Introduction to Jacques Lacan through Popular Culture*, Cambridge and London: MIT Press.
Žižek, S. (2008) *The Sublime Object of Ideology*, London: Verso.
Žižek, S. (2010) *Living in the End Times*, London: Verso.

Part III
The technocratization of climate change

9 My space
Governing individuals' carbon emissions[1]

Matthew Paterson and Johannes Stripple

Introduction

In recent years, there has been a veritable explosion of projects designed to enable individuals to 'do their bit' in the struggle to limit climate change. Previously, the focus of action had been on states and firms, but in the early 2000s this started to be complemented by a focus on individual practice. For example, in 2006 the UK environment minister proposed a system of Personal Carbon Allowances. Others have exhorted us to go on a low-carbon diet. There are now many organizations offering to help you measure and manage your carbon footprint, or to go 'carbon neutral' through carbon offsetting. Community groups have established voluntary carbon rationing systems. All of these practices have been accompanied by a plethora of books focusing on 'what you can do' to help limit climate change (e.g. Goodall 2007; Marshall 2007; Reay 2006; Spence 2005). The common denominator in all of these projects is the focus on individual practice in relation to climate change. We invoke the metaphor of 'My Space' deliberately. It is suggestive of how the forms of individualization in these projects simultaneously operate through the sorts of communicative rationality involved like those in 'Web 2.0' technologies like Myspace, Facebook, Twitter, Jaiku, Tagged and Flickr. At the same time, the phrase implies the appropriation of climate change for an individual, almost narcissistic subject, who thinks of 'their emissions' and their responsibilities regarding them. But this subject, while narcissistic, is also forced to problematize her/his practices through peer pressure, comparison and communication.

Two sorts of question drive our motivation for writing this chapter. One is to try to understand the reasons for this proliferation of discourses focusing on individuals. Why is it that these elements have quickly become commonplace currency and seem to many to make obvious common sense? Our second is to engage in a more interpretive reflection on the character of these practices as parts of global climate governance. How should we understand the complicated relationship between individual practice and identity (which is clearly central to these projects) and the broad collective understanding of the need to respond to climate change that underpins the legitimacy claims of these projects? Our argument is that these projects entail a complex and interesting shift in the way that subjects are being formed around climate change. This complexity is missed by either managerial/normative analyses which seek to establish how they can be made to work best (e.g. Seyfang 2007) or those making the critical arguments that these practices are simply scams for companies to make money out of people's sense of guilt, while enabling continued overconsumption by the rich (Lohmann 2006; Smith 2007). Both of these intellectual exercises are worthwhile, but we aim here to complement them with an interpretation of these practices in terms of governmentality – the way they entail shaping individual subjects through exhorting them to manage their climate-related practices themselves. The chapter draws on debates about advanced liberal governmentality to develop an account of how the government of carbon operates by mobilizing individual subjectivity. Following that, we turn in more detail to an analysis of the five principal sorts of individualized carbon practice outlined above; footprinting, offsetting, dieting, voluntary carbon rationing, and Personal Carbon Allowances. We argue that there is an emergent governmentality that entails the 'conduct of carbon conduct' through moulding and mobilizing a certain subjectivity (the individual as concerned carbon emitter) to govern their own emissions in various ways – as counters, displacers, dieters, communitarians or citizens.

The conduct of carbon conduct

Since first introduced by Michel Foucault in the 1970s, the governmentality concept (see also Chapters 3 and 4 in this volume) has been used and developed across numerous disciplines such as critical sociology, history, cultural studies and political geography (Rose *et al.* 2006; Rose-Redwood 2006; Rutherford 2007). Governmentality, as a form of thinking, enables us to develop a perspective on climate change and its government which focus on the creation of appropriate subjectivities and self-regulating, carbon-conscious citizens. Let us very briefly introduce governmentality in general terms before we develop a specific account of people's governing of their own emissions. Michel Foucault showed in the recently published lectures held at the *Collège de France* in 1977–8 how the meaning of the word 'government' in the sixteenth century contrasts markedly to its modern connotation to centralized structures of authority. In addition to control/management by the state or the administration, 'government' also signified problems of self-control, guidance for the family and for children, management of the household, directing the soul, etc. (Lemke 2001: 191). Hence, the art of government was about the correct manner of managing individuals, goods and wealth within the family but applied to the state as a whole (Foucault 1991: 92). Similarly, Gordon, writing in the introduction to the edited book where the 'governmentality lecture' was first made available for a wider English-speaking audience, understood the essence of government as an activity concerning: the relation between self and self; the relation between self and others involving some sort of guidance; relations within social institutions or communities; or relations related to the exercise of political sovereignty (Gordon 1991: 2–3).

To understand government as the 'conduct of conduct' is, in a well-known formulation, to understand power as the possibility to 'structure the possible field of actions of others' (Foucault 1982: 221). But how is this actually done? Miller and Rose (2008) and Dean (1999) have usefully conceptualized what it means to govern, what it means to conduct conduct. First, government is a problematizing activity. Issues and concerns have to be made to appear problematic. Problems are not pre-given, but have to be constructed and made visible. This process can occur in different ways, in different sites and by different agents (Miller and Rose 2008: 14). The result is a notion of government that illuminates 'the way in which an individual questions his or her own conduct so that he or she may be better able to govern it' (Dean 1999: 12). Second, the conduct in question has to be amenable to intervention. In this respect, governmentality combines two aspects of governing. On the one hand, it entails representing and knowing a phenomenon and, on the other hand, acting upon the same phenomenon in order to transform it.

The concept of governmentality draws attention to the moulding and mobilizing of individual subjectivity and individuals' capacity to govern themselves (Merlingen 2006: 184). Government as the 'conduct of conduct' is a calculated and rational (clear and systematic) activity, undertaken by a multiplicity of authorities and agencies, that shape our behaviour according to particular norms for a variety of ends (Dean 1999: 10–11). This enables us to talk about the 'conduct of carbon conduct', by which we mean a government of people's carbon dioxide emissions that does not work through the authority of the state or the state system, but through people's governing of their own emissions. Different regimes of 'carbon calculation' operate so that individuals either work on their emission-producing activities or to 'offset' their emissions elsewhere. The conduct of carbon conduct is therefore a government enabled through certain forms of knowledge (measurements and calculations of one's own carbon footprint) certain technologies (the turning of carbon emissions into tradable commodities) and a certain ethic (low-carbon lifestyle as desirable).

What is therefore particularly interesting about the emergence of what we conceptualize as 'the conduct of carbon conduct' is precisely the way that it articulates the relationships between individual and collective responsibilities to address climate change. The neoliberal relationality at the heart of these practices is not so much that their individualizing character attempts to effect a depoliticization of climate change, but rather that it reshapes the boundary between these two dimensions of social life, as well as what each concretely means. Climate politics as 'My Space' simultaneously operates as a vanity-oriented, virtue politics of self-denial, sacrifice and neo-colonial offsetting, *and* something that calls into question the freedom-oriented discourse of neoliberal politics. Individualism becomes interpreted increasingly as responsible agency, not quite active citizenship in the republican sense, but nevertheless acting in the *private* sphere to pursue a *public* good.

Drawing on a framework developed by Dean (1999) and Angela Oels (2005), Table 9.1 distinguishes between five different sorts of practice that we discuss below. It illustrates how they operate in relation to the sorts of 'rationalities of government' and 'technologies of government' elaborated above. From these two general aspects of governmentality, four themes are identified. What aspects of

Table 9.1 Different forms of individualized carbon governance

Analytical category	Key questions	General features common to all	Carbon footprinting	Practice of governance — Carbon offsetting in the project based markets	Carbon dieting	Carbon rationing action groups	Personal carbon allowances
Fields of visibility	What is illuminated? What is obscured?	Focus on the individual's contribution to climate change as object of governance. Focus on dilemmas individuals face in responding to climate change.	'Rule by visibility': aim simply to illuminate impact of individual practice.	Markets as means for commensuration. Relation between emissions and practices elsewhere – a political geography of emissions. The dilemma is enhanced – the question of 'virtue'. Particular visibility of air travel.	Universalist image – the equality of people as potential dieters. A morality of excess and self-denial.	Social group/peer group. Community action. Practices of concrete others, and visibility of our practices to them.	Nationalist frame. Markets as means. Equality of allocation.
Technical aspects	By what instruments, procedures and technologies is rule accomplished?	Techniques of measurement of greenhouse gas emissions.	Calculative technologies. Technologies of representation and visualization ('footprints'). The basic unit – a tonne of carbon dioxide equivalent.	Baselines, additionality and credits (like CDM or Verified Emissions Reduction). Standards and systems of certification. Technical infrastructure (firms, websites, carbon calculators).	Constant monitoring of minutiae of behaviour. 'Guidance manuals' like for Weightwatchers – a 'how-to guide'.	Constitutions of CRAG groups. Rules of the group (variable). Relationship of CO_2 to money – the annual reckoning. Wiki software to share experiences and knowledge.	Rules for permit allocation and about trading. Boundaries of systems – geographical, social (who has to participate?), emissions included (boundaries work/personal, direct/embodied energy, etc).

Forms of knowledge	Which forms of thought arise from and inform the activity of governing?	Knowledge concerning practices that generate emissions and options for reducing them.	Market-calculating behaviour. Choices of projects – trees vs HFCs. Focus on 'big-ticket items' (air travel).	Knowledge of carbon content of every item. Focus on details. Restraint in some areas to get the 'treats'.	Trust – knowledge of trustworthiness of group members. Knowledge of the limit.	Market practices. Translation of tons CO_2 to money (commensuration). Knowledge of the limit.
Formation of identities	What forms of self are presupposed? What transformations are sought?	Presupposes a calculative capacity and orientation. Conduct of carbon conduct. Pursuit of a carbon managing subject.	The carbon displacer. Guilt and absolution. Charitable dimension – the do-gooder.	Subject prone to guilt as motivation. Relationship between guilt and pleasure. Smugness of achievers. Climate practice as a 'bodily' experience – focus on the *work* entailed in producing the subject.	Solidaristic. Competitive ascetism. Collective learning.	Cost-optimizers/ profit maximizers. Limits and markets.

Notes
The analytical schema follows Dean (1999) and Oels (2005).
In the columns for individual approaches, the elements in the 'general features' column should also be assumed. We only add elements where they either add to or are slightly different to the general features.

practice do they render visible or invisible? By what instruments, procedures and technologies is rule accomplished? What sorts of knowledge are required to act or brought about through action? What sorts of subjectivities are produced through the action?

Carbon footprinting

Carbon footprinting has become perhaps the elemental form of practice as individuals self-govern in relation to climate change. In order to affect one's practice, so the idea of carbon footprinting at least claims, one must first measure it. There is now thus a huge range of carbon calculators available enabling individuals to make such calculations. Most are online, and many can be reached by links from other sources, such as from newspapers, websites such as that associated with Al Gore's film/PowerPoint presentation *An Inconvenient Truth* (at www.climatecrisis. net), or in books such as the Collins Gem series *Carbon Counter: Calculate Your Carbon Footprint* (Lynas 2007). All carbon calculators share a basic set of features. They enable users to plug in a set of figures regarding energy use – kwh of electricity, cubic metres of gas, litres of petrol, kilometres travelled by air, in particular – to estimate their annual carbon emissions. They usually enable the reader to compare their own emissions to standard figures – the average in their country, the average globally, what would be needed to stabilize the planet, and so on. They often combine this with advice and ideas about how to limit one's footprint. Footprinting of course entails calculative choices which can serve to render visible some things and invisible others. There is always a question concerning what sorts of emissions are to be included and excluded. For example, should the embodied energy in products purchased be included? How should aircraft emissions be calculated given the indirect effects on climate arising from the altitude at which aeroplanes operate?

Carbon footprinting thus serves to contribute to the production of reflexive subjects, reflecting on their carbon emissions and engaging in a sort of calculative practice – combining rough and ready calculations with constant evaluation of the practices that make up the numbers. The numbers are never simply numbers, they represent immediately moralized activities on which the footprinter is invited, exhorted to act. But it is only the first step. What is one to do with these numbers?

Carbon offsetting

Carbon offsetting is the best known of the specific practices that target individuals. It entails the purchase of credits which are claimed to be equivalent to the emissions produced by an individual's actions, either from a specific activity (often offsetting firms target air travel as a source of emissions) or overall emissions for a given period of time. In principle, an individual can offset his or her emissions by any type of carbon unit. In practice, offsetting has come to be associated mainly with the project-based carbon markets, where the money is used to invest in forestry, renewable energy or energy efficiency in developing countries, in return for carbon credits. Offsetting renders visible carbon emissions in particular through their marketization – turning them into credits or commodities, abstract units, which make the individuals' emissions equal to the emissions (apparently) foregone elsewhere. As such it makes the geography of emissions visible, but also the dilemma faced by offsetters; it is always apparent in the websites of carbon offset firms that individuals are engaged in a problematic attempt to compensate for their overconsumption.

Carbon markets can broadly be understood as 'calculable spaces' subjected to particular 'calculative regimes' (Stripple and Lövbrand 2010; see also Miller 1992). A whole series of calculative technologies is deployed to construct the emissions foregone through the investment in an offset project as equivalent to those emissions the individual is attempting to compensate for. These entail in particular: (1) the calculation of baseline emissions (what would have happened in the absence of the investment); (2) the calculation of the 'additionality' of the project – what amount of emissions are therefore foregone through the investment; (3) the means of verifying that the project in fact realizes this promise; (4) the systems of certification (Methodological guidelines, Gold Standard, Voluntary Carbon Standard, etc.) through which verification firms and the CDM executive board operate; (5) the legal/contractual infrastructure to exchange carbon units like a CERs (Certified Emission Reductions) or a VERs (Verified Emissions Reductions) produced by this process.

While it entails such elaborate detailed technical knowledge for the firms operating in the offset market, for the individuals, such knowledge is largely delegated. Rather, individuals largely rely on their already-existing knowledge of how market transactions work, most commonly online transactions. The market gives broad sets of choices about what types of projects to invest in. As to subjectivity, the critiques of carbon offsetting call attention to the way that this produces what might be called a 'carbon displacer' – a subject who simply displaces onto others (via a monetary exchange) the responsibility for reducing overall collective emissions. This is the origin of the claim that the offset market is a market in the 'new indulgences' (Smith 2007). It entails a guilty subject seeking absolution for their sins. But it also engages a charitable subject – the discourse in most offset firms is expressly couched in North–South terms, where the offsetter will not only be absolved of their emitting sins but contributing more positively to development in the South.

Carbon dieting

In 2006, major US environmental NGO the Sierra Club exhorted people to go on a 'low-carbon diet' (Zuckerman 2006). *Time Magazine* picked up the theme (Stukin 2006) in a feature article, as did the Observer Magazine in the UK (Siegle 2007), where the article was complete with a tape running across the pages for measuring your carbs as if they were your waistline (and interspersed with ads for Mediterranean cruises and Hellmans *light* mayonnaise). The chapter in Mayer Hillman's book *How We Can Save the Planet* (Hillman and Fawcett 2004) on managing your personal carbon emissions is entitled 'Watching your figure'. In the US version (Hillman *et al.* 2007), this chapter is called 'Carbon watchers', alluding to Weight-Watchers. An organization called the Empowerment Institute produced an entire book entitled *Low Carbon Diet: A 30 Day Program to Lose 5000 Pounds – Be Part of the Global Warming Solution!* (Gershon 2006).

The explicit analogy of dieting goes beyond the simple exhortation to 'calculate your carbon footprint', as discussed above, although the dieting metaphor appears occasionally in those involved in footprinting. Mark Lynas' *Carbon Counter* (2007) starts with the following line: 'You've heard of counting carbs. This book is about counting carbon.' The dieting metaphor however invokes a whole series of connections between self-denial and sacrifice, self-discipline and virtue. It articulates climate change fundamentally as a question of forgoing things we want in return for getting things which are 'good for us'. Carbon dieting operates through a register of guilt, similarly to offsetting, but without the absolution through market exchange. Dieting is a powerful metaphorical device and much advice about the 'how to' of carbon emission reductions is now given in terms of the diet metaphor.

Carbon dieting proceeds from the logic of measuring individual carbon emissions and renders this visible in two different ways. It makes carbon emissions visible on an individual, emotional level, through the analogy with the management of one's body through dieting. Such a connection is at once visceral (literally) and (allegedly) universal – speaking to the purportedly universal concern of rich Westerners with nutrition, body image and weight. But it also engages with us in a moral register, suggesting that like the management of our body, the management of our emissions is something which we have an obligation to address. The dieting metaphor of course invokes a morality that is at the same time narcissistic – our obligation to reduce our emissions connects immediately to competitive desires to impress those around us. Carbon dieting thus entails a form of subjectivity centred on the relationship between guilt and emotional reward, peer pressure and mutual judgement. It also makes climate action a specifically *bodily* practice, entailing *work*. This marks as a significant contrast to offsetting – while in the latter, emissions can be eliminated through the artifice of the offset project investment, in carbon dieting, one is stuck with one's own bodily practice, the only way to act is through self-discipline and restraint.

Technically, a dieting metaphor draws attention to the minutiae of practice in a way that goes beyond simple carbon footprinting. With footprinting, we could stay at the macro-level of overall consumption; with dieting, we count calories for every single tiny practice. One carbon dieting book for example, contains appendices for carbon emissions from a huge range of practices, distinguishing even between different cuts of meat; beef tenderloin apparently produces 68kg of CO_2 per kg of meat, beef top-round only 42kg (Harrington 2008: 174). Within the rationality of dieting, consumers must know this in order to manage their emitting behaviour. But the relationship of denial to luxury is also established; this knowledge enables them to plan their self-denial in order to allow themselves specific treats. To earn a couple of bottles of wine from New Zealand, you must save 3.6kg of CO_2; to fly from London to Paris, you need to find 88kg (Siegle 2007: 29).

Carbon Rationing Action Groups

Like offsetting, carbon dieting is resolutely individualistic – it engages the individual as the atomized subject of liberal thought – what will *you* do to save the climate? But other practices engage the individual precisely in relation to a collectivity. One such initiative is the development of Carbon Rationing Action Groups (CRAGS). CRAGS started in the UK and are spreading to other places (particularly the United States and Canada) as means through which individuals collectively work to reduce their emissions (Howell 2008; see also Redgrove and Roberts 2007). They have a variety of means of understanding the way that individuals can pursue emissions reduction in a collective context – for some it operates through competition between those individuals as to who can reduce the most, for some it entails an emissions trading system and a collective attribution of emissions budgets to individuals, for others it simply operates through a mutual learning process, sharing information about means of reducing emissions. CRAGS typically set quantitative goals for individuals to reduce their emissions, impose financial penalties on those who don't meet them, and often involve regular meetings where members report on their efforts to reduce their emissions. CRAG groups are also connected with each other through a network website for the group (available at www.carbonrationing.org.uk).

CRAGS make visible the judgement of others about individuals' practices, and force a collective reflection on these practices. They make the practices of others visible, in order to facilitate collective learning. Technically, they rely on Wiki software to enable the sharing of knowledge about emissions reductions, and their members' experience in attempting to reduce their emissions. They also usually entail specific constitutions that articulate individuals to the group in specific ways, and the face-to-face meeting is of course itself a technology through which the individuals interact.

Carbon offsetting schemes entail a certain amount of trust in the technologies and calculations through which projects are defined as equivalent to the offsetter's emissions. In CRAGS, trust is also central, but operates in terms of the reciprocity of group members, their trust that each is making a similar effort. As such, it operates with (and perhaps builds on) solidaristic subjects, seeking to build their emissions reductions efforts in the context of mutual obligations to group members. At the same time, it can operate through a sort of competitive asceticism – not unlike dieting, but without narcissistic overtones, perhaps. It also entails subjects recognizing both their interdependence and their intersubjectivity – who need both the pressure from and the knowledge gained by working with others.

Personal Carbon Allowances

In a speech on 19 July 2006, the UK Environment Secretary, David Miliband, announced that the UK government would look into the option of tradable Personal Carbon Allowances and he provided a thought experiment for how carbon emissions could be driven down:

> Imagine a country where carbon becomes the new currency. We carry bank cards that store both pounds and carbon points. When we buy electricity, gas and fuels we use our carbon points, as well as pounds. To help reduce carbon emissions, the Government would set limits on the amount of carbon that could be used.
>
> (Miliband 2006)

Personal Carbon Allowances were floated as an idea in 2006, but remain only an idea; no state is seriously developing proposals for them. But they are a logical extension of the premise of neoliberal climate governance – to extend the logic of market efficiency underpinning emissions trading schemes, so far only applied at firm level, to individuals. PCAs is therefore a 'downstream' system that target emissions from individual energy consumption. In a PCA system, individuals would be allocated a specific amount of permits to emit CO_2, which would, as in the various emissions trading systems already operating, be tradable. Individuals who were able to reduce their emissions below the level of the permits they held (or whose emissions were lower for other reasons, such as poverty) would be able to sell the surplus to those who were not.

They also reflect a significantly more egalitarian logic than the neoliberal policy alternative of carbon taxes. PCAs would allocate allowances evenly, enabling for the most part the poor to have surplus allowances which they could sell to rich overconsumers. As such their logic is worth exploring here. Personal Carbon Allowances extend part of the logic of CRAGS to the regulatory sphere. They remain collectivist, but lose both the voluntary character and thus the way that the inter-subjective character of CRAGS builds on the normative identities of the participants, and enables individuals to learn from and with others. In its place it makes the individual's relation to a national space visible – PCAs would be operated by states acting through their individual citizens.[2] The market character would also be transformed in consequence – instead of being a small-scale market amongst specific individuals, it becomes an abstract market amongst anonymous actors.

As with other emissions trading markets, a PCA scheme entails a series of technical questions concerning the rules for allocating permits, the rules for trading allowances amongst individuals (or between individuals and firms), penalties for non-compliance, decisions about the boundaries of the system (the geographical scope, who has to participate, what sorts of emissions are included and excluded). Such technical features entail individuals who need to develop skills and knowledge of how to translate their CO_2 emissions (as calculated through footprinting techniques) into money figures, to know where their emissions are in relation to a limit, and to be able to engage in trading activity to sell surplus or buy needed allowances. It thus entails subjects who are cost-optimizers or even profit-maximizers, incorporating into their daily carbon-emitting practice a calculation about the cost-implications in terms of permit requirements for each activity.

Conclusions

We have outlined and compared five different practices governance that aims at calculating, measuring and managing emissions of greenhouse gases at the level of the individual (footprinting, offsetting, dieting, rationing and trading with Carbon Rationing Action Groups or through a system of Personal Carbon Allowances). These five sets of practices are *problematizations* of individuals' emissions of carbon dioxide. Emissions are seen as a problem that need to be rectified and the issue is articulated in a fairly formalized language, such as tons per person. These practices, or technologies of carbon government, are principally interesting because they shape individual subjects through exhorting them to manage their climate-related practices themselves. We argue that there is an emergent government of carbon that entails the 'conduct of carbon conduct' through moulding and mobilizing a certain subjectivity (the individual as carbon emitter) to govern their own emissions in various ways – as counters, displacers, dieters, communitarians or citizens. This carbon governmentality is enabled through calculative practices that simultaneously totalizes (aggregating social practices, overall greenhouse gas emissions) and individualizes (producing reflexive subjects actively managing their greenhouse gas practices).

We have articulated a politics of climate change that is largely invisible in contemporary discussions, which focus on the 'policy architecture' (e.g. Aldy and Stavins 2007; Compston and Bailey 2008). Our examples of climate politics do not entail 'power over', with the state, or an international treaty, enforcing rules over states, companies and individuals, but rather acting through all such subjects, shaping not only their behaviour but their internal rationalities, identities, what they fundamentally regard as 'normal' behaviour. The element that we have focused on draws this point out particularly clearly. The various practices of carbon footprinting, rationing, offsetting, and so on, all share this character. They articulate individuals as agents managing their own carbon practice in relation to an articulated global public goal of minimizing climate change. This is closely connected to the 'privatized' character of many of these elements, but the critiques widely seen of such 'marketized' governance misses the mark. To operate by shaping and producing individuals as particular types of subjects (managing their carbon budgets, etc.) is precisely how power operates in neoliberalism. Rather than by using individual freedom as a depoliticization strategy, it acts through channelling ways that individuals exercise their freedoms (Rose 1999). 'Freedom in the marketplace' goes hand in hand with increasingly elaborate practices of self-monitoring and management. And this relationship between market freedom and governmentality applies not only to individuals but to firms, states and others. In fact, in a climate change context, it is difficult to envisage how limiting global warming to 2°C (emission reductions by 50–75 per cent below 1990 levels by 2050) might be avoided without such an intensive, managerial (and self-managerial) effort.

Notes

1 This is a shortened and revised version of a previous article, published in *Environment and Planning D: Society and Space* 28(2): 341–362. We thank the publishers, Pion, and the editor, Stuart Elden, for permisson to reproduce the paper here. The original benefited from comments by Sara Kalm and from colleagues at the fourth ECPR general conference in Pisa, Italy, 6–8 September, 2007, and at the ENERGI conference on 'energizing markets', Copenhagen Business School, October 2008. We are grateful in particular to excellent research assistance by Philippe Descheneau.
2 While the national community has often been the assumed entity in the design of different PCA schemes, this might change with the contemporary voluntary trends towards engaging individuals in relation to different collectivities (such as CRAGs). The Royal Society of Arts (RSA) foresee in their final report a localization of PCA to community based carbon trading. Such schemes would be 'more likely to be cost effective and would not compromise the unique selling point of being able to change people's behaviour and attitudes' (Prescott 2008: 4).

References

Aldy, J.E. and Stavins, R.N. (2007) *Architectures for Agreement: Addressing Global Climate Change in the Post-Kyoto World*, Cambridge: Cambridge University Press.

Compston, H. and Bailey, I. (eds) (2008) *Turning Down the Heat: The Politics of Climate Policy in Affluent Democracies*, London: Palgrave.

Dean, M. (1999) *Governmentality*, London: Sage.

Foucault, M. (1982) 'The subject and power', in H. Dreyfus and P. Rabinow (eds) *Michel Foucault: Beyond Structuralism and Hermeneutics*, Hemel Hempstead: Harvester Wheatsheaf, pp. 208–226.

Foucault, M. (1991) 'Governmentality', in G. Burchell, C. Gordon and P. Miller (eds) *The Foucault Effect*, Chicago: The University of Chicago Press, pp. 87–104.

Gershon, D. (2006) *The Low-Carbon Diet: A 30 Day Program to Lose 5000 Pounds – Be Part of the Global Warming Solution!*, Woodstock: Empowerment Institute.

Goodall, C. (2007) *How to Live a Low-Carbon Life: The Individual's Guide to Stopping Climate Change*, London: Earthscan.

Gordon, C. (1991) 'Governmental rationality: an introduction', in G. Burchell, C. Gordon and P. Miller (eds) *The Foucault Effect*, Chicago: The University of Chicago Press, pp. 1–51.

Harrington, J. (2008) *The Climate Diet: How You Can Cut Carbon, Cut Costs, and Save the Planet*, London: Earthscan.

Hillman, M. and Fawcett, T. (2004) *How We Can Save the Planet*, London: Penguin.

Hillman, M. with Fawcett, T. and Rajan, S.C. (2007) *The Suicidal Planet: How to Prevent Global Climate Catastrophe*, New York: St Martins Press.

Howell, R. (2008) *The Experience of Carbon Rationing Action Groups: Implications for a Personal Carbon Allowances Policy*, London: UK Energy Research Centre.

Lemke, T. (2001) 'The birth of bio-politics: Michel Foucault's lecture at the Collège de France on neo-liberal governmentality', *Economy and Society* 30: 190–207.

Lohmann, L. (2006) 'Carbon trading: a critical conversation on climate change, privatization and power', *Development Dialogue* 48: 1–359.

Lynas, M. (2007) *Carbon Counter: Calculate Your Carbon Footprint*, Glasgow: HarperCollins.

Marshall, G. (2007) *Carbon Detox: Your Step-by-Step Guide to Getting Real about Climate Change*, London: Gaia Books.

Merlingen, M. (2006) 'Foucault and world politics: promises and challenges of extending governmentality theory to the European and beyond', *Millennium: Journal of International Studies* 35: 181–196.

Miliband, D. (2006) 'Government to look at personal carbon allowances to combat rising domestic emissions', News Release 19 July 2006. Online. Available at: www.defra.gov.uk/news/2006/060719b.htm (retrieved: 22.7.2006).

Miller, P. (1992) 'Accounting and objectivity: the invention of calculating selves and calculable spaces', *Annals of Scholarship* 9(1/2): 61–68.

Miller, P. and Rose, N. (2008) *Governing the Present*, Cambridge: Polity Press.

Oels, A. (2005) 'Rendering climate change governable: from biopower to advanced liberal government?', *Journal of Environmental Policy and Planning* 7(3): 185–207.

Prescott, M. (2008) 'A persuasive climate: personal trading and changing lifestyles', The Royal Society for the Encouragement of Arts, Manufactures and Commerce (RSA).

Reay, D. (2006) *Climate Change Begins at Home: Life on the Two-Way Street of Global Warming*, London: Macmillan.

Redgrove, Z. and Roberts S. (2007) 'Making carbon personal? A snapshot of community initiatives', a report to Defra, Centre for Sustainable Energy.

Rose, N.S. (1999) *Powers of Freedom: Reframing Political Thought*, Cambridge: Cambridge University Press.

Rose, N., O'Malley, P. and Valverde, M. (2006) 'Governmentality', Annual Review of Law and Social Science 2(1): 83–104.

Rose-Redwood, R.S. (2006) 'Governmentality, geography, and the geo-coded world', *Progress in Human Geography* 30(4): 469–486.

Rutherford, S. (2007) 'Green governmentality: insights and opportunities in the study of nature's rule', *Progress in Human Geography* 31(3): 291–307.

Seyfang, G. (2007) 'Personal carbon trading: lessons from complementary currencies', Norwich: Centre for Social and Economic Research on the Global Environment, University of East Anglia.

Siegle, L. (2007) 'The low-carbon diet (or how to lose half a tonne in just one month)', *Observer Magazine*, 21 January, 24–29.

Smith, K, (2007) 'The carbon neutral myth: offset indulgences for your climate sins', Amsterdam: Carbon Trade Watch.

Spence, C. (2005) *Global Warming: Personal Solution for a Healthy Planet*, London: Palgrave Macmillan.

Stripple, J. and Lövbrand, E. (2010) 'Carbon market governance beyond the public-private divide', in F. Biermann, P. Pattberg and F. Zelli (eds) *Global Climate Governance Post 2012: Architectures, Agency and Adaptation*, Cambridge: Cambridge University Press, 165–183.

Stukin, S. (2006) 'The low-carbon diet', Time, 30 October. Online. Available at: www.time.com/time/health/article/0,8599,1552237,00.html (retrieved 27.11.2012).

Zuckerman, S. (2006) 'My low-carbon diet', Sierra Magazine, September/October. Online. Available at: www.sierraclub.org/sierra/200609/carbon.asp (retrieved: 19.3.2012).

10 Governing knowledge through START and the expansion of global environmental change research

Ola Uhrqvist

Introduction

Early in December 1990, 18 men from the most industrialized countries, plus one from China, two from Brazil and one from Venezuela, gathered at the Rockefeller Foundation's conference facility in Bellagio, Italy. Their task was to establish and coordinate a global research network to meet the needs of the emerging research agendas concerning global environmental change (IGBP 1991). This network was to strengthen the research conducted by the World Climate Research Programme established in 1980 and that of two emerging research agendas. In the mid 1980s, the International Geosphere-Biosphere Programme (IGBP) had set out to predict the Earth system, and around 1990 the Human Dimensions of Global Environmental Change Programme widened the natural science agenda by adding social components. All three programmes were dependent on reliable, long-term global data. In 1992, based on the results of the Bellagio meeting, the three programmes jointly launched *SysTem for Analysis, Research and Training* (START) to organize regional research networks that would enable worldwide coordination of global environmental change research and policy (IGBP 1993b). However, despite its initial global ambitions, START today works mainly in Africa, Asia and Oceania, annually engaging over 1,000 scientists and policy-makers. By tracing the history of START, this chapter highlights how tensions between scientific rationalities and practical challenges emerge as regimes of practice expand.

In this chapter, I examine the constitutive effects of the 'knowledge infrastructure' (Edwards 2010) produced by the START programme. Drawing on a performative understanding of knowledge derived from sociological studies of scientific knowledge and post-humanist thought, I trace discourses on governing of the START project's network of people, artefacts, and institutions to understand how it has shaped understandings of global change, generating certain ways of seeing and knowing the global environment. Unlike previous studies of the role and influence of epistemic communities in global environmental politics (Haas 1992), my analysis rests on a post-structuralist understanding of how the performativity of scientific knowledge emerges in regimes of scientific practice.

The connection between knowledge and politics has been analysed in a range of ways. Liberal approaches have attributed actors the ability to use scientific knowledge as a tool to advance various interests and reveal how strategic networks are formed to influence policy-making (Haas 1992). In her analysis of the Montreal Protocol on Substances that Deplete the Ozone Layer, Karen Litfin elevates the 'role of scientific discourses in regime formation' (Litfin 1994: 7). This step takes the analysis beyond the rational and autonomous actor and shows how scientific knowledge and other cognitive factors enable and restrict the formation of policy regimes. Based on the importance of images that shape scientific and lay understandings of the objects to be governed, Jasanoff analyses how the global images produced by the IGBP, IPCC and other international institutions can 'serve as a basis for global policy' (Jasanoff 2004: 45). Although the analysis mostly concerns the beneficial and dangerous effects of the global images produced, she argues that more attention needs to be paid to the processes that win acceptance for these images. Following up that argument, this chapter takes a slight detour from the usual analytics of climate governance and ventures into territories where scientific practices produce trustworthy images of the Earth as a calculable and governable object.

The IGBP envisioned a 'truly global study' (IGBP 1986: 2) to ensure the capacity to predict the Earth system. However, though its research agenda was formulated mainly by scientists in the United States and Europe, it had to be operationalized on a global scale. Analysing documents related to START from 1986 when the planning began to 2002 when the network was consolidated visualize how this global knowledge infrastructure problematized the role of scientists, their practices and the connections with politics. Rutherford (1999: 117) argues that relations between power and knowledge need to be understood through the dynamic social interactions in which they are shaped. Closely examining the emergent knowledge infrastructure of scientific networks therefore offers a key for understanding the discourses operating at the science–policy interface. The present analysis draws on accounts of how performative knowledge – or what Foucault called power/knowledge – emerges as fields of relationships in which ideas, subjectivities, practices and artefacts shape each other (Foucault 1991: 102).

This chapter also traces the history of START to grasp the rationalities of Earth system science emerging in the governing of the processes rendering global environmental change thinkable and trustworthy. START has been portrayed as a 'truly equal collaboration between scientists from developed and developing countries' (START 1999: 5). I analyse the extent to which the knowledge infrastructure of START enabled such equitable collaboration. The chapter is organized as follows: after introducing the chapter's theory and method, I first consider how the problematization changed from a highly centralized science-driven project to a more regionalized and policy-related project around 1990. Second, the chapter draws attention to how subjectivities related to policy-making and funding were produced when START's networks were put into practice after 1992. A central finding is that the character of START's networks changed considerably as they expanded among researchers and into the science–policy contexts of the developing world. In light of the social production of trust and performative power in knowledge infrastructures, this is understood as both a project aiming to govern policy and scientific practice in developing countries and, simultaneously, as the expansion of a research agenda seeking to decentralize the scientific practices involved in knowing the planet as a governable object.

Theoretical approach

This chapter draws on two main analytical traditions to understand the emergence of performativity and power relationships in global scientific networks. The first tradition stems from the sociology of scientific knowledge (SSK), which analyses scientific truths as the result of social processes. The perspective of the 'strong programme' of SSK is that scientific programmes produce their own rationality (Bloor 1976). This insight provides this chapter with a basis of methodological relativism according to which truth claims and authority are understood as dependent on a range of social practices, but not on any intuitive recognition of 'true' reality. Drawing on SSK and historical analysis, Shapin and Schaffer (1985) argue that science is as dependent on systematic scepticism as on the production of systematic trust. Without trust, scientific networks would crumble. So how is trust produced? In connection with his analysis of governmentalities, Foucault suggests that an important factor is the knowledge that emerges in processes by which people try to make sense of and organize reality to make it governable, i.e. enable strategies to reach desired ends (Foucault 1991). Rooted in this will to power, any production of knowledge therefore contains intentions and direction (Foucault 1976: 95). The institutions of global environmental change research are thus both rooted in the imagery and rationalities of the Earth system and produce legitimacy by enacting this perspective.

Clearly, operationalizing this post-structural understanding of truth requires another view of the results of knowledge production. Underlying the above assumption is the claim that identifying objects, analysing them and putting them back together risks overlooking how these objects emerge in relation to each other. Foucault (1991) argues for a shift from studying objects to studying fields of power. Karen Barad (2003) develops this point, asserting that matters come to matter not by virtue of their essence, but in tension between temporary assemblages. In other words, we should not focus on what objects *are* but what they *do*. This is also found in her post-humanist understanding of performativity in discursive practices, in which speech acts do not represent but rather perform reality (Barad 2003). Drawing on Foucault and Barad, this chapter directs attention to governing practices as working in performative fields of power enabled by and enabling the Earth system concept.

A second and closely related approach drawn on here also concerns the links between the ideational and material dimensions of scientific knowledge practices. Examining how knowledge travels in space and time (Jasanoff and Martello 2004; Mahony and Hulme 2011) provides tools for localizing scientific practices. To that end, this chapter draws primarily on the concept of global knowledge infrastructure. As a concept, global knowledge infrastructure directs attention to the circulation of scientific information in coupled technological–human networks for data gathering, analysis and distribution. Such an understanding of START as an expanding research network provides a frame for analysing the discourse about the practices involved in combining data gathered from all parts of the planet – land, sea and sky. From this vantage point, the infrastructure mobilized by START emerges as a technology of government that enables the assembling and mobility of knowledge and legitimacy (Ilcan and Phillips 2008). From this perspective, understanding possible experiences of global environmental change is dependent on practices that enable the stabilization of particular images and ways of calculating, i.e. the social production of truth and trust.

Research strategy

Drawing on Foucault (1991), this chapter argues that governing should be understood as any calculated attempt to arrange things to convenient ends. Although studies of governmentality usually turn to the practices within the state (Foucault 1991; Miller and Rose 2008), their analytical tools are equally useful in studies of any calculated attempt to conduct the conduct in a specific domain, such as science. Analogously, START is interpreted as the institutionalization and intensification of governmental rationalities and practices already present in the network. START is especially interesting from a power perspective since participation in it is voluntary. However, analytics of governmentalities have problematized this liberal idea of autonomy. By analysing how governing through freedom works, studies have demonstrated that subjects are produced in particular ways to fit these kinds of governing practices (Dean 2007). The organization's ability to harmonize a global research network requires that scientists and others accept being arranged or governed in a particular way. Simultaneously, the emergence and stabilization of START highlights the production of subjectivities and rationalities in a phase that is often overlooked in the interpretation of climate governance discourses. In order to understand Earth system rationalities through how they materialize and expand performativity the main strategy in this chapter is to provide a genealogical study of the discourses on governing the practices of START's knowledge infrastructure.

Using START as a lens also allows me to analyse an empirical material and an organization previously studied only briefly. The analysis is based on the IGBP's Global Change Reports from 1986 to 2002, a central information channel by which the IGBP network presented important meetings and new projects. Three periodicals were also examined: the *Global Change Newsletter*, 1989–2002; the *START Newsletter*, 1997–2002; and *IHDP Update*, 1996–2002. These periodicals enabled the tracing of events and discussions within the START networks. All four sources serve as central channels for coordinating the global environmental change research networks and are as such central elements of the START programme's global knowledge infrastructure. Aiming for both internal communication between scientists and external communication with policy-makers and funders, this material constitutes well-considered formulations reproducing the rationalities of the relevant practices. It is rich material in which to trace problematizations of the knowledge infrastructure, its subjectivities and governing rationalities. Central to the governing of the START networks, these documents are understood as a part of the practices that stabilized and fostered the authority of this emerging global network. Accessing the material dimensions of the knowledge infrastructure is more difficult. This chapter uses the argument of science and technology studies (STS), that science as a social practice has to be located somewhere (Shapin 1998; Mahony and Hulme 2011), as a lens through which to see how these practical aspects are approached.

Acknowledging that all knowledge is situated (Haraway 1988) enables the study of START as a social process while questioning the positions that enable my interpretation of the material. Therefore, avoiding the 'God trick' – i.e. constructing a view from nowhere (Shapin 1998) – calls for transparent points of departure. Situated in studies of governmentality, the document analysis asks: what governance objects and subjects have been produced in problematizing the START networks, and how are they related to each other? I first examine how the practical needs of global change research are presented in the texts and how the subjects of Earth system governance are portrayed. Then these presentations are interpreted by filtering them, first, through the lens of Shapin and Schaffer's (1985) understanding of the social production of truth and trust. A second round of interpretation relates the objects and subjects to the problematization of practical conditions for gathering, circulating and analysing data informed by Edwards' (2010) knowledge infrastructure. Here my focus will be on the governing of the network, not on the research per se. The assumption is that the documents manifest problematizations of ongoing research practices including both proposals and the evaluation of strategies for changing these.

From a network of geo-biosphere observatories to regional research centres

Closely connected to the emerging research into the Earth system in the mid 1980s was the rationality of establishing a coordinated global research network (IGBP 1986: 4). The coordination and disciplining of this network received significant attention in order to secure long-term datasets suitable for predictively modelling the Earth system (Uhrqvist and Lövbrand forthcoming). Global databases had been set up by the United Nations Environmental Programme in the 1970s, but the IGBP saw a need for long time series of 'coordinated physical, chemical and biological measurements' (IGBP 1986: 7). The first network proposal that emerged under the auspices of IGBP was a 'network of geo-biosphere observatories' (IGBP 1987: 13).

Growing out of the rationalities in the planning process of the IGBP, this network primarily reflected the scientific challenges of modelling the Earth system. At the launch of the IGBP in Stockholm in 1988, a very hierarchical structure was outlined to harmonize the gathering and distribution of data in a consistent manner (IGBP 1988a: 20). The nodes in the network were supposed to ensure the long-term global implementation of the IGBP (1988b: 27). These five to ten nodes were to function as regional research and training centres as well as fostering cooperation across national and disciplinary boundaries. Training was supposed to ensure that the interdisciplinary objectives of the IGBP were put into practice (IGBP 1989a: 122). This in turn problematized current scientific practices and aimed to foster a knowledge production based on voluntary, interdisciplinary and technologically advanced global knowledge infrastructure. This infrastructure echoed the self-understanding that the emerging global change research community was on the brink of developing a new paradigm for research (Malone and Roederer 1985: xi). The architecture of the network also strengthened the understanding of scientists as being in an exclusive position to formulate relevant aims and results that could then be made 'available to the global community' (IGBP 1988b: 104).

The early research agenda of IGBP did not problematize the possibility that the interests of scientists in developing countries might differ from those of their industrialized-world counterparts. IGBP stated that the 'transfer of new technological advances in experimental research, data management, and simulation modelling are only a few areas where local and regional researchers could benefit from access to the GBO [geo-biosphere observatory] network' (IGBP 1988b: 107). In the report from the first meeting of the IGBP's Scientific Advisory Council in 1988, the sections on the global network and on the least developed countries were clearly separate (IGBP 1989a: 127). Soon after the launch of IGBP this research agenda was questioned. Noting that just one of 19 members of the special committee planning the IGBP was from the southern hemisphere, a workshop in Africa raised questions about the implementation of the geo-biosphere observatories (IGBP 1989b: 10). Scientists in the southern hemisphere called for a programme more open to different relationships to global changes and global change research in different parts of the world. This seems to have had an effect on the IGBP planning process.

In the 1990 presentation of the IGBP's initial core projects, regional research centres (RRCs) were promoted instead of geo-biosphere observatories (IGBP 1990), signalling a shift in how the organization of global research was discussed. 'Unless RRCs are established, it is likely that developing country scientists will be only involved in data collection and will be outside the mainstream of global change research including participation in data analysis, interpretation and modelling' (IGBP 1990: 11–13). This double problematization stressed the need for scientists at the RRCs to become fully integrated in the entire knowledge infrastructure. Simultaneously it signalled that this had not been the case earlier. Relationships to policy also became more central. These changes in desired ends performed new attributions of roles and responsibilities in the expanding network. As stated in a 1990 IGBP report, to have impact on policy, global change research and Earth system models had to 'be interpreted in the regional context' (IGBP 1990: 11–13). Clearly, the policy impact of the Earth system research agenda was seen as a problem in need of governing when it came to both scientific and policy practices.

A global knowledge infrastructure requires economic resources and, unlike many other institutions, IGBP and the other two global environmental change programmes had very limited resources of their own. They had to compete for funding in regular funding regimes (Kwa 2006). IGBP's early planning did not problematize funding. Soon, however, questions of securing resources were considered in the governing of the network and the relationship to a range of local funders was rendered problematic. Funding had to be secured without jeopardizing the scientific rationale: 'RRC activities should be directed by global change scientific concerns and IGBP Core Project needs as opposed to individual interests of funding bodies' (IGBP 1990: 11–16). To attract major outside donors, it was also seen as important that governmental bodies specify 'global change research to be a national priority' (IGBP 1990: 11–17). These formulations strengthened the image of a science-driven project producing a rationality to which other regimes of practices, such as funding, were supposed to adapt.

With this background, it is time to return to the Bellagio workshop of 3–7 December 1990. The task was to organize the global system of research networks (IGBP 1991). The topic had ascended the political and scientific agenda in the wake of IPCC work noting that greater developing country involvement was needed to raise the awareness of policy-makers in these countries (IPCC 1990; IGBP 1991). So, 'policy-makers' was produced as an object that had to be governed and involved regional researchers as a technology to do so. In Bellagio climate, bio-geochemical and social scientists jointly developed a shared knowledge infrastructure for global change research. IGBP implementation was now to be governed through 'a global system of *regional* networks' (IGBP 1991: 5). The new framing departed from regional networks and the SysTem for Analysis, Research and Training (START) project emerged to harmonize and coordinate these at the global level. The architecture of START expressed emphasis on the need to mobilize financial and human resources, implying increased education and the inclusion of 'more members from the developing countries' (IGBP 1991: 3).

Still, nothing had changed in the central project rationality: 'the underlying objective of an RRN [Regional Research Network] is to mobilize scientific manpower and resources to address scientific questions concerned with global environmental change, as these are defined by the Core Projects', continuing that 'any regional network must also take into account the societal, cultural, and political needs of the region' (IGBP 1991: 7). It was also argued that each RRC should bring together policy-makers and funders to present results and get feedback on 'how well the RRC is serving the needs of the region' (IGBP 1991: 13). In this closer connection between science and policy, it is the scientific community that takes the initiative of organizing the rapprochement. Relating to the concept of 'analytical responsibility' (Foucault 2007: 227), studies of governmentality usually find that this responsibility is assumed by the state (Hannah 2000; Whitehead 2009). Here START gives the impression of a science-driven project formulated in the most industrialized regions and then implemented in the rest of the world due to the rationalities of data gathering and ensuring policy impact.

The tracing of START's history up to this time highlights the challenge of securing a stable global knowledge infrastructure. START's global reach was dependent on its ability to balance a research agenda primarily formulated in

Governing knowledge through START 159

the industrialized countries with the positions of scientists, funders and policy-makers in the rest of the world. In producing the network, developing regions were assigned a more active role, but there was still a clear emphasis on the command structure in the system of networks in which the RRCs' scientific committees were appointed and monitored by the START Standing Committee. The need to ensure 'full complementary interaction both within and among the RRNs' (IGBP 1991: 29) indicates that research practices were by no means seen as self-regulating, due to the performative impact of the agenda of Earth system science.

So far the planning had primarily concerned scientists, but with the Bellagio report, START was to be implemented and made operational. The world was divided into 14 networks based on the research needs of the core projects, bio-geochemical characteristics, and national boundaries (IGBP 1991: 18). The resulting map (see Figure 10.1) proposed regions unfamiliar to the geographical frameworks known by policy analysts and in that sense challenged nation states as the taken-for-granted object of knowledge and governance in a world characterized by global change.

However, the scientific community was not alone in arranging global change research networks at this time. In 1990, US President Bush organized a conference and 'invited the countries of the world to join the United States in creating three regional networks' (APN 1999: 5). After 1992, the proposed governmental Inter-American Institute for Global Change Research shouldered the responsibility for organizing global change research on both American continents (Liverman 2009). As shown in Figure 10.2, this disrupted the rationality informing the Bellagio meeting and excluded the activities of START, while the networks organized in Europe and Japan were designed to work alongside START in coordinating research in their regions (APN 1999; Contzen and Ghazi 1994). In all regions, cooperation continued with the core projects of the international programmes. In the redrawn map of scientific networks, northern Europe organized a scientific network, but this soon faded away and left little documentation of its activities.

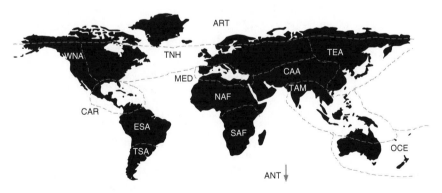

Figure 10.1 Regional research networks proposed by START in 1991 (based on IGBP 1991: 18).

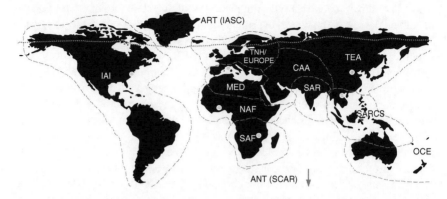

Figure 10.2 Regional networks under development in 1994 (based on IGBP 1994: 116).

Overall, the implementation of START indicates how an initially uniform network structure could change into a heterogeneous system of cooperating but not necessarily coordinated networks. Discussions under the auspices of START now turned to institutionalizing interdisciplinary and stable research networks in the developing world.

Fine-tuning the roles in the regional research networks

The production of the global knowledge infrastructure as an object of government had undergone significant change including the adjustment to the intergovernmental initiatives, closely connected to the funding agencies. START became operational in 1992 with its secretariat in Washington, DC and was working to expand the Earth system research agenda into new regions (IGBP 1994). Recalibration to help the developing world brought a new set of subjectivities to be governed for the sake of a harmonized global network. The rationalities of government strove to arrange the relationships between the functions of governing, science, policy-making and funding to achieve a performative whole. As the research network was implemented in Africa, Asia and Oceania, the division among scientists, policy-makers and funders became more complex. Although the establishment of RRCs had to be based on long-term government support (IGBP 1994), it was clear that developing countries lacked funding to prioritize such research. External funding had to be provided. START itself was not a funding agency; rather, 'it should facilitate funding through links with the relevant agencies' (IGBP 1993a). The primary agency in mind was the International Group of Funding Agencies for Global Change Research (IGFA) established in 1990. It had emerged to reduce tension arising from the mismatch between national science funding regimes and the global cooperation characteristic of Earth system science. IGFA also tipped the balance regarding formulating research agendas from the international programmes back to national funding agencies (Kwa 2006).

When global change research expanded beyond the core of industrialized countries, the impact on regional policy emerged as a problem. It was repeatedly noted that local decision-makers seemed to disregard results if there was no significant regional participation in their production. START sought to ensure that regional scientists would be involved in research, from planning to synthesis, to develop the 'knowledge and information required by their own governments to formulate effective national policies' (IGBP 1992: 13). There was also the understanding that scientific knowledge of global change would only have policy impact if developed into regional scenarios and policy strategies in cooperation with regional policy-makers (Knight 1999: 17; IGBP 1998: 8). Interpreting these strategies of involving policy-makers in light of Litfin's (1994) emphasis on the power of discourse at the science–policy interface suggests that the performativity of discourse must include intersectional practices that develop trust.

As Edwards (2010) has demonstrated, producing global predictive models was (and still is) a very expensive activity affordable only in the richest countries. Bringing trust in global models to the developing countries was dealt with by means of an extensive fellowship programme in which promising researchers from developing countries could visit advanced modelling environments in the United States, Europe, and Japan (START 1999: 22). Again, the ambition to inform policy is interesting from the perspective of 'analytical responsibility', where legitimate governing is based on the responsibility to know what is needed to know. As START strove to invite policy-makers into the new partnership, it was still not the governments in these parts of the world that welcomed the international programmes, but the other way around. However, motivated by a perceived mistrust of Western perspectives, the programmes avoided giving the advice themselves, but instead educated promising local scientists to provide the link.

Understanding the performativity of scientific knowledge as a matter of the production of trust rather than truth (Shapin and Schaffer 1985), the difficulties of achieving policy impact must be interpreted as social. In this light, fields of power/knowledge can be understood to be based on trust developed in local relationships and practices of governing; achieving performativity then must either replace or transform the knowledge production processes related to fields of governing. START shifted from the first strategy to the second, which suggests that the power of local relationships of trust outweighed the 'truth' produced by global models.

A global knowledge infrastructure as an object of government

How does scientific knowledge become performative? Here this grand question is approached by analysing how the production of this global scientific knowledge transformed as an object of government. The tensions produced between an initial scientific vision of predictive Earth system models and the, assumed necessary, geographical expansion of global environmental change research networks provides a fertile ground for a genealogical discourse analysis. By tracing the history of START, this chapter has sought to visualize rationalities of government embedded in the production of global change knowledge. Both Litfin (1994) and Jasanoff

(2004) argue that the connection between scientific knowledge and policy-making must be studied as a discursive field. Combined with Barad's (2003) understanding of performativity it implies that discourse must be understood in relation to how scientific knowledge is attributed with authority in local regimes of practice. By doing so, this analysis ventures beyond the discourses at the science–policy interface and looks into the transforming field of power/knowledge that enables the co-production of scientific knowledge and trust.

The analysis indicates that a centralized and homogeneous global network of geo-biosphere observatories had to be reframed as more decentralized to perform scientific networks in developing countries. A second shift in the rationalities governing the network was the reformulation from a clear division between scientists, funders and policy-makers towards a network characterized by close relationships. In that context, rationality also shifted from scientific efficiency producing universal truth to a rationality of producing trust and relevance in different contexts. This could be a practical implication of what Kwa (2006) describes as a situation in which the funding agencies started to demand interdisciplinarity and policy relevance. Understanding global environmental change research as embedded in this changing context is an important component in understanding the performativity of this kind of knowledge.

The empirical material also suggests that these changes can be interpreted as the recalibration of strategies of government that emerged when the network widened and trust in the produced knowledge had to be renegotiated. The 'analytical responsibility' taken by START when inviting regional policy-makers, instead of the reverse, suggests that it was not regional funders that pushed for more policy relevance. 'Regional policy-makers' was produced as a subject and attributed an increasingly central role in defining and evaluating future research. Meanwhile promising scientists in the developing world were given grants to visit key institutions in the knowledge infrastructure to interact with the research frontier. These grants, encouraging interdisciplinarity, advanced technology and international cooperation, can be interpreted as a technology of government 'conducting the conduct' of a new generation of researcher by simultaneously exemplifying ideal science and rewarding role models. The efforts to establish networks of regional scientists and policy-makers were explicitly used as a technique to overcome suspicion of Western science said to exist among regional policy-makers. These two threads, Western dominance and increasing regional influence, coexist and are now embodied in the global knowledge infrastructure of START.

The analysis also suggests that performative research practices works on local scales where power/knowledge performs and preforms in networks. Central to the rationality of Earth system science is the importance of being relevant to policy-making. The production of this kind of knowledge became an object of government, and START emerged as a technology to conduct the conduct of researchers, funders and policy-makers worldwide. However, the limited success – at least considering the initial ambition – indicates that the rationale of a disciplined global network was not as performative as initially envisioned among IGBP planners. Recalibrations had to be made to cope with regional tensions, funders and governmental interventions. Instead, START translated into a project for bringing global environmental change research into the developing world. The continuous problematization of subjects and objects of government in START activities clearly indicates that there was little faith in a naturally emerging network. Scientists, funders and networks had to be governed to keep them in line with the research objectives of the core projects. Dean (2007) suggests that liberalism is governed thorough freedom but subjects first have to be conducted in a particular way to be able to live together as free. This argument fits well with the findings in this chapter. Visible in START, the challenges of predicting the Earth system produced an understanding of mutual dependency that made governing a network of independent scientists possible, even if roles and responsibilities had to be recalibrated.

This chapter has traced the history of START as an embodiment of rationalities and technologies of government related to the scientific regimes of practice that, from the mid 1980s, produced a global knowledge infrastructure to develop predictive models of the Earth system. The chapter illustrates how the governing of this infrastructure depends on and co-produces governable objects and subjectivities. It also shows how the relationships between these components became increasingly decentralized and intertwined as the infrastructure was implemented in order to influence policy. However, throughout the studied period (1984–2002), the commitment remained firm that the networks was needed and should be coordinated to meet the scientific needs formulated in the core projects and to have policy impact. In conclusion, this chapter argues that in '(de)constructing the greenhouse', it is valuable to complement the discourses at the science–policy interface with analytics of the rationalities emerging in the government of tensions between scientific knowledge, visions and practice in 'knowledge infrastructures'. Infrastructures that perform trust and, thereby, potentially, perform policy impact as well.

Acknowledgements

I would like to thank Linköping University's LiU FoAss programme for its financial support and all commentators on earlier versions of this chapter for their valuable recommendations.

References

APN (1999) *Asia-Pacific Network for Global Change Research Strategic Plan 1999–2004*, Kobe: APN-secretariat.
Barad, K. (2003) 'Posthumanist Performativity: Toward an Understanding of How Matter Comes to Matter', *Signs: Journal of Women in Culture and Society*, 28: 801–830.
Bloor, D. (1976) *Knowledge and Social Imagery*, London: Routledge & Kegan Paul.
Contzen, J. and Ghazi, A. (1994) 'The Role of the European Union in Global Change Research', *Ambio*, 23: 101–103.
Dean, M. (2007) *Governing Societies*, Maidenhead: Open University Press.

Edwards, P.N. (2010) *A Vast Machine: Computer Models, Climate Data, and the Politics of Global Warming*, Cambridge, MA: MIT Press.

Foucault, M. (1976) *The History of Sexuality*, New York: Pantheon Books.

Foucault, M. (1991) 'Governmentality', in: G. Burchell and P. Rabinow (eds) *The Foucault Effect: Studies in Governmentality: with Two Lectures by and an Interview with Michael Foucault*, London: Harvester Wheatsheaf, 87–104.

Foucault, M. (2007) *Security, Territory, Population – Lectures at the college de France 1977–1978*, New York: Palgrave Macmillan.

Haas, P.M. (1992) 'Introduction: Epistemic Communities and International Policy Coordination', *International Organization*, 46: 1–35.

Hannah, M.G. (2000) *Governmentality and the Mastery of Territory in Nineteenth-Century America*, Cambridge: Cambridge University Press.

Haraway, D. (1988) 'Situated Knowledges: The Science Question in Feminism and the Privilege of Partial Perspective', *Feminist Studies*, 14: 575–599.

IGBP (1986) *Global Change Report 1 – The International Geosphere-Biosphere Programme: A Study of Global Change*, Stockholm: International Geosphere-Biosphere Programme.

IGBP (1987) *Global Change Report 2 – A Document Prepared by the First Meeting of the Special Committee*, Paris: International Council of Scientific Unions.

IGBP (1988a) *Global Change Report 3 – A Report from the Second Meeting of the Special Conunittee*, Stockholm: International Geosphere-Biosphere Programme.

IGBP (1988b) *Global Change Report 4 – The International Geosphere-Biosphere Programme: A Study of Global Change, IGBP: A Plan for Action*, Stockholm: International Geosphere-Biosphere Programme.

IGBP (1989a) *Global Change Report 7:1 – The International Geosphere-Biosphere Programme: A Study of Global Change, IGBP: A Report from the First Meeting of the Scientific Advisory Council for the IGBP*, Stockholm: The Royal Swedish Academy of Sciences.

IGBP (1989b) *Global Change Report 9 – Southern Hemisphere Perspectives of Global Change: Scientific Issues, Research Needs and Proposed Activities*, Stockholm: International Geosphere-Biosphere Programme.

IGBP (1990) *Global Change Report 12 – The International Geosphere-Biosphere Programme: A Study of Global Change, IGBP: The Initial Core Projects*, Stockholm: International Geosphere-Biosphere Programme.

IGBP (1991) *Global Change Report 15 – Global Change System for Analysis, Research and Training (START)*, Boulder: International Geosphere-Biosphere Programme.

IGBP (1992) *Global Change Report 22 – Report from the START Regional Meeting for Southeast Asia*, Stockholm: The International Geosphere-Biosphere Programme.

IGBP (1993a) 'Future Direction of the IGBP', *Global Change Newsletter*, 13: 3–10.

IGBP (1993b) 'Global Change and Regional Research Networks', *Global Change Newsletter*, 14: 7–8.

IGBP (1994) *Global Change Report 28 IGBP in Action: Work Plan 1994–1998*, Stockholm: International Geosphere-Biosphere Programme.

IGBP (1998) *Global Change Report 44 – START Implementation Plan 1997–2002*, Stockholm: The International Geosphere-Biosphere Programme.

Ilcan, S. and Phillips, L. (2008) 'Governing through Global Networks: Knowledge Mobilities and Participatory Development', *Current Sociology*, 56: 711–734.

IPCC (1990) 'Summary for Policymakers', in: *First Assessment Report – Working Group III Geneva:* Intergovernmental Panel on Climate Change.

Jasanoff, S. (2004) 'Heaven and Earth: The Politics of Environmental Images', in: S. Jasanoff and M.L. Martello (eds) *Earthly Politics Local and Global in Environmental Governance,* Cambridge, MA: MIT Press, 31–52.

Jasanoff, S. and Martello, M.L. (eds) (2004) *Earthly Politics Local and Global in Environmental Governance,* Cambridge, MA: MIT Press.

Knight, G.C. (1999) 'Regional Assessment', in: *START Annual Report 1998–1999,* Washington, DC: International START Secretariat.

Kwa, C. (2006) 'Speaking to Science: The Programming of Interdisciplinary Research through Informal Science-Policy Interactions', *Science and Public Policy,* 33: 457–467.

Litfin, K.T. (1994) *Ozone Discourses – Science and Politics in Global Environmental Cooperation,* New York: Columbia University Press.

Liverman, D.M. (2009) 'Institutions for Collaborative Environmental Research in the Americas: A Case Study of the Inter-American Institute for Global Change (IAI)', in: G.C. Knight and J. Jäger (eds) *Integrated Regional Assessment of Global Climate Change,* Cambridge: Cambridge University Press, 352–366.

Mahony, M. and Hulme, M. (2011) 'Model Migrations: Mobility and Boundary Crossings in Regional Climate Prediction', *Transactions of the Institute of British Geographers,* 36: 1–15.

Malone, T.F. and Roederer, J.G. (eds) (1985) *Global Change,* Cambridge: ICSU Press.

Miller, P., and Rose, N.S. (2008) *Governing the Present: Administering Economic, Social and Personal Life,* Cambridge: Polity.

Rutherford, P. (1999) 'Ecological Modernization and Environmental Risk', in: É. Darier (ed.) *Discourses of the Environment,* Oxford: Blackwell, 95–118.

Shapin, S. (1998) 'Placing the View from Nowhere: Historical and Sociological Problems of the Location of Science', *Transactions of the Institute of British Geographers,* 23: 5–12.

Shapin, S. and Schaffer, S. (1985) *Leviathan and the Air-Pump: Hobbes, Boyle, and the Experimental Life,* Princeton: Princeton University Press.

START (1999) *START Annual Report 1998–1999,* Washington, DC: International START Secretariat.

Uhrqvist, O. and Lövbrand, E. (forthcoming) 'Rendering the Earth System Problematic: The Constitutive Power of Global Change Research in the IGBP and IHDP'.

Whitehead, M. (2009) *State, Science and the Skies: Governmentalities of the British Atmosphere,* Chichester: Wiley-Blackwell.

11 Climate engineering

Spectacle, tragedy or solution?
A content analysis of news media framing

Holly Jean Buck

Introduction

The relationship between news media and global climate governance is not often the focus of international relations literature, yet it is vital to explore: media portrayals of both climate change and climate politics can change the course of national policies and enable or disable political support for different approaches to international governance. This chapter examines the relationship between media and governance by focusing on media coverage of climate engineering.

Climate engineering, or geoengineering – large-scale technological interventions in the climate system – is an emerging area of interest. As a relatively new field, there is a manageable amount of media on it, thus making it a feasible case study to examine the interplay between news media and governance. Social scientist Anthony Leiserowitz (2010a) added a question about geoengineering to a recent poll on attitudes about climate change in the United States, and found that 74 per cent of respondents had never heard of geoengineering – and only 3 per cent of the respondents had a correct idea about what it actually is. As Leiserowitz told scientists, gathered for an international geoengineering conference at Asilomar, 'The first impression, frame, and narrative has yet to be set' (Leiserowitz 2010b).

This chapter presents a content analysis of both print news media and online content, designed to address two key questions. First, who has voice or authority in current media treatments of geoengineering? Second, how is geoengineering framed in the news media? That is, what interpretive storylines emerge that suggest boundaries for how to think about the issue? Through studying authority and framing, I hope to glean some insight how these stories write the audience into the text – how they position the reader – which could lay the groundwork for a discussion of how media portrayals enable or hinder specific forms of climate governance.

Theoretical background: seven premises about media

1   *Media is an environment*. The media sphere is where humans interact, especially in the 'developed' world. Throughout this chapter, I employ Roger Silverstone's concept of the *mediapolis*: 'the mediated space of appearance in which the world appears', where we are constructed as human (or not), and where public and political life emerges (Silverstone 2007: 31).

Climate engineering 167

2   *This environment is interactive, but that does not make it equally authored.* Digital media is not a true 'public sphere', *à la* Habermas; as Silverstone (2007: 27) puts it, 'the world is shareable but not necessarily shared'. It is often intimated that we are stepping into a brave new interactive world: rhizomatic, democratic. Yet while digital code is a beautiful technology that allows us to manipulate, write and rewrite the media, the mediapolis is still shaped by the hands of large corporations: those who own the literal infrastructure of backbone cables and data farms, those who create the code of the programs we use, those who host and organize the content, and those who produce much of the content. The power to interact is moulded by many hands before it gets handed down to the consumer/creator/end-user.

3   *Media produces both content and audiences as commodities.* Media sells content (texts, images, video) as commodities, but audiences are also made into commodities and sold to advertisers. This is a fairly obvious point, but it often goes unnoticed. How does the creation and selling of audiences influence coverage of geoengineering? A trial assumption could be that it can influence the angle of the stories being told. Certainly, the media-influenced fragmentation of 'the public' into a multiplicity of publics does have implications for democratic politics, as far as it limits a true public debate, perhaps even a public reality (see Sunstein 2007; Hajer 2009). While the collective term 'the public' is used occasionally throughout this chapter, it is more as a *goal* than an actually-existing entity.

4   *Both media texts and audience have an active part in making meaning.* When we experience media, should we describe ourselves as audiences, users, consumers, producers, citizens, participants? Where is the agency? Social scientists studying climate change communication have faced difficulties trying to employ the 'information deficit model', which presumes that 'the public are "empty vessels" waiting to be filled with useful information on which they will then rationally act' (Ockwell *et al.* 2009: 321). Geoengineering will likely suffer from the same communication difficulties as climate change in general, until we alter the model of thinking about the challenge. I believe the agency is shared. The 'empty vessel' perspective is as passé in media studies as it is in education – few believe that humans are blank slates to be injected with media – but neither are the readers/watchers/participants completely free to construct their own interpretations; the author is not dead.

5   *Communication serves a ritual function.* The transmission view of communication has to do with the Euroamerican legacy of colonization, geographical expansion and conquering distance – early mass communication equalled sending a telegram. The ritual view of communication, however, views communication as being grounded in ideas of sharing, participation and communion (Carey 1992). Hence, using media is not just about transmitting information: it consists of us telling stories about ourselves. This is particularly fascinating when considering geoengineering: what function does it serve within our culture to share these stories about climate?

6   *Media does not just relate events, it also performs them.* It represents the world, but also enacts social relations and identities (Fairclough 1995: 15). This is explored by Beck (2010: 261), who writes that 'the news media do not only function in terms of a global focusing of events; rather, the news media adopt a more performative stand, actively enacting certain issues as "global risks"'. This is especially relevant with geoengineering, which is often staged as the insurance policy for climate risks.
7   *Language can create conceptual changes.* There are certain opportunities that living in a mediapolis affords us for rapid societal change. A new concept, given life by a word, can spread quickly: 'geoengineering', while not a freshly minted word, has almost done this. Imagine talking about 'geoengineering' without the signifier 'geoengineering': for one, vastly different approaches like biochar and aerosols in the stratosphere would probably not be lumped together in the same news article, and 'geoengineering' would not have the dread-inspiring gravitas that it carries.

New terminology and new metaphors do not just reflect changing realities; they create shifts in the narrative, open the way for reality to change. Language does not simply innovate to accommodate the new ways of seeing the world – it plays an active role in creating new views. There is not enough space to fully elaborate this point here, but it is fundamental to understanding what is going on with public perceptions of geoengineering.

Method: reading stories about the world

Content analysis is the 'systematic, objective, quantitative analysis of message characteristics' (Neuendorf 2002: 1). This method of working with and studying discourse and language is invaluable in examining just how prevalent the discourses were. By undertaking a quantitative content analysis of stories on climate engineering, I did not expect to find definitive numbers about all media ever generated on the topic. However, I do believe the sample is representative of English-language news media, and that some rough truths can be gleaned from this method.

The sample consists of two parts, print and online. The print news media study collected articles from the Nexis UK Global News database, using the search strings 'geoengineering' or 'climate engineering' from the category 'Major World Newspapers – English'. Ninety-three of the 208 articles found were selected for analysis, on the basis of having more than 300 words and three or more sentences pertaining to geoengineering. They span the years 1990 to mid-2010, though almost all of them were written in 2006 or afterwards. They are compiled from English-language publications from ten countries (see Figure 11.1).

The online media sample was compiled using Digg (www.digg.com), a site where users submit content from all over the web and other users vet this content for popularity. All content appears on the front page for a period. After the initial display, content with the highest number of votes rises to the top, thus using peer review to democratically and collectively select items users like best.

Climate engineering 169

Eighty-five text-based items which were rated over eight points for the search strings 'geoengineering' or 'climate engineering' were selected. These are items which range from articles published from sources such as *Reader's Digest* online and the *Financial Times* online to blogs like *The Daily Green* and *Wired*.

My interest in drawing samples from these two sources is the idea that they represent two different (though interlinked) media ecologies. The first is a traditional broadcast media environment, where content is packaged with all other important 'news' and the audience buys the whole package (whether or not they are interested in geoengineering). The second is an online media ecology where the audience has the power to choose which stories they like and want to read about; an environment in which there may be more freedom to write in-depth stories with different angles.

The content analysis examined various attributes:

1. *Trigger event* of each publication (is the publication inspired by a politician's statement, the release of a study, a meeting of scientists, the release of a popular book?).
2. *Location* of both where the news is generated and where the news is published.
3. *Voices*: who does the article cite, and what is their role? This is an attempt to directly investigate who has the authority to make assertions about geoengineering. Do some actors have more power to speak than others? Only the 71 news articles from the print sample which were standard news articles (i.e. reportage) were coded for voice; the commentary/opinion pieces/editorials were omitted for this evaluation as these whole texts could be assumed to be an assertion from the author. The evaluation looked at each *assertion* or declarative statement made about geoengineering by a specific person or body (direct quotes or paraphrases of declarations); general statements in passive voice were not included.
4. *Frames*: 'Frames are interpretive storylines that set a specific train of thought in motion communicating why an issue might be a problem, who or what might be responsible for it, and what should be done about it' (Nisbet 2009: 15). As Koteyko *et al.* (2010: 27) observe, 'framing creates the boundaries around an issue and allows certain actors to claim ownership of it'. In this analysis, I am interested in the question: which actors do the framings privilege, and how do the different framings write the audience into the text?

Climate change framing studies often divide a set of texts into broad categories such as a 'progress' frame, a 'conflict and strategy' frame or a 'science fiction' frame (Nisbet 2009; Weaver *et al.* 2009). This study looked at two distinct aspects of the frames employed: the *spatial* aspect and the *narrative* aspect. For the spatial aspect, I modified a framework used by Liu (2010), dividing the spatial dimension into five levels: individual, regional, societal (or national), international and biospheric (articles in which the dominant frame is addressing the earth system, rather than human societies or nation-states).

Narrative frames relate to which story is being told. After reading all the articles, I identified five dominant frames: catastrophic, managerial, cautionary, spatiotemporal struggle and bildungsroman (climate change as a coming-of-age for humanity). Frames can be combined (for example, the catastrophic and cautionary frames have synergies), and so the articles were not simply sorted into different categories by frame: this would have been too arbitrary. Instead, I coded the presence of 11 discursive elements (see Table 11.1), which were identified by cues (framing devices) in the text. Table 11.2 shows the different discursive elements and the devices that show evidence of the element. These devices include headlines and catchphrases from the article text, and can also include images, though images were not analysed as a part of this chapter.

Results

Where does the news happen? Trigger events and geography of coverage

Geoengineering coverage has increased over the past few years, peaking with the release of the Royal Society report in September 2009. The topic is especially prominent in UK newspapers (see Figure 11.1).

Table 11.1 Narrative framings and discursive elements

Narrative framing	Discursive elements that contribute to the frame
1. Catastrophic	Crisis, inevitability
2. Cautionary	Doubting our place, fantastic ideas
3. Spatiotemporal struggle	Geopolitics, justice
4. Managerial	Cheap solutions, risks vs. rewards, ecological modernization, science education
5. Bildungsroman	Doctors and nurses

Table 11.2 Discursive elements in the text

Discursive element	Framing devices that indicate this element	The story being told
Crisis	Statements that convey urgency, danger, or catastrophe, e.g. headlines like 'Bombing the sky to save us from global warming' or 'Can the ecohackers save us?'	The world/the planet/ 'we' are in urgent trouble and need to be saved.
Inevitability	Statements which give a sense of fatalistic likelihood to geoengineering, from strong inevitability, e.g. 'the world will need to suck carbon from the atmosphere to avoid permanent damage to the climate' (Pagnamenta 2009) to statements that introduce the possibility of inevitability, like the headline 'Life may depend on giant sunshade'.	We have screwed up and now these climate engineering technologies may/will be necessary.

Doubting our place	Statements which doubt our *right*, or our existential ability, to be doing climate engineering. Phrases about 'playing God', 'hubris' or 'tinkering with Mother Nature'.	The planet is messed up because of technology, so technology cannot solve this; humans are not wise enough to mess with Mother Nature.
Fantastic ideas	Mentions of 'science fiction', 'fantastic' or 'futuristic' ideas; statements about 'wacky' or 'loony' ideas, either for entertainment appeal or to be derisive. Example: headlines like 'Wild and Crazy Ideas to Cool the Planet'.	A far-out, awesome future is coming: or it's already here.
Geopolitics	Statements darkly warning about 'rogue states' that are 'difficult to restrain' by other 'powers', e.g. headlines like 'Global Climate Engineering: Who Controls the Thermostat?'	The world is a geopolitical game of strategy. Climate engineering will be used in this game of great powers.
Justice	Statements that give a justice dimension to the problem, either by questioning the actors, questioning the spatial impacts of geoengineering, or intergenerational issues.	There are winners and losers in geoengineering.
Cheap solutions	This evaluation does not count attention to cost (many articles feature cost estimates), but statements which are explicitly comparing the cost of geoengineering to mitigation, e.g. headlines like 'Global Warming's Cheap, Effective Solution', statements like 'It would be 100 times cheaper to shield the Earth from sunlight with a man-made "sun block" than to cut emissions of greenhouse gases' (Connor 2010).	It is cheaper to geoengineer than to cut emissions.
Risks vs. rewards	Talk of risks of both geoengineering and climate change, metaphors about geoengineering as 'insurance', discussions of 'rolling the dice' with our planet.	'Life is about weighing risks' (Gorrie 2008).
Ecological modernization	Statements which create a vision of the future where the earth has become ecologically modernized, and is successfully managed, e.g. 'in 200 years the earth will be "an artifact", a product of human design' (Keith, qtd. by Dean 2007). This discourse is admittedly hard to distinguish, since it is implied in the very idea of geoengineering – most stories contain a grain of it.	With cooperation and technology, we can make the future work. We can still modernize, and take care of the planet, too: caring for the planet is a question of proper management.
Science education	Any material which attempts to enhance the reader's understanding of science. Many stories relay facts; here only those which make a genuine attempt to explain the underlying concepts are counted.	Climate engineering has scientific groundings, which you can learn about.
Doctors and nurses	Metaphors with the earth as patient, geoengineering as 'planetary medicine', statements like 'we should be the heart and mind of the Earth not its malady' (Lovelock 2008).	The earth is sick, but maybe humans have the power to heal her.

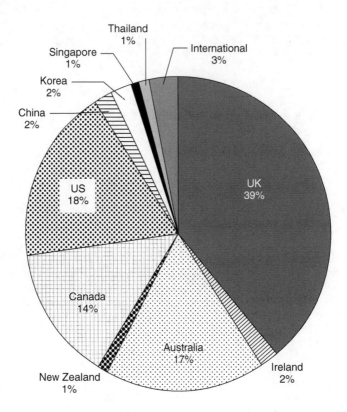

Figure 11.1 English print newspaper articles by country.

About 10 per cent of the collected articles were triggered by events in North America, 12 per cent in Europe and 25 per cent with unclear trigger events (e.g. feature stories that ran somewhat independently of specific moments). At least half of the stories (49 per cent) were triggered, however, in what I call the 'mediasphere': the stories were written in response to publications, such as an article in *Nature*, a book, the release of a report, or another newspaper article. In some sense, these *events* take place in a space which transcends borders – a realm of discourse or ideas. Geoengineering is not yet something that *happens* in the physical realm: it is enacted in this mediasphere.

Voice: who is speaking?

In his book *Hack the Planet*, science writer Eli Kintisch refers to what he calls the 'Geoclique': the network of scientists who are working on geoengineering. This geoclique, to borrow the neologism, is responsible for about 36 per cent of the 500 assertions made about geoengineering in the sample of 93 print articles (see Table 11.3).

Table 11.3 Most frequently cited authorities

Most-quoted geoengineering scientists		Other heavily cited authors	
David Keith	9.4% (47)	The Royal Society	6.4% (34)
Ken Caldeira	6% (30)	Stephen Chu	5% (25)
John Shepherd	3.2% (16)	Martin Rees	3.2% (16)
Paul Crutzen	3% (15)	J. Eric Bickel	1.8% (9)
Roger Angel	3% (15)	Lee Lane	1.8% (9)
Alan Robock	1.8% (9)	David Victor	1.6% (8)
John Latham	1.8% (9)	Bjorn Lomborg	1.6% (8)
Mike MacCracken	1.6% (8)		
Steven Schneider	1.6% (8)		

Notice that natural scientists and engineers together create 70 per cent of the assertions on geoengineering, followed in much smaller parts by government officials and political scientists (14 per cent) and economists (7 per cent) – see Figure 11.2. By and large, it is voices in the scientific community who are making assertions about this topic. As asked by political ecologist Joan Martinez-Alier

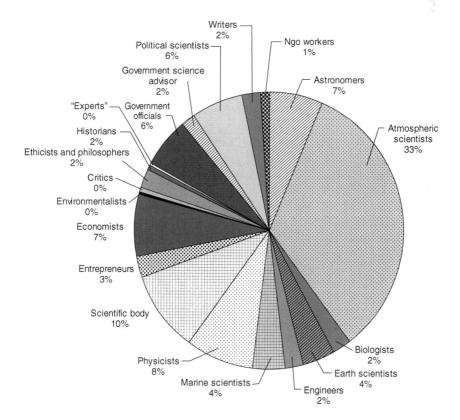

Figure 11.2 Who is making assertions about geoengineering?

174 H.J. Buck

(2002: 271), with regards to environmental governance: 'Who has the power to simplify complexity, and impose their language of valuation?'. Those who are speaking have the power to simplify complexity; it is in some crude sense those who have voice that have the power, the authority, the ability to author reality.

Who is not speaking? Citizens. Social scientists and philosophers are fairly unquoted on the topic, as well. There is little attention to geoengineering from a cultural perspective. Economists and politicians are also surprisingly quiet, given how prominent they are in Western society.

But the loudest silence, so to speak, is from women. Only 3 per cent of assertions of geoengineering were made by women (15 statements out of 500). Furthermore, none of these statements were encouraging of geoengineering: all of them expressed scepticism or even hostility to the idea. Is this because there are simply less women scientists? Can we attribute the voicelessness to the media – perhaps it is simply not representing the women scientists who are out there, somehow? Or is it that geoengineering is a male project?

Framing: what is being spoken about?

Spatial frames

Most stories are framed internationally (see Table 11.4). This is none-too-surprising, given the existing definition of geoengineering as large-scale. It also reflects what Hulme has observed about the universalization of the idea of climate: he argues that we have 'detached it from its cultural settings' (Hulme 2008: 9). Both the 'de-culturization' of climate and the universalization of 'the human plight' under climate change have implications for the governance structures that can be imagined. Further research could investigate whether individual, regional or societal frames would increase public engagement with geoengineering.

Narrative frames

Print news media and online articles employ similar discursive elements. Online stories were more likely to frame things in terms of justice or geopolitics, less

Table 11.4 Spatial frames

Print newspapers – percentage of stories possessing this spatial frame*		Online content – percentage of stories possessing this spatial frame*	
Individual	7%	Individual	1%
Regional	7%	Regional	0%
Societal	10%	Societal	15%
International	88%	International	93%
Biospheric	8%	Biospheric	11%

Note
* some stories employ two frames, so the numbers do not add up to 100%

likely to focus on the cheapness of geoengineering, and more likely to educate their readers on the science (see Table 11.5). Most of these slight differences between print and online stories, I attribute to narrowcasting – the fragmentation of audiences – and the on-demand nature of online media. People who read online stories are often seeking topics they are interested in, and they are often reading stories written for audiences interested in science or the environment. Potentially, narrowcasting could allow writers to go more in-depth in certain areas, but it also makes it difficult to have a wider public debate.

The most dominant discursive element has been the 'crisis' element: most journalists are telling a story about 'saving the world'. What does this signify? Is 'saving the world' simply a story with classic appeal? Or do we actually believe that 'the world' is in such grave danger? Social science research on climate change attitudes indicates that people are indeed concerned: as of June 2010, about half of people in the United States were worried about climate change; 11 per cent think it will harm their families and communities 'a great deal' (Leiserowitz *et al.* 2010). In Europe, a Eurobarometer (2009) poll found that 67 per cent of respondents think that climate change is a very serious problem, and 65 per cent believe that the seriousness of climate change has not been exaggerated. Despite a recent drop in belief in global warming (in the United States, anyway), the catastrophic frame is not out-of-line with how people are feeling.

Discussion and conclusion

In this part of the chapter, I will reflect upon what stories are not being told by news articles, how the issue is bounded, and what governance implications these framings and omissions have.

Table 11.5 Narrative frames

Discursive elements	Print newspaper stories	Online media stories
Crisis	60%	43.5%
Ecological modernization	59%	30.5%
Risks vs. rewards	31%	35 %
Fantastic ideas	29%*	33%*
Inevitability	29%	29%
Doubt	24%	23.5%
Cheapness	21%	12%
Justice	12%	23.5%
Geopolitics	11%	23.5%
Science education	7.5%	18%
Doctors and nurses	6.5%	3%

Notes

* of these stories, 33% of print publications and 25% of online publications present geoengineering as something which *used* to be 'science fiction' or 'far-out', but is now being considered seriously.

Absent stories

Anyone who has read a few articles on geoengineering could guess that articles are often framed in terms of saving the planet, managing the planet, and weighing risks and benefits. We reach richer material when we ask: what stories are *not* being told?

First, despite the managerial framing and the elements of ecological modernization, almost nobody is framing the article with attention to the positive power of humans to transform their societies or environments. Humans, even when they are cast as fixers, are rarely protagonists. Even the articles which featured ecological modernization were not exactly enthusiastic or positive: more often, they approached managing the earth as a chore, rather than a creative activity. The actors featured seem unable to act. If there is a protagonist, he is more a jaded, reluctant Hamlet than a Hollywood disaster-flick hero. We might have never been modern, but if the lack of enthusiasm about the human potential to transform the planet is any indication, we have definitely been postmodern: the modernist dream of order and progress for better living seems to have lost its lustre. It is necessary to stabilize the climate to avert chaos – as Boykoff *et al.* (2010: 60) explain, 'a guiding ethos of climate stabilization is the imagined future, safe, secure, stable climate, which can be engineered by our actions now'. Yet this stability is about averting the negative, not about establishing something positive.

Second, the articles analysed tend to treat warming as the problem, and examine whether geoengineering is the potential answer, but rarely do they take a comprehensive look at the problems with our energy system. The input, i.e. the extraction and burning of fossil fuels, is excluded from view. Generally, the comprehensive nature of the dilemma is acknowledged with a few sentences, but it is not examined; the focus is elsewhere. A fairly typical article will mention that 'the battle to contain emissions seems every day less winnable', and that geoengineering would be 'a last resort because we could not curb our excesses' (Boyer 2010) – yet the articles always muse within the bounds of this geoengineering topic. The question is, of course, how did those bounds come to be set? Can any topic have 'natural' bounds? Because geoengineering looks at the waste disposal aspect of our energy woes, not the waste creation aspect, it would be easy to say the boundaries are inherent in the topic. A more material reason for the limited scope is the for-profit nature of the media system: in print media, each page is valuable 'real estate'. Hence, it's quite expensive to write an in-depth treatment of any problem. With online media, the limits are not space, but attention span: it is hard to get engrossed in a computer screen, and hypertext makes for hyperactivity. There are few forms with mass appeal that can treat the issue with a wide scope.

Third, the justice issue is seldom considered; even when it was present, it was rarely the dominant frame. Of course, it is hard to write about the justice aspects of specific geoengineering situations when the science is still so speculative. As for considering the justice aspects of geoengineering *as an idea*, this also requires a comprehensive look at our fossil fuel dilemma. The antagonist in the dominant frames is CO_2, which mundanely threatens everyone, making questions of justice invisible (see Swyngedouw 2010: 222).

Bounding the issue

When we look at who is speaking in these stories, geoengineering emerges as the province of experts, as it becomes an object which can only be understood at long time scales by complex models and specialized techniques. This is consonant with ecological modernization discourses, where the layperson is disqualified. As Hajer (1995: 10) observes:

> this disqualification in fact not only affects the proverbial man in the street: specialist natural scientists, politicians, philosophers, or social scientists, all experience how their stocks of knowledge and normative theories about proper procedural roles of reaching social agreements are devalued too.

As the environment is no longer understood through direct experience, the layman is dependent upon these experts and can only be educated (Hajer 1995).

Two ways of looking at the role of the individual reader appear, depending on how the topic is bounded:

1. *Educated chooser.* Especially where the risks versus rewards element is present, the audience is written in as an 'educated chooser' which is encouraged to weigh the risks and benefits; to make informed choices along with the people who are actually doing the decision-making. While we are not invited to weigh in directly, we are presented the rudimentary information to make evaluative decisions. As consumers, we possess and use these decision-making skills daily, at least in the rational-choice model of economics. In the articles analysed here, this role is marginal compared to the role of the reader as spectator.
2. *Spectator.* The topic is bounded as something which civil society should *keep watch on*, but the audience is written into the text simply *as an audience*, meant to observe while geoengineering matures into whatever it will become. NGOs have a role in this story (as vigilant watchers, or 'watchdogs'). Government has a role: that of watcher (over*sight*), and a role which is expanded to that of protector, in the 'strategic realism' of geopolitical discourse. Think tanks have a slightly more dynamic role; they can provide ideas-as-food for this growing project. The media is the stage upon which geoengineering is performed, and it also actively performs geoengineering. Scientists are usually the stars – but the conflicts and characters take place *within* the scientific community; it is a self-enclosed dramatic system which usually provides the necessary dramatic elements without venturing into political landscapes. Civil society, however, has an uncertain place in this story.

Governance implications

Many scholars have written about the governance implications of catastrophic discourse (e.g Swyngedouw 2010; Methmann and Rothe, Chapter 7, this volume). The sinister thing about the catastrophic-managerial geoengineering frame is that it excludes idealism and possibility: there may be no alternative. The frame is based on the premise that we are in fact *incapable* of positive action. I would like to be absolutely clear that I am not arguing against the science which suggests that we are in a difficult climatic predicament: this is probably true. The focus here is on the narratives which we create out of this scientific data, and to whom they give authority; the forms of governance they may imply.

The frames suggested by the news media could act to encourage public participation (if they position the readers as agents with authority, whose participation is important – that is as 'educated chooser') or discourage public participation (if they position the audience as subject to the inevitability of geoengineering – as 'spectator'). At the moment – looking at the frames featured by the articles which have been analysed – authority rests with natural scientists, though this will likely change in the future if more actors become familiar with the topic, and if geoengineering becomes more of a 'real' possibility.

Are there narrative framings that would open up climate engineering governance to other authorities and other political possibilities? If we abandon the 'strategic realism' storyline that pits nation-states against each other, and the grim neo-Malthusian scenarios of scarcity and conflict, we could frame climate engineering as a task that challenges us to evoke the best of human traits: altruism and innovation. Nordhaus and Shellenberger (2007: 127) ask, 'How might history have turned out differently had we imagined the solution to global warming as *unleashing* rather than *restricting* human activity?'. The governance that would come from this framing would not place nations in competition, but encourage cooperation (a trait much needed if a UN body is going to govern geoengineering). Framing climate change as an innovation challenge, rather than employing the politics of limits, might generate and unlock research funding, spur new grants, and promote international science cooperation. In this generative climate of cooperation, perhaps other alternatives to dealing with the climate situation beyond climate engineering could be discovered. Climate engineering could be an entrance into a kind of science diplomacy.

Other frames could focus on the local: instead of large-scale, industrial initiatives, we could imagine smaller-scale, locally managed carbon dioxide removal projects – regional and community carbon management – done in conjunction with decentralized, regional food systems and permaculture, organized so that individual gardeners and farmers could take part, and executed with a culturally-variable sense of beauty. 'Geoengineering' as a conceptual category could give way to 'mega-gardening' or 'tending the wild' (à la Brand 2009), phrases that essentially invite some level of ecological management, but that imply governance and involvement at regional and local scales.

Still another frame for geoengineering could focus on development. Like climate change, geoengineering is fundamentally a development issue. 'Climate politics is precisely not about climate but about transforming the basic concepts and institutions of first, industrial, nation-state modernity', writes Beck (2010: 256). If climate engineering was framed in terms of development, it could find a place in the aid/development regime of governance, which would put it into regimes of evaluation and funding with a humanitarian/human security emphasis. This might not be altogether useful (see Buck 2012), but it could focus attention upon the impacts geoengineering would have upon various vulnerable populations, and serve as a reminder that the stated goal is to stabilize the climate for all.

The current narratives about geoengineering – that it is a reluctant choice we may have to make after failing to mitigate emissions, or that it is an insurance policy we should invest in – are unlikely to galvanize public interest in any direction, because they are stories of failure, and of insurance. Furthermore, they do nothing to address justice issues, or the fundamental drivers of the climate change problem. Yet there are other frames out there to invent and deploy. I suggest that some of this initial framing could be done by scientists, because in the case of geoengineering, a small group of atmospheric scientists has a large share of voice on the topic. This is an interesting situation, where a small group of people has power to really frame a topic, at least in the mass media or traditional press. Since the news media is where many of the stories in the blogosphere are sourced from, this power is significant. The scientists involved in geoengineering research should choose to actively frame their work in ways that enable creative, democratic governance possibilities.

References

Beck, U. (2010) 'Climate for Change, or How to Create a Green Modernity?', *Theory, Culture & Society* 27(2–3): 254–266.
Boyer, P. (2010) 'Grand Measures the Last Resort', *Hobart Mercury*, 25 May.
Boykoff, M., Frame, D. and Randalls, S. (2010) 'Discursive Stability Meets Climate Instability: A Critical Exploration of the Concept of "Climate Stabilization" in Contemporary Climate Policy', *Global Environmental Change* 20: 53–64.
Brand, S. (2009) *Whole Earth Discipline: An Ecoprgamatist Manifesto*, New York: Viking.
Bronson, D. (2009) 'Geoengineering: A Gender Issue?', *Women in Action*, 2: 83–87.
Buck, H. (2012) 'Geoengineering: Re-making Climate for Profit or Humanitarian Intervention?', *Development and Change* 43: 1–18.
Carey, J. (1992) *Communication as Culture: Essays on Media and Society*, New York: Routledge.
Connor, S. (2010) 'Simulated Volcanoes and Man-Made "Sun Blocks" can Rescue the Planet; Scientists Back Radical "Geoengineering" Projects to Stop Climate Change', *Independent*, 28 January.
Dean, C. (2007) 'Experts Discuss Engineering Feats, Like Space Mirrors, to Slow Climate Change', *The New York Times*, 10 November.
Eurobarometer (2009) 'Europeans' Attitudes Towards Climate Change', *Special Eurobarometer 313 / Wave 71.1 – TNS Opinion & Social*. Online. Available at: ec.europa.eu/public_opinion/archives/ebs/ebs_313_en.pdf (retrieved: 15.8.2010).
Fairclough, N. (1995) *Media Discourse*, London: Edward Arnold.
Gorrie, P. (2008) 'Climate Change', *The Toronto Star*, 21 June.
Hajer, M. (1995) *The Politics of Environmental Discourse: Ecological Modernization and the Policy Process*, Oxford: Oxford University Press.

Hajer, M. (2009) *Authoritative Governance: Policy-Making in the Age of Mediatization*, Oxford: Oxford University Press.

Hulme, M. (2008) 'Geographical Work at the Boundaries of Climate Change', *Transactions of the Institute of British Geographers* 33: 5–11.

Kintisch, E. (2010) *Hack the Planet: Science's Best Hope – or Worst Nightmare – for Averting Climate Catastrophe*, Hoboken: John Wiley & Sons.

Koteyko, N., Thelwall M. and Nerlich, B. (2010) 'From Carbon Markets to Carbon Morality: Creative Compounds as Framing Devices in Online Discourses on Climate Change Mitigation', *Science Communication* 32(1): 25–54.

Leiserowitz, A. (2010a) 'Geoengineering and Climate Change in the Public Mind'. Presentation given to the Asilomar International Conference on Climate Intervention Technologies, Pacific Grove, 24 March.

Leiserowitz, A. (2010b) 'Fact Check: Percent of Americans Having Heard of Geoengineering' [email] (personal communication, 15 August).

Leiserowitz, A., Maibach, E., Roser-Renouf, C. and Smith, N. (2010) 'Climate Change in the American Mind: Americans' Global Warming Beliefs and Attitudes in June 2010'. Online. Available at: environment.yale.edu/climate/files/ClimateBeliefsJune2010.pdf (retrieved: 15.8.2010).

Liu, B.F. (2010) 'Distinguishing How Elite Newspapers and A-List Blogs Cover Crises: Insights for Managing Crises Online', *Public Relations Review* 36: 28–34.

Lovelock, J. (2008) 'Climate Change is Inevitable. We Must Adapt to it', *Independent*, 2 September.

Martinez-Alier, J. (2002) *The Environmentalism of the Poor: A Study of Ecological Conflicts and Valuation*, Cheltenham: Edward Elgar Publishing.

Neuendorf, K. (2002) *The Content Analysis Guidebook*, Thousand Oaks: Sage Publications.

Nisbet, M. (2009) 'Communicating Climate Change: Why Frames Matter for Public Engagement', *Environment* 51(2): 12–23.

Nordhaus, T. and Shellenberger, M. (2007) *Break Through: From the Death of Environmentalism to the Politics of Possibility*, New York: Houghton Mifflin.

Ockwell, D., Whitmarsh, L. and O'Neill, S. (2009) 'Reorienting Climate Change Communication for Effective Mitigation: Forcing People to be Green or Fostering Grass-Roots Engagement?', *Science Communication* 30(3): 305–328.

Pagnamenta, R. (2009) 'Carbon Cuts Won't be Enough: We May Have to Suck it Out of the Atmosphere', *The Times*, 1 December.

Silverstone, R. (2007) *Media and Morality: On the Rise of the Mediapolis*, Cambridge: Polity Press.

Sunstein, C. (2007) *Republic.com 2.0*, Princeton: Princeton University Press.

Swyngedouw, E. (2010) 'Apocalypse Forever? Post-Political Populism and the Spectre of Climate Change', *Theory, Culture & Society* 27: 213–232.

Weaver, D., Lively, E. and Bimber, B. (2009) 'Searching for a Frame: News Media Tell the Story of Technological Porgress, Risk, and Regulation', *Science Communication* 31(2): 139–166.

Part IV
Between de- and re-politicization

12 White ponchos dripping away?

Glacier narratives in Bolivian climate change discourse

Anna Kaijser

Introduction

Anyone who has come into contact with the majesty of a glacier understands the emotional and symbolic significance of these overwhelming masses of ice. It is no surprise that their large-scale melting incites concern and gloomy newspaper headlines. The scientific, social and cultural values attributed to glaciers and the material implications of their retreat have made them a powerful symbol for the impacts of global warming. Melting glaciers have, using Maarten Hajer's (1995) terminology, turned into an emblematic issue in climate change discourses, and a strong narrative that portrays glaciers as an endangered species, risking extinction due to global warming (Carey 2007), has emerged. This narrative on glacier retreat, however, mostly embodies a mainstream western perspective, suggesting that climate change can and should be managed through political and technical interventions within the existing political-economic system – a view that is compatible with the framework of green governmentality–ecological modernization.

Bolivia here comes forward as a unique case due to the cultural and material importance of glaciers in the Bolivian Andes, and the ways glacier narratives are employed in local discourse formation on climate change. Glaciers have increasingly assumed a central place not only in the hydrologic system of the country, but also in its political landscape.

The Bolivian government has recently promoted an alternative climate discourse that John Dryzek and Hayley Stevenson (Chapter 15 in this volume) label 'green radicalism', in which the western, capitalist system is identified as the root cause of climate change and incompatible with its solution. Andean glacier retreat plays a significant role in this discourse, as an illustrative example of how people are adversely affected by climate change impacts to which they have contributed little and which local actions cannot do much to prevent. The issue of glacier retreat is thus employed in Bolivia to support a discourse of green radicalism, which, I will argue, is connected to a greater political project. I will show how glaciers are embedded in Bolivian discourses of climate change, and how the stories about their melting assume a different emblematic function in Bolivia than in mainstream climate discourses. Furthermore, I will discuss how Bolivia's remarkable positioning in international climate politics is related to formation of state and national identity within Bolivia.

This chapter's analysis of how Bolivian actors mobilize narratives of melting glaciers at the crossroads of national political projects and global climate politics touches upon issues that go well beyond the Andes. Besides presenting an empirical case, I discuss the broader question of how narratives are drawn into discourse formation on climate change, and how climate change discourses may be incorporated as an element in wider political projects. I want to add to the understanding of how climate change is de-politicized and re-politicized through discursive practices, and the power imbalances and frictions (Tsing 2005) within these processes. By studying discourse formations and dynamics on climate change, we may in turn achieve a more profound understanding of climate politics which may facilitate appropriate action.

I will now move on to some theoretical and methodological remarks, after which I will explore glaciers and the meanings assigned to them. Thereafter, I turn to the empirical case of Bolivia and the ways glacier narratives are constructed and employed by Bolivian actors.

Theory and methods

In this chapter, I employ Hajer's definition of discourse as 'a specific ensemble of ideas, concepts, and categorizations that are produced, reproduced, and transformed in a particular set of practices and through which meaning is given to physical and social realities' (1995: 44). Environmental politics involve various dominant and alternative discourses, which challenge and influence each other in specific contexts. The arena of environmental politics is thus a dynamic discursive battleground where struggles over meaning and definition take place. The relation between power and knowledge – what is considered legitimate knowledge in any given context – is a central feature of these discursive struggles (Bäckstrand and Lövbrand 2006).

Discourses of ecological modernization and green governmentality arguably dominate international climate change politics today (Hajer 1995; Bäckstrand and Lövbrand 2007; see also Chapters 2 and 3 in this volume). The ecological modernization discourse reconciles economic growth and environmental protection (Hajer 1995; Bäckstrand and Lövbrand 2006; Mol and Spaargaren 2000). As Karin Bäckstrand and Eva Lövbrand put it, within ecological modernization 'ecological degradation is decoupled from economic growth; capitalism and industrialization can be made more environmentally friendly' (2006: 53). This is reflected in international climate politics for instance in the popularity of carbon trading systems. Bäckstrand and Lövbrand (2007) argue that in international climate change politics, ecological modernization is paralleled with a discourse of green governmentality which proposes that the problem of climate change requires high-level administration and monitoring by state, advanced science and large private actors. Climate change is, from the outlook of ecological modernization–green governmentality, framed as a threat to all of humanity, which has occurred through flaws in the current political and economic system, but should still be dealt with within this same system; through consensual and concerted global effort and large-scale management by states, international institutions and private companies. Solving the problem of climate change is thus perceived as compatible with – and often only imaginable within – a sustained economic-political global order. The ecological modernization–green governmentality regime is the space where accounts about climate change and its solution take form and gain legitimacy. It is in the context of this dominant discourse formation that Bolivia's promotion of an alternative discourse of green radicalism takes place.

One way to understand how discourses are conveyed and made meaningful is to look at the narratives used to promote them. Narratives can be regarded as 'a frame through which people make sense of their lives' (Leavy 2009: 27). By studying narratives we may explore 'not just how stories are structured and the ways in which they work, but also who produces them, and by what means; the mechanisms by which they are consumed; and how narratives are silenced, contested or accepted' (Squire *et al.* 2008: 2). Analysing narratives can be a beneficial approach for understanding climate change discourses, as shown for instance by Kjersti Fløttum (2010). I seek to show how narratives may be employed to strengthen particular discourses, and argue that the narration of a phenomenon, such as glacier retreat, is a discursive practice that has implications for how the phenomenon is perceived in public and political spheres, what explanations are considered true and legitimate and what strategies are suggested in response to it. While the melting of glaciers is a physical process with strong material impacts, it gains meaning for humans through narration.

The methods used for this chapter are a combination of ethnography and discourse analysis. Empirical material was generated through ethnographic studies in Bolivia in 2010 and 2012, during which I carried out semi-structured interviews with representatives from government authorities, environmental activists, staff of local and international NGOs, development cooperation personnel and scientists. I also participated in climate-related meetings and events arranged by government units, civil society and international cooperation agencies. Additional empirical data consists of statements and publications from the Bolivian government and other relevant actors. Analysing the data was a continuous interpretive process in which I looked for references to glaciers and glacier retreat in the material and studied closely the characteristics of these accounts.

Narrating glaciers

Glaciers appear in places where winter snowfall exceeds melting in the summer for an extensive amount of time, accumulates and turns to ice. As long as there is balance between snowfall and melting, the glacier remains, but if the losses surpass the gains – for instance due to warmer climate or changed precipitation patterns – the glacier loses mass.

Glaciers occupy a central position in scientific research and public recognition of climate change. Studies of glacier mass variations provide valuable data for assessing climate change and predicting its future impacts (Soruco *et al.* 2009).

Glacier retreat is often brought forward as a canary-in-the-coalmine indicator for impacts of global warming, and the prediction of ice sheet melting at the poles and subsequent sea level rise is a main source of worry in public climate change debates. Furthermore, glaciers serve as archives for historical climate data. Through analysing ancient ice accessed through ice core drilling, scientists can learn about climatic changes several hundred thousand years back in time.

There is scientific consensus around the retreat of glaciers as an effect of human-induced climate change. However, as argued by Hajer and Versteeg, the fact that a particular environmental issue receives widespread attention 'cannot be deduced from a natural-scientific analysis of its urgency, but from the symbols and experiences that govern the way people think and act' (2001: 176). The reason why glacier melting has turned into an emblematic issue in climate change discourse is not only scientific – symbolic meanings play an important role in this process.

Glaciers 'transcend glaciology and bear upon altogether bigger issues of the environment and its changing future' (Knight 2004: 392). They also possess a majestic, almost transcendental appeal, which may be referred to as nonhuman charisma: 'the distinguishing properties of a non-human entity or process that determine its perception by humans and its subsequent evaluation' (Lorimer 2007: 921). Drawing on theories of nonhuman agency and human relations to nature,[1] Jamie Lorimer identifies a number of characteristics that make humans perceive certain other species as charismatic, which has implications for nature conservation ideals and practices. While Lorimer refers only to animals as bearers of nonhuman charisma, I extend the concept to cover also places and natural phenomena, in this case glaciers.

Some of the charisma of glaciers could be explained by their constant movement and ability to change. A long cultural history exists in both western and nonwestern societies of depicting glaciers as living beings with their own agency (Carey 2007; Cruikshank 2005; Rhoades et al. 2008). Mark Carey argues that '[i]n recent decades, glaciers have become both a key icon for global warming and a type of endangered species' (2007: 497). He identifies a narrative which he refers to as the 'endangered glacier narrative' and which has emerged in light of climate change. In this narrative, glaciers are portrayed as a species in danger of extinction due to human-induced climate change; mourned and in need of protection. This narrative contains elements of earlier perceptions of glaciers. Tracing glacier discourses in Europe and the United States several centuries back and up until present time, Carey shows how glaciers have been seen as menace; as sublime; as scientific laboratories; as sites for mountaineering and tourism; as remote, empty spaces to conquer; and as wilderness. All these understandings, he argues, seep into the endangered glacier narrative of today. As glaciers embody such a multitude of meanings, they 'offer a platform to implement historical ideologies about nature, science, imperialism, race, recreation, wilderness and global power dynamics' (Carey 2007: 497).

Glaciers are usually located in remote places. Most people do not live close to a glacier; most have never even seen one, but are nevertheless concerned about their disappearance (Orlove et al. 2008; Cruikshank 2005). Gretel Ehrlich points out that glaciers seem to be ascribed an intrinsic value that goes beyond their direct usefulness to humans and which makes their destruction appear as nearly immoral (in Orlove *et al.* 2008).

Carey argues that the endangered glacier narrative is rooted in certain discourses, which construct nature and environmental issues in specific ways: '[a]t the center of the endangered glacier narrative are questions of power – the power to define nature and, in turn, the power to create specific laws and policies (and not others)' (2007: 501).

The contemporary endangered glacier discourse is situated in a post-colonial setting, reproducing patterns of scientific power-knowledge and western domination; it may encourage top-down intervention and control over glaciated areas through scientific missions, tourism and protection initiatives. One example is the recent discussions about the Arctic region, where melting of glaciers and ice sheets open up new possibilities for transport, oil extraction and other profitable projects. This incites foreign interest and concern, reflected for instance in the US Ambassador Mark Brezinski's plea to the Swedish government to keep working for a 'responsible development in sensitive Arctic areas', based on scientific expertise and diplomacy (Brezinski 2012, my translation).

The endangered glacier narrative may thus be employed to support a discourse of ecological modernization–green governmentality in relation to climate change. However, as I will show, narratives do not have fixed meanings, but can be altered and employed within different discourses and for different political purposes. I will now turn to Bolivia, where a local version of the endangered glacier narrative is employed to support a perspective of green radicalism.

Andean glacier retreat: embodying climate change

Within view from the Bolivian administrative capital of La Paz, surrounded by Andean mountain peaks, are several glaciers, and, nowadays, ex-glaciers. Among those, two are especially symbol-laden. Chacaltaya used to be the world's highest and most equatorial lift-served skiing resort. Since 2009 the glacier has entirely disappeared, leaving the skiing infrastructure on bare ground as an eerie monument of what has been and a reminder of what the future may bring more of. The cabin, which used to shelter cold and tired skiers, has been turned into a museum; its walls decorated with diplomas, photos of the old days of glory and a pair of antique wooden skis. Instead of skiers, the place is now frequented by tourists and visiting politicians and development cooperation staff, who want to take a look at climate change (see for instance Commission on Climate Change and Development 2009). Worse than the tourists and the local elite being deprived of a winter playground, the communities below Chacaltaya have seen an essential water resource, on which they were heavily dependent, disappear with the glacier.

Illimani, the second highest mountain in Bolivia, is crowned by another glacier, which on clear days makes a beautiful and dramatic backdrop to La Paz. It figures on most postcards of the city and on its official shield. For *paceños*, the inhabitants of La Paz, it is a basis for identification, representing the city and its Andean surroundings: 'the residents identify not only with the city and with the nation but also with the highland region of the country, embodied in the summits of Illimani' (Orlove et al. 2008: 13). The glacier is an important water reservoir for downstream communities, as well as a powerful symbol. Over recent years, numerous journalists, development cooperation officials and researchers – including myself – have travelled the winding roads to villages on the mountainsides to hear the local residents mourn the shrinking ice and blame it on climate change.

The disappearing glaciers in the Andes have received great attention during the past few years (Carey 2010). Glacier retreat in the Bolivian Andes frequently appears in scientific and public discussions on climate change and has become a common reference in international mass media (see Rosenthal 2009; Shukman 2009). Glacier narratives are also a common feature in the discourse on climate change promoted by the Bolivian government. This discourse, I argue, must be understood in relation to past and current political processes. Therefore, I will now provide brief outlines of the Bolivian political context and recent actions in the field of climate change.

The Bolivian political context

Bolivia is one of the poorest countries of South America, with wide gaps between the rich and the poor and a turbulent political history. There are deep tensions along economic and ethnic lines, owing to the country's colonial history and persisting post-colonial patterns of segregation and discrimination. Between 60 and 70 per cent of the ten million inhabitants are estimated to belong to one of the 36 recognized indigenous groups, out of which Quechua and Aymara – historically inhabiting the Andean highlands – amount to half of the total population; however, ethnicity in Bolivia is quite fluid, and has been ascribed various meanings across time (Postero 2007; Mamani Ramirez 2011a).

Since 2006, Bolivia is governed by President Evo Morales and MAS, the Movimiento al Socialismo (Movement towards Socialism), a coalition rooted in indigenous and popular movements and workers' organizations. MAS's political agenda is characterized by critique against preceding neoliberal regimes, with the overarching ambition of decolonizing the country; decolonization here referring to freedom from a post-colonial order (Howard 2010; Bolivian Government 2006). Re-framing politics in line with a resurrection of local values and traditions is an important element of MAS's agenda. Depictions of indigenous, predominantly Andean, practices and worldviews are employed in the re-definition of the state and a national identity contrasting the 'western' equivalent (Widmark 2009; Albro 2010). Some main features are *Pachamama*, or Mother Earth, a central figure in Andean tradition, and the concept of *vivir bien* (to live well), which is generally defined as living in harmony with other people and the environment.[2] Environmental issues, particularly climate change, have, as I will explain, played an important role in this project. It is against this general backdrop that Bolivian glacier narratives gain meaning.

Politicization of climatic change under MAS

Since MAS came to power, climate change has emerged as a central issue in Bolivian politics. This may be related to the rise of climate change on the international political, scientific and media agendas, in combination with accounts of climate change impacts in Bolivia. However, it should also be understood in light of MAS's project of re-defining and re-positioning Bolivian politics and the state itself, a project into which climate issues have been drawn.

Climate change was initially handled as a predominantly technical issue by Bolivian authorities, but a couple of years after MAS took office it started to seep into a higher-level agenda and was increasingly politicized. Bolivia's standpoint during international climate negotiations since 2008 is characterized by sharp criticism against the capitalist system, which is identified as the driving force behind climate change. This system is associated with western values and lifestyles, depicted as diametrically different to Andean and other indigenous traditions. Spiritual dimensions are often invoked, for instance in the frequent references to Mother Earth. Two central ideas are those of climate justice and a climate debt that industrial countries should pay back to developing countries (see for example People's Agreement of Cochabamba 2010).

At COP 15 in Copenhagen 2009, the Bolivian government together with a number of other countries rejected the resulting document – the Copenhagen Accord – claiming that the document was too weak and only served the interests of rich, western nations. Furthermore, they disapproved of the arguably non-inclusive and undemocratic process in which it had been produced. A year later, at COP 16 in Cancun, Bolivia alone refused to sign the agreement approved by all the other participant countries. At the most recent climate conference, COP 17 in Durban, Bolivia maintained a critical position but kept a lower profile and attracted less attention than before.[3]

In climate politics, the Bolivian government has taken on the task of speaking not only for the Bolivians, but for 'the people' in general (Aguirre and Cooper 2010). Denouncing the UN-led climate negotiation process, the government organized an alternative summit in Cochabamba, Bolivia; the World People's Conference on Climate Change and the Rights of Mother Earth, in April 2010, in which the official Bolivian standpoint was promoted as an alternative to dominant climate politics (Turner 2010). The outcome of the summit was a 'People's Agreement' – essentially a list of the proposals that Bolivia has presented in UN negotiations (People's Agreement of Cochabamba 2010; Turner 2010).

During and after the Cochabamba conference, the government has been criticized by indigenous movements, which are customarily among their main supporters, for keeping double standards on environmental issues and not living up to their radical discourse at home (Aguirre and Cooper 2010; Turner 2010). This criticism increased in 2011 during a conflict around a highway, which is planned to be constructed through TIPNIS, a national park and indigenous territory (Mamani Ramirez 2011b; Bjork-James 2011). While climate change has clearly been politicized in Bolivia, this recent critique against the government has made it more difficult for them to frame themselves as a green alternative. Nevertheless, although the field of Bolivian environment politics has become increasingly complex, it is interesting to follow the recent politicization and discursive unfolding of the climate issue in Bolivia.

Glacier narratives in Bolivian climate discourse

Narratives about glacier retreat are frequently employed in the green radicalism climate discourse promoted by the Bolivian government and related actors. I will now turn to a number of documents produced by government units, as well as oral and written statements by Evo Morales and publications by a foundation with – at the time – close links to the government, in order to explore how narratives around glacier melting are constructed and mobilized. The examples are obviously not exhaustive, but they give an indication of the main features of these narratives. I have chosen the actors and examples to shed light on the government's discourse, which represents the Bolivian standpoint externally, and also influences national debates. The examples are primarily from 2007 to 2010, the period in which politicization of climate change was most lively in Bolivia.

Government documents

Climate change was brought into Bolivian high-level politics around 2007 and 2008, which is reflected in documents released by government authorities during the past decade. Glacier retreat is a reoccurring feature in these documents.

In 2007, the National Mechanism for Climate Change Adaptation was presented, which outlines areas of vulnerability to climate change impacts and suggests strategies for reducing this vulnerability. The actions of developed countries are posed as the cause for climate change and for the global lack of success in mitigating emissions; however, the approach is mainly technical. Glacier retreat is mentioned in a section on hydrological resources. It is stated that glaciers lose mass due to elevated temperatures, causing risks for floods and droughts, which compromise the availability of water for human consumption and hydropower generation (Bolivian Government 2007).

In the subsequent years, climate change travelled, from being handled as a primarily technical issue, onto the centre stage of politics. In 2009, Bolivia's second National Communication[4] was presented to the UNFCCC. This document can be compared with the first National Communication which was produced in 2000, six years before MAS came to power. Although the two documents were largely prepared by the same people, they differ greatly, illustrating the advancing politicization of climate change in Bolivia. The first Communication is focused on the more technical side of climate change. It mentions glacier retreat only briefly as a possible future effect of climate change impacts (Bolivian Government 2000: 68). The second, while also describing the technical aspects, is much more politicized, reflecting the augmented attention to climate change and the standpoints of the

MAS government. Here, glacier retreat is given a more elevated position as an evidence of increased temperature. The shrinkage of glaciers is presented as 'the most significant impact of climate change' (Bolivian Government 2009: 25) and illustrated with a series of pictures showing Chacaltaya in 1982, 1992 and 2005 – indeed a dramatic transformation. The text asserts that 'Bolivia's glaciers are definitely receding as a result of climate change' (Bolivian Government 2009: 25). The implications for water availability are pointed out, and funds to cover adaptation measures are requested from developed countries as a part-payment of climate debts. This later document thus echoes and supports the green radicalism discourse promoted by the government in international forums (Bolivian Government 2009).

Statements by Evo Morales

Statements given by Evo Morales to the UN and during international climate negotiations from 2007 to 2010 reflect the Bolivian government's position and exemplify how glacier narratives are employed to add weight to a green radicalism discourse.[5]

On 23 April 2008 Morales made a statement to the 7th Session of the UN Permanent Forum on Indigenous Issues, listing '[t]he 10 sins of capitalism and the 10 commandments to save the planet, humanity, and life'. Here he blamed capitalism for causing overexploitation of natural resources that leads to climate change. Among the proposed commandments are 'End capitalism', 'A world without imperialism or colonialism' and 'Respect for Mother Earth'. Under the fourth commandment, 'Water as a human right belonging to all living beings', it is claimed that '[t]he biggest impact of climate change is in water sources. Our snows and glaciers are disappearing'. The last sentence of the statement, under commandment number ten ('Live Well. Don't live better at others' expense. Build communitarian socialism in harmony with mother earth') reads: '[i]ndigenous communities will not be silenced until we achieve real change, because our voice is the voice of the snowcapped mountains losing their white ponchos' (UNPFII 2008).

During COP 15, Morales gave a press conference in which the Bolivian proposals were presented. Again, respect for Mother Earth and ending capitalism were central features. The Bolivian or Andean culture was termed a 'culture of life', contrasted to the western/capitalist 'culture of death', and exploitation of Mother Earth was equated with colonization and exploitation of indigenous people. Morales argued that a one-degree centigrade decrease of the temperature must be realized in order to prevent disaster and, for instance, 'save our sacred glaciers and lakes' (Morales Ayma 2010).

Publications by Fundación Solón

As climate change has moved onto the high-level agenda, its political dimensions have been subsumed under the wings of the Ministry of Foreign Relations, which has taken on a strong role in positioning Bolivia in international climate negotiations. During the peak of Bolivian discourse formation on climate change, in 2007–10, the former Bolivian UN Ambassador and lead climate negotiator Pablo Solón was frequently pointed out as 'the man' behind the country's position.[6] Pablo Solón has personal linkages to Fundación Solón, an influential foundation that produces campaigns on social and cultural themes and was created by his father, the famous artist Walter Solón. Fundación Solón receives financial support from a number of international NGOs. Though not formally associated with the government, it has to a great extent promoted the government's position on climate change, and provided intellectual material to support it (personal interviews with the head of Fundación Solón on 10 April 2012, former government officials on 22 October 2010 and 24 October 2010 and a representative from a La Paz-based climate research institute on 15 November 2010, La Paz, Bolivia). Since Pablo Solón left his two formal positions, he has continued to participate in climate and environment debates both internationally and within Bolivia (personal interview with Pablo Solón on 11 April 2012, La Paz, Bolivia). In September 2011 he publicly criticized the Morales government for its actions during the TIPNIS conflict (Climate Connections 2011). Thereby, the ties between Fundación Solón and the government have weakened. However, given the great influence of the foundation on the radical shift in Bolivian climate politics, it is still interesting and important to analyse their publications on this matter.

Fundación Solón has emphasized glacier retreat in their climate change campaigns. The theme is highlighted in several issues of their bulletin Tunupa. Especially, Tunupa No 62, from August 2010, is dedicated to the topic. Its title is 'Víctimas silenciosas del cambio climático: Los glaciares y el agua' ('Silent victims of climate change: The glaciers and the water'). The issue features articles that draw on scientific data to explain the melting of glaciers, as well as more policy-oriented texts covering themes such as human rights, water security and proposals for glacier protection. The scientific importance of glaciers as repositories for information on historical climate changes is addressed, as well as their symbolic and religious meanings. One article titled 'El "resplandeciente" Illimani pierde su poncho blanco' ('The "luminous" Illimani loses its white poncho') discusses the cultural and spiritual significance of Illimani and other glaciers. Here it is stated that 'the disappearance of Illimani would be a great disaster for the Bolivians, much larger than what happened to the twin towers in New York' (Fundación Solón 2010a, my translation). In the editorial, the capitalist system is explicitly pointed out as the cause for climate change, and glaciers are identified as victims and paradigmatic examples of climate change impacts.

The editorial of Tunupa No 64, also from August 2010, dwells on glacier retreat as a threat to water availability and a loss of cultural values and climatic memories (Fundación Solón 2010b). In an earlier issue, No 47 from February 2009, the disappearance of Chacaltaya is shown in diagrams and a series of pictures ranging from 1940 to 2007, as an illustration of climate change effects. The same issue also contains a general introduction to climate change impacts and a stern political positioning in which responsibility and climate justice is a main focus. Bolivia's minor emissions in relation to the impacts it is facing are emphasized (Fundación Solón 2009).

Discussion

In the statements made by Evo Morales, and reflected by Fundación Solón in the contents of Tunupa, glaciers are assigned an important symbolic value. The powerful allegory of the snow-capped mountains losing their ponchos establishes a kinship between culture and territory, between the mountains and their indigenous inhabitants among whom the poncho is, famously, a traditional piece of clothing. The people are envisioned to speak with one voice, which is also the voice of the mountains; humans and mountains are suffering the same tragedy, together. This exemplifies the claim of speaking for 'the people' and for Mother Earth; the cultural, spiritual and material environment in which humans are embedded, against the threat of a western, capitalist 'culture of death'.

These accounts may be viewed in light of the ongoing political project aiming towards a reformulation of the Bolivian state and national identity. Andean culture is predominant in this project, further adding to the symbolic importance of glaciers and the highland communities threatened by their retreat. The cultural value of glaciers is explicitly emphasized in this narrative, not least clearly expressed in the bold comparison with the emblematic demolition of the World Trade Center in New York – a place which may well symbolize the capitalist west – in 2001.

In the exemplified official publications, the Bolivian government employs technical rather than cultural arguments in the accounts on glacier retreat, but also here, elements of the same narrative are invoked and disappearing glaciers are placed within a green radicalism approach, attributing climate change to western capitalism. Studying the two national communications and the mechanism for adaptation, it becomes evident how climate change has, over a short time period, been increasingly politicized and tied to a greater political project, and how glaciers have been assigned an increasingly significant symbolic role.

The glacier narrative employed by the Bolivian government and Fundación Solón reflects and supports the recent Bolivian positioning in international climate negotiations. The narrative includes local features, such as references to indigenous culture and to the importance of glaciers to local communities. Yet, it can be seen as a version of the endangered glacier narrative identified by Carey. The narrative draws on natural scientific accounts in presenting glaciers as archives for climate data, indicators of climate change and invaluable water reservoirs. Glaciers are also depicted as carriers of cultural and spiritual values; they are named, personalized, sacralized and portrayed as silent victims, and their disappearance is bemoaned. Glacier retreat is attributed to human action; however, the responsibility is placed outside the local area, on western capitalist exploitation. The primary solution presented is not to mitigate emissions within a sustained global order or to physically protect the remaining glaciers – which would be the case within an ecological modernization–green governmentality discourse – but to end capitalism and radically change the global world order. A local variety of the endangered glacier narrative is thus employed by Bolivian actors in order to support a green radicalism discourse, and in turn strengthen a political project, which promotes decolonization and a revival of local – primarily Andean – values.

The Bolivian government has until this point not been very successful in terms of gaining wider support for its claims. Bolivia has not had much influence on the outcomes of international climate negotiations; its proposals have been largely ignored. Bolivia's radical position during COP 15 and the subsequent Cochabamba Conference attracted positive interest from international climate justice movements, but the public and media attention to the COPs, and the climate issue in general, has faded since the interest peak around COP 15. At COP 17, Bolivia also kept a lower profile than at the two prior meetings.

Within Bolivia, climate and environment has recently been a topic of fierce public debate. The MAS government has received heavy criticism from actors that usually support it, confronting it with its own arguments and accusing it of not living up to its green rhetoric. It may however be assumed that the government's promotion of a green radicalism discourse – backed up by elements such as the endangered glacier narrative – has partly incited these discussions and popular engagement in environmental issues within Bolivia.

The case of Bolivia is illustrative of the complexity and fluidity that characterize the formation and mobilization of narratives on climate change. Where, and how, do narratives appear? Which stories can be told by whom, and at which moment? As we have seen, the emblematic issue of glacier retreat has emerged carried by the powerful and evocative narrative of the endangered glacier. This narrative has appeared under certain conditions: within post-colonial regimes of power-knowledge, in times marked by climate change concerns formed under a dominant discourse of ecological modernization–green governmentality. Nevertheless, as the case of Bolivia shows, the narrative does not necessarily stay within this discourse, and the meaning(s) it loads glaciers with can be mobilized for different political purposes.

Bolivia is one of the places on Earth facing glacier retreat as a material reality. It is also a place where climate change politics have become part of recent political transformations. Various factors, including the specific post-colonial setting, a change of national government, vibrant popular movements, geophysical aspects and a moment of international attention to climate change, can be traced behind the emergence and promotion of the green radicalist climate discourse, which challenges the ecological modernization–green governmentality regime.

By drawing on existing symbolic and material meanings of glaciers in the Andes, Bolivian actors construct a continuum between culture and territory, human and nature, tradition and an ongoing political project; here, the mountains losing their ponchos of ice become victims of the same 'culture of death' as the indigenous people inhabiting them. Thereby an established narrative of endangered glaciers is appropriated and adjusted, a story which is recognized and resonates well in international forums, but also with local perspectives and identity formations. Perhaps the only possible story right there and then. Here, using Anna Tsing's term, a friction can be identified, where the local and the global are entangled in awkward and uneven encounters (Tsing 2005). The global, universal or hegemonic is never smooth or unchallenged; it is a dynamic space of constant negotiation taking place in a zillion instants of friction. The stories that we tell about the world, and how we make them make sense to us, reflect these frictions.

Notes

1 As developed by for instance Bruno Latour (2004) and Donna Haraway (1991).
2 For instance, Bolivia recently passed a law defining the rights of Mother Earth, and *vivir bien* is a central idea in the new constitution, which was approved by referendum in 2009.
3 This has to do with a fading international interest in climate conferences as well as internal political tensions and the replacement of key individuals on the negotiating team.
4 All parties to the UNFCCC are required to submit national reports on their implementation of the Convention to the Conference of the Parties (COP). On the UNFCCC webpage it is stated that: '[t]he core elements of the national communications... are information on emissions and removals of greenhouse gases (GHGs) and details of the activities a Party has undertaken to implement the Convention' (UNFCCC 2010).
5 Morales has later been less outspoken on climate change issues, due to a changed political environment.
6 This account was given by several of my informants in La Paz.

References

Aguirre, J.C. and Cooper, E.S. (2010) 'Evo Morales, Climate Change, and the Paradoxes of a Social-Movement Presidency', *Latin American Perspectives* 37: 238–244.
Albro, R. (2010) 'Confounding Cultural Citizenship and Constitutional Reform in Bolivia', *Latin American Perspectives* 37: 71–90.
Bäckstrand, K. and Lövbrand, E. (2006) 'Planting Trees to Mitigate Climate Change: Contested Discourses of Ecological Modernization, Green Governmentality and Civic Environmentalism', *Global Environmental Politics* 6(1): 50–75.
Bäckstrand, K. and Lövbrand, E. (2007) 'Climate Governance Beyond 2012: Competing Discourses of Green Governmentality, Ecological Modernization and Civic Environmentalism', in Pettenger, M.E. (ed.) *The Social Construction of Climate Change: Power, Knowledge, Norms, Discourses*, Farnham: Ashgate, 123–148.
Bjork-James, C. (2011) 'Indigenous March in Defense of Isiboro Sécure Arrives in La Paz, Challenges Evo Morales Government. Background Briefing'. Online. Available at: www.scribd.com/doc/69142514/TIPNIS-Background-Sheet-16Oct11 (retrieved: 13 March 2012).
Bolivian Government (2000) *First National Communication to the UNFCCC*, La Paz.
Bolivian Government (2006) *Bolivia Digna, Soberana, Productiva y Democratica para Vivir Bien 2006–2010* (National Development Plan), La Paz.
Bolivian Government (2007) Mecanismo Nacional de Adaptación al Cambio Climático, La Paz.
Bolivian Government (2009) *Second National Communication to the UNFCCC,* La Paz.
Brezinski, M. (2012) 'Arktis vårt gemensamma intresse', *Svenska Dagbladet,* 6 August.
Carey, M. (2007) 'The History of Ice: How Glaciers Became an Endangered Species', *Environmental History* 12: 497–527.
Carey, M. (2010) *In the Shadow of Melting Glaciers: Climate Change and Andean Society*, Oxford: Oxford University Press.

Climate Connections (2011) 'Letter from Pablo Solon on the TIPNIS Highway Controversy'. Online. Available at: http://climate-connections.org/2011/09/29/letter-from-pablo-solon-on-the tipnis-highway-controversy (retrieved: 13 March 2012).

Commission on Climate Change and Development (2009) *Closing the Gaps*, Stockholm: Ministry for Foreign Affairs.

Cruikshank, J. (2005) *Do Glaciers Listen? Local Knowledge, Colonial Encounters, and Social Imagination*, Vancouver: UBC Press.

Fløttum, K. (2010) 'A Linguistic and Discursive View on Climate Change Discourse', *Revue du GERAS* 58: 19–37.

Fundación Solón (2009) *Tunúpa* No 47, La Paz, Bolivia.

Fundación Solón (2010a) *Tunúpa* No 62, La Paz, Bolivia.

Fundación Solón (2010b) *Tunúpa* No 64, La Paz, Bolivia.

Hajer, M. (1995) *The Politics of Environmental Discourse: Ecological Modernization and the Policy Process*, London: Clarendon Press.

Hajer, M. and Versteeg, W. (2001) 'A Decade of Discourse Analysis of Environmental Politics: Achievements, Challenges, Perspectives', *Journal of Environmental Policy & Planning* 7(3): 175–184.

Haraway, D. (1991) *Simians, Cyborgs and Women: The Reinvention of Nature*, London and New York: Routledge.

Howard, R. (2010) 'Language, Signs, and the Performance of Power: The Discursive Struggle over Decolonization in the Bolivia of Evo Morales', *Latin American Perspectives* 37: 176–194.

Knight, P.G. (2004) 'Glaciers: Art and History, Science and Uncertainty', *Interdisciplinary Science Reviews* 29: 385–393.

Latour, B. (2004) *Politics of Nature: How to Bring the Sciences Into Democracy*, Cambridge, MA: Harvard University Press.

Leavy, P. (2009) *Method Meets Art: Art-Based Research Practice*, New York: The Guilford Press.

Lorimer, J. (2007) 'Nonhuman Charisma', *Environment and Planning D: Society and Space* 25(5): 911–932.

Mamani Ramirez, P. (2011a) 'Cartographies of Indigenous Power: Identity and Territoriality in Bolivia', in Fabricant, N. and Gustafson, B. (eds) *Remapping Bolivia: Resources, Territory, and Indigeneity in a Plurinational State*, Santa Fe: School for Advanced Research Press, 30–45.

Mamani Ramirez, P. (2011b) '¿Por qué pensar fuera de los marcos de izquierda y derecha? Reflexión crítica desde *Qullasuyu/Bolivia'*, in Gutiérrez, R. (ed.) *Palabras para tejernos, resistir y transformar en la época que estamos viviendo*, Cochabamba: Textos Rebeldes, 171–202.

Mol, A. and Spaargaren, G. (2000) 'Ecological Modernisation Theory in Debate: A Review', *Environmental Politics* 9(1): 17–49.

Morales Ayma, E. (2010) *The Earth Does Not Belong to Us, We Belong to the Earth: Messages from President Evo Morales Ayma about the Pachamama (the Earth Mother) and Climate Change*, La Paz: The Ministry of Exterior Relations.

Orlove, B., Wiegandt, E. and Luckman B.H. (eds) (2008) *Darkening Peaks: Glacier Retreat, Science, and Society*, Berkeley: University of California Press.

People's Agreement of Cochabamba (2010) 'People's Agreement of Cochabamba'. Online. Available at: 1191406429 http://pwccc.wordpress.com/2010/04/24/peoples1191406429 -1191406429 agreement/ (retrieved: 13 March 2012).

Postero, N.G. (2007) *Now We Are Citizens: Indigenous Politics in Postmulticultural Bolivia*, Stanford: Stanford University Press.

Rhoades, R.E., Ríos, X.Z. and Aragundy Ochoa, J. (2008) 'Mama Cotacachi: History, Local Perceptions, and Social Impacts of Climate Change and Glacier Retreat in the Ecuadorian Andes', in Orlove, B., Wiegandt, E. and Luckman, B.H. (eds) *Darkening Peaks: Glacier Retreat, Science, and Society*, Berkeley: University of California Press, 216–228.

Rosenthal, E. (2009) 'In Bolivia, Water and Ice Tell of Climate Change', *The New York Times*, 13 December.

Shukman, D. (2009) 'Glacier Threat to Bolivia Capital', *BBC News*, 4 December.

Soruco, A., Vincent, C., Francou, B. and Francisco Gonzalez, J. (2009) 'Glacier Decline between 1963 and 2006 in the Cordillera Real, Bolivia', *Geophysical Research Letters* 36, L03502.

Squire, C., Andrews, M. and Tamboukou, M. (2008) 'Introduction: What is Narrative Research?', in Squire, C., Andrews, M. and Tamboukou, M. (eds) *Doing Narrative Research*, Thousand Oaks: Sage, 1–21.

Tsing, A.L. (2005) *Friction: An Ethnography of Global Connection*, Princeton: Princeton University Press.

Turner, T.E. (2010) 'From Cochabamba, a New Internationale and Manifesto for Mother Earth', *Capitalism Nature Socialism* 21(3): 56–74.

UNFCCC (2010) *National Reports*. Online. Available at: unfccc.int/national_reports/items/1408.php (retrieved: 12 April 2012).

UNPFII (2008) 'Statement by Evo Morales to the 7th United Nations Permanent Forum on Indigenous Issues'. Online. Available at: www.un.org/esa/socdev/unpfii/documents/statement_morales08.pdf (retrieved: 10 March 2012).

Widmark, C. (2009) 'The Power of "Andean Culture" – Bolivian Debates on the Decolonization of Gender Equality Within and Outside the Framework of the State'. Paper prepared for the 2009 Congress of the Latin American Studies Association, Rio de Janeiro, Brazil, 11–14 June 2009.

13 'Climate justice', 'green economy' or 'a one planet lifestyle'

Hegemonic narratives in transnational NGOs and social movements

Philip T. Bedall

Introduction

> [I]t should be remarked that the general notion of the state includes elements which need to be referred back to the notion of civil society (in the sense that one might say that state = political society + civil society, in other words hegemony protected by the armour of coercion).
>
> (Gramsci 1971: 262f.)

This famous equation by the Italian philosopher and politician Antonio Gramsci referring to the conception of the state has not been widely established among the dominant approaches to global environmental politics so far. When it comes to explaining how regimes such as the UNFCCC are formed, regime theory is dominant (Okereke and Bulkeley 2007). It is characterized by state-centrism, to a large extent neglecting non-state actors (cf. Newell 2000: 2ff., 23ff.).[1] In Gramsci's terms they focus on the political society only, i.e. on the state in the narrower sense (institutions with administrative and legal duties). The relevance of the civil society is mostly neglected. It is the civil society, where social conflicts are turned into balanced compromises, hence into a hegemonic consensus that is essential to develop political strategies and to handle collective problems. A Gramscian understanding, by contrast, implies that hegemonic struggles in the field of global environmental politics do not exclusively take place at international conference tables. They are also being fought within civil society.[2]

This chapter analyses the re-production of hegemonic projects in the global civil society, where climate change is interpreted in many different ways (cf. for example Hulme 2009). As many of the contributions in this volume show, there are various competing representations, all of which come along with different ideas about how to govern climate change. Civil society, then, is the arena in which struggles over a hegemonic representation of climate change are fought out (see also Chapter 15 in this volume). The hegemonic representation of climate change decides over the question, which particular political demands are accepted, excluded or marginalized in climate governance. Civil society, hence, is the place in which hegemonic conditions – such as governing climate change through the deployment of market instruments – can be legitimized; at the same time, it is also the place where criticism can be expressed and where alternative projects emerge.

This chapter explicitly focuses on the activities of transnational NGOs and social movements as part of the discursive arena, in which modes of global climate governance are fought out. In contrast to existing studies (for example Arts 1998; Newell 2000), this contribution takes up a micro-perspective on the (re-)production of hegemony in discursive struggles: it investigates the articulated (competing) demands and narratives on climate change. The analysis is based on interviews conducted during COP 15 in Copenhagen in 2009. In doing so, the chapter also presents an approach to integrate close-to-the-text interview research with research on broader hegemonic discourses and thus contributes to the elaboration of discourse analysis.

This chapter seeks to analyse how articulations in the discursive arena of the civil society reaffirm or challenge existing forms of global climate governance. The chapter's perspective on hegemony departs from essentialist positions and lends more weight to agency: hegemonic or 'counter'-hegemonic political activity is not understood as a historic necessity resulting from the economy or the properties of certain actors. In other words, institutionalized civil society actors are not necessarily affirmative, the same way as grassroots movements are not essentially more critical – even if there might be a lot of empirical evidence for these assumptions.[3] To understand hegemonic struggles, it is more useful to ask: what is the *critical* or what is the *affirmative* substance of discursive articulations? Who are the actors putting them forward? Which coalitions are being formed? To deal with these questions, the present analysis draws on the discourse theory of Ernesto Laclau and Chantal Mouffe (1985).

The results of the empirical study show that narratives at the level of the individual text are not *either* hegemonic *or* counter-hegemonic, as some of them can articulate demands that are affirmative *as well as* demands that are critical. We thus have to distinguish between two types of narratives: on the one hand the *individual narrative* that individuals use to make sense of the world and which is articulated in the single interview. On the other hand the *discursive narrative*, which crystallizes civil society discourses as the cumulative effect of repeated articulations. The individual narrative is characterized by the multiplicity of demands articulated within it. The discursive narrative – as an outcome of hegemonic struggles – however, condenses this complexity into rather simple storylines that promote certain demands and exclude others. It is thus either reproducing or challenging existing hegemonies.

I start by outlining the concepts of Laclau and Mouffe's hegemony and discourse theory that are decisive for the argument of this chapter. I then present a possibility to identify and study critique, as understood in the theory of Laclau and Mouffe, in concrete empirical texts. An analysis of narratives from the actors' field serves to transfer the conceptual framework to the empirical sphere. To do this, I first outline what has to be considered as the object of criticism: the manifestation of a neoliberal hegemony in climate politics.

Conceptualizing hegemony – the discourse theory of hegemony

Hegemony is often understood in terms of dominance. A Gramscian perspective, by contrast, highlights the exertion of power through consensus. Drawing on this general insight, Laclau and Mouffe have put forth a theory of hegemonic discourses (cf. Torfing 1999). In their view, the whole social world is discursive in nature. Discourse is 'a differential and structured system of positions' constituted by 'linguistic and non-linguistic elements' (Laclau and Mouffe 1985: 108). More recently Laclau has argued that the elements of political discourses can be regarded as political 'demands' (see Laclau 2007: 72–77). The signifying system, and hence the meaning of single demands, is constituted by establishing discursive relations (Laclau and Mouffe 1985: 127ff.; Nonhoff 2006: 86ff.). These relations follow two general logics. On the one hand, there is the logic of difference: the meaning of individual demands is constituted by their differentiation from each other. The logic of equivalence, on the other hand, links demands into broader classes – or chains of equivalences in Laclau and Mouffe's terminology. Every discourse includes an antagonism: there are always two chains of equivalence, opposing each other. One represents the demands that, once fulfilled, lead to social harmony and 'fullness', while the other represents the challenges that constitute an obstacle for realizing this harmony.

The social meaning established through such an (ontic) antagonism is never an ultimate one. There is always an excluded *other* vis-à-vis the *common* of the discourse. This social heterogeneity – or rather the excluded other – bears witness to the possibility of an alternative (Laclau 2007: 140). Following Laclau and Mouffe, only a partial fixation of social meaning is possible in discourse. This fixation is based on privileged demands, which serve as common labels (Laclau 1996: 36ff.; Laclau and Mouffe 1985: 112ff.). These labels represent the Common and, at the same time, the negation of the excluded Other. Those demands are defined as empty signifiers – more precisely signifiers, which have been *made empty* as they represent a whole series of different demands (Laclau 1996: 42).

To give an example: *growth* as used in the neoliberal discourse functions as a symbolic representative of the *common* (in particular of the fullness and harmony) because it is linked to, among other things, the prosperity of the market economy, an individual promise of happiness or the solution of problems. Accordingly, there is 'a variety of possible antagonisms in the social', i.e. 'any position in a system of differences, insofar as it is negated, can become the locus of an antagonism' (Laclau and Mouffe 1985: 131). In hegemonic struggles – like those taking place in climate politics – various ensembles of demands – subsequently defined as *hegemonic projects* – compete for discursive hegemony. They attain hegemony if they have a broad 'discursive "circulation"' (Nonhoff 2006: 141, my translation): they have to be repeatedly articulated a) over time and b) by a multiplicity of actors in the discursive arena from very different positions.

The latter assumption, that demands have to be re-articulated to become hegemonic, is of special interest for the present analysis. First of all, it is assumed that the primary means by which ensembles of demands *travel* across subjects is their representation in (fantasmatic) narratives. The notion of fantasy, as developed by the French psychoanalyst and structuralist Jacques Lacan, provides us with a means to understand why subjects become grip and hence re-produced certain discursive narratives. This issue is of particular interest for the analysis of the (re-)production of hegemony based on interviews:

> The role of fantasy . . . is not simply to set up an illusion that provides a subject with a false picture of the world. Instead, fantasies 'teach' us how to desire by incorporating references to features which are societally prohibited, or which tend to resist public-official disclosure. Typically, this involves the construction of a narrative that promises a fullness-to-come once a named or implied obstacle is overcome – the beatific dimension of fantasy – or which foretells of disaster if the obstacle proves too threatening or insurmountable: the horrific dimension of fantasy.
>
> (Glynos *et al.* 2009: 11f.)

Fantasmatic narratives in either their beatific or horrific dimensions reveal the ideological character of hegemonic struggles when they cover up the 'radical contingency of social relations' (Glynos and Howarth 2007: 14). Fantasies serve to give '*direction* and *energy*' to a variety of discursive elements (Glynos and Howarth 2007: 147), i.e. they serve to connect various demands in an imaginative way. Through the concept of fantasy, the processes of (re-)production and/or contestation of hegemony can be examined empirically. What follows will clarify this argument.

The 'moment of antagonism' – how to get hold of it empirically

So how can one conceptualize the abstract notion of criticism and – furthermore – operationalize it for an empirical analysis? Laclau and Mouffe's understanding of dislocation helps us to answer this question: a dislocation constitutes a moment of politicization when the contingency of discourse becomes manifest. Through a dislocation, established and taken-for-granted knowledge and ideas are called into question (Laclau 1990: 39ff.). '*What is*' is confronted with '*what might be*'. Hence, a dislocation can be conceived as a *critical* moment. It is '[t]he moment of antagonism where the undecidable nature of the alternatives and their resolution through power relations becomes fully visible' (Laclau 1990: 35). To get hold of criticism empirically, one has to focus on dislocations.

Two levels must be separated for the purpose of analysis. On the *level of discourse*, coalitions of actors are reproducing hegemonic projects through discursive narratives. By contrast, one has to distinguish ensembles of articulations produced by individual subjects (individual narratives). These ensembles – if they are constituted by linguistic articulations – can be grasped by analysing texts. In the case of the present study, these texts are the interview transcriptions. Even on the *level of individual texts*, demands are differentiated and equated, so that two chains of equivalence contrary to one another as well as symbolic representatives emerge. The structure prevailing in a specific text can be called its hegemonic structure (see also Nonhoff 2008: 321). It is by no means identical with a hegemonic project at the level of the discourse. At the same time, the hegemonic structure is not constituted by subjects in a voluntary manner. Subjects only possess a partial autonomy: they operate within the constraints of the existing discursive context, which for example provides the vocabulary they can use or the ideas they can link up to. Their articulations are hence contingent articulations (see Laclau 1990: 29f.).

On both levels – the discourse level as well as the level of an individual text – critical moments can be found by examining narratives. On the discourse level hegemonic projects emerge as specific fantasmatic narratives. I assume that even in an individual text a narrative is constructed. And just as in discursive narratives an antagonistic division can be observed in these individual articulations: the division into a beatific and a horrific dimension of fantasy. Here it should be noted that the fantasmatic narratives on the level of the individual text are not by themselves hegemonic or counter-hegemonic. This is what distinguishes individual narratives from discursive narratives, which constitute representations of different hegemonic projects. As a set of different articulations, individual narratives on the contrary may (re-)produce various (competing) hegemonic projects.[4]

What would focusing on dislocations and, with it, on criticism in hegemonic struggles mean? On the discourse level it would mean asking if the fantasies of different hegemonic projects are antagonistic towards hegemony. On the level of the individual text it would mean focusing on the demands articulated in the narratives and scanning them for their critical character.

Glynos and Howarth (2007: 150f.) have developed a classification to examine the struggle for hegemony on the *discourse level*. Its point of reference is the antagonism of a hegemony, i.e. of a hegemonic project that has reached hegemony: the antagonism of the common versus the other. They classify according to how the *dimensions of fantasy* of a hegemonic project fit into the antagonistic relation of the hegemony (see Figure 13.1).

To be more concrete, Glynos and Howarth on the one hand question narratives in regard to what is articulated as *beatific* – is it *what exists* or *what is to come*? On

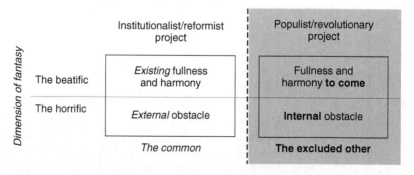

Figure 13.1 Classification of hegemonic projects (on discourse level) in hegemonic struggles (figure based on Glynos and Howarth (2007: 145ff.)).

the other hand they question what is articulated as a threat – an *external obstacle* to the fullness already attained or an *internal obstacle* to the fullness aimed for? In hegemonic projects classified by Glynos and Howarth as '*institutionalist* or *reformist*', fantasmatic logics can 'be articulated by means of a narrative in which an external obstacle or enemy is deemed to be a threat to an already existing fullness and harmony' (Glynos and Howarth 2007: 151). By contrast, in hegemonic projects classified as '*populist* or *revolutionary*', 'fantasmatic logics may take the form of a narrative in which an *internal* obstacle (or "enemy within") is deemed responsible for the blockage of identity, while promising a fullness or harmony to come' (Glynos and Howarth 2007: 150). Hegemonic projects like those are characterized by *dislocatory* fantasmatic logics confronting the seemingly ultimate fixing of meaning with alternatives.

How then is it possible to take hold of the critical content of a fantasmatic narrative on the *level of the individual text*? It depends on which dimension of hegemony (the *common* or the excluded *other*) is reproduced when specific demands are articulated, i.e. whether an articulation is an affirmation or a pejoration of the hegemonic fantasy. Basically, demands in an individual narrative can be classified with one of the two dimensions of fantasy (see Figure 13.2).

An *affirmative* demand is a demand which fits in with the hegemonic chains of equivalence. If, however, demands are articulated from the terrain of the excluded *other*, dislocatory effects will emerge. Such pejorative demands disrupt the established hegemony so that 'the fact that things could be otherwise . . . becomes apparent' (Marchart 2004: 4). Such demands shall be called *critical*.

Hegemony in climate politics – the neoliberalization of the climate

In the following I will sketch the established hegemony in order to illustrate the battleground of the discursive struggle to be analysed below. The aim, however,

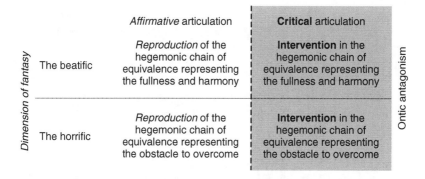

Figure 13.2 Classification of articulations in the hegemonic structure (on the level of the individual text).

is not to provide a general and comprehensive overview of neoliberal discourses and practices, but to show what is taken for granted in contemporary climate governance and which positions are demarcated to the discursive outside. This is a precondition for the subsequent examination of the criticism of the established hegemony as expressed in the narratives.

The market orientation of the Kyoto Protocol and its flexible mechanisms, competition and economic growth play a decisive role in global climate politics. This is, at least partly, due to 'a larger, more longstanding historical wave of neoliberalism' (Lohmann 2006: 54) – a wave that, since the 1970s, has brought about essential changes in the global economy (for more details see Harvey 2005; Saad-Filho and Johnston 2005). Neoliberalism seeks to reduce direct governmental intervention into the society. Instead, markets must be created in all social spheres, if necessary by state activities (see also Chapters 3 and 5 in this volume). By the 1990s this neoliberal dogma increasingly pervaded all areas of life:

> [I]t became a far broader project of regulating social life through market imperatives ... Neoliberalism had become the political form in which political and social relations are reproduced at the local as well as the national level of the state, and across the international state system.
>
> (Albo 2007: 356)

Likewise, neoliberalism was of great influence wherever climate change was treated politically (see Newell and Paterson 2010: 11ff.). In climate negotiations, first steps towards trade mechanisms were taken in the mid-1990s by free market environmentalists in the Clinton administration (Lohmann 2006: 49). The initial opposition between Europe and the South was abandoned in favour of the view that market mechanisms were without alternative: a 'global consensus' that sees market mechanisms as 'the only show in town' (Lohmann 2006: 50). Since then, a 'new global regulation system' is emerging (Brunnengräber *et al.* 2008: 191, my translation) that guarantees the reproduction of the economy. On the one hand it ensures access to and consumption of fossil resources, and on the other hand handles externalities – greenhouse gas emissions – politically to reduce conflicts, though mainly in a symbolic way. This is made possible by a 'strategic selectivity' (Jessop 2004: 70) that reconciles the regulation of the socio-ecologic crises with the regulation of fossilistic competition (Paterson 2010; Brunnengräber 2013).

This selectivity is found in the dominant problematization of climate change as well as in the political measures that are deemed appropriate for solving the problem (cf. Brunnengräber *et al.* 2008: 188ff.). Through this selectivity the complexity of the problem of anthropogenic climate change is reduced: climate change is not understood as revealing a crisis of society's present relation with nature, but merely as an ecological crisis that is not an intrinsic feature of the present society: a 'global environmental problem' (Brunnengräber *et al.* 2008: 188, my translation). This narrows the crisis down to a problem of overstraining the global carbon budget and so views emissions, not social relations, as the primary cause for the problem (see also Swyngedouw 2010: 216ff.). With regard to the hegemonic climate change discourse, these remarks imply that the continued existence of the contemporary global economic system is taken for granted and positions that call for more substantial social-economic transformations are excluded from the discourse.

At the same time, strategies to regulate emissions are preferred, whereas the production of energy itself is left untouched. This 'institutional separation of an input and an output side' of the fossilistic energy regime (Brunnengräber *et al.* 2008: 188, my translation) is particularly apparent in the context of the commodification of emissions through the flexible mechanisms of the Kyoto Protocol (emission trading, Clean Development Mechanism and Joint Implementation) and with regard to the focus on technological solutions such as efficiency strategies or sequestration. Any articulation that questions the fossilistic energy regime hence constitutes a dislocation to the dominant climate governance discourse.

For analytical purposes, several characteristics of climate neoliberalism have to be highlighted (see Figure 13.3). It should be noted that empirically neoliberalism is not presenting itself as a 'homogenous and universal thing', but rather as 'a spatiotemporally differentiated process' (Castree 2008a: 155). In fact, the outlined characteristics need to be understood as ideal types (Jessop 2002: 460, as cited by Castree 2008b: 142). Similar translocal or transnational processes, mechanisms or rules, which are results of a '"fast policy transfer" between national and international policy elites' manifest themselves in different places and at different times (Castree 2008a: 156).

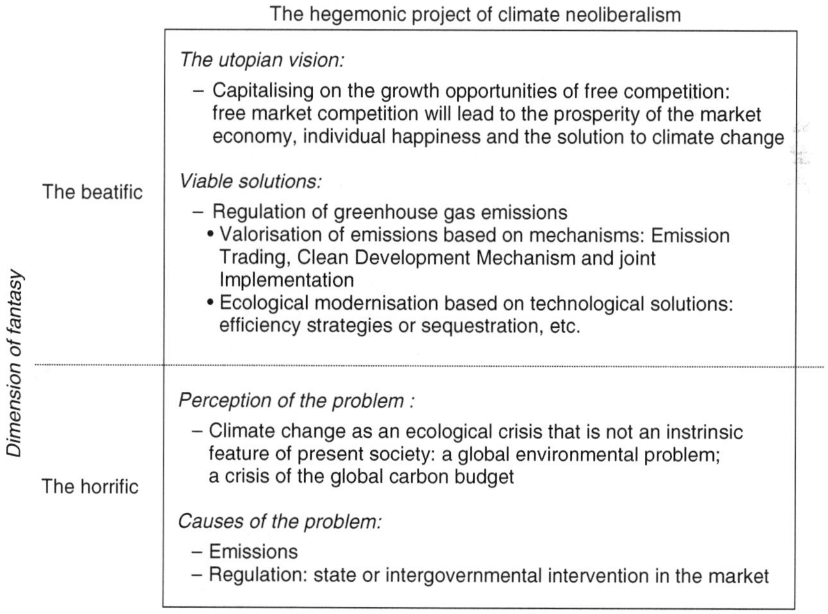

	The hegemonic project of climate neoliberalism

The beatific	*The utopian vision:*
	– Capitalising on the growth opportunities of free competition: free market competition will lead to the prosperity of the market economy, individual happiness and the solution to climate change
	
	Viable solutions:
	– Regulation of greenhouse gas emissions
	  • Valorisation of emissions based on mechanisms: Emission Trading, Clean Development Mechanism and joint Implementation
	  • Ecological modernisation based on technological solutions: efficiency strategies or sequestration, etc.

The horrific	*Perception of the problem :* – Climate change as an ecological crisis that is not an instrinsic feature of present society: a global environmental problem; a crisis of the global carbon budget *Causes of the problem:* – Emissions – Regulation: state or intergovernmental intervention in the market

Dimension of fantasy

Figure 13.3 Ideal-typical characteristics of climate neoliberalism.

At the time of the Copenhagen climate negotiations it seemed that unless the parties to the Kyoto Protocol can agree on a second commitment period, its regulatory mechanisms lose any effect after 2012. Without these market mechanisms central elements of the neoliberal hegemony within global climate politics would be lost.[5] For the neoliberal hegemony to continue, the coherence of growth and socio-ecological problems must be ensured institutionally beyond that period. Consequently, negotiations for a post-Kyoto protocol open up a terrain of hegemonic struggles for either the maintenance or contestation of the neoliberal hegemony and its institutions, with a great variety of actors participating. It is on this terrain that the narratives chosen for analysis have been articulated.

From the interviews towards the hegemonic structure

To select the civil society actors focused on in this study – the transnational NGOs and social movements oriented towards international climate politics – a set of criteria for inclusion and exclusion[6] was formulated. To grasp actors based on these criteria I consulted the UNFCCC's register of NGOs accredited to the UN climate conference COP 15 at Copenhagen, analysed social movements' websites and conducted participatory observations at preparatory meetings of social movements. This procedure allowed including a range of actors: accredited organizations with observer status *and* actors that worked outside the official UNFCCC process. I clustered the actors on the basis of their *membership in political networks* like the Climate Action Network (CAN), Climate Justice Now! or Climate Justice Action as well as (if existing) on the basis of their *thematic orientation* (indigenous, religious, conservation, gender). Subsequently, a representative set of 17 actors was chosen from this spectrum. The semi-structured qualitative interviews with these actors were conducted during the COP 15 (supplemented by three telephone interviews in the aftermath of the conference).

It is a distinctive feature of interviews to collect extensive information about actors' articulations of particular issues. In contrast to documents, which may differ as to content, structure and length, interviews allow for a structured collection, applying heuristic categories relevant to the research project. The interviewees offer an individual and spontaneous impression of discursive patterns of meaning, which exist in a particular field, at a particular time (see Hansen and Sørensen 2005: 99).

Presenting a possibility to reconstruct the hegemonic structure from an interview narrative is a particular contribution of this chapter. This novel perspective draws on aspects of the narrative-analysis of Feldman *et al.* (2004), which are linked to hegemony and discourse theory. This procedure has been divided into three steps.

In the first step – *identification* – distinctive stories are identified in the text body, i.e. specific textual sequences are segmented intuitively. Here, 'Stories are instantiations, particular exemplars, of the grand conception. They respond to the questions of "And then what happened?" or "What do you mean?"' (Feldman *et al.* 2004: 153). The following segment from an interview with a representative of the 'Hopenhagen' campaign may serve as an example:

[The 'It's Going to be Companies Not Countries' story:]
I think the right solutions to climate change they – I'll start with what they can't be. I don't think that they can come from [above] . . . mandate[d] from any authoritative intergovernmental body. You know, [this] kind of rules out the United Nations' ability to 'solve climate change'. Solutions to climate change are going to come from market forces. From free competition to really capitalize on the growth opportunities of finding the solutions to global warming and finding the ways to limit greenhouse gases without hurting productivity and it's going to be companies not countries, but companies that really drive this and really create the innovation that will allow us to achieve a carbon neutral economy.

The *second step – evaluation –* is based on the assumption 'that an argument could be identified and represented in an inferential, logical form' (Feldman *et al.* 2004: 155). Here the story can be reproduced in the form of syllogisms[7] (Feldman *et al.* 2004: 155). Syllogisms can be reconstructed from explicit as well as implicit statements in the text body. The concept of enthymeme can also be used to describe implicitly expressed arguments. The rhetorical figure of the enthymeme is the short form of a syllogism where one of the two premises or the conclusion is not made explicit (Feldman *et al.* 2004: 152). Implicit statements may be identified by 'impressions of the stories as a whole and . . . deduction from the explicit elements of the argument that appear more readily' (Feldman *et al.* 2004: 158). Especially the statements implicit in the syllogisms reveal 'what is either controversial or taken for granted' (Feldman *et al.* 2004: 167).

The story quoted above can thus be reproduced in the form of the following syllogisms (implicit parts are capitalized):

The right solutions to climate change cannot be mandate from any intergovernmental body. MARKET FORCES ARE NOT MANDATED. *Therefore, solutions to climate change can come from market forces.*

The right solutions to climate change can not come as a mandate from any intergovernmental body. The rules of the United Nations are like a mandate. THEREFORE THE RIGHT SOLUTIONS TO CLIMATE CHANGE WILL NOT COME FROM THE UNITED NATIONS.

Free competition capitalizes on the growth opportunities. Capitalizing on the growth opportunities means finding solutions to global warming and limiting greenhouse gases without hurting productivity. Therefore, free competition means finding solutions to global warming and limiting greenhouse gases without hurting productivity.

Companies will create innovation. Innovation will allow us to achieve a carbon neutral economy. THEREFORE, COMPANIES WILL ALLOW US TO ACHIEVE A CARBON NEUTRAL ECONOMY.

Countries will not create innovation. Innovation will allow us to achieve a carbon neutral economy. THEREFORE, COUNTRIES WILL NOT ALLOW US TO ACHIEVE A CARBON NEUTRAL ECONOMY.

In a third step – *interpretation* – the syllogisms can be coded to make further interpretation possible. Their elements – premises and conclusions – are taken as textual units, and the coding of the single transcripts of interviews – that is I (a) to I (n), see Figure 13.4 – uses 'a list of relatively concrete, descriptive categories focusing on specific content' (see Feldman *et al.* 2004: 165). In this *longitudinal analysis* I used the fantasmatic structure of the narratives – the beatific and the horrific dimensions of fantasy – as a guideline to determine the descriptive categories: what is the perception of the problem, and what is articulated as causing the problem? Or: what is the utopian vision? What solutions are articulated as viable? The categories assume the role of heuristic lenses which are used to look at the realm of the empirical – the discourse. Coding according to subjects makes it possible to draw up case excerpts for each interview that represent the hegemonic structure of the narrative. Those excerpts assemble articulated demands. From the hegemonic structure of a narrative, one can deduce symbolic representations of the beatific or of the horrific (cf. the concept of the 'empty signifier' above).

The texts can also serve as the basis for a comparative analysis of the interviews, carving out typological patterns. In this study this *cross-sectional analysis* is analysing whether the articulated demands can be found on the *common*-side or on the excluded *other*-side of the antagonism of the established (neoliberal) hegemony. Following the previous discussion (see Figure 13.2), this translates to an either affirmative or critical character of an articulation.

Empirical results

In this section, I present some of the results from my empirical study. I start with an analytical distinction between the affirmative and the critical demands as articulated in the empirical material.

The full range of the demands that have been articulated in the material becomes visible when considering the narratives collected from members of the 'Hopenhagen' project and from members of the 'People's Protocol on Climate Change'. These narratives for the most part either contain *purely affirmative* or *purely critical* demands and thus can be grouped accordingly. In fact, they display a connection between the type of organization and the critical substance articulated, as 'Hopenhagen' is a highly institutionalized campaign while the 'People's Protocol on Climate Change' is a project mainly based on grassroots structures. The narratives provided by other actors in the sample, however, do not confirm such a connection; on the contrary, the heterogeneity of the articulated demands becomes apparent. The divide between criticism versus conformity does not correspond to the degree of organization. Members of NGOs and social movements articulate *both* affirmative *and* critical demands in their narratives. These heterogeneous demands can be further specified by drawing on the analytical categories developed above, i.e. problem perception, perception of its causes, utopian visions and viable solutions.

Problematization: as demonstrated above, it is typical of the neoliberal project to have a selective problem perception framing climate change as a mere ecologi-

Figure 13.4 Categories used for encoding the data – longitudinal and cross-section analysis

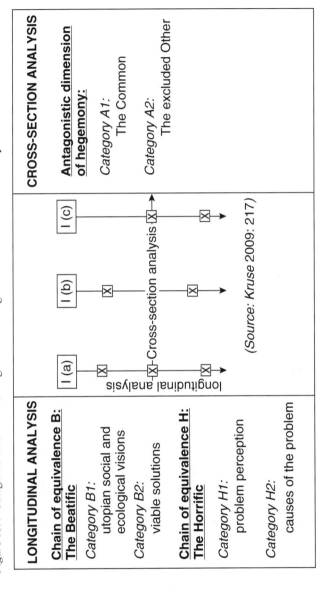

cal problem – a global environmental problem. Such an affirmative problem articulation is found only in one narrative ('Wetlands International'). When considering all narratives it becomes clear that the critical articulation of climate change as a social problem has largely become sedimented.

Causes of the problem: in many narratives emissions are articulated as the cause of the problem. Articulations like these can be identified as affirmative as they reproduce the neoliberal view of climate change as a crisis of the global carbon budget. Critical articulations of the problem and its causes (such as identifying 'growth', 'market mechanisms' or the 'energy system' as causes of the problem) seem to be loosely scattered over the narratives. With regard to the categories 'problem perception' or 'causes of the problem', many narratives already show the concurrence of critical and affirmative articulations. This concurrence becomes even more apparent when it comes to the articulated 'viable solutions'.

Viable solutions: the narratives articulate a large number of solutions. There are affirmative demands like those for 'market mechanisms', for an ecological modernization based on technology ('techno-fix') or for the enhancement of 'energy efficiency'. Critical articulations demand turning away from fossil resources ('leaving fossils in the ground'), ask for 'changes in the economic organization of the world' or call for 'new ways of production'. The heterogeneity of solutions has been illustrated in Figure 13.5: the example of the '350.org'-narrative shows that affirmative and critical demands can be articulated simultaneously.

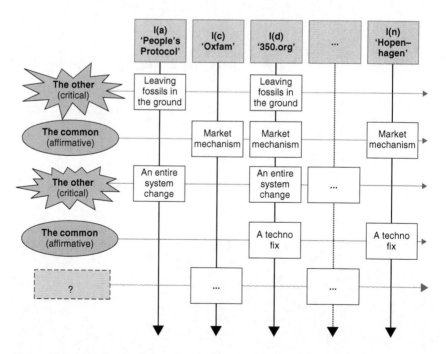

Figure 13.5 Articulated solutions (longitudinal and cross-section analysis).

The *utopian vision*: the utopian vision illustrates a specific type of demand. Various narratives articulate 'sustainability' as a central feature of the utopian vision, but the character of the demand cannot be ascertained unambiguously. The demand must be regarded as 'floating'[8] as for example in one instance it is articulated as a principal change of the development paradigm ('CIDSE', 'OXFAM'), while in another instance it is used to question a specific exploitation of wetlands, where the development paradigm is not challenged ('Wetlands International').

When making a distinction between affirmative and critical demands, assessing the *quantity* of these demands enables us to estimate how close to an established hegemony a narrative is. However, in order to assess the *quality* of a narrative with regard to the reproduction (or contestation) of the established hegemony, it is not sufficient to ask what kind of demands have been *articulated*. In addition, it is necessary to consider the specific manner in which demands are *linked*. On closer examination the interaction of demands may turn out to be strategic and serve to universalize the fantasy of the narrative.

This could be seen quite clearly in the 'Hopenhagen'-narrative. Among the large number of affirmative demands, such as the demand for 'free competition' for 'investments in innovation' (i.e. 'capitalizing on the growth opportunities') or for 'investments in technologies', there is the positive reference to the UN as 'incredibly good at setting a large enough table that everyone can come and sit down and talk'. This is linked to the demand for 'raising awareness of the UN's role in creating the international standards and frameworks'. Is this possibly a call for the success of an international institution whose task is the regulation of the climate policy? At first sight, this is astonishing, as it is part of the neoliberal dogma – which can be perceived in most of the articulations – to totally reject a regulation by the state or by intergovernmental institutions (cf. above). In fact, a closer look at the narrative reveals a fundamentally contradicting articulation: 'Solutions to climate change ... can [not] come from [above] ... mandate[d] from any authoritative intergovernmental body – which kind of rules out the United Nations' ability to truly quote-unquote solve climate change. Solutions to climate change are going to come from market forces.'

The positive reference to the UN serves a different purpose than a contestation of the neoliberal paradigm. The articulation itself marginalizes other actors and their demands, which is expressed in another quotation: 'You saw a lot of the protest and the anger coming from activists from the developing world ... all it did was discredit them as people who would be unwilling to come to the table as equal partners in dialogue and as contributors to any solutions'. The demand, though of a *critical* character, serves to marginalize alternatives ('unwilling') and thus to universalize the fullness articulated in the narrative. As Glynos and Howarth point out: 'fantasies seek directly to conjure up ... an impossible union between incompatible elements' (Glynos and Howarth 2007: 147).

The coding of the demands on the basis of the beatific and the horrific dimensions of fantasy constitutes two chains of equivalence per individual narrative. From each of those chains of equivalence we can derive a symbolic representative – one either beatific or horrific. Figure 13.6 provides an overview of these rep-

212   P.T. Bedall

Figure 13.6 The symbolic representatives of the beatific/the horrific

Lines of discourse		Symbolic representative of the BEATIFIC	The Narrative	Symbolic representative of the HORRIFIC	Lines of discourse	
A Comprehensive Transformation		A social transformation/reconstruction of society	'People's Protocol'	The (economic) system	The Economy	
		A whole new system/social structure in place	'Global Justice Ecology Project'	The (economic/capitalist) system		
		A social transformation/a systemic change	'Focus on the Global South'	Capitalism		
		A radical change on the municipal level	'Climate Alliance'	Economic functioning		
		Climate Justice (social & ecological transformation)	'AVAAZ'	Climate Injustice (responsibility vs. vulnerability)	Injustice	
A Paradigm Shift		A transformation of society	'GenderCC'	Androcentrism	The (Development) Paradigm	
		A change of the development model	'Oxfam'	The development model		
		A paradigm-shift	'CIDSE'	The paradigm of development & well-being		
		A changed paradigm of development	'GROOTS'	The paradigm of development		
		A paradigm-shift	'World Council of Churches'	The paradigm of development & well-being		
An Eco-managerial Transformation	Carbon Management	A CO_2 concentration of 350 ppm	'350.org'	CO_2 concentration above 350 ppm	A Deficient Management	
		A carbon neutral society	'Greenpeace'	Excessive CO_2 concentration		
	Ecological Modernisation	A sustainable ecological footprint worldwide	'Global Footprint Network'	The 'overshoot' (imbalanced consumption of bio-capacity)		
		An ecological/modernization (technologies & lifestyles)	'CAN'	The business models of the fossil fuel industry		
		A one planet lifestyle	'WWF'	A three planet lifestyle		
	Conservation	Conserved ecosystems worldwide	'Wetlands International'	The unsustainable use of ecosystems		
Climate Neoliberalism		A green economy	'Hopenhagen'	Interventions into the free market	Regulation	

resentatives that were revealed throughout the analysis. They span a wide range from a more populist to a more reformist pole: regarding the beatific dimension, several of the narratives reproduce a revolutionary fantasy promising a fullness via a *'comprehensive transformation'*. Those narratives are similar, concerning demands for a transformation of the social as well as the ecological sphere. They differ from discourses which primarily highlight only one of these spheres. These discursive lines remain closer to the hegemonic project of *'climate neoliberalism'*, which is pushed by the 'Hopenhagen' narrative in its almost ideal-typical form. This hegemonic fantasy does not consider the conjunction of both spheres, but is narrowing the problem and its solutions to the ecological one.

It is a coalition of actors – notably from the development sector, including 'Oxfam', 'CIDSE' or the 'World Council of Churches' – which bundles their demands into a *'paradigm shift'* focusing primarily on the way of development, i.e. exclusively on the social sphere. By contrast, there is a discourse coalition that mainly wants to improve the ecological conditions by promoting eco-managerial approaches in order to gain a fullness and harmony with nature. In contrast to climate neoliberalism's focus on the freedom of market forces this coalition is highlighting active management. Although this pattern ties all of the coalitions' narratives together, they differ in what exactly is privileged to reach the ecological improvement. Several sub-lines of the eco-managerial project can be carved out. Whereas some actors – like '350.org' or 'Greenpeace' – stress a management of CO_2 emissions (a *'carbon management'*), others – including 'CAN' or 'WWF' – emphasize the enhancement of the ways of consumption and production (an *'ecological modernization'*) or just a *'conservation'* of ecosystems worldwide – like 'Wetlands International'. It is noticeable that the more revolutionary lines of discourse are pushed by grassroots groups – like the 'People's Protocol', 'Global Justice Ecology Project' or 'Focus on the Global South'. However, it is the more institutionalized groups that are pushing reformist lines of discourse.

In the studied text body, the lines of discourse at large can be accurately divided in terms of their fantasy. The narratives can be grouped the same way regarding their beatific as well as their horrific fantasy. Only the narratives of 'GenderCC' and of 'AVAAZ' stand out in this regard. Most of the narratives that reproduce the 'comprehensive transformation' line of discourse believe in the economy as the obstacle to be overcome. The 'GenderCC' narrative in contrast is in line with the paradigm-shift discourse naming an androcentric development model as the determining obstacle. The 'AVAAZ' narrative actually identifies a moral irresponsibility, which it labels 'climate injustice' – a further line of discourse. On the empirical level both narratives show that individual narratives as unique sets of demands can reproduce several hegemonic projects. A hegemonic project has to be conceived as an analytical entity that is not connected to empirical entities like individual texts or even actors.

Conclusion

The analysis of individual texts allows us to make statements about the way particular actors (re-)produce or contest hegemony through specific demands and narratives they articulate. Following Laclau and Mouffe's theoretical perspective, one can understand struggles for hegemony as struggles for the universalization of antagonisms. Accordingly, I developed a concept of criticism based on the theory of hegemony. It is based on the idea that the critical content of narratives or demands can be determined according to their character as an affirmation or a pejoration of the hegemonic fantasy – i.e. the hegemonic articulation of the 'fullness and harmony' or of the 'obstacle to overcome'.

On the basis of these interview narratives it became clear that actors could not be simply grouped into two poles, either reproducing or contesting the established hegemony. The demands articulated in a narrative may in parts (A) confirm the established hegemony while other aspects (non-A) may oppose the hegemony. They can be affirmative demands or critical ones. An analysis of only the demands, however, is not sufficient to judge the quality of a narrative regarding the reproduction (or contestation) of the established hegemony. It is also necessary to consider the manner in which demands are linked in the narrative.

The method presented qualifies as a sub-step for the study of the role of specific actors in hegemonic struggles. Such a study of the role of actors in discourse clearly cannot be based on single interviews or individual texts. It has to aim at the discursive level as a whole. This means broadening the scope of articulations of the examined actors – beyond the linguistic articulations gathered in text documents. In this way the varying degree to which the actors have resources at their disposal and their discursive effect would be included in the study. Furthermore, in contrast to the archaeological examination of individual texts, one has to consider the hegemonic struggles as a process and has to draw on a genealogical perspective.

Notes

1 Some authors contributing to the regime theory literature are aware of the fact that non-state actors such as NGOs are trying to influence intergovernmental negotiations (Corell and Betsill 2001; Gulbrandsen and Andresen 2004). States remain the central actors, though.
2 However, a Gramscian perspective is not negating the significance of negotiations regarding the constitution of hegemony (Gramsci 1971: 208f.).
3 A fundamental connection of the degree of institutionalization or organization with socio-political practice has often been discussed in studies of social movements and parties or of NGOs (see for example Barker 2001). In recent empirical studies a connection has frequently been proven (see for instance Teune *et al.* 2007: 165ff.; Walk and Brunnengräber 2000: 217). Even if there is at present only a *probabilistic* basis for a connection, studies often suggest a *causal* connection.
4 Nonhoff is aware of this (Nonhoff 2008: 318). In his discourse-analytical examination, the texts he examines – as they are seen as 'sufficiently representative' of the discourse (Nonhoff 2006: 51, my translation) – seem to represent a hegemonic project.
5 At Copenhagen finally no agreement could be reached. The Durban climate negotiations in December 2011 brought about a signing of a second commitment period to the Kyoto Protocol. Although main actors like Canada, Australia and Japan dropped out of the process, it remains a broad and powerful discourse coalition, including a whole newly formed branch of business around carbon markets, which is pushing forward market mechanisms. Thus, the withdrawal of several industrialized countries from Kyoto does not have to entail a decreased prominence of market mechanisms in future global climate politics.
6 *Criteria for inclusion*: non-profit; non-governmental; transnational network; oriented towards international climate politics (UNFCCC/Kyoto process); main activities focusing on climate politics; membership groups active in at least five nations. *Criteria*

for exclusion: networks of government or international organizations; organizations or networks of political parties; think-tanks; foundations; nationally based charity or conservation organizations with an international operational area; regionally limited organizations (with the exception of indigenous unions); exclusively advisory – management consultants; exclusively capacity building.
7 Syllogisms are core elements of Aristotelian logic. A syllogism consists of a first premise, a second premise and a conclusion. Example: all humans are mortals (first premise). Greeks are humans (second premise). Greeks are mortals (conclusion).
8 A floating signifier or demand is one that is called upon from very different hegemonic projects, articulating it in very distinct contexts. It is thus simultaneously part of quite different chains of equivalence (see Laclau 1990: 28).

References

Albo, G. (2007) 'Neoliberalism and the Discontented', in L. Panitch (ed.) *Global Flashpoints: Reactions to Imperialism and Neoliberalism*, London: Merlin Press, 354–362.
Arts, B. (1998) *The Political Influence of Global NGOs: Case Studies on the Climate and Biodiversity Conventions*, Utrecht: International Books.
Barker, C. (2001) 'Robert Michels and the "Cruel Game"', in C. Barker, A. Johnson and M. Lavalette (eds) *Leadership and Social Movements*, Manchester, Manchester University Press, pp. 24–43.
Brunnengräber, A. (2013) 'Multi-Level Climate Governance: Strategic Selectivities in International Politics', in J. Knieling and W. Leal Filho (eds) *Climate Change Governance*, Frankfurt: Springer, 67–84.
Brunnengräber, A., Dietz, K., Hirschl, B., Walk, H. and Weber, M. (2008) *Das Klima neu denken: Eine sozial-ökologische Perspektive auf die lokale, nationale und internationale Klimapolitik*, Münster: Westfälisches Dampfboot.
Castree, N. (2008a) 'Neoliberalising Nature: Processes, Effects, and Evaluation', *Environment and Planning A* 40: 153–173.
Castree, N. (2008b) 'Neoliberalising Nature: The Logics of Deregulation and Reregulation', *Environment and Planning A* 40: 131–152.
Corell, E. and Betsill, M.M. (2001) 'A Comparative Look at NGOs in International Environmental Negotiations: Desertification and Climate Change', *Global Environmental Politics* 1(4): 86–107.
Feldman, M.S., Sköldberg, K., Brown, R.N. and D. Horner (2004) 'Making Sense of Stories: A Rhetorical Approach to Narrative Analysis', *Journal of Public Administration Research and Theory* 14: 147–170.
Glynos, J. and Howarth, D. (2007) *Logics of Critical Explanation in Social and Political Theory*, London: Routledge.
Glynos, J., Howarth, D., Norvall, A. and Speed, E. (2009) *Discourse Analysis: Varieties and Methods*, ESRC National Centre for Research Methods Review paper, NCRM/014. Online. Available at: http://eprints.ncrm.ac.uk/796/1/discourse_analysis_NCRM_014.pdf (accessed 1 February 2011).
Gramsci, A. (1971) *Selections from the Prison Notebooks*, ed. by Q. Hoare. London: Lawrence & Wishart.
Gulbrandsen, L.H. and Andresen, S. (2004) 'NGO Influence in the Implementation of the Kyoto Protocol: Compliance, Flexibility Mechanisms and Sinks', *Global Environmental Politics* 4(4): 54–75.
Hansen, A.D. and Sørensen, E. (2005) 'Polity as Politics: Studying the Shaping and Effects of Discursive Politics', in D. Howarth and J. Torfing (eds) *Discourse Theory in*

European Politics: Identity, Policy and Governance, Hampshire and New York: Palgrave Macmillan, 93–116.

Harvey, D. (2005) *A Brief History of Neoliberalism*, Oxford: Oxford University Press.

Hulme, M. (2009) *Why We Disagree about Climate Change: Understanding Controversy, Inaction and Opportunity*, Cambridge: Cambridge University Press.

Jessop, B. (2004) 'Multi-Level Governance and Multi-Level Metagovernance', in I. Bache and M. Flinders (eds) *Multi-level Governance*, reprinted, Oxford: Oxford University Press, pp. 49–74.

Kruse, J. (2009) *Reader: Einführung in die Qualitative Interviewforschung*. Online. Available at: www.soziologie.uni-freiburg.de/kruse (accessed 12 November 2009).

Laclau, E. (1990) *New Reflections on the Revolution of Our Time*, London: Verso.

Laclau, E. (1996) *Emancipation(s)*, London: Verso.

Laclau, E. (2007 [2005]) *On Populist Reason*, London: Verso.

Laclau, E. and Mouffe, C. (1985) *Hegemony and Socialist Strategy: Towards a Radical Democratic Politics*, London: Verso.

Lohmann, L. (2006) *Carbon Trading: A Critical Conversation on Climate Change, Privatisation and Power*, Uppsala (development dialogue, 48).

Marchart, O. (2004) *Staging the Political: (Counter-)Publics and the Theatricality of Acting*. Online. Available at: www.republicart.net/disc/publicum/marchart03_en.pdf (accessed 10 February 2011).

Newell, P.J. (2000) *Climate for Change: Non-State Actors and the Global Politics of the Greenhouse*, Cambridge: Cambridge University Press.

Newell, P.J. and Paterson, M. (2010) *Climate Capitalism: Global Warming and the Transformation of the Global Economy*, Cambridge: Cambridge University Press.

Nonhoff, M. (2006) *Politischer Diskurs und Hegemonie: Das Projekt 'Soziale Marktwirtschaft'*, Bielefeld: Transcript.

Nonhoff, M. (2008) 'Hegemonieanalyse: Theorie, Methode und Forschungspraxis', in R. Keller, A. Hirseland, W. Schneider and W. Viehöver (eds) *Handbuch Sozialwissenschaftliche Diskursanalyse*, 3rd edn, Wiesbaden: VS Verlag für Sozialwissenschaften, pp. 299–331.

Okereke, C. and Bulkeley, H. (2007) 'Conceptualizing Climate Change Governance Beyond the International Regime: A Review of Four Theoretical Approaches', *Tyndall Centre Working Paper*, 112. Online. Available at: www.scribd.com/doc/5283233/Conceptualizing-climate-change-governance-beyond-the-international-regime-a-review-of-four-theoretical-approaches (accessed 28 August 2009).

Paterson, M. (2010) 'Legitimation and Accumulation in Climate Change Governance', *New Political Economy* 15: 345–368.

Saad-Filho, A. and Johnston, D. (2005) *Neoliberalism: A Critical Reader*, London: Pluto.

Swyngedouw, E. (2010) 'Apocalypse Forever? Post-Political Populism and the Spectre of Climate Change', *Theory, Culture & Society* 27(2–3): 213–232.

Teune, S., Rucht, D. and Yang, M. (2007) 'Moving Together? Global Justice Movements in Germany', in D. Della Porta (ed.) *The Global Justice Movement: Cross-National and Transnational Perspectives*, Boulder: Paradigm Publishers, pp. 157–183.

Torfing, Jacob (1999) *New Theories of Discourse: Laclau, Mouffe and Žižek*, Oxford: Blackwell.

Walk, H. and Brunnengräber, A. (2000) *Die Globalisierungswächter: NGOs und ihre transnationalen Netze im Konfliktfeld Klima*, Münster: Westfälisches Dampfboot.

14 Building legitimacy

Consensus and conflict over historic responsibility for climate change

Mathias Friman

Introduction

During the past two decades, negotiations under the UN Framework Convention on Climate Change (UNFCCC) have been the central forum for the organization of global climate governance. However, when it comes to decision-making, the UNFCCC is indeed a rather odd bird in the UN family. The UNFCCC is an independent treaty body that entered into force in 1994 and has yet to adopt rules of procedure, especially with respect to the role and function of voting. In the absence of voting procedures, all decisions have required, if not unanimous agreement, at least consensus in that there are no declared objections (Depledge 2005).

Depledge (2005) underscores that states' understanding of UNFCCC consensuses as legitimate is particularly important: if the process fails to build consensuses that are judged as legitimate, UNFCCC outcomes are unlikely to be effectively implemented. In this connection, Hurd (1999) argues that there are three reasons for sovereign states to obey international law: coercion, maximized self-interests, and legitimacy. The first two have, according to Hurd, gained a disproportionate amount of attention in international relations studies. However, it no longer seems controversial to claim, with Hurd, that they are insufficient on their own (Okereke *et al.* 2009; Risse 2004).

This chapter aims to account for and understand legitimacy, particularly in relation to consensus and conflict in negotiating historic responsibility under the UNFCCC. The case embodies a general principle in multilateral environmental negotiations, which differentiates responsibility based on contribution to a problem (Stone 2004). The long history of negotiating historic responsibility serves to account for and understand legitimacy in connection with consensus and conflict: while it has been endorsed by a number of consensuses, the question of how to operationalize the concept of historic responsibility has been subject to intense debate since the early 1990s (Friman and Linnér 2008).

This contribution uses discourse theory of Ernesto Laclau and Chantal Mouffe to approach legitimacy. As indicated in the introduction to this book, Laclau's and Mouffe's discourse theory is in general agreement with the departure points for interpretative perspectives. How this position differs from other approaches will be exemplified by contrasting it with an understanding of legitimacy derived from Jürgen Habermas. Both of these theories approach legitimacy in procedural terms, which leads me to start this chapter by discussing definitions of legitimacy and rules of procedure under the UNFCCC. The chapter continues with discussing how this definition relates to the two theories and how they can be applied to the case of negotiations on historic responsibility. One of the four dominant interpretations of climate change (see Hulme 2009 and Chapter 1, this volume), the scientific, has played a particularly important role in building consensus on historic responsibility while avoiding to deal with core conflict. For a long time, this did not promote legitimacy. On the other hand, this chapter concludes that the capacity and consensuses built during the years of negotiating historic responsibility in scientific terms have now created a situation where negotiators may draw on the scientific understanding to explicate conflict in other areas, such as that of social change. How to treat this resurfacing conflict while building legitimacy is still an open question; the chapter ends by tentatively proposing a new long-term negotiating forum under the UNFCCC to deal with core questions on different understandings of responsibility, designed to use conflict to build legitimacy.

Legitimacy and negotiations for consensus under the UNFCCC

This chapter borrows the definition of legitimacy from Hurd (1999: 381): legitimacy is 'the normative belief by an actor that a rule or institution ought to be obeyed' because it has come about in a procedurally fair manner or is substantially important. This connects legitimacy to perception, here focusing on perceptions among the Parties' representatives at the negotiations. Although clearly not the only important subjects in climate governance (cf. Okereke *et al.* 2009), states are validated stakeholders in negotiations under the UN system. They have an important role in national implementation, thus evoked legitimacy among Parties is one essential part of global climate governance for reasons that will be discussed below.

The focus of this chapter is on what Scharpf (1997: 19) originally termed 'input accountability', later rephrased as 'input legitimacy'. 'Input legitimacy relates to the participatory quality of the decision-making process and asks whether the process conforms to procedural demands, such as representation of relevant stakeholders, transparency and accountability' (Bäckstrand 2006a: 473). Thus, connecting this refinement of legitimacy to Hurd's definition, Parties will more likely obey outcomes from the UNFCCC negotiations if they perceive the participatory quality in deliberations as being relatively high.

The contrasting concept, output legitimacy (Scharpf 1997), has it that if a political outcome is sufficiently effective, it is argued to be legitimate. Output legitimacy is often described as balancing input legitimacy (Bäckstrand 2006b; Risse 2004). However, this chapter is motivated by a slightly different take: instead of balancing low-input legitimacy with high-output legitimacy, or vice versa, it sees high-input legitimacy as the *foundation for effective* international climate policy (cf. Scholte 2011: 117). This approach paraphrases Depledge (2005): achieving outcomes perceived as highly legitimate is likely to spur ratification and implementation of international policy, which is absolutely necessary when there are few other means to do so.

This is not the same as saying that agreed outcomes from the UNFCCC will be viewed as sufficiently effective to deal with climate change by all Parties or non-state actors. It may well turn out that the substantive performance (output legitimacy) of the UNFCCC is or will not be viewed as sufficient to address climate change, but the degree to which efficiency should be a legitimacy requirement is still an open question (Bernstein 2011: 33). It is, however, to say that the effectiveness by which states will implement agreed outcomes would increase if they perceive the agreements as having come about in a procedurally fair manner. This in turn does not prevent states, or other actors, from taking further actions or negotiate climate-related issues in other forums than the UNFCCC to make up a regime complex, with initiatives that add to achievements by the UNFCCC (see e.g. Keohane and Victor 2011).

Input legitimacy is especially important in the UNFCCC regime for two reasons: (1) it lacks legitimated voting procedures and (2) it is centred on a truly transnational and intergenerational objective to prevent dangerous anthropogenic interference with the climate system. Voting is commonly the last step in negotiations in multilateral forums concerning the environment. The lack of formal voting procedures in the UNFCCC derives from the aforementioned inability to agree on rules of procedure. UNFCCC Article 18 stipulates that every party to the convention has the right to vote. The Convention further demanded that the first Conference of the Parties (COP) to the UNFCCC set up its own rules of procedure (UN 1992a: Articles 18 and 7.3). The procedures were drafted in preparation for COP 1 in 1995 and accepted with the exception of rule 42: 'Voting' (UNFCCC 1996b). Attempts have been made to change the negotiation procedures to enable majority rule, yet in the absence of voting procedures the demand for consensus has so far blocked these attempts (Blobel *et al.* 2006: 41; UNFCCC 1996b). Both the Kyoto Protocol (KP) Articles 20 and 21 and UNFCCC Articles 15 and 16, on adopting amendments and annexes, allow a three-fourths majority rule, yet it also allows for non-acceptance of Parties so that amendments or annexes taken by vote need not enter into force for Parties that vote against them (for details, see UNFCCC 1998: Articles 16, 20 and 21; UN 1992a: Articles 15 and 16). In this context, consensus has come to mean the absence of any Party's formal objection.

Proceeding with this chapter, the UNFCCC draft rules of procedure have been taken for granted given that, over the last 15 years, attempts to change the status quo have failed. For good or bad, the UNFCCC is likely stuck with the above definition of consensus in the foreseeable future. However, I'd like to exemplify how consensus decisions have been taken while the continued process of deliberations indicates conflict over these agreements. In itself, this does not necessarily pose a problem. In fact, it can be argued that it is a feature inherent to all politics (Glynos and Howarth 2007). Simply put, without conflict we would not have politics. The problem, as I will argue, is in illegitimacy, not in conflict per se.

The second reason why legitimacy, as defined above, is of special interest to UNFCCC politics is in fact common to most multilateral environmental negotiations. Due to the transnational nature of global environmental/developmental problems, national or regional responses are more effective if they are coordinated and regulated on an international scale. Therefore, multilateral negotiations concerning the environment generally tend to avoid voting, even if it is a procedural option, to foster the greatest possible legitimacy (in turn, fostering ratification and implementation).

Approaching legitimacy through discourse theory

This chapter approaches the question of legitimacy in negotiations by drawing on the discourse theory of Ernesto Laclau and Chantal Mouffe. This theory allows for the analysis of how discursive dynamics both enable and restrict articulation in policy-formulating processes, assuming that legitimacy of a consensus outcome is likely to suffer if it is arrived at through rationales that submerge rather than deal with conflict (Laclau 1996: 15–16; Laclau and Mouffe 2001: 111 and 129; Mouffe 2000: 98–105). This point of departure – neo-Gramscian in character – will be contrasted with Jürgen Habermas' liberal approach, which has been taken to the international arena by scholars such as Thomas Risse (2000, 2004). Both strains of thought offer explanations as to why a lack of legitimacy occurs, and both propose solutions to address the issue.

Habermas and his followers see communication as containing an inherent logic that seeks mutual understanding. This inborn force could be cultivated to build consensuses, perceived as legitimate, by designing speech situations that generate rationally based deliberations, free from self-interest and power. For the purpose of contrasting with the approach of Laclau and Mouffe, the important point to note is that the criteria are meant to create an objective reasoning, even if may well result in consensuses that are regarded by the participants as having limited legitimacy. Thus, objectivity does not have to line up with truth claims in a traditionally positivistic sense. Rather, the idea is that criteria can be designed so that self-interests and partial perspectives can be assumed to be left aside. If an interest, under Habermasian conditions, cannot be backed by reasonable arguments it would lose legitimacy and be willingly left aside (Habermas 1995; Kapoor 2002; Risse 2004: 296).

With this understanding of Habermas, the contours of Laclau's and Mouffe's arguments can be made more distinct. Laclau and Mouffe are of the opinion that a Habermasian consensus would in fact lead to either (1) hiding power relations under a rhetorical mask, making already powerful statements more powerful; or (2) the creation of a situation devoid of power, which actually removes the foundational cornerstones of democratic negotiations (Butler *et al.* 2000; Laclau 1996; Mouffe 2000, 2005).

The argument that a successful Habermasian consensus would conserve, and veil, power relations is ultimately based on the claim that all objects are constituted through discourse. Differently put, the meanings of phenomena are not inherent to the phenomena themselves. Instead, they are given meaning through discourse and cannot be understood outside of discourse. Taken at face value, this means that it is impossible to take decisions on grounds external to discourse, and that possibilities to construct meaning are theoretically endless although practically limited by already existing discourses. In this perspective, no political decisions can be judged as good or bad based on any extra-discursive criteria.

The taken-for-granted impossibility of taking decisions on grounds external to discourse elevates the importance of choice, struggle and the exertion of power associated with all political outcomes (Laclau and Mouffe 2001). From the same perspective, power is seen as both oppressive (meaning that it is constraining what can be said) and creative (in that it is making it possible to communicate with a somewhat shared understanding to begin with).

Thus, a consensus, claim Laclau and Mouffe, cannot evade power. If it appears that a consensus has been reached without anyone exerting power, it is a sign of a hegemonic relation; a naturalized discourse that erases the possibility of debate and hides contingency in favour of a totalitarian system of repetition (Laclau 2000; Laclau and Mouffe 2001; Mouffe 2000). As such, it would hide the endless horizon of alternative interpretations. To quote Dryzek (2001: 661), whose argument in this case aligns well with the perspective of Laclau and Mouffe, such consensuses can only be imagined 'if the discourses were themselves either merged or dissolved — a prospect that is both unlikely and undesirable, inasmuch as it would erase the difference that makes deliberation both possible and necessary'.

To build legitimacy, Laclau and Mouffe explore a different path that could be summarized as an anti-universal universality. With this, they want to sidestep two endpoints in negotiations, both representing the impossibility of democratic negotiations. First, they avoid generating totalities based on, for example, reasoning that a certain discourse embodies a correct approach that other discourses cannot challenge since there is nothing substantially important to add or change; second, they avoid situations of more or less sheer flux where meaning is hard to capture due to fragmented and autonomized discourses (Friman 2010).

Rather than closing boundaries of discourse around content, Laclau and Mouffe explore ways to close boundaries on the *logic* of the possibility of boundary crossing. Under such circumstances, discourses would be constructed in a context in which subjects of discourses would understand the boundaries around the content of discourse as temporary and permeable. Differently put, achieving discursive closure on substance/content would be understood as a procedural compromise between inclusion and exclusion that manifests certain power relations rather than erasing power. Legitimacy, in this perspective, is built by creating firm ground for the logic of boundary crossing in all discourse. In discussing the results of the analysis, I'll return to how these ideals could line up with future negotiations on historic responsibility.

Analytical framework and empirical material

The analysis first accounts for whether and to what extent striving for consensus on historic responsibility has followed the logic of the more rational (Habermasian) or agonistic (Mouffian) ideals. Recognizing that this is not at all an exhaustive taxonomy for understanding consensus, it can provide partial but important insights into climate negotiations. Second, a scale between the perceptions of outcomes as legitimate or not is applied in which the logic(s) for striving towards and creating consensus on historic responsibility is tested against its ability to build (input) legitimacy among Parties in the negotiation process (see Figure 14.1). Departing from Laclau and Mouffe, the results from this analysis will be used in exploring whether there is unrealized potential to increase legitimacy in historic responsibility negotiations.

Müller (1994: 38, own translation) highlights that researchers who put the above definition of legitimacy at centre stage start out with an empirical as well as a theoretical focus that differ from those in more traditional IR studies: 'Unlike in a rational choice approach, the point of departure is not pre-fixed interests or negotiated outcomes; instead, it puts the interactive process of negotiation in the foreground.'

To capture this process, three broad sets of material have been examined: (1) official documents from the negotiating process and expert groups; (2) observations of the negotiating process (on site, through webcasts, and through the reporting service *Earth Negotiations Bulletin*) and expert groups; and (3) interviews with Party delegates and relevant scientists.

The official documents constitute the empirical backbone. They are used to track historic responsibility negotiations, especially regarding what has been agreed upon or officially discussed. Observations of eight negotiating rounds and webcasts, as well as reporting services and complementary interviews, have been used to encircle what has been negotiated but not agreed upon, and to determine the perceived legitimacy of several negotiated outcomes. Tracking the process represents producing a 'raw' discourse on historic responsibility that is filtered through the analytical framework to understand legitimacy in relation to consensus and conflict.

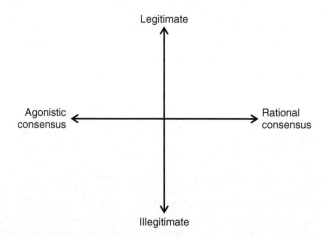

Figure 14.1 Analytical framework.

Legitimacy of consensuses in negotiating historic responsibility

A first phase of negotiating historic responsibility is distinguishable between 1991 and 1995. During that period, conflict over historic responsibility was hidden by the creation of high levels of interpretative flexibility around its central components. The UNFCCC was concluded by mid-1992. The preamble notes that the largest historic contributors to climate change are located in the global North. This is most often understood in connection to Article 3.1 on common but differentiated responsibility (CDR): differentiating responsibility for climate change, it is argued, should take historic contributions into account (Müller 2002; UN 1992a). This presumption is indeed understandable given that up until the final round of official negotiations before the conclusion, historic contribution and differentiated responsibility were almost always structured in direct connection to each other (see e.g. UN 1991a: 13; 1991b: 2, 4, 6 and 13–16; 1992b: 27; 1992c: 28).

At the Party level, the vague understanding of historic responsibility in the Convention has since enabled several parallel interpretations of how to operationalize the concept (Interview 2008b). The fundamental discursive rationale of how to build a UNFCCC consensus on this issue, for this era, thus seems to relate to emptying the central signifiers of historic responsibility discourse of content to allow all Parties to inscribe their own understanding of what it amounted to in practical terms.

This phase of negotiating historic responsibility led to a second phase where the archetypical categories of agonistic and rational consensus make more sense. Shortly after the Convention entered into force in 1994, the issue of differentiation was again brought to the agenda. Countries such as Australia, Russia, Switzerland, Norway and Japan, for example, argued that it was not enough to differentiate between the global North (roughly concurrent with Parties listed in Annex 1 of UNFCCC (A1)) and South (non-Annex 1 (NA1)). Within A1, they argued, differentiation should be downscaled to the Party level, for example, by calculating commitments based on energy efficiency of technology in a country or emissions per square kilometre of a country (ENB 1995, 1996; UN 1995; UNFCCC 1996a). According to representatives of the Brazilian government, this brought to bear differentiation at the country level and opened the door to the challenge that sorting countries into Annexes attached with distinctive responsibilities had settled the issue of differentiating, including then the vaguely defined issue of historic responsibility (Interview 2008a, 2008b).

The government of Brazil responded by introducing differentiation based on a causal link between countries' past emissions and climate change (UNFCCC 1997a). Thus according to their proposal, countries that had an energy-efficient development path, or little development to begin with, would have less responsibility to address the present climate change. This simultaneously specified Parties' emissions allowances under a global cap. A fine based on the Polluter Pays Principle would be imposed on any emissions above the allowance. The fines would, in turn, enter a fund to finance adaptation and mitigation in developing countries (ENB 1997; Interview 2008b; UNFCCC 1997a).

No elements of the Brazilian proposal were included in the draft protocol that was forwarded to COP 3 in Kyoto (UNFCCC 1997b). However, the COP reacted to an oral report by asking for further consideration by the Subsidiary Body for Scientific and Technological Advice (SBSTA) (UNFCCC 1998: 59). Under the SBSTA, the Brazilian proposal came to be subjected to intense scientific debate.

During a set of SBSTA-endorsed workshops organized by the Brazilian government, the original Brazilian proposal was criticized for what was seen as a number of methodological flaws (for workshop reports, see Appendix A in den Elzen et al. 1999). Even though Brazil seemingly never intended the model as anything but a simple illustrative example of how historic responsibility could be quantified, the Brazilian government tried to correct these flaws (Interview 2008b; Meira Filho and Miguez 2000; Miguez 1997). Out of this grew a specific focus on methods to establish relations between contribution and indicators of change that would continue to engage researchers and negotiators for a long time.

Responding to the workshops, the first of what would become two UNFCCC expert meetings on the issue touched upon what 'science and methodology' ought to be, opening up for a 'thin' as opposed to a 'thick' interpretation (UNFCCC 2001). Unable to settle this debate, the meeting participants adopted a thin definition in practice and reinforced it at the second meeting with continued modelling exercises. Their report (UNFCCC 2002) was forwarded to the SBSTA, which eventually referred the issue to the 'scientific community' (UNFCCC 2003a). An expert group, soon known as MATCH (the ad-hoc group on Modeling and Assessment of Contribution to Climate Change), formed with a clear ambition to foster inclusiveness (MATCH 2003a). However, the group's terms of reference and practical focus continued to restrict participation to the benefit of some Parties' core perspectives, especially through resting on a strong and traditional notion of science (Friman and Linnér 2008; MATCH 2003b). In several instances the SBSTA took note of MATCH's reports (see e.g. UNFCCC 2003b, 2004, 2006) and eventually, in 2008, closed the agenda item noting that the results of the work could be useful in other negotiation settings (UNFCCC 2008).

This phase of negotiating historic responsibility, which lasted roughly from 1997 to 2007, was organized on the principle of reaching a well-reasoned consensus in which arguments were evaluated against a norm of objective science (Friman and Linnér 2008). In literature on scientific knowledge production it is argued that knowledge, understood as objective, is commonly considered more valuable than knowledge perceived as normative. Further, the so-called *human component* or *soft dimension* of the 'earth system' is seen as complex and hard to predict, generating more uncertainty. The result is a hierarchy of scientific knowledge where 'objective', 'reliable' and 'certain' have become favoured adjectives that are also more often ascribed to natural than social sciences (see e.g. Bourdieu 1981; Fuller 1991; Lahsen 2005).

Some studies suggest that the above view of science prevails in the UNFCCC (cf. e.g. Sundberg 2007). Sociology of knowledge studies of the Intergovernmental Panel on Climate Change (IPCC) mirror this pattern. In a study of the IPCC's Third Assessment Report, Bjurström and Polk (2011: 1) argue that it 'is strongly dominated by Natural sciences, especially the Earth sciences'. Whereas the predominant focus on natural science in the IPCC has become more challenged over time, the focus on objectivity has remained more or less intact. The IPCC's governing principles say the Panel should 'be neutral with respect to policy, although they may need to deal objectively with scientific, technical and socio-economic factors relevant to the application of particular policies' (IPCC 2006).

The general view on science in the UN climate negotiations provides a context in which to understand the negotiations on historic responsibility. Originally, the Brazilian proposal explicitly combined several justice principles, inspired by moral philosophy, with simple climate modelling. In their proposal, the Brazilian government argued for objective criteria to establish a link between past emissions and responsibility (UNFCCC 1997a). Two consequences followed from putting forward their proposal in the context of objectivity and the view of science described above. First, the components of the Brazilian proposal explicitly focusing on justice were devalued as political and subjective. Second, the simple modelling, originally intended for illustrative purposes (Interview 2008b), became challenged on grounds of being too uncertain and scientifically biased (ENB 1998).

Using science on climate change as one example among others, Carolan (2008: 735) argues that demands for more objective science 'will only further squeeze out those people whose positions cannot easily be quantified'. The UNFCCC outcomes on historic responsibility, during the second phase of negotiations, have been taken precisely under conditions to generate rational consensuses where arguments have been evaluated against a contextual norm based on objective science. This has not fostered legitimacy.

Although, admittedly, the perceived legitimacy of conclusions and decisions on historic responsibility are hard to get at with consistency, observations and interviews indicate that the legitimacy of outcomes on historic responsibility has not been particularly high or widespread. At least one important case strengthens the more general sense of illegitimacy: negotiators from both the Chinese and Brazilian delegations have clearly indicated that, in hindsight, although they were not against the work of the SBSTA and MATCH per se, they would have preferred a different framing of historic responsibility to begin with (Interview 2008b, 2009).

Furrow (1995) has suggested that Habermas (in his discussion on reasonable arguments) does not resort to classic positivism. Rather, Habermas represents a case of arguing for objectivity within contexts. That is to say that reason is confined in social contexts. Furrow continues, however, that even if this is a general non-fundamentalist view, within the social contexts fundamentalism persists. Reason in such cases becomes more of a disciplined consensus than a rational consensus since the 'background theories . . . to help determine which facts about individuals and societies are morally relevant' (Furrow 1995: 27) are in themselves no less problematic to judge than the moral perspectives put forward in the first instance. In the context of negotiating historic responsibility, the framing that grants objectivity isn't, from this perspective, objective.

In order to build legitimacy, Mouffe provides an alternative to 'unbiased' or 'disinterested' reasonable agreements. In her perspective conflict does not necessarily connote something negative. Instead she underscores that the presence of conflict is at the core of democracy (Mouffe 2000, 2005). With the view that various perspectives on historic responsibility, especially in international politics, are more or less incommensurable, complete commensurability would connote the hegemony of a certain perspective. This points towards a different consensus from that of Habermas, one that acknowledges the impossibility of erasing power relations from any negotiated outcome. The current negotiations on historic responsibility may possibly open up space for testing this potential.

Compared to the second phase of negotiating historic responsibility, the current negotiations are differently geared. In the lead-up to COP 15/CMP 5 in Copenhagen, in December 2009, numerous causal interpretations of historic responsibility were put on the table and inscribed into text to facilitate negotiations (Bolivia 2009; Brazil 2009; India 2008; UNFCCC 2009a, 2009b). As with the Brazilian proposal, the current proposals that establish causal links between contribution and responsibility clearly limit the interpretative flexibility, which has resulted in illuminating what the core conflict is about: it is not a conflict over accepting language of historic responsibility in emblematic terms, but over how to interpret its more precise meaning.

In 2009, the Group of 77 and China made a collective statement in favour of a causal understanding, wanting 'historical responsibility' (rather than 'past contribution') to be inscribed both as an amendment to the Kyoto Protocol (which has not so far included any such or similar language) and as a principle in a new deal on long-term cooperation under the Convention. Further, they proposed that the common interpretation of the UNFCCC should be made explicit through connecting historic responsibility to differentiation in precise legal text, and making clear that it refers to a causal view of historic responsibility (rather than, for example, a more conceptual view).

The Russian Federation, Switzerland and Japan thought references to historical responsibility would be inappropriate to begin with (ENB 2009). Although still resisting anything beyond an emblematic reference, the 2010 Cancún outcome for the first time under the COP (as compared to the subsidiary level) explicitly acknowledges the importance of historic responsibility (UNFCCC 2011). This renewed debate on historical responsibility carries the potential to generate outcomes perceived as more legitimate through treating conflict in more explicit ways.

Using conflict to build legitimacy

Exclusion per se is not the core problem of historic responsibility in the UNFCCC. Laclau and Mouffe (2001) argue that exclusion of alternatives is inevitable to all articulation. The problem is that negotiating historic responsibility under the UNFCCC has excluded perspectives of stakeholders that the very same regime has accepted as legitimate. Accepting Parties' equal voices while leaning on discursive mechanisms that exclude some interests and include others under claims to objectivity is unlikely to be very productive in terms of building legitimacy in international politics. Carolan (2008: 735) proposes a potential solution to the problem of excluded, yet legitimated, perspectives: 'Instead, what are required are more and/or better political mechanisms to bring those hidden values, which lie within science, to the forefront of the discussion.'

Considerations of how to model historic responsibility could have been more closely coupled with an analysis of what moral foundations the modelling rested on and how the results could be translated into responsibility using various moral perspectives. For example, making a clear distinction between contribution and responsibility to allow for a more nuanced debate could indeed be helpful (cf. Müller *et al.* 2007). However, even quantifications of contribution depend on choices between numerous defining aspects. Some choices have been particularly highlighted in the academic literature, notably start year, composition of gases and choice of indicator to measure change (den Elzen *et al.* 1999; Höhne 2006; UNFCCC 2002). Yet, a review of the literature shows a rather complex field with a large number of defining aspects which, collectively, can more thoroughly explain why quantifications differ as much as they do and also partly explain why referring the issue to the scientific community cannot solve the fundamental conflict concerning the issue, namely, how to understand equity. Supplementing science by showing its normativity could somewhat level the negotiating field between those favouring natural scientific framings (which are largely endorsed by an aura of objectivity) and those favouring more social scientific framings of climate change.

In the case of historic responsibility under the UNFCCC, this could contribute to more passionate debates in attempts to level, and accept, inevitable power relations by pointing to them. It would not eradicate power, in fact not even hierarchy. It would, however, demand a consensus to approach contested issues in an agonistic context in line with Butler's (2000: 41) call 'to provoke a political discourse that sustains the questions and shows how unknowing any democracy must be about its future'.

What marks a legitimate decision is not that it serves all interests but that all interests are included in the course of a truly adversarial decision-making process. Even if not all interests are served in an outcome, they are heard and passionately discussed while honestly seeking (or attempting to seek) understanding. The desire to generate such a climate of discussion under the UNFCCC is rather clear, yet the practice of negotiating historic responsibility shows that it has been operationalized, at least in that case, through a more rational than agonistic logic. The rational logic has generated technocratic discussions with the aim of generating universally valid and seemingly disinterested conclusions. Agonism would refute such an attempt since such logic discursively erases what is seen as a fundamental feature of social relations – the plurality of interests – and undermines meaningful politics. However, to avoid agonism in order to take on antagonistic forms, careful attention needs to be paid to how anti-hegemony is institutionalized.

The interface between explicitly stated ethical principles and an implementation policy based on an implicit ethical grounding is precisely where the core of conflict seems to be located. Neither the COP nor the CMP have enough time to deal with this. This deficit has become, I believe, a great source of illegitimacy and slows down real progress. To gradually introduce and evaluate a more careful balance between rational and agonistic consensus, it would be beneficial, at least in the case of historic responsibility, for negotiators to deliberate more fully, in the early stages, over how principles connect to detailed policy. It would serve to confine the principles within structures, giving them meaning and guarding against excessive flexibility in interpreting them when designing policies and measures; at the same time, it would also allow room for negotiating on conflict over core ethical perspectives.

Tentatively pointing towards an opening to increasing legitimacy, I'll turn to the regime design that could extend the scope of negotiations while keeping to its procedural praxis. This means that consensus prevails as a starting point. Under these circumstances, creating a forum to pinpoint the location of conflict and to congregate and comprehensively lift it into explicitness could potentially motivate the creation of a new subsidiary body. Such a body could, if molded carefully, balance the current bias towards natural science and its traditional view of rationality.

A new subsidiary body could mediate between principles and policies on the one hand, and, on the other hand, already established principles and the need for new, or clarified, ones, as established through amendments or decisions. In the case of negotiating historic responsibility, the terms of reference of neither the SBSTA nor the SBI have been interpreted as including a mandate to do so. This also indicates that in order to avoid 'more of the same', the mandate for a new group would have to be very carefully managed. The proposal should be seen as a first tentative promotion to balance an institutional bias between interests that favour turning conflict into a momentum to build much-needed legitimacy, speed up implementation and increase the long-term efficiency of compliance. However, exactly how to design the mandate would need much more attention from researchers and policy-makers alike.

References

Bäckstrand, K. (2006a) 'Democratizing Global Environmental Governance? Stakeholder Democracy after the World Summit on Sustainable Development', *European Journal of International Relations* 12(4): 467–498.

Bäckstrand, K. (2006b) 'Multi-Stakeholder Partnerships for Sustainable Development: Rethinking Legitimacy, Accountability and Effectiveness', *European Environment* 16: 290–306.

Bernstein, S. (2011) 'Legitimacy in Intergovernmental and Non-State Global Governance', *Review of International Political Economy* 18(1): 17–51.

Bjurström, A. and Polk, M. (2011) 'Physical and Economic Bias in Climate Change Research: A Scientometric Study of IPCC Third Assessment Report', *Climatic Change (Online First)*: 1–22.

Blobel, D., Meyer-Ohlendorf, N. and Schlosser-Allera, C. (eds) (2006) *United Nations Framework Convention on Climate Change: Handbook*, Bonn: UNFCCC.

Bolivia (2009) 'AWG-LCA6: Technical Briefing (Angelica Navarro)'. Online. Available at: http://unfccc.int/files/meetings/ad_hoc_working_groups/lca/application/pdf/4_bolivia.pdf (retrieved 26.5.2010).
Bourdieu, P. (1981) 'The Specificity of the Scientific Field', in Lemert, C.C. (ed.) *French Sociology: Rupture and Renewal Since 1968,* New York: Columbia University Press, 257–292.
Brazil (2009) 'AWG-LCA6: Technical Briefing (José Miguez), Historical Responsibility: A Brazilian Perspective'. Online. Available at: http://unfccc.int/files/meetings/ad_hoc_working_groups/lca/application/pdf/5_brazil.pdf (retrieved 26.5.2010).
Butler, J. (2000) 'Restaging the Universal: Hegemony and the Limits of Formalism', in Butler, J., Laclau, E. and Žižek, S. (eds) *Contingency, Hegemony, Universality: Contemporary Dialogues on the Left,* London and New York: Verso, pp. 11–43.
Butler, J., Laclau, E. and Žižek, S. (eds) (2000) *Contingency, Hegemony, Universality: Contemporary Dialogues on the Left,* London and New York: Verso.
Carolan, M.S. (2008) 'The Bright- and Blind-Spots of Science: Why Objective Knowledge Is Not Enough to Resolve Environmental Controversies', *Critical Sociology* 34(5): 725–740.
den Elzen, M., Berk, M., Schaeffer, M., Olivier, J., Hendriks, C. and Metz, B. (1999) *The Brazilian Proposal and Other Options for International Burden Sharing: An Evaluation of Methodological and Policy Aspects Using the FAIR Model.* Report 30-07-1999, The Hague and Bilthoven: Netherlands Environmental Assessment Agency.
Depledge, J. (2005) *The Organization of Global Negotiations: Constructing the Climate Change Regime,* London: Earthscan.
Dryzek, J. (2001) 'Legitimacy and Economy in Deliberative Democracy', *Political Theory* 29(5): 651–669.
ENB (1995) 'AGBM2 Report: Oct 30 – Nov 3, 1995', *Earth Negotiation Bulletin* 12(24).
ENB (1996) 'AGBM3 Report: March 5–8, 1996', *Earth Negotiation Bulletin* 12(27).
ENB (1997) 'AGBM Highlights: July 31, 1997', *Earth Negotiation Bulletin* 12(50).
ENB (1998) 'SB Highlights: June 5–6, 1998', *Earth Negotiation Bulletin* 12(81).
ENB (2009) 'AWG-LCA5 -KP7 Highlights: April 2, 2009', *Earth Negotiation Bulletin* 12(402).
Friman, M. (2010) 'Understanding Boundary Work through Discourse Theory: Inter/disciplines and Interdisciplinarity', *Science Studies* 23(2): 5–19.
Friman, M. and Linnér, B.-O. (2008) 'Technology Obscuring Equity: Historical Responsibilities in UNFCCC Negotiations', *Climate Policy* 8(4): 339–354.
Fuller, S. (1991) 'Disciplinary Boundaries and the Rhetoric of the Social Sciences', *Poetics Today* 12(2): 301–325.
Furrow, D. (1995) *Against Theory: Continental an Analytical Challenges in Moral Philosophy,* London: Routledge.
Glynos, J. and Howarth, D. (2007) *Logics of Critical Explanation in Social and Political Theory,* Abingdon: Routledge.
Habermas, J. (1995) *Diskurs, rätt och demokrati,* Göteborg: Diadalos.
Höhne, N. (2006) *What Is Next After the Kyoto Protocol? Assessment of Options for International Climate Policy Post 2012,* Amsterdam: Techne Press.
Hulme, M. (2009) *Why We Disagree about Climate Change: Understanding Controversy, Inaction and Opportunity,* Cambridge: Cambridge University Press.
Hurd, I. (1999) 'Legitimacy and Authority in International Politics', *International Organization* 53(2): 379–408.
India (2008) 'AWG-LCA4: Workshop Presentation (Shared Vision for Long-Term

Cooperative Action), Poznan 2008'. Online. Available at: http://unfccc.int/meetings/ ad_hoc_working_groups/lca/items/4668.php (retrieved 25.5.2010).

Interview (2008a) Meira Filho, Luiz Gylvan, Instituto de Estudos Avançados da USP, São Paulo, 12.11.2008.

Interview (2008b) Miguez, José Domingos Gonzalez. Federative Republic of Brazil, Ministry of Science and Technology, Brasilia, 31.10.2008.

Interview (2009) Teng Fei. Bela Center, Copenhagen, 9.12.2009.

IPCC (2006) 'Principles Governing IPCC Work'. Online. Available at: www.ipcc.ch. (retrieved 9.4.2009).

Kapoor, I. (2002) 'Deliberative Democracy or Agonistic Pluralism: The Relevance of the Habermas-Mouffe Debate for Third World Politics', *Alternatives: Global, Local, Political* 27(4): 459–488.

Keohane, R.O. and Victor, D.G. (2011) 'The Regime Complex for Climate Change', *Perspectives on Politics* 10(1): 7–23.

Laclau, E. (1996) *Emancipation(s)*, London and New York: Verso.

Laclau, E. (2000) 'Identity and Hegemony: The Role of Universality in the Constitution of Political Logics', in Butler, J., Laclau, E. and Žižek, S. (eds) *Contingency, Hegemony, Universality: Contemporary Dialogues on the Left*, London and New York: Verso, 44–89.

Laclau, E. and Mouffe, C. (2001) *Hegemony and Socialist Strategy: Towards a Radical Democratic Politics*, London: Verso.

Lahsen, M. (2005) 'Technocracy, Democracy, and U.S. Climate Politics: The Need for Demarcations', *Science Technology Human Values* 30(1): 137–169.

MATCH (2003a) '3rd Meeting Report, Berlin, 2003'. Online. Available at: www.match-info.net/data/report 3rd Expert Meeting_final.PDF (retrieved 30.12.2005).

MATCH (2003b) 'Terms of Reference'. Online. Available at: www.match-info.net/data/ Terms_of_reference.PDF (retrieved 12.1.2007).

Meira Filho, L.G. and Miguez, J.D.G. (2000) 'UNFCCC Technical Note: Note on the Time-Dependent Relationship between Emissions of Greenhouse Gases and Climate Change'. Online. Available at: http://unfccc.int/resource/brazil/documents/proposta.pdf (retrieved 25.1.2011).

Miguez, J.D.G. (1997) 'Speech, AGBM7'. Online. Available at: www.mct.gov.br/index. php/content/view/18355.html (retrieved 11.10.2010).

Mouffe, C. (2000) *The Democratic Paradox*, London and New York: Verso.

Mouffe, C. (2005) *On the Political*, London and New York: Routledge.

Müller, B. (2002) *Equity in Climate Change: The Great Divide*, Oxford: Oxford Institute for Energy Studies.

Müller, B., Höhne, N. and Ellermann, C. (2007) *Differentiating (Historic) Responsibilities for Climate Change: Summary Report*, Oxford: Oxford Climate Policy.

Müller, H. (1994) 'Internationale Beziehungen als kommunikatives Handeln. Zur Kritik der utilitaristischen Handlungstheorien', *Zeitschrift für Internationale Beziehungen* 1(1): 15–44.

Okereke, C., Bulkeley, H. and Schroeder, H. (2009) 'Conceptualizing Climate Governance Beyond the International Regime', *Global Environmental Politics* 9(1): 58–78.

Risse, T. (2000) '"Let's Argue!": Communicative Action in World Politics', *International Organizations* 54(1): 1–39.

Risse, T. (2004) 'Global Governance and Communicative Action', *Government and Opposition* 39(2): 288–313.

Scharpf, F.W. (1997) 'Economic Integration, Democracy and the Welfare State', *Journal of European Public Policy* 4(1): 18–36.

Scholte, J.A. (2011) 'Towards Greater Legitimacy in Global Governance', *Review of International Political Economy* 18(1): 110–120.

Stone, C.D. (2004) 'Common but Differentiated Responsibilities in International Law', *The American Journal of International Law* 98(2): 276–301.

Sundberg, M. (2007) 'Parameterizations as Boundary Objects on the Climate Arena', *Social Studies of Science* 37(3): 473–488.

UN (1991a) *INC1: Report, Washington, 1991. A/AC.237/6.*

UN (1991b) *INC2: Possible Elements for a UNFCCC, Geneva, 1991. A/AC.237/Misc.5/Add.3.*

UN (1992a) *The Framework Convention on Climate Change. A/AC.327/18 (Part II)/Add.1.*

UN (1992b) *INC4: Report, Geneva, 1991. A/AC.237/15.*

UN (1992c) *INC5, Part I: Report, New York, 1992. A/AC.327/18 (Part I).*

UN (1995) *INC11: Comments from Parties, New York 1995. A/AC.237/Misc.43/Add.1.*

UNFCCC (1996a) *AGBM3: Comments from Parties. FCCC/AGBM/1996/Misc.1/Add.3.*

UNFCCC (1996b) *COP2: Rules of Procedure, Geneva 1996. FCCC/CP/1996/2.*

UNFCCC (1997a) *AGBM7: Add. Proposals from Parties. FCCC/AGBM/1997/MISC.1/Add.3.*

UNFCCC (1997b) *AGBM8: Consolidated Negotiating Text. FCCC/AGBM/1997/7.*

UNFCCC (1998) *COP3: Report, Addendum 1, Kyoto 1997. FCCC/CP/1997/7/Add.1.*

UNFCCC (2001) *SBSTA14: Progress Report. FCCC/SBSTA/2001/INF.2.*

UNFCCC (2002) *SBSTA17: Report of the Expert Meeting. FCCC/SBSTA/2002/INF.14.*

UNFCCC (2003a) *SBSTA17: Report, New Delhi 2002. FCCC/SBSTA/2002/13.*

UNFCCC (2003b) *SBSTA18: Report, Bonn 2003. FCCC/SBSTA/2003/10.*

UNFCCC (2004) *SBSTA19: Report, Milan 2003. FCCC/SBSTA/2003/15.*

UNFCCC (2006) *SBSTA24: Report, Bonn 2006. FCCC/SBSTA/2006/5.*

UNFCCC (2008) *SBSTA28: Report, Bonn 2008. FCCC/SBSTA/2008/6.*

UNFCCC (2009a) *AWG-LCA6: Negotiating Text, Bonn, 2009. FCCC/AWGLCA/2009/8.*

UNFCCC (2009b) *CMP5: Proposal for Amendments (Algeria, Benin, Brazil and 34 other States), Copenhagen 2009. FCCC/KP/CMP/2009/9.*

UNFCCC (2011) *COP16: Report (addendum 1), Cancún 2010. FCCC/CP/2010/7/Add.1.*

15 Democratizing the global climate regime[1]

John S. Dryzek and Hayley Stevenson

Introduction

Climate change is commonly seen as a global problem that demands a global solution. The fact that measures to mitigate and adapt to climate change are ever increasingly debated and enacted in international, transnational and supranational settings begets multiple challenges for effective and legitimate governance. Such settings beyond the national state largely transcend the reach of democracy, at least as traditionally conceptualized in liberal terms. Yet, decisions on climate mitigation and adaptation will affect many people with diverse values, needs and interests. Legitimacy demands that global climate governance reflects this diversity. Legitimacy, in other words, demands the democratization of the global climate regime. While democratic legitimacy may rightly be pursued as an end in itself, there is also evidence to suggest that democratic decision-making is more conducive to environmental protection than non-democratic forms of governance.[2] Moreover, consensual democracies demonstrate a higher level of environmental performance than adversarial democracies (Scruggs 2003; Poloni-Staudinger 2008). There are multiple possible reasons for this: one possible factor is the effort they make to integrate seemingly conflicting values; another is that consensual systems are more deliberative, that is, politics involves a greater ratio of communicative action to strategic action than in adversarial democracies (see Steiner *et al.* 2004).

Deliberative, communicative action ought in theory to promote environmental values because in such action, argument is effective to the degree it proceeds in terms generalizable to all parties concerned (Dryzek 1987: 204–205). Ecological values are examples of such values, so there is every reason to expect such values to come to the fore to the degree interchange is deliberative. On contemplating the democratization of global regimes, lessons can be drawn from the experience of nation-states. Although it is clearly not possible to replicate the entire democratic architecture of consensual democracies at the global level, it is possible to promote the deliberative features of this architecture. In this chapter we explain how this can be approached with reference to a post-Westphalian, post-liberal, and post-electoral theorizing on democracy. The central idea in this approach is the 'deliberative system', which treats democratization as deliberative capacity building. From this perspective, enhancing the inclusivity and authenticity of deliberation across the system is key to producing collective decisions that resonate with public opinion. Inclusivity here is understood in terms of discourses, namely, shared sets of concepts, categories and ideas that provide their adherents with a framework for making sense of situations (Dryzek 2005: 1). Later we will elaborate on the discursive dimension of this democratic project. First, though, we introduce the concept of a *deliberative system*. In the following it is shown that this concept allows analysing, evaluating and providing prescriptions for enhancing legitimacy in global climate governance. Methodically the chapter draws on a discourse analysis (Dryzek 1987) of side-events at the Conference of the Parties (COP 15) in Copenhagen 2009 as well as interviews with UNFCCC delegation members.

The deliberative system

The notion of a deliberative system was first introduced by Mansbridge (1999). Hers and subsequent treatments by Parkinson (2006), Hendriks (2006) and Goodin (2005) were limited by their close ties to the institutions of a liberal democratic state. A more generally applicable conceptualization of a deliberative system (presented initially in Dryzek 2009) proceeds with the following elements:

1 *Public space.* In public space a diversity of viewpoints and discourses can interact, ideally without legal restriction. Discourses might be engaged by activists, social movements, journalists, bloggers or ordinary citizens. Spaces might exist or be created in connection with, for example, physical places (classrooms, bars, cafés), virtual locations (Internet forums), the media, social movements, public hearings and designed citizen forums.
2 *Empowered space.* Empowered space is where authoritative collective decisions get produced, and can feature, for example, legislatures, constitutional courts, corporatist councils, empowered stakeholder dialogues, international negotiations, governance networks or international organizations. Empowered space in some kinds of governance arrangements may take on a more informal character (for example, in many of the cases of community-based governance of common pool resources described by Ostrom (1990)).
3 *Transmission.* Public space can influence empowered space through for example political campaigns, the argument and rhetoric of political activists, and cultural change initiated by social movements that eventually changes the outlooks of those in empowered space.
4 *Accountability.* Democratic legitimacy requires that empowered space be held accountable to public space. The most common means within democratic states is through elections, though these are not necessarily very deliberative affairs. But accountability means, quite literally, having to give an account; it does not have to involve the possibility of sanction through, for example, removal from office.
5 *Meta-deliberation.* Meta-deliberation is the reflexive capacity of those in the deliberative system to contemplate the way that system is itself organized, and if necessary change its structure. As Thompson (2008: 15) puts it, not all

practices and arrangements need to be deliberative all the time, but they do need to be justifiable in deliberative terms.
6   *Decisiveness.* The deliberative system should be consequential when it comes to the content of collective outcomes. That is, deliberation should not be a sideshow that obscures where key decisions actually get made. This sixth aspect drives home the idea that democratic deliberation should be consequential as well as authentic and inclusive.

This conceptualization of the deliberative system yields a general template for the analysis and evaluation of any real-world political process. Its underpinning is the philosophical claim (which has empirical support) that deliberative democracy yields legitimate outcomes. In the context of environmental affairs in particular, the desirability of its applicability rests in addition on both theoretical and empirical claims about the efficacy of deliberative democracy in resolving complex problems and providing public goods. The conceptualization is not in itself a normative *model* because there are many different ways each of the elements could conceivably be realized. This kind of thinking can be applied to all kinds of settings, including 'post-Westphalian' ones involving transnational networked governance (Braithwaite 2007), whose democratization turns on a differentiation of empowered space and public space within the network, and the presence of contestation within public space. Such contestation can be impeded by discursive hegemony (see Chapter 14, this volume); so it is important to have multiple and contesting discourses, engaged by all those affected by network decisions (or their representatives).

In the following section, we use this theoretical account of a deliberative system to analyse, evaluate and provide prescriptions for democratizing the global governance of climate change. A rudimentary deliberative system already exists in this arena but its shortcomings are significant. The challenge for democracy and ecologically effective climate governance is to find ways to overcome these shortcomings.

The global governance of climate change

Public space

The public space of global climate governance is populated by a large and diverse range of actors including business leaders, entrepreneurs, activists, church groups, youth groups, trade unions, non-government organizations, journalists and bloggers (sometimes grouped under the heading of global civil society). Major inequalities of access to global public space exist (as they of course do nationally). Nevertheless it is plausible to think in terms of representation of the discourses that go some way towards capturing the diversity of values, interests and needs of the world's peoples – including the least advantaged and most vulnerable to the effects of climate change. So rather than attempt to define the contributions of all the various actors, a more fruitful exercise is to identify the set of discourses represented within the public space. This move is consistent with normative theories of deliberative democracy that emphasize de-centred communication within the broad public sphere (Benhabib 1996; Habermas 1996; Dryzek 2000). The growing range of issues being absorbed into the climate agenda has been accompanied by a growing number of climate discourses. Identifying the character of distinct discourses and their inter-relationships is important for assessing the health of the public space itself, as well as the inclusiveness of representation in the wider deliberative system.

The programme of side events that runs alongside the annual Conference of the Parties (COP) to the United Nations Framework Convention on Climate Change is a good place to examine empirically the discourses found in public space. The fifteenth COP, held in Copenhagen in 2009, attracted 560 side event applications from groups in the North and South. These provided data for a discourse analysis consistent with the approach Dryzek (2005: 17–19) presents in *The Politics of the Earth*. For the purpose of identifying discourses in public space, events proposed by governmental bodies were excluded, as were multiple proposals by the same organization. The remaining 344 applicants were categorized on the basis of their principal theme (for example, justice, adaptation, indigenous peoples, security, technology), to ensure that the sample was representative of all key topics. From these categorized, a sample of 120 applicants was compiled for a discourse analysis. The selection was affected by two limitations: material on the applicant and their presentation topic had to be available on the Internet, and it had to be available in either English or Spanish (namely, a language in which at least one author is proficient). The majority of sourced materials were written texts (including declarations, brochures and publicity, press releases, website text, research and position briefings); visual and audio material constituted a small part of the sample. These materials provided the basis for identifying and recording the constitutive element of discourse (ontology; assumptions about natural conditions and relationships; agents and their motives; key metaphors) (see Dryzek 2005: 17–19). The overall message of each piece of material was also recorded to assist with identifying patterns across them. The patterns discussed below were discerned from this data.

Climate discourses can be classified on two dimensions: one broadly economic and the other broadly political. The economic orientation can be understood as either reformist or radical in relation to the parameters of the existing liberal capitalist international economic system. Reformists accept these basic parameters. From a radical perspective, existing economic objectives and values are themselves deeply implicated in the problem of climate change and ought to be the focus of more transformative action.

The political orientation of climate discourses can be understood as either conservative or progressive. The conservative position envisages that strategies to address climate change will be designed and enacted within the parameters of existing institutions and power structures. The progressive position is that the existing distribution of power is inadequate and inappropriate. Authority for designing and enacting strategies should thus be shared with, or transferred to, presently disempowered actors at global, national or local levels.

Bringing together these two analytical dimensions (the economic and the political) generates a four-cell typology of climate discourses, as shown in Figure 15.1.[3]

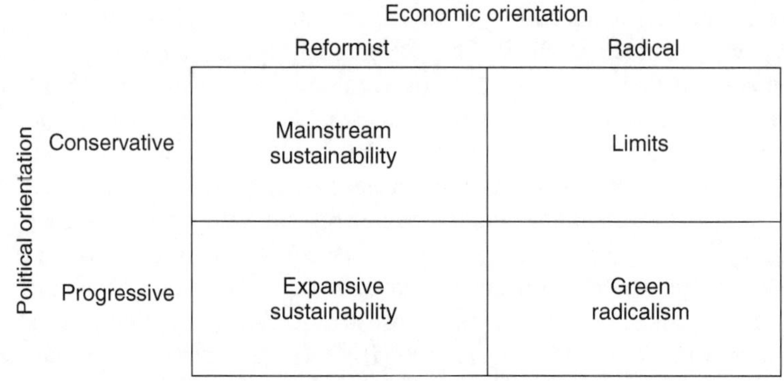

236 J.S. Dryzek and H. Stevenson

	Economic orientation	
	Reformist	Radical
Conservative	Mainstream sustainability	Limits
Progressive	Expansive sustainability	Green radicalism

(Political orientation on vertical axis)

Figure 15.1 Classifying climate discourses.

The discourses captured in this typology are those that accept the hypothesis of anthropogenic climate change as valid and thus engage with the debate of how the international community should respond to the problem. In the background there is a persistent discourse of scepticism of the existence of climate change and denial of the need to do much about it.

First, Mainstream Sustainability is economically reformist and politically conservative. Action to address climate change can be defined within the parameters of the existing economic order by actors and institutions already endowed with power and authority. Competition and the profit motive are inherent in human relations, but sustainability and material growth prove compatible. Three distinct discourses within this category diverge in terms of *how* and *why* climate change ought to be absorbed into existing development.

Climate marketization. All aspects of global climate governance can effectively be brought under the logic of the market. Emissions can be reduced most efficiently through cap and trade schemes. Emissions from deforestation can be reduced through market mechanisms that make felling trees less profitable than keeping them in the ground (see Chapter 4, this volume). Industries and individuals can then purchase offsets that negate the impact of their emissions. Global carbon markets could allow impoverished communities in the global South to profit by auctioning their inaccessible allocations of atmospheric space. Development and climate change mitigation are thus rendered compatible. Businesses are motivated to contribute to mitigation by a desire to profit from new markets, compliance with legislation, propagating a responsible image, and genuine concerns about climate change. While the agency of business is stressed, governments too have a role in creating carbon markets.

Ecological modernization is premised on the mutually supportive relationship between economic development and climate change mitigation. Reducing greenhouse gas (GHG) emissions presents an opportunity for efficient and productive economies in which green technologies become the motor of economic development. Recognizing that 'pollution prevention pays' will spur a shift away from emissions-intensive production towards clean technologies (renewable energy, biochar, carbon sequestration). But in the absence of appropriate policy and regulation, climate-friendly technologies and services will not be able to compete. Governments therefore must encourage ecologically rational decisions from the private sector by negotiating GHG stabilization targets, and creating voluntary or mandatory sectoral standards, a monetary value applied to greenhouse gases, publicly-funded research and development, and strong intellectual property rights regimes.

Energy security interprets climate change through the prism of existing energy and security concerns rather than ecological ones. This discourse focuses on opportunities climate change presents for promoting changes in the supply and source of energy. The energy responsible for emitting carbon dioxide is the same energy imported from politically and economically volatile regions. A safe climate is thus synonymous with energy independence and domestic security. For some, this lends new legitimacy to nuclear power. Energy security emphasizes the agency of national policy-makers, whose decisions affect both climate and security. These actors are primarily motivated by a concern for economic growth and national security.

Second, Expansive Sustainability is economically reformist but politically progressive in its stress on a redistribution of power.

Equitable modernization. Climate change mitigation is potentially profitable so it can be reconciled with decarbonized economic development. However, unlike ecological modernization, the objective should not be simply decoupling profit and pollution within industrial economies; instead, modernization should serve human rights and needs while evening out inequalities between industrialized and developing countries. This may require carefully designed and monitored market mechanisms, or transfer of mitigation and adaptation technology from North to South. Wealthy governments have a duty to transfer technology to developing countries to enable future development and trade to occur on a clean and even playing field. Participation in decision-making should be extended to a wider range of actors at multiple levels. The potential agency of (for example) local communities, indigenous peoples, forest-dependent populations, youth and non-government organizations is recognized.

Natural integrity accepts 'sustainable growth' but insists that strategies for addressing climate change while promoting 'green capitalism' should aim as far as possible to maintain the integrity of the natural world and to empower its advocates. The natural world provides services that ought to be valued as an alternative to artificially manufactured strategies and products. Manipulating natural processes through genetic engineering or the displacement of organic products for synthetic ones may yield unexpected adverse consequences due to the inherent complexity of ecosystems. The agency of national policy-makers is highlighted. Recognized but condemned is the agency of unscrupulous corporate actors that seek to profit by promoting mitigation strategies involving manipulation of natural processes.

Third, the Limits discourse is economically radical yet politically conservative: it questions the viability of existing neoliberal development, criticizing unconstrained economic growth, population growth and profligate consumption. But while the economy needs to be radically reorganized, this does not require a redistribution of power. Changes can be implemented either under the guidance of existing authorities or by individuals voluntarily modifying their own behaviour. Adaptation is perceived not as mere risk management, but as coping with destabilization attending massive human displacement and conflict over resources (see Chapter 6, this volume). The military may be an important agent here.

Fourth, Green Radicalism is economically radical and politically progressive, seeking fundamental reorientation of economic development through a redistribution of power. Unconstrained material growth cannot be reconciled with a safe climate and sustainability. Structural causes underlying the problem are stressed. Concerns relating to human rights, justice and equity are prioritized over short-term economic concerns.

Ecofeminism connects climate injustice and gender injustice. Ecofeminists observe that negotiations as well as economic and political institutions are overwhelmingly dominated by men, masculine interests, masculine concerns and masculine rationality. Existing governance arrangements thus tend to marginalize women and their concerns and experiences, including their increased vulnerability to both climate change and mitigation measures. Responding effectively to climate change requires fundamental transformation of patriarchal institutions.

Radical decentralization, 'small is beautiful', identifies the structural cause of climate change in a development model that privileges industrial-scale production; this needs replacing by small, local-scale production. Global governance is dominated by big businesses, state elites and international institutions. Community-level development, mitigation and adaptation can better respond to human needs and the environment. Carbon markets and offsetting are rejected because they shift responsibility and accountability away from the local level. Decision-making processes also need to be de-centralized to allow for genuine participation by marginalized and affected peoples.

New globalism avers that an effective and just response to climate change will only be possible if the presently unequal international system is transformed into an equitable global community, featuring low-carbon economies. Basic human needs should be prioritized over material wealth. In principle, a per capita emissions allocation may be appropriate but global equity may demand preferential treatment for vulnerable and marginalized people. Governance ought to be democratic and foster cooperation between individuals, cultures, nations, social movements and NGOs. Existing institutions are clearly unable to deliver such a fair and sustainable economic and political order; citizens and civil society can instead drive the transition.

The presence of such a wide range of discourses, some of which stand at a healthy critical distance from empowered space, is one indication of vibrant public space. But this in itself is insufficient. A well-functioning public space should also feature engagement of discourses in such a way that induces critical reflection on the part of people articulating different discourses. The level of genuine inter-discourse engagement in global public space remains quite low. As we have demonstrated elsewhere (Stevenson and Dryzek 2012), enclaves of likeminded individuals are pervasive. Enclave deliberation has its place (Karpowitz et al. 2009), but in light of the requirements of a deliberative system, only as a place for creating competence prior to engagement with other discourses. A further problem is that organized scepticism can undermine the authenticity of deliberation in public space by seeking to discredit the climate science that informs many of the discourses we have highlighted; and scientists have often responded with dogmatic assertion, rather than admit real uncertainties.

Empowered space

Authoritative decisions on climate change are made in a number of venues. From a deliberative democratic perspective, these decisions may be considered legitimate to the extent they reflect inclusive and authentic dialogue responsive to the needs of all affected parties. There are three principal empowered spaces in global climate governance: state-based multilateral arrangements; network-based arrangements that coordinate the activities of private or public and private actors; and market-based arrangements (see Pattberg and Stripple 2008; Andonova et al. 2009). Given the present space constraints, we report an empirical analysis of just one empowered space: the United Nations Framework Convention on Climate Change (UNFCCC), in which member states meet to develop collective agreements for mitigating and adapting to climate change. The UNFCCC features a lot of bargaining. While deliberative theorists have traditionally contrasted bargaining and deliberation, they are not mutually exclusive (Risse 2000). Mansbridge (2009: 2) defines deliberative negotiations as those open to all potentially affected by a decision, in which all participants speak truthfully, are treated with mutual respect, protected by basic rights, have equal resources and an equal opportunity to influence the process. Participants should exchange reasons that are mutually comprehensible and acceptable, and seek a desired outcome through mutual justification rather than coercion (threats, sanctions and manipulation).

Assessing the *authenticity* of negotiations against such criteria is rendered difficult by their closed nature. Such assessments must rely on the accounts of negotiators and privileged UNFCCC staff. Interviews carried out by the authors with senior negotiators in the two-track process set out in the Bali Action Plan,[4] reveal that deliberative quality is quite low.

Participation: among those interviewed there was fairly broad agreement that procedural openness is undermined by differentiated capacity. Small, poor and non-Anglophone parties are at a disadvantage. Limits apply to the number of contact group meetings that may be held simultaneously, but not to informal meetings. The Secretariat covers the cost of two delegates from each least developed country to attend UNFCCC sessions, but there are frequently more than two meetings running simultaneously. Challenges facing small delegations are not only logistical; large inter-ministerial delegations have a greater capacity to genuinely participate in all political, technical and legal aspects of a debate than do small specialized delegations. Interpretation between the six languages of the United Nations is provided, but only in high-level plenary sessions. Actual negotiations are conducted in English without formal interpretation.

Truthfulness: perceptions of truthfulness in negotiations are affected by the level of trust that exists between parties, as well as between parties and chairs. Among those interviewed, none claimed that a high level of trust exists among participants of UNFCCC negotiations. Most observed varying levels of trust across issue areas. Several observed that trust is low or entirely absent due to previous broken promises; suspicions that some parties seek to abolish existing mandates and agreements; or perceptions that some negotiators were promoting more extreme positions than their ministers. Lack of trust was cited as an issue between and within the North and South; within some negotiating blocs; between parties and chairs; and between parties and civil society observers. Beyond the impact of trust, truthfulness in the UNFCCC is affected by the nuances of negotiation norms. Negotiating in bad faith is considered a 'cardinal sin' but it is expected and accepted that negotiators will maintain reserved positions until the final stage of negotiation. Similarly, several interviewees observed that parties may hide their true positions in the presence of observers but speak more openly behind closed doors.

Respect: despite the observed lack of trust, most agreed that negotiators generally treat one another with respect. Despite frequent disagreements over positions, this rarely entails personal disrespect. Many empathized with their colleagues and recognized that unfavourable positions could not be associated with their speakers. However, several either admitted to finding it difficult to separate the person from the position, or observed rare impolite behaviour. More positively, many interviewees commented on the collegiality and even friendships that have developed among long-serving negotiators and diplomats, which is seen to aid the negotiating process.

Justification: observations of the level and quality of reason-giving in UNFCCC negotiations were quite mixed. Many claimed that the mutual exchange of reasons was quite prevalent, citing that diplomats have a talent for making compelling cases. However, this claim was often qualified with observations that reasons were provided *ad nauseam* without actually listening and reflecting. Some suggested that the extent of reason-giving depends on the nature of the underlying reasons: scientifically or morally legitimate positions tend to be explained, but not purely strategic positions. Of course, the general lack of trust impacts on this indicator of deliberative quality: there are sometimes suspicions that the reasons provided are insincere or incomplete. One interviewee noted that the culture of mistrust made it hard to seek explanations because to do so may be perceived as cruel, harsh or negative, or as a lack of one's own political will to allow progress. While some suggested that informal corridor conversations were useful for understanding the reasons behind parties' positions, several observed that time constraints preclude seeking or exchanging reasons. According to a couple of interviewees, delegates sometimes are simply unable to provide reasons because they do not adequately understand all technical and political aspects of an issue or position. A few interviewees drew a distinction between rational positions and ideological ones: open plenary can be a venue for venting ideological statements (perhaps for domestic audiences), while behind closed doors delegates will move beyond these given that it is not possible to reach agreement on the basis of ideology. A couple of interviewees articulated this distinction in North/South terms, or associated ideology only with seemingly unconstructive positions such as the rejection of markets or the focus on historical responsibility.

Mutual justification without coercion/threats: deliberative negotiations are those that seek a desired outcome through mutual justification rather than coercion (Mansbridge 2009: 2). According to the observations of interviewees, the UNFCCC does not perform well on this condition. Several commented that the process is one of give-and-take in which the best outcome is one in which everyone is unhappy. Often this results in lowering ambitions to the lowest common denominator by finding the most flexible language that all parties can support. Delegates are reportedly rarely persuaded by the force of the better argument but rather come into the negotiations knowing their thresholds of acceptability. Shifts that do occur tend to concern minor details of mechanisms and procedures. A few were more sanguine noting that good ideas can get traction; the paradox, according to one interviewee, is that good ideas are less likely to prevail later in the process once suspicion sets in, but if introduced early on there is a larger pool of competing ideas in which good ones may be lost. The absence of threats, sanctions and manipulation is crucial in deliberation, yet such instances were observed by two interviewees. One cited threats being issued in corridors; another cited external pressure on small states to vocally support the less ambitious position of a more powerful state. On the basis of our interviews, debate and negotiation in the UNFCCC appear to perform weakly against the standards of authentic deliberation.

Transmission, accountability and meta-deliberation

The means of *transmission* from the engagement of discourses in public space to the empowered space of the UNFCCC are many and varied. An inside/outside distinction can be drawn between the strategies used by actors in public space to transmit ideas to the empowered space of the UNFCCC (Fisher 2010). Those outside the UNFCCC tend to engage in protest, publicity and performance outside the venues of actual negotiations as well as in activists' home countries as they seek to influence the positions of their governments prior to international meetings. Insider status is secured through the observer accreditation process of the UNFCCC secretariat. Close to 1,000 organizations (business and industry groups, environmental organizations, local governments, research institutions, trade union associations, and women, youth and church groups) have taken advantage of this opportunity to gain access to the venue of UNFCCC meetings (UNFCCC 2010). We can think of them as representatives of particular discourses (though that is not how they think of themselves). Once inside, their access is confined to open meetings (formal and informal plenary sessions, workshops and side events). Influence within these confines is pursued in a variety of ways. Developing relationships with governments may eventually yield a coveted 'pink badge', which denotes membership of a government delegation and widens the scope of access to talks and negotiations. In some cases, NGOs may also sponsor a delegate for a Least Developed Country delegation to bolster the inadequate representation assured by the UNFCCC Secretariat. Climate Action Network (CAN) has sought to convey its ideas by distributing a widely-read daily newsletter, *Eco*, which ridicules, shames, and occasionally praises, the positions of specific countries. Other organizations and networks opt to hover outside closed meeting rooms to present departing delegates with suggested negotiating texts.

There is some blurring of the inside/outside distinction as actors on the 'inside' do sometimes employ strategies of performance, publicity and protest, such as CAN's Fossil of the Day ceremony. Another blurring of the inside/outside distinction stems from the efforts of some 'post-neoliberal' governments to establish relationships with social movements representing Green Radical discourses. The Bolivian president, Evo Morales, with the support of Venezuela, Cuba, Ecuador and Nicaragua, has been the driving force of this 'discourse coalition' (Hajer 1995). Through public meetings and the commissioning of a negotiating text drafting group in Copenhagen, as well as the convening of a World People's Summit on Climate Change and Mother Earth Rights in the Bolivian city of Cochabamba in 2010, Bolivia has sought to bring the voice of one version of 'the people' to the empowered space of the UNFCCC (Stevenson 2011). But the receptiveness of this empowered space to marginal discourses remains limited.

Accountability mechanisms in global climate governance are quite weak. Within states, the main accountability mechanism is that of elections, as voters can hold governments to account for their actions. Supranational elections rarely occur. National elections make very little contribution to transnational accountability, except at two removes: negotiators are accountable to their own governments, who in turn are sometimes accountable to voters. Within the UNFCCC, the principal accountability mechanism is the Compliance Committee of the Kyoto Protocol, comprising a Facilitative Branch and an Enforcement Branch. The former is designed to support parties in complying with their commitments, while the latter branch may impose 'consequences' on parties in the second commitment period of the Protocol in the event of non-compliance in the first commitment period. Specifically, failure to comply with an emission reduction or limitation commitment will result in a 30 per cent deduction from a party's assigned emissions in the second commitment period of the Kyoto Protocol; in addition, the non-complying party is required to submit a compliance action plan, and will be rendered ineligible to participate in emissions trading (Stokke *et al.* 2005: 1–3; Yamin and Depledge 2004: chapter 12). As the future of the Kyoto Protocol remains uncertain, it is unclear whether this compliance system will be of any consequence.

Opportunities for those in the empowered space of the UNFCCC to provide more direct public accounts of their positions and decisions are minimal but not absent. At their own discretion, national delegations may arrange briefing sessions during international climate talks to update their compatriots within civil society, and respond to questions about their own position and that of other parties.

In addition, an increasing number of delegations arrange press briefings during the annual conferences of the parties and inter-conference negotiating sessions. Again, these briefings are at parties' own discretion but they do allow parties and negotiation groups to explain their positions and respond to questions from the media. Access is restricted to accredited journalists so the potential for these briefings to serve as an accountability mechanism is dependent on critical and capable media representation. The growing number of activist media groups enhances the diversity of questions directed at governments during press briefings, but the exclusive nature of press and observer briefings, together with the absence of any sanctioning power, limits accountability.

The style of briefing described here reflects what Mansbridge (2009: 2) has called 'narrative accountability' rather than 'deliberative accountability'. Narrative accountability is a one-way process in which the representative provides the represented with an account or explanation of their actions. Some negotiators are expected by their governments to remember storylines about the government's positioning: as frontrunner, as vulnerable, as mainstream, or as objector. Deliberative accountability, by contrast, involves two-way communication between the representative and the represented in which both ask questions and give answers. In enhancing the deliberative democratic capacity of global climate governance, special attention will need to be directed to institutionalizing opportunities for deliberative accountability.

Meta-deliberation is weak. There is no developed reflexive capacity to work on the deliberative system itself. In one sense this is not surprising because no important actors explicitly conceive of the global governance of climate change in the systemic deliberative terms set out here. However, in the aftermath of Copenhagen much attention has been focused on the perceived deficiencies of the empowered space of the UNFCCC. Two features in particular have been the subject of debate: representation and decision-making. In the final plenary of COP 15, a handful of countries including Tuvalu, Venezuela, Bolivia, Ecuador, Cuba, Nicaragua and Sudan rejected the final text not only on the basis of its contents but also for the exclusive manner in which it was drafted and presented to the world as a finalized deal prior to consideration by all parties (UNFCCC 2009). Although it is not unusual for negotiations to move to smaller groups of Friends of the Chair or President, what appears to be crucial is that adequate representation of positions (and discourses) is assured and that all parties be provided an opportunity to consider a document before it is adopted. Both of these requirements were violated in the final days of the Copenhagen climate meeting. In the first instance, the ALBA countries,[5] many of whom espouse a post-neoliberal and anti-capitalist position, were not represented in the smaller negotiating group.[6] In the second instance, US President Barack Obama announced to the world that a deal had been reached before this document was presented to the parties for consideration.

The impact of this controversy on the outcome of the meeting was profound given that the Conference of the Parties operates on the basis of consensus (in that if any party vocally objects to any clause, that objection must somehow be accommodated). At the beginning of the Copenhagen meeting, the chief negotiator for

Papua New Guinea, Kevin Conrad, made a impassioned plea to adopt the rule on voting which had been consistently disallowed since the parties failed to adopt the Rules of Procedure in 1995 (Yamin and Depledge 2004: 432). He argued that 'consensus means that any agreement here can only aspire to the lowest common denominator amongst us. From our perspective . . . making decisions based only on the lowest common denominator is beyond irresponsible, it's gravely negligent' (Conrad 2009). Yet the consensus requirement means that there has to be a lot of persuasion of actors on points that matter to them. Such persuasion might be coercive, but it might also involve reason giving that induces reflection. The problem remains that states (such as Saudi Arabia) interested only in blocking progress have every incentive to object frequently. If the rule had been implemented as Conrad proposed, the Copenhagen Accord would have been adopted rather than merely 'taken note of', as it was supported by more than three-quarters of the parties. Of course, as dissenting parties pointed out in the final plenary, even if it had been adopted, the Copenhagen Accord would not achieve its stated objective of keeping global warming to below 2°C. In fact, scientists estimate that the emission pledges accompanying the accord imply a greater than 50 per cent chance that global temperatures will exceed 3°C by 2100 (Rogelj et al. 2010).

What these two controversies over representation and decision-making ultimately point to is the need for better contemplation of how global climate governance is organized. Such contemplation has occurred when it comes to the governance of the global economic and financial order, ever since the Bretton Woods conference of 1945. By contrast, the current system for climate governance arose in very haphazard fashion. As we pointed out earlier, not all arrangements need be deliberative all the time, but they must be amenable to deliberative justification.

Even after lapses in transmission, accountability and meta-deliberation, the global deliberative system for climate change governance often fails to be *decisive* when it comes to determining outcomes. Any agreements reached will have to be implemented by states. Even if they get to the point of formal acceptance of an agreement, states are quite capable of failing to enforce its provisions and meet targets – as the experience of the Kyoto Protocol illustrates. And states are quite capable of negotiating compliance in such a way as to meet the letter of agreements while interpreting it in such a way as to promote their own interests at the expense of global sustainability concerns (Stevenson 2011). Energy corporations that have failed in public space may exert power behind the scenes upon states in order to secure the fossil fuel economy (and their own profits).

Conclusion

We conclude this contemplation of the global governance of climate change with the following observations.

- Public space, some of whose actors and discourses stand at an appropriate critical distance from empowered space, is in good shape in terms of the sheer variety of available discourses – though often they fail to engage each other

as effectively as they might. This might seem unremarkable, until we contrast with cases where hegemony of a single discourse prevails – such as in the global financial system pre-2008.
- Empowered space features a lot of bargaining, but some real deliberation.
- Means of transmission from public to empowered space, notably the UNFCCC, do exist, if imperfectly. However, some discourses (for example Green Radicalism) do not make it through in very effective fashion.
- There is some narrative accountability but very little deliberative accountability in the system.
- Meta-deliberative capacity is currently weak.
- The deliberative system is not as decisive as it should be.

Any lacunae notwithstanding, the elements of a deliberative system can be discerned, even if only in putative or compromised form. Thus it is worthwhile to examine global governance in deliberative democratic terms. The democratization of global climate governance will need to draw on the lessons of experience, not simple application of normative reasoning. And to develop lessons, we need analysis of the sort that our conceptualization and application of the deliberative system concept supplies. There is a long way to go before anything adequate in the way of global governance seems attainable. But however long and hard the road, in the end the question is one of 'how' rather than 'whether'.

Notes

1 This chapter is partly based on a previous publication in *Ecological Economics* (Dryzek and Stevenson 2011).
2 For a review of this evidence see Dryzek and Stevenson (2011: section 2).
3 Further evidence of these discourses in public space, together with empirical examples, can be found in Stevenson and Dryzek (2012).
4 Eighteen negotiators were anonymously interviewed either in person or by telephone between September 2009 and July 2010. Interviewees represented 13 parties, however several spoke from the perspective of their negotiating bloc rather than their individual party.
5 Bolivia, Venezuela, Cuba, Dominica, Ecuador, Antigua and Barbuda, Nicaragua, Saint Vincent and the Grenadines, and Venezuela (Bolivarian Alliance for the Peoples of Our America).
5 For a list of participants in the Friends of the President see Bodansky (2010).

References

Andonova, L.B., Betsill, M.M. and Bulkeley, H. (2009) 'Transnational climate governance', *Global Environmental Politics* 9(2): 52–73.
Benhabib, S. (1996) 'Toward a deliberative model of democratic legitimacy', in: S. Benhabib (ed.) *Democracy and Diffference: Contesting the Boundaries of the Political*, Princeton: Princeton University Press, 67–94.
Bodansky, D. (2010) 'The Copenhagen climate change conference – a post-mortem', *American Journal of International Law* 104(2): 230–240.
Braithwaite, J. (2007) 'Contestatory citizenship, deliberative denizenship', in: G. Brennan,

F. Jackson, R. Goodin and M. Smith (eds) *Common Minds*, Oxford: Oxford University Press, 161–181.

Conrad, K. (2009) 'Statement to the 1st meeting of the Fifteenth Conference of the Parties, Copenhagen', 7 December, 11:45 am. Online. Available at: http://cop15.metafusion.com/kongresse/cop15/templ/play.php?id_kongresssession=2281&theme=unfccc (retrieved: 24.5.2010).

Dryzek, J.S. (1987) *Rational Ecology: Environment and Political Economy*, New York: Basil Blackwell.

Dryzek, J.S. (2000) *Deliberative Democracy and Beyond: Liberals, Critics*, Oxford: Oxford University Press.

Dryzek, J.S. (2005) *The Politics of the Earth: Environmental Discourses*, 2nd edition, Oxford: Oxford University Press.

Dryzek, J.S. (2009) 'Democratization as deliberative capacity building', *Comparative Political Studies* 42: 1379–1402.

Dryzek, J.S. and Stevenson, H. (2011) 'Global democracy and earth system governance', *Ecological Economics* 70(11): 1865–1874.

Fisher, D.R. (2010) 'COP-15 in Copenhagen – how the merging of movements left civil society out in the cold', *Global Environmental Politics* 10: 11–17.

Goodin, R.E. (2005) 'Sequencing deliberative moments', *Acta Politica* 40: 182–196.

Habermas, J. (1996) *Between Facts and Norms: Contributions to a Discourse Theory of Law and Democracy*, Cambridge, MA: MIT Press.

Hajer, M.A. (1995) *The Politics of Environmental Discourse*, Oxford: Clarendon Press.

Hendriks, C.M. (2006) 'Integrated deliberation: reconciling civil society's dual roles in deliberative democracy', *Political Studies* 54: 486–508.

Karpowitz, C.F., Raphael, C. and Hammond, A.S. IV. (2009) 'Deliberative democracy and inequality: two cheers for enclave deliberation among the disempowered', *Politics & Society* 37(4): 576–615.

Mansbridge, J. (1999) 'Everyday talk in the deliberative system', in: S. Macedo (ed.) *Deliberative Politics*, Oxford: Oxford University Press, 211–239.

Mansbridge, J. (2009) 'A "selection model" of political representation', *The Journal of Political Philosophy* 17(4): 369–398.

Ostrom, E. (1990) *Governing the Commons*, Cambridge: Cambridge University Press.

Parkinson, J. (2006) *Deliberating in the Real World: Problems of Legitimacy in Deliberative Democracy*, Oxford: Oxford University Press.

Pattberg, P. and Stripple, J. (2008) 'Beyond the public and private divide: remapping transnational climate governance in the 21st century', *International Environmental Agreements* 8: 367–388.

Poloni-Staudinger, L.M. (2008) 'Are consensus democracies more environmentally effective?', *Environmental Politics* 17: 410–430.

Risse, T. (2000) '"Let's argue!": communicative action in world politics', *International Organization* 54(1): 1–39.

Rogelj, J., Nabel, J., Chen, C., Hare, W., Markmann, K., Meinshausen, M., Schaeffer, M., Macey, K. and Höhne, N. (2010) 'Copenhagen Accord Pledges are Paltry', *Nature* 464: 1126–1128.

Scruggs, L. (2003) *Sustaining Abundance: Environmental Performance in Industrial Democracies*, Cambridge: Cambridge University Press.

Steiner, J., Bächtiger, A., Spörndli, M. and Steenbergen, M.R. (2004) *Deliberative Politics in Action: Analyzing Parliamentary Discourse*, Cambridge: Cambridge University Press.

Stevenson, H. (2011) *Discursive Representation in Global Climate Governance*, Working

Paper, Australian National University: Centre for Deliberative Democracy and Global Governance.

Stevenson, H. and Dryzek, J.S. (2012) 'The discursive democratization of global climate governance', *Environmental Politics* 21(2): 189–210.

Stokke, O.S., Hovi, J. and Ulfstein, G. (eds) (2005) *Implementing the Climate Regime: International Compliance*, London: Earthscan.

Thompson, D. (2008) 'Deliberative democratic theory and empirical political science', *Annual Review of Political Science* 11: 497–520.

UNFCCC (United Nations Framework Convention on Climate Change) (2009) On demand webcast, Conference of the Parties serving as the meeting of the Parties to the Kyoto Protocol (CMP), resumed 12th Meeting, Copenhagen, 19 December, 3:10 am and 5 am. Online. Available at: http://cop15.meta-fusion.com/kongresse/cop15/templ/ovw.php?id_kongressmain=1&theme=unfccc (retrieved: 24.5.2010).

UNFCCC (United Nations Framework Convention on Climate Change) (2010) 'List of admitted NGOs'. Online. Available at: http://maindb.unfccc.int/public/ngo.pl?mode=wim&search=A (retrieved: 24.5.2010).

Yamin, F. and Depledge, J. (2004) *The International Climate Change Regime: A Guide to the Rules, Institutions, and Procedures*, Cambridge: Cambridge University Press.

16 Reflections

*Chris Methmann, Delf Rothe and
Benjamin Stephan*

This book can be told as the story of John Doe, an everyday working man, and Jane Doe, an average International Relations scholar. On a regular day, John Doe is woken up by his radio alarm. The news anchorman reports one of the worst droughts affecting the United States, connecting it to man-made climate change. John Doe gets up and takes a shower. He likes to shower long, but today he feels uncomfortable because of the drought. The more water goes down the drain, the more energy he consumes. The more energy he consumes, the more coal is burned in a power plant around 40 miles away from his house. The coal is imported from Colombia. The more coal is burned, the more CO_2 gets into the atmosphere. We are not yet half an hour into the day of John Doe, but we cannot escape global warming. The story of John Doe is entwined with a story of climate change. Maybe John Doe works in a car factory. And although he thus enormously contributes to raising GHG emissions, quitting the job, especially in times of economic crises, is not an option. The the car he drives (instead of using the local train, whose ticket price exceeds the gasoline prices for the trip by far), the flat he lives in (which is not properly insulated because his landlord has no interest to invest in insulation): all these routines and landmarks of his daily life form a story John Doe could tell about climate change.

Yet, the stories that John Doe generally hears about climate change are radically different ones. John knows from the newspaper that scientists go to the Arctic and drill deep in order to analyse and measure climate change. He knows that genius inventors have developed possibilities to capture the emissions from coal-fired power stations to store them underground. A friend has told John that climate change is a great business opportunity and pays off for a number of people, while making others pay. Last summer, John Doe saw a movie in which global warming took the form of a global apocalypse – it seemed as if it was an external enemy to be fought by militaries and global political leaders. In all these stories, climate change is a remote issue, somehow detached from the social, political and economic structures who are at the root of the problem and which we (unconsciously) encounter in our everyday lives. Of course, John Doe's story about climate change is not more or less true than the others are – but it is less often told.

Depoliticization revisited

The contributors of this book have engaged with three such stories: the technocratization, the economization and the securitization of climate change. And they found that most of the plots in these stories are highly depoliticized; that is, these stories picture a superficial and highly contingent picture of climate change; a picture that downplays the structural entanglement of climate change with the basic structures of our lives – the story of John Doe – and narrows it down to a technical problem, an economic risk, or a security threat.

In Chapter 1 we argued that 'the political', seen from an interpretive perspective is not (only) located in parliaments and governments and it is not (only) the business of politicians and diplomats. The political acquires its distinct shape in contrast to the social: the realm of sedimented and routine social structures that nobody questions or contests. When these structures are called into question, they enter the realm of the political, where the undecidable is decided through political struggle. Politicization, then, is the movement from the social to the political. Depoliticization denotes the opposite: attempts to re-settle disrupted structures in times of dislocation. When we talk about depoliticizing stories, we mean that these stories tackle climate change in a way that prevents John Doe from seriously questioning his entanglement with the causes of global warming; preserving its image as a remote and abstract phenomenon.

If we were to isolate a general conclusion from the richness and plurality of the previous chapters, it would be this: global climate governance is being depoliticized through processes of technocratization, economization and securitization. But what does generalization actually mean from an interpretive perspective? We think that a good vehicle for generalizing empirical findings is that of a logic. In line with Glynos and Howarth we see logics as a promising alternative to a causal law or mechanism approach in social science. In contrast to laws, which are universally applicable and reproduceable, a logic points to a 'set of *family resemblances*' among different empirical phenomena (Glynos and Howarth 2007: 136). Logics help to study the patterning of social and political practices, while avoiding claims of a universal generalizability of these patterns. According to Glynos and Howarth 'the logic of a practice comprises the rules or grammar of the practice, as well as the conditions which make the practice both possible and vulnerable' (Glynos and Howarth 2007: 136).

This means that a logic of depoliticization is not a general feature of global climate governance, and it does not have to be the same in every case. A logic is a conceptual abstraction that is articulated differently in various contexts. For example, the logics of carbonification, upon which Mert and Stephan focus in their analyses, have a certain family resemblance in the sense that things are converted into carbon. However, there are differences in both cases, in the sense that both display different modes of calculation, different actors involved and the like. So, in this sense, the logics we are about to sketch out, are analytical abstractions of things that the researchers assembled in this book came up with during their research. In our opinion, condensing the findings of interpretive analysis as logics is particularly helpful. It does enable researchers to use the findings revealed in one case as precedent cases (Glynos and Howarth 2007: 4) that help to illuminate other phenomena without turning them into hard knowledge as the quasi-transcendental law in a positivist perspective.

We thus propose to condense the findings of this book into three logics linked to depoliticization: the logics of technocratization, economization and securitization.

Technocratization is probably the most sedimented logic of global climate governance. Climate change is nothing we can actually see or experience. It is worth noting that people created the first theories of the greenhouse effect before they could actually experience any signs of unusual warming. Climate change, so to speak, is a virtual problem. More than other forms of social and economic problems, we depend on scientific shortcuts, such as the atmospheric concentration of certain gases, which enable us to govern climate change. And this peculiar genealogy of the problem at hand empowers a whole armada of scientists and 'carbon professionals'. They make climate change countable, visible, understandable and hence malleable (Chapter 10, this volume). And they are legitimated as inventors of solutions to the problem – solutions, which again, are merely technical ones (Chapter 11, this volume). Moreover, also politics becomes an art and a technique. This is most clearly visible in the apparatus of UN climate negotiations, the UNFCCC and the Kyoto Protocol, in which, for example, we speak of flexible *instruments* or of Clean Development *Mechanisms*. Technocratization turns global climate governance into a 'political machine' (Barry 2001). And today, even individuals are inserted into this machine (Chapter 9, this volume). This technocratization of global climate governance depoliticizes. It focuses on the output (GHG emissions) instead of the underlying social and economic practices that produce these outcomes (buying of fossil fuels). Finally, the technocratization ties neatly into the second strand of discourses: the economization of global climate governance.

The *economization* is rooted in the neoliberal revolution that took place since the 1970s and 1980s and materialized as ecological modernization in environmental politics (Hajer 1995). Lohmann (Chapter 5, this volume) describes the long genealogy of neoliberal environmental thought that led to the prominence of carbon trading in global climate governance. As proponents of ecological modernization still insist, it is both necessary to understand environmental problems as economic (external) costs, and use the toolkit of economic instruments to internalize these costs. In this sense, climate change is valorized, and climate politics marketed. Moreover, these two processes build heavily on the technocratization of global warming. As Stephan (Chapter 4, this volume) demonstrates, one can only valorize and trade such an abstract thing as forest carbon, if one can somehow measure it. Disentangling forest carbon through technical means enables policy-makers to put a price tag on forests, and trade the carbon value of these forests on global markets. Economization mainstreams climate change into the global economy, with a lot of investment practices focusing on carbon emission reductions (Chapter 3, this volume). This economization is an instance of depoliticization, because it downplays the role of politics and empowers market forces, thereby reducing democratic control and the possibility to intervene into markets. And again, it narrows the social conditions of climate change down to a very specialized and limited language. Climate protection is what pays off, and not what necessarily protects the climate in the best way.

The *securitization* of global warming, finally, is the newest trend in the field of global climate change. Scholars and politicians have been debating environmental security since the 1980s (Floyd 2008). But security concerns in global climate governance only had their breakthrough during the last decade. Popular culture – *The Day After Tomorrow, An Inconvenient Truth* – as well as high politics – UN Security Council debates in 2007 and 2011, a UN General Assembly debate in 2009 – started to engage with the issue. Hartmann (Chapter 6, this volume) demonstrates that this new fashion in global climate governance reproduces much of the older debates on environmental security – especially their neo-Malthusian touch. It strikes the eye that most substantiated empirical investigations conclude that environmental change or climate change is unlikely to lead to conflicts in the near future, whereas many politicians promote the opposite opinion. And although a number of developing countries challenge the notion of climate change as a threat multiplier, there is an underlying apocalyptic consensus within global climate governance (Chapter 7, this volume). From our interpretive perspective, we find it quite interesting that the lack of scientific evidence makes proponents of climate security base their claims on emblematic examples – such as the Darfur conflict or the fate of climate refugees. Bettini (Chapter 8, this volume) explores the symbol of climate refugees in detail, its apocalyptic undertone as well as its depoliticizing effect. Securitization focuses on the impacts of climate change at the cost of its consequences and so downplays the possibility of mitigation. Through this logic, climate change tends to be articulated as the most important driver of conflict or migration, neglecting other social and economic grievances that might play a decisive role. Finally, it tends to picture those affected by climate change as passive victims and somehow dangerous. They oscillate between objects of and dangers for Western security policies.

We have painted these three logics of depoliticization with bold strokes. Of course, the closer one looks, the more nuanced the picture gets. Take for example Chapter 9 by Paterson and Stripple. In a nutshell, they argue that individual carbon accounting in fact empowers many individual subjects to take action on climate change in times where the performance of the official political system is rather poor. And although these subjects are inserted into the depoliticizing machine of carbon accounting, they at the same time gain scope for action they did not have before. In terms of John Doe's story, carbon accounting helps him to realize his own entanglement with climate change. In this sense, we would line up with Foucault, who noted that being critical does not mean

> that everything is bad, but that everything is dangerous, which is not exactly the same as bad. If everything is dangerous, then we always have something to do. So my position leads not to apathy but to hyper and pessimistic

activism. I think that the ethico-political choice we have to make every day is to determine which is the main danger.

(Foucault 1982: 231)

In this sense, we would not claim that depoliticization is a coherent and overwhelming process – this is what the notion of logic entails. Bedall shows how social movements, who attempt to repoliticize global climate governance, often end up playing the song of depoliticization. Likewise, the strongest symbols of a particular depoliticizing discourse are most prone to subversion. The British activist group 'Cheat Neutral' (http://www.cheatneutral.com/) provides a good example. Through a mock-up website they advertise a service for offsetting cheating in relationships. Through irony they expose the flaws of technocratic climate governance's flagship – carbon trading – and thus help to repoliticize the issue.

As the last part of the book shows, there are indeed possibilities for repoliticization. In our view, one way to repoliticize global climate governance is to (re-)connect it to the story John Doe could tell about climate change – the entanglement of our everyday lives, our social and political structures, our routine and unquestioned social practices that cause climate change in the first place. Based on the previous chapters, we think that there are at least two strategies to do bring John Doe's story back in.

1 Creating new fora and arenas to incite discursive struggle and deliberation. Friman (Chapter 14, this volume), for example, explores the idea of a new body to the UNFCCC, in which states could discuss and engage with the ethical and political principles that underwrite their positions, but which are seldom explicitly part of the negotiations. In this line, we think that repoliticization of climate change should entail the creation of various fora and participatory mechanisms, in which citizens instead of carbon professionals could discuss and take action on causes of climate change (Leggewie and Welzer 2011).
2 Connecting climate change to other grievances and social problems. Many frame climate change as the 'threat multiplier' and as the outstanding 'most important challenge of our generation' (Ban 2009). By contrast, we think that it is most useful to demonstrate the intertwinement of global warming with other problems without reducing these to aspects of global warming. The Bolivian government for example – which framed glaciers so successfully as images of climate justice – organized the Cochabamba summit, which brought together activists from a broad range of countries in order to create more radical discourses of global warming. And indeed these discourses are necessary (Chapter 15, this volume). We contend that the most successful acts of climate activism are those which connect the issue to other grievances – the other stories of John Doe.

Methodology

The second story that runs through this book is that of Jane Doe. She is John Doe's counterpart, an IR scholar, in academia. On her road to wisdom, Jane Doe one day came to a crossing. She was startled, because no one had told her that there would be any crossing. So far, she had been sure that there was simply one way to truth – the positivist highway. Yet, that morning, her neo-positivist journey came to an end. She came to a crossing and took the linguistic turn. This radically changed the way she worked. She entered a widely ramified realm of approaches and perspectives. Delving into the realm of language and meaning, Jane Doe developed what we call an interpretive perspective.

We intended this book to be a travelogue of Jane Doe's advent in the field of global climate governance, which could serve as a guidebook for other scholars that seek to explore this territory beyond the popular routes. In Chapter 1, we argued that rationalist approaches to climate politics have been somewhat exhausted when it comes to making sense of present day climate politics. The chapters in this book provide snapshots of new perspectives on global climate governance that can be gained when travelling off the beaten path.

In the introduction we argued that the interpretive perspective is not a coherent approach. The different approaches and methods instead share a family resemblance. The previous chapters have corroborated this. There is not *one* interpretive perspective. This becomes clear when looking at how the different authors have operationalized what it means to be interpretive. While some focused entirely on linguistic discourse (Buck, Chapter 11), others engaged with practices (Wolf, Chapter 3). Some discussed material factors (Stephan and Lohmann, Chapters 4 and 5), whereas others included the dimension of the affective (Bettini, Chapter 8). Some drew on auto-ethnographic experiences (Kaijser, Chapter 12), others have conducted interviews (Bedall, Chapter 13). Some adopted a historical-genealogical approach (Uhrqvist, Chapter 10), while others worked archeologically (Methmann and Rothe, Chapter 7). Yet again, others remained mostly on the conceptual-theoretical level (Friman, Dryzek and Stevenson, Chapters 14 and 15), drawing on different theories of discourse.

We think that these differences fit quite well with the different turns that Jane Doe encountered once she had left the beaten path. These differences also point to the paths not taken by the researchers assembled in this book. In our view, exploring why some of these paths are less taken than others, reveals some of the methodological challenges that come with choosing an interpretive perspective. Obviously, all contributions have followed the *linguistic turn*. They all engage with language, meaning and discourse. A couple of years ago, some researchers declared that the focus on discourse had come at the cost of neglecting practices. Neumann has called this phenomenon 'armchair research' (Neumann 2002). Such a *practice turn* is reflected only in few of the contributions. Wolf (Chapter 3 this volume), for example, explores in a Foucauldian spirit how changing investment practices have triggered a shift in investment discourses – and not vice versa, which is a common assumption. Uhrqvist (Chapter 10, this volume) demonstrates how scientific practices have shaped a certain globalist discourse of global environmental change. The renewed focus on practices has triggered a growing interest in adopting ethnographic methods for the study of political phenomena (Vrasti 2008, 2010; Rancatore 2010). However, this is also the reason why only a few contributions actually engage with practices. It requires effort and time. Thus, the contributions in this book engage with practices only indirectly – only one of them, Kaijser (Chapter 12), has actually used ethnographic methods. The others have solved this dilemma by studying practices on the basis of secondary literature. This is obviously legitimate, but it leads to the problem that language is brought back in as an intermediate level, which makes the analysis even more complicated.

Some scholars have promoted an emotional turn (Crawford 2000; Ross 2006). They contend that the idea of a rationalist subject is an illegitimate abstraction, and that emotions have to be included into the study of social phenomena. The emotional turn is almost entirely absent, which reflects its marginal role in interpretive studies in general. Only the contribution by Bettini in this volume (Chapter 8) dealt with the dimension of the affective, by introducing the psychoanalytic notion of fantasy. Also Glynos and Howarth – whose *Logics of Critical Explanation* have provided much inspiration for some chapters – call for acknowledging the importance of fantasmatic logics. However, we think that the reluctance to do so is rooted in the fact that emotions are easy to acknowledge but difficult to operationalize. How do we distinguish emotions analytically from other linguistic or practical data? How can we capture it without bringing too much of our own perspective into the analysis? Emotions are deeply rooted in subjects, and they are easily mis-recognized.

Finally, there is a material turn, which argues that interpretive perspectives, due to their focus on language, have systematically underscored the political role of the material – such as new technologies. Given the centrality of technology, but also economic structures, the material turn is highly relevant for phenomena such as environmental change. In our view only Actor-Network Theory (Chapter 5, this volume) really accounts for this fact. Here, we see how things become things, so to speak, as tangible and discrete entities. Other contributions, however, deal of course with material phenomena, but always already bound up with language. Such contributions follow-up on post-structuralist notions of discourse, arguing that the material world is only meaningful and hence perceivable against the backdrop of particular discourses. This includes an epistemological argument: even though technologies and other materialities have a major impact on climate politics, they cannot be directly researched. Even if we would directly observe them, our very perception would already be influenced by the dominant discourses that surround these technologies. Hence, we would contend that it is the wrong approach to make a distinction between the discursive and the material. While it is important to account for the technologies of satellite monitoring, carbon measuring or allowance trading, this should be done alongside and not instead of a study of prevalent climate change discourses.

In addition, some scholars flagged the role of visual media, for example in the study of securitization (Williams 2003; Hansen 2011). They argue that much content is not only contained in linguistic discourse, but often paradigmatically condensed in images, graphs, illustrations, photos and the like. The study of visuals is absent from this book – and it took us writing these reflections to even take note of this (although some of the authors have engaged with visual material before). In our view, this perfectly symbolizes the focus on text in academic discourses that needs to be overcome.

In this sense, the whole story of Jane Doe that runs through the book is one of paths taken as well as it is one of paths not taken. The dominant perspective is that on speech and language. But the various subsequent turns show that it would be a short-circuit to limit interpretive methodology to the linguistic turn. We have to think about how to develop techniques and methods to deal with these other turns. Some of the chapters assembled in this book provide some inspiration to do so.

Outlook

To conclude: there is as much power in the story of John Doe as there is in that of Jane Doe for renovating global climate governance. The contributors have shown that the new interpretive toolkit for understanding global climate governance is helpful to reveal the depoliticizing tendencies that characterize global climate governance today. In this sense, Jane Doe helps us to reveal the contingency of dominant accounts of global climate governance. And it opens avenues to think about how to connect these accounts with John Doe's story of global warming. Let us be clear: by insisting on John Doe's story, we do neither say that this is the definite version, nor do we advocate a common-sense perspective on climate politics! We want to pull the attention to the social, economic and political structures that govern our everyday lives. This is what John Doe's story is about. And Jane Doe helps us to recover it.

What can Jane Doe, what can social scientists do to achieve this? Our first answer would be: continuing to work off the beaten path; by fleshing out interpretive perspectives in more detail; by answering the questions raised by the linguist, practice, emotional and material turns. This book has shown how interpretive approaches can open up new perspectives on global climate governance. And this is a valuable achievement. But we think that to become even more relevant, Jane Doe has to turn once more. This time not so much in methodological terms, but rather with respect to the scope and scale of her empirical interest.

We have argued that the governance perspective has done a great deal to widen the focus on governing climate change: away from inter-state negotiations, towards new types of actors, new modes of governance, and the interplay of various political levels. The notion of the political, however, which we have adopted throughout this book, makes it necessary to radicalize this ambition. For – as we have seen – most arenas of global climate governance are deeply depoliticized. We think that politicization thus cannot come from within what is generally defined as global climate governance. It has to come from a closer engagement with John Doe's story. Jane Doe should study the discourses and practices that challenge depoliticization. She has to investigate the counter-discourses of global warming that are not yet reflected in the 'official' and institutionalized governance arenas. She should investigate the discourses of those affected by global warming, bringing in the perspective of those supposed to become 'climate refugees'. She should take into account the perspectives of those that creatively spur new discourses of global warming by organizing local resistance against new power plants, motorways or airport runways: the counter-discourses emerging in the critical conversation between states and non-state actors such as in the Cochabamba declaration. She has to engage with those places where social movements seek to reclaim the climate, to occupy global warming. She has, in other words, to stretch the notion of global governance even further, beyond its own limits to those spaces and actors that refuse 'being governed like that and at that cost' (Foucault 2007: 28–29). This is where an interpretive perspective would turn into a truly critical perspective.

References

Ban, K.-M. (2009) 'The sky is the limit', *Our Planet. Magazine of the UNEP*, December, 6–7.
Barry, A. (2001) *Political Machines: Governing a Technological Society*, London: Athlone Press.
Crawford, N.C. (2000) 'The passion of world politics: proposition on emotion and emotional relationships', *International Security* 4: 116–156.
Floyd, R. (2008) 'The environmental security debate and its significance for climate change', *The International Spectator* 43(3): 51–65.
Foucault, M. (1982) 'On the genealogy of ethics: an overview of work in progress', in H.L. Dreyfus and P. Rabinow (eds) *Michel Foucault: Beyond Structuralism and Hermeneutics*, Brighton: Harvester Press, 231–232.
Foucault, M. (2007) 'What is critique', in S. Lotringer (ed.) *The Politics of Truth*, Los Angeles: Semiotexte, 41–81.
Glynos, J. and Howarth, D. (2007) *Logics of Critical Explanation in Social and Political Theory*, London and New York: Routledge.
Hajer, M.A. (1995) *The Politics of Environmental Discourse: Ecological Modernization and the Policy Process*, Oxford: Oxford University Press.
Hansen, L. (2011) 'Theorizing the image for security studies: visual securitization and the Muhammad cartoon crisis', *European Journal of International Relations* 17(1): 51–74.
Leggewie, C. and Welzer, H. (2011) Das Ende der Welt, wie wir sie kannten: Klima, Zukunft und die Chancen der Demokratie [online]. *Fischer Taschenbuch*. Available from: http://scholar.google.de/scholar?hl=de&q=leggewie+welzer&btnG=&lr= [accessed: 27 August 2012].
Neumann, I.B. (2002) 'Returning practice to the linguistic turn: the case of diplomacy', *Millennium* 31(3): 627–651.
Rancatore, J.P. (2010) 'It is strange: a reply to Vrasti', *Millennium: Journal of International Studies* 39(1): 65–77.
Ross, A.A.G. (2006) 'Coming in from the cold: constructivism and emotions', *European Journal of International Relations* 12(2): 197–222.
Vrasti, W. (2008) 'The strange case of ethnography and international relations', *Millennium: Journal of International Studies* 37(2): 279–301.
Vrasti, W. (2010) 'Dr Strangelove, or how I learned to stop worrying about methodology and love writing', *Millennium: Journal of International Studies* 39(1): 79–88.
Williams, M.C. (2003) 'Words, images, enemies: securitization and international politics', *International Studies Quarterly* 47(4): 511–531.

Index

2°C target 114, 116–17, 149, 244

absent narratives 176
accountability 233;242–3, 245
activism 15, 72–87
accumulation cycles 80–2
actor-network theory 73–5, 254
adaptation 98–9, 117–18
advanced liberal government 15, 59, 140
affirmative articulations 203, 208–11
Africa 92, 93–4
AFRICOM 97–8
agency 7, 176
agonistic logic 220–2, 227–8
aid, militarization of 96–9
analytical responsibility 158, 161, 162
analytics of government 45–7, 59; individual carbon accounting 141–8
Andes: culture 193–4; disappearing glaciers 187–8; *see also* Bolivia
antagonism 127, 201–3, 208, 213
anti-universal universality 221
apocalypse: apocalyptic reading of climate-induced migration 16, 122–36; logic of 116–18
archaeological-synchronic interpretive perspective 6
archaeology 6, 44, 47, 108
Arctic region 187
argumentative discourse analysis 123–4
attitudes to climate change 175
audience 177
authenticity of negotiations 239
avoided deforestation, commodification of 14–15, 57–71

Bali Action Plan 62
Ban Ki-Moon 30, 43, 91, 105
bandwagoning 36

baselines: REDD+ 63–4, 65; wetlands banking 80
beatific dimension of fantasy 201, 202–3, 205, 209, 211–13
Beck, U. 168
Beckett, Margaret 33
bildungsroman frames 170–1
biodiversity 31, 64–5
biodiversity credits 74
biofuels 32
biospheric frame 174
black swan events 99
Blühdorn, I. 1
Bolivia 242, 252; climate change discourse 17, 183–97; climate change politics 189–90; government documents 190–1; Ministry of Foreign Relations 191–2; National Mechanism for Climate Change Adaptation 190; political context 188
Brazil 191–2; proposal on historic responsibility 223–4, 225
Bush, George W. 27

Callon, Michel 73
Cancun Adaptation Framework 122, 189, 226
cap and trade 75; and fishery quotas 76–8
capitalistic discourse on climate change 125–31
carbon calculators 144
carbon dieting 139, 142–3, 145–6, 149
carbon dioxide equivalent (CO_2e) 63, 79–80
carbon footprinting 139, 142–3, 144, 149
carbon forester 60, 65–6
carbon governmentality 117
carbon market professionals 65

Index

carbon markets 50–1, 57, 144–5; *see also* carbon trading, commodification
carbon offsetting *see* offsetting
carbon rationing action groups (CRAGS) 139, 142–3, 147, 148, 149
carbon trading 75–82, 250; *see also* market environmentalism, offsetting
carbonification 6, 14, 24, 31–6, 249
Castles, S. 130
catastrophe 107, 116
catastrophic frame 170
cautionary frames 170–1
Center for American Progress 98, 99
Center for Naval Analysis (CNA) 33, 91, 98–9
Chacaltaya 187, 191, 192
cheap solutions 171, 175
Cheat Neutral 252
China 82, 226
Christian Aid 125–31
civil society: hegemonic narratives 17, 198–216; public space and global climate governance 234–9
clean development mechanism (CDM) 57, 64, 78; reform proposals 50–1, 52
Clean Technology Fund 50
Climate Action Network (CAN) 242
climate bandwagoning 36
climate change attitudes 175
climate conflict 92–4; narratives 112–13, 115–16
climate engineering 17, 166–80 see also geoengineering
climate finance funds 47–8
climate-induced migration (CM) 16, 122–36
Climate Investment Funds (CIFs) 48, 50
climate marketization 236
climate refugees 91–104, 115–16, 251; apocalyptic discourses and climate-induced migration 16, 122–36; estimated numbers of 128
Club of Rome 73
Coalition for Rainforest Nations 62
Coase, R. 75
Cochabamba Conference 125–31, 189, 194, 252
co-constitution, discursive 14, 23–39
coercion 217, 241
Cold War 106–7
commensuration 60, 62–5
commodification 59–61; of avoided deforestation 14–15, 57–71; of nature 59–60

communication 167
compensation 47–8
complexity 128–9
comprehensive transformation 212, 213
conduct of conduct 58, 140–4
Conference of the Parties of the UNFCCC: Copenhagen Conference *see* Copenhagen Conference; side events to 235
conflict 226; climate conflict *see* climate conflict; conflict–migration nexus 127–8; environmental 91–2, 92–4, 95; legitimacy, consensus and in negotiations over historic responsibility 217–31; neo-Malthusianism, militarism and migration 15, 91–104; using to build legitimacy 226–8
Conrad, Kevin 243–4
consensus 244; legitimacy of consensuses 223–6; legitimacy, conflict and in negotiations over historic responsibility 217–31
conservativeness principle 63
content analysis 17, 166–80
contingency 6–7; 13; 18; 201; 221
cooperation 178
Copenhagen Accord 189, 244
Copenhagen Conference (COP 15) 1, 189, 191, 194, 199, 206, 226, 243–4; civil society discourses 17, 198–216
Copenhagen School 105, 106, 107, 108
'Corporate Governance Framework for Climate Change' 35
corporate social responsibility (CSR) 23; 66
Costanza, R. 74–5
corporations 29–30
counterfactual arguments 64
coverage of news media 169, 170–2
crisis 107; discursive element 170, 175; environmental 13–14; financial 30–1, 34–5; narratives 92
critical articulations 203, 208–11
critical moments 201–3
critical security studies 106–8
cross-sectional analysis 208, 209

Darfur 91
Day After Tomorrow, The 28
Dean, M. 14, 45, 47, 59, 141
decision-making 243–4
deforestation 52–3; commodification of avoided deforestation 14–15, 57–71

degradation narratives 91–104
Deleuze, G. 45
deliberative system 18, 232–47, 234–44
democratization 18, 232–47
depoliticization 12–14, 17–18, 131, 249–52
developing countries 47–8
development assistance, militarization of 96–9
development framing 178–9
dieting, carbon 139, 142–3, 145–6, 149
difference, logic of 25–6, 200
differentiation of responsibility 223
disaster 107
discourse, definition of 5–6
discourse theory: of hegemony 200–1; of legitimacy 220–1
discursive co-constitution 14, 23–39
discursive elements 170–1, 174–5
discursive interplay 14, 23–39
discursive narratives 199, 201–2
discursive practices 6
disease metaphors 110, 112
disentanglement 60; 66
dislocations 201–2
dispositif 45–9; climate investment dispositif 47–9; combining with regimes of practice 45–7
dominant discourses 26–7
doubt 170–1, 175
Durban climate conference 189

Earth 2100 96
ecofeminism 238
ecological modernization 74–5, 171, 175, 184–5, 236–7, 250
ecological paradox 1
eco-managerial transformation 212, 213
economic discourses of climate change 2–3, 6; financialization 14, 43–56, 73; public space 235–9
economization 14–15, 249, 250–1
ecosystem services 74
ecosystems 75
emissions trading *see* cap and trade
emotional turn 254
empowered space 233; global governance of climate change 239–41, 245
empty signifiers 127, 132, 200
endangered glacier narrative 186–7; Bolivia 187–95
energy security 237
ensuring state 52
enthymeme 207

environmental conflict 91–2, 92–4, 95
environmental crisis 13–14
Environmental Defense Fund 61
Environmental Justice Foundation (EJF) 125–31
environmental refugees 94–6
environmental regulation 73
environmental risk 74
environmentalist/modernist paradigm 25
equitable modernization 237
equivalence, logic of 200
European research network 159
European Union Emissions Trading Scheme (ETS) 75, 76, 77–8, 80
exceptional measures 15, 105, 117, 118–19
expansive sustainability 236, 237
explanation: plausibility 11–12; vs understanding 9–11
externalities 75

fantastic ideas 171, 175
fantasy 201, 254; dimensions of 201, 202–3, 205, 209, 211–13
Feldman, M.S. 206–8
field inventories 63, 68
financial crisis 30–1; and carbonification 34–5
financialization 14, 43–56, 73
fishery quotas 76–8
floating signifiers 123–4, 127
footprinting 139, 142–3, 144, 149
forest carbon content, measuring 63, 65
fossil fuels 176
Foucault, Michel 10, 13, 47, 108, 153, 154, 155, 251–2; dispositif 46; governmentality 58, 140; knowledge and power 44–5; problematization 46
framing 12; news media framing 17, 166–80
Fundación Solón 191–3
funding: climate finance funds 47–8; for global research 157–8, 160

genealogy 6, 44–5, 47
Generation IV International Forum (GIF) 33–4
geo-biosphere observatories, network of 156–7
geoclique 172–3
geoengineering 17, 166–80
geographical coverage of news 169, 170–2
geopolitics 171, 174–5
glaciers 5; glacier narratives 17, 183–97

Index

Global Circulation Models 75
Global Compact 30
global environmental change research network 16–17, 152–65
global knowledge infrastructure 152–65; as an object of government 161–3
global predictive models 161
Glynos, J. 201, 202–3, 249
Gore, Al 32, 91
governance: climate-induced migration 130–1; implications of new media framing of geoengineering 177–9; perspective 255–6
governmentality 57–8, 155; climate politics as investment 43–56; commodification of avoided deforestation 57–71; individuals' carbon emissions 139–51; perspective on commodification 15, 58–61
Gramsci, A. 198
Granjas Carroll de Mexico 80
Green Economy Initiative 30
Green Finance Initiative 34–5
green governmentality 184–5
Green Investment Bank (GIB) 49–50
Green New Deal (GND) 30, 34–5, 48
Green New Deal Group 53
green radicalism 183, 193–4, 236, 238
Greenpeace 34–5, 49
Group of 77 226

Habermas, J. 220, 226
Hajer, M.A. 123–4, 177, 184
Harvey, D. 81
hegemonic projects 200, 202–3
hegemonic structure 201–2, 206–8
hegemony: in climate politics 203–6; discourse theory of 200–1; hegemonic narratives in transnational NGOs and social movements 17, 198–216
High Level Advisory Group on Climate Finance 43
historic responsibility, negotiations over 18, 217–31
historical accumulation cycles 80–2
holism, methodological 12
Homer-Dixon, T. 91, 93
'Hopenhagen' project 208–13
horrific dimension of fantasy 201, 202–3, 205, 209, 211–13
Howarth, D. 202–3, 249
Hulme, M. 1, 2–3, 174
human body metaphors 110, 112

Human Dimensions of Global Environmental Change Programme 152
humanitarian assistance, militarization of 96–9
humanitarian discourse on climate change 125–31
hybrids 74

identities 45, 54, 59; commodification of avoided deforestation 65–6; individualized carbon governance 141–8
Illimani glacier 187–8, 192
individual carbon accounting 7, 16, 139–51, 251
industrial disasters 28
industrialist/modernist paradigm 25
inevitability 170, 175
Informal Working Group on Interim Financing for REDD+ 52–3
information deficit model 167
innovation framing 178
input legitimacy 218, 219; *see also* legitimacy
institutionalist/reformist hegemonic projects 202–3
Inter-American Institute for Global Change Research 159
Intergovernmental Panel on Climate Change (IPCC) 23, 61, 63, 122, 224–5; Nobel Peace Prize 32, 91; scientific discourse on climate change 125–31
international climate regime 1–3
international frame 174
International Geosphere-Biosphere Programme (IGBP) 152, 153, 155–6, 156–8
International Group of Funding Agencies for Global Change Research (IGFA) 160
International Political Economy (IPE) 3–4
International Relations 1–4
interplay, discursive 14, 23–39
interpretive methodology 8–12, 252–5
interpretive theory 4–8
investment 14, 43–56; climate investment dispositif 47–9; governing investment for climate protection 49–51

Jackson, P.T. 8
Johannesburg Declaration 30
justice 171, 174–5, 176
justification 240–1; mutual without coercion 241

Kenya 94
knowledge: forms of and individualized carbon governance 141–8; global infrastructure produced by START 152–65; power and 44–5, 153, 154; and rationalities of government 45, 59
Kurki, M. 10
Kuznets curve 74
Kyoto Protocol 105, 204, 205, 219, 226, 250; carbon trading 75, 76, 77; Compliance Committee 242

Lacan, J. 201
Laclau, E. 13, 123–4, 200, 201, 220, 221
language 168; linguistic turn 8, 253
Law of the Sea 77
legitimacy 232; building and negotiations over historic responsibiilty 17–18, 217–31; of consensuses 223–6; discourse theory of 220–1; using conflict to build 226–8
legitimization 60
Leiserowitz, A. 166
liberal environmentalism 29
liberal migration policy 130
liberalism 163
limits discourse 236, 238
linguistic turn 8, 253
local framing 178
logics: of depoliticization 249–52; logic of apocalypse 116–18; logic of difference 25–6, 200; logic of equivalence 200
low-carbon diet 139, 142–3, 145–6, 149
low-carbon investment strategies 48–9, 53

mainstream sustainability 236–7
managerial frame 170–1
market creation processes 58–61
market environmentalism 15, 72–87
market failure 74
market mechanisms 204
marketization, climate 236
MATCH, ad-hoc group on Modeling and Assessment of Contribution to Climate Change 224, 225
material turn 254
maximized self-interests 217
McKinsey Global Greenhouse Gas Abatement Cost Curve 48
mechanical metaphors 113
media framing 17, 166–80
mediapolis 166

meta-deliberation 233–4; 243–4, 245
metaphor analysis 12, 15–16, 108;
methodological holism 12
methodological relativism 154
methodology, interpretive 8–12, 252–5
migration: climate-induced 16, 122–36; neo-Malthusianism, militarism and 15, 91–104; migration–conflict nexus 127–8
Miliband, D. 147–8
militarism 91–104; military intervention and aid 96–9
Miller, P. 141
mind-world-dualism 8
mind-world-monism 8
Mitchell, Timothy 73
mitigation 117–18
Monterrey Consensus 27
Montreal Protocol 1, 153
Morales, Evo 188, 191, 242
Mother Earth 188, 189, 195
motional metaphors 109–10, 111–12, 114–15
Mouffe, C. 200, 201, 220, 221, 226
Movimiento al Socialismo (MAS) (Movement towards Socialism) 188, 189
mutual justification without coercion/threats 241
Myers, N. 94, 95

narrative analysis 12, 15–16, 108–9; apocalyptic narratives and climate-induced migration 16, 122–36; identification-evaluation-interpretation approach 206–8; Security Council debates 109–18
narrative frames 169–70, 174–5
narratives 123, 185, 199, 201–2; degradation 91–104; discursive 199, 201–2; glacier narratives 17, 183–97; precautionary 111–12, 114–15
National Communications to the UNFCCC 190–1
NATO 98
natural integrity 237
natural resource management 75
negotiations: empowered space and global climate governance 239–41; on historic responsibility 18, 217–31
neoliberal institutionalism 2
neoliberalism 73, 149, 250; climate neoliberalism 203–6, 212–13; development of in environmental matters 73–5

neo-Malthusianism 15, 91–104
neorealism 2
Netherlands, the 81
network of geo-biosphere observatories 156–7
new fora 228, 252
new globalism 238
New Public Management 29
news media framing 17, 166–80
Nigeria 93–4
no net loss 74
Nobel Peace Prize 32, 91
non-discursive practices 6
non-governmental organizations (NGOs) 23; transnational 17, 198–216
North American Free Trade Agreement 75
Norway 62, 76, 77
nuclear energy partnerships registered with the UNCSD 33–4

Obama, Barack 243
objectivity 224–5
offsetting 75; individual carbon governance 139, 142–3, 144–5, 149; and wetlands banking 78–80
online news media 166–80
output legitimacy 218
outside/inside distinction 241–242
owner–worker divides 77
Oxfam America 99

Pachamama (Mother Earth) 188, 189, 195
Pachauri, Rajendra 32
pairs of opposition 109–18
paradigm shift 212, 213
participation in negotiations 239–40
People's Agreement of Cochabamba 125–31, 189
People's Protocol on Climate Change 208–12
performativity 154, 161–3
personal carbon allowances (PCAs) 139, 142–3, 147–8, 149
personification metaphors 109, 110–14
Pew Global Stewardship Initiative (PGSI) 95
Pigou, A.C. 75
plausibility 11–12
policy-making: global research network and 157, 161, 161–3; scientific knowledge and 152–3
political, the 12–14, 249
political discourses on climate change 235–9

politicization 249, 255–6
population growth 100; *see also* neo-Malthusianism
populist/revolutionary hegemonic projects 202–3
positivism 9–11
postfoundationalism 5–6, 123
post-modernism 5
post-positivism 9–11
post-structuralism 5
power 7–8, 220–1; 149; and knowledge 44–5, 153, 154
practice turn 253–4
precaution 107, 117
precautionary narratives 111–12, 114–15
preemption 107
preparedness 107, 118
primacy of the political 13
print news media 166–80
private investment 47–8
privatization of environmental governance 24, 28–30; and carbonification 33–4
problem perception 205, 208–10
problematization 4, 6, 44, 46–7, 106; new problematization of climate change 51–3
project-based carbon markets 144–5
Public Finance Mechanisms (PFMs) 49–50, 52
public space 233; global governance of climate change 234–9, 244–5

qualification; commodification 60

radical decentralization 238
radical discourse on climate change 125–31
rational logic 220–2, 227–8
rationalities of government 45, 59; commodification of avoided deforestation 61–2; individual carbon accounting 141–8
realism 5
Reducing Emissions from Deforestation and Degradation (REDD+) 57, 62–7
reduction of emissions 32
reflectivism 5
reformist/institutionalist hegemonic projects 202–3
refugees: climate *see* climate refugees; environmental 94–6
regime theory 25, 198
regimes of practice 45–7, 59

regional frame 174
regional research centres (RRCs) 157–60
regional research networks (RRNs) 158–61; fine-tuning roles in 160–1
religious metaphors 110
remote sensing 63, 68
renewable energies 49
re-normalization of climate change 129
repoliticization 17–18, 252
representation 243–4
regressive migration policy 130
revolutionary/populist hegemonic projects 202–3
Rio Earth Summit (1992) 1
Rio+20 Summit (2012) 24, 30
risk: environmental 74; vs reward 171, 175; security, apocalypse and 106–8
risk management 15–16, 105–21
ritual view of communication 167
Rockefeller Foundation Bellagio Conference 152, 158
Roe, E.M. 92
Rose, N. 141

scenario-building 99
science: objective 224–5; scientific discourse on climate change 2–3, 125–31, 218
science education 171, 175
securitization 15–16, 27–8, 249, 251; and carbonification 32–3; risk and security 106–8
self-government technologies 16, 139–51
social-constructivism 3
social media 139
social movements 2–3, 7, 252; hegemonic narratives 17, 198–216
social problems 252
societal frame 174
sociology of markets 59–60
sociology of scientific knowledge (SSK) 154
Solón, Pablo 192
spatial frames 169, 174
spatiotemporal struggle frame 170–1
spectator role 177
speech acts 106, 108
stability operations 97
stakeholder view of the corporation 29
START (SysTem for Analysis, Research and Training) 7, 16, 152–65; history of development 156–60
state 198; ensuring state 52; return of in climate governance 52

statistical persons 74
Stern Review 30, 62; capitalist discourse on climate change 125–31
Strategic Climate Fund (SCF) 50
Subsidiary Body for Scientific and Technological Advice (SBSTA) 224, 225, 228
Sudan 93
surface changes 27
sustainability, expansive 236, 237
sustainable development 28, 29–30
syllogisms 207–8, 215
symbolic political acts 24–6

technocratization 16–17, 249, 250
technologies of government 45, 59; individual carbon accounting 141–8
temporality 116
threat multiplier 115
TIPNIS conflict 189, 192
tipping point metaphor 114
ton of carbon dioxide equivalents (tCO$_2$e) 63
tradable quotas (TQs) 76–8
transnational NGOs 17, 198–216
trigger events 169, 170–2
trust 161
truthfulness 240
Tunupa bulletins 192–3

uncertainty 128–9
understanding vs explanation 9–11
United Kingdom (UK): Fund for Green Growth 49; Green Investment Bank 49–50; historical accumulation cycle 81
United Nations 211; Permanent Forum on Indigenous Issues 191
United Nations Commission on Sustainable Development (UNCSD) 30; nuclear energy partnerships registered with 33–4
United Nations Conference on Environment and Development 29
United Nations Conference on Financing for Development (Monterrey Conference) 27
United Nations Environment Programme (UNEP) 34, 93, 95, 96, 156; Finance Initiative (FI) 49
United Nations Framework Convention on Climate Change (UNFCCC) 47, 57, 117–18, 122, 195, 250; deliberative system and 18, 235–45; High Level

UNFCCC (*cont.*):
  Advisory Group on Climate Finance 43;
  legitimacy and negotiations over
    historic responsibility 217–31; National
    Communications to 190–1; new
    subsidiary body proposed 18, 228, 252
United Nations General Assembly 109–18
United Nations Refugee Convention 96
United Nations Security Council 33, 105;
  debates 109–18
United States (US) 33, 76, 93, 100, 159;
  Department of Defense (DoD) 96–7;
  historical accumulation cycle 81,
  82; military intervention and climate
  change 96–9; wetlands trading 78–80
unleashing solution 178
utopian vision 205, 209, 211

Van Munster, R. 106–7
viable solutions 205, 209, 210
victims, climate refugees as 130, 131
visibility: climate investment 52–3; fields
  of 45, 59, 142; individualized carbon
  governance 141–8; making forest
  carbon visible 62–5

visual media 254–5
vivir bien (to live well) 188, 195
voices 169, 172–4
voluntary carbon rationing 139, 142–3,
  147, 148, 149
voting 219

Wæver, O. 26–7
war gaming 99
war metaphors 109, 110–14, 117
wetlands banking 78–80
Wildlifeworks 66
win-win narrative 30–1
women 174
Woodrow Wilson Center Environmental
  Change and Security Program 100
worker–owner divides 77
World Bank 43, 62; Climate Investment
  Funds (CIFs) 48, 50
World Climate Research Programme 152
World Nuclear University (WNU) 33–4
World People's Conference (WPC)
  on Climate Change and the Rights
  of Mother Earth (Cochabamba
  Conference) 125–31, 189, 194, 252